Cliffs Advanced Placement™

CliffsAP™
English Language and Composition

2ND EDITION

by

Barbara V. Swovelin

Consultant
Jerry Bobrow, Ph.D.

WILEY

Wiley Publishing, Inc.

About the Author

Barbara Swovelin has taught AP and gifted classes since 1982. She is an experienced AP Reader and conducts workshops for teachers for the College Board. Ms. Swovelin also has taught graduate test preparation classes in the LSAT and GMAT at California universities since 1986. She currently teaches at Torrey Pines High School in Del Mar, California.

Publisher's Acknowledgments

Editorial

Project Editor: Suzanne Snyder

Acquisitions Editor: Roxanne Stanfield

Production

Proofreader: Arielle Carole Mennelle

Wiley Indianapolis Composition Services

CliffsAP™ English Language and Composition, 2nd Edition

Published by:
Wiley Publishing, Inc.
111 River Street
Hoboken, NJ 07030
www.wiley.com

Copyright © 2001 Barbara V. Swovelin.

Published by Wiley Publishing, Inc., New York, NY
Published simultaneously in Canada

Library of Congress Control Number: 00-109060

ISBN: 0-7645-8685-8

Printed in the United States of America

10 9 8

2B/TQ/QV/QU/IN

Author's Acknowledgments

This book is dedicated to my husband, Jerry, who assisted and inspired me when I needed it most. I would also like to thank Dr. Jerry Bobrow for believing in me and Dr. Allan Casson for his technical assistance. Finally, I would like to thank all of my students and acknowledge Carrie Cunningham, Bill Danielson, Jessica Grossman, Tim Hong, Oliver Miao, Cindy Mong, and Cheya Pope for their invaluable help with the essays.

Table of Contents

PART III: DIAGNOSTIC MINI-TEST

PART IV: PAST AP ENGLISH LANGUAGE ESSAYS

PART V: GLOSSARY OF IMPORTANT TERMS FOR THE AP LANGUAGE EXAM

PART VI: FIVE FULL-LENGTH PRACTICE TESTS

PART VII: SUGGESTED READING LIST

Study Guide Checklist

❑ 1. Become familiar with the test format, page 3.

❑ 2. Familiarize yourself with the answers to Questions Commonly Asked about the AP English Exams, page 5.

❑ 3. Carefully read Part II: Analysis of Exam Areas, beginning on page 13.

❑ 4. Take the Mini-Test section by section, strictly observing the time allotments, beginning on page 53.

❑ 5. Check your answers, analyze your results, and read the sample essays and analysis, beginning on page 59.

❑ 6. Familiarize yourself with the AP exam terminology by carefully reading the Glossary of Important Terms for the AP Language Exam, beginning on page 75.

❑ 7. Take Practice Test 1 section by section, strictly observing time allotments, beginning on page 89.

❑ 8. Check your answers and analyze your results, beginning on page 109.

❑ 9. While referring to each item of Practice Test 1, study ALL the Answers and Explanations, including the student essays and analysis, beginning on page 113.

❑ 10 Take Practice Test 2 section by section, strictly observing time allotments, beginning on page 135.

❑ 11. Check your answers and analyze your results, beginning on page 155.

❑ 12. While referring to each item of Practice Test 2, study ALL the Answers and Explanations, including the student essays and analysis, beginning on page 159.

❑ 13. Take Practice Test 3 section by section, strictly observing time allotments, beginning on page 179.

❑ 14. Check your answers and analyze your results, beginning on page 197.

❑ 15. While referring to each item of Practice Test 3, study ALL the Answers and Explanations, including the student essays and analysis, beginning on page 201.

❑ 16. Take Practice Test 4 section by section, strictly observing time allotments, beginning on page 219.

❑ 17. Check your answers and analyze your results, beginning on page 237.

❑ 18. While referring to each item of Practice Test 4, study ALL the Answers and Explanations, including the student essays and analysis, beginning on page 241.

❑ 19. Take Practice 5 section by section, strictly observing time allotments, beginning on page 261.

❑ 20. Check your answers and analyze your results, beginning on page 278.

❑ 21. While referring to each item of Practice Test 5, study ALL the Answers and Explanations, including the student essays and analysis, beginning on page 283.

PART I

INTRODUCTION

Format and Scoring of a Recent AP Language and Composition Exam

Format	
Section I: Multiple-choice questions (approximately 55)	60 minutes
Section II: Free-response sections (3 essays)	120 minutes
Total time:	180 minutes

Scoring
1. In the multiple-choice section, you earn one point for each correct answer. To eliminate random guessing, a quarter point is deducted from the total for each wrong answer. Unanswered questions do not count for or against your score. The multiple-choice section equals 45% of the total exam score.
2. The three essays are each scored holistically; the scores range from one to nine (or zero for a blank paper or one that does not attempt to answer the question). These scores are then calculated to equal 55% of the total exam score. You can find more detailed information on the scoring of the essays in the Introduction to the Essay in this book.
3. The multiple-choice section score is added to the free-response section score to produce a composite (or total) score. Finally, this composite is translated into a five-point scale that is reported in July to the student, the student's secondary school, and any college designated by the student.
4. AP final scores are reported as follows:
5 = extremely well qualified
4 = well qualified
3 = qualified
2 = possibly qualified
1 = no recommendation

General Description

The AP English Language and Composition exam is used by colleges to assess your ability to perform college-level work. Actual college credit (either for one semester or for an entire year) may be offered by colleges and universities. The test lasts three hours and consists of two major sections. The multiple-choice section includes 55–60 questions that address four reading passages. All the questions in this section have equal value. The second portion of the test is called the free-response section. You are given three essay topics, and you must write an essay on each of the three topics in two hours. The suggested time allotment for each essay is 40 minutes. Each of the essays is of equal value in your final score.

The multiple-choice questions are designed to test your ability in analyzing prose passages; these passages are drawn from a variety of sources, rhetorical modes, historical or literary periods, and disciplines. You will be asked questions about the passages' style, content, and rhetoric. Expect four reading passages with between 12 and 15 questions per passage. However, do not be surprised if you receive five reading passages, which can occasionally happen. If this is the case, the number of questions for each passage will be reduced accordingly. The multiple-choice questions are carefully written and screened by a committee of eight English teachers. The committee is ethnically and geographically balanced, and its members represent public and private high schools, as well as colleges and universities. The committee is responsible for choosing the passages for both the multiple-choice section and the essay portion of the exam. All of the multiple-choice questions are pretested in college classes before they are used on AP examinations.

The essays test your writing ability in a variety of modes and for a variety of purposes. These timed essays measure your expository and analytical writing skills, skills that are essential to success in many college exams. In general, expect the three different essays to give you an opportunity to demonstrate that you can do the following:

1. Analyze how an author's rhetoric and style create meaning
2. Analyze how an author develops an argument or idea
3. Create a persuasive argument of your own for a given topic

The Essay examinations are read and scored during a seven-day period in early June. In the year 2000, more than 300 readers representing the entire United States and Canada read more than 115,000 AP English Language exams. More than half of the AP readers are college or university instructors; less than half are high school teachers. Each reader is assigned to score only one essay question during the reading session; therefore, each student's work is read by at least three readers. Some essays are read and chosen as samples to be examined by all the readers, while others are checked by the table leaders after an individual teacher has scored the essay. You can trust that the essay scoring is as professional and accurate as possible. All readers are thoroughly trained and retrained throughout the week of scoring.

Each essay is scored on a scale from zero to nine. After reading a large number of randomly selected essays, a committee creates a scoring guide that differentiates between the numerical scores for each of the three essay questions. Therefore, the scoring guide is based on the students' *actual performance* in writing the essays, not how the question writers *anticipate* they should perform.

Overall, the entire exam is designed to show student awareness of how an author creates meaning through language use, genre conventions, and rhetorical choices. A qualifying score demonstrates your ability to perform college-level work.

Questions Commonly Asked About the AP English Exams

Q. WHO ADMINISTERS THE TEST?

A. The Advanced Placement exams are sponsored by the College Entrance Examination Board.

Q. WHAT MATERIALS MAY I BRING TO THE TEST?

A. Bring your identification card, plenty of pens for the essays, and pencils for the multiple-choice questions. You may not bring a dictionary, a thesaurus, or any other reference book.

Q. MAY I CANCEL MY SCORE FOLLOWING THE EXAM?

A. Yes. You always have this option.

Q. IS THERE A PENALTY FOR A WRONG ANSWER?

A. Yes. To discourage random guessing, a quarter point is deducted for each wrong answer. You should make only educated guesses.

Q. HOW CAN I PREPARE?

A. Practice! Become comfortable with the test and its format. Take several practice exams to work on your timing. Learn new or unfamiliar terms that you might be expected to know for the exam. Practice your essay planning and timed writing. Practice paraphrasing what you read so that this skill becomes second nature before the exam.

Q. HOW DO I REGISTER FOR AN AP EXAM?

A. See your school counseling office for registration information. Most schools register candidates in March for the upcoming May AP exams.

Q. IS PAPER PROVIDED FOR THE ESSAYS?

A. Yes. In fact, you'll write all of your essays in a special book that conceals your identity from the readers who score it.

Q. HOW MANY STUDENTS A YEAR TAKE THE AP ENGLISH EXAMS?

A. Each year, the number of students taking the test increases, but in 2000, more than 115,000 students took the AP English Language Exam, while more than 189,000 took the AP English Literature Exam.

Q. WHY ARE THERE TWO ENGLISH EXAMS?

A. Because not all colleges offer the same curriculum for freshman English. The two separate exams permit each college to designate the exam that best reflects its curriculum.

Q. WHAT'S THE DIFFERENCE BETWEEN THE TWO ENGLISH EXAMS?

A. Basically, the two tests are similar; they test your ability to analyze the written word and to prove that you can communicate intelligent ideas on a give subject. However, the language exam asks more questions about nonfiction; there is no poetry on the language exam. The language test also places more emphasis on rhetorical analysis and the ability to write and analyze persuasive arguments. In contrast, the literature exam places greater emphasis on literature; it includes poetry, fiction, and drama. You should expect to analyze several poems on the literature test.

Q. WHICH EXAM SHOULD I TAKE?

A. The best way to be sure of which exam to take is to ask the college that you plan to attend. A college may offer either one or two semesters of credit depending on its freshman English curriculum. Generally, a school that has a literary component combined with expository writing skills in its freshman English course gives up to a full year's course credit for the literature exam. Conversely, a school that has a full year of freshman writing in various rhetorical modes may give up to a full year's credit for the language exam. In addition, you must know your own strengths and weaknesses, your likes and dislikes. If you enjoy prose reading and persuasive, analytical writing, then the language exam is for you. If you have a strong literary background, especially in American and British literature and poetic analysis, then AP literature exam will be your goal.

Q. IS EITHER EXAM EASIER THAN THE OTHER?

A. They are equally rigorous.

Q. WHAT IS AN AVERAGE SCORE?

A. To earn an average score of three, you must answer about 50% to 60% of the questions correctly on the multiple-choice section and also write three adequate essays. At a typical test administration, two-thirds of all test takers receive a grade of three or higher.

Q. CAN I TAKE BOTH THE LITERATURE EXAM AND THE LANGUAGE EXAM IN THE SAME SCHOOL YEAR?

A. Yes, they are given on different days.

Q. HOW CAN I FIND OUT HOW MUCH CREDIT I'LL GET AT COLLEGE IF I PASS THE TEST?

A. Contact the college and ask the admissions office for a clear, written response. Do not be surprised to find that this is a somewhat confusing issue, compounded by the fact that two English exams exist. Additionally, some colleges and universities consider an overall score of three as passing, while some require a four. In addition, some schools or programs within a college have different requirements.

Q. DO COLLEGES GET MY MULTIPLE-CHOICE SCORE SEPARATE FROM MY ESSAY SCORE? MAY I GET THE TWO SEPARATE SCORES?

A. No to both questions. Only your overall score, based on one to five will be released to you or to any college.

Q. WHAT IF MY SCHOOL DOES NOT OFFER AN AP COURSE OR I DID NOT ENROLL IN THE COURSE? MAY I TAKE THE TEST ANYWAY?

A. Sure! While an AP course is designed theoretically to prepare students for the test, much of that "preparation" consists of reading quality literature — both fiction and non-fiction — and practicing analysis, critical thinking, and close reading, over and above taking practice AP exams and understanding the format of the exam. You can do this on your own, especially if you have disciplined study habits. However I do strongly recommend that you read this test preparation book carefully, and, if you can, also explore the College Board Web site (www.collegeboard.org/ap).

Q. WHEN WILL I RECEIVE MY AP EXAM SCORES?

A. Approximately in early July; schools receive your scores at the same time.

Q. HOW CAN I OBTAIN OLD EXAMS TO USE FOR PRACTICE?

A. You may order previously released exams directly from the College Board at the Advanced Placement Program, P.O. Box 6670, Princeton, New Jersey, 08541-6670. You may also order materials online: the AP section of College Board information can be found at www.collegeboard.org/ap.

Q. HOW OFTEN ARE PREVIOUS EXAMS RELEASED TO THE PUBLIC?

A. Multiple choice exams are released only every five years; essay topics are released every year.

Q. IF I AM NOT CERTAIN OF THE CORRECT ANSWER, SHOULD I GUESS ON A MULTIPLE-CHOICE QUESTION?

A. Don't be afraid to make an educated guess if you can eliminate at least two of the answer choices. Remember that you get no credit for a question you skip, but lose a quarter of a point for a wrong answer. If a question seems really hard for you, or if you know from your pre-testing practice that it is a question type that tends to stump you, let it go and skip it. Don't forget to leave that answer space blank on your answer sheet when you do fill in the next answer. You will find more information on guessing and eliminating answers in the Introduction to the Multiple-Choice Section.

Q. CAN I STILL PASS THE TEST EVEN IF I DON'T FINISH ALL THE MULTIPLE-CHOICE QUESTIONS IN TIME?

A. Yes! Many students don't finish all the questions and still receive a passing score. Naturally, anyone who does not finish needs to exhibit good accuracy on the questions they do complete and write three good essays. If you are running out of time, do not randomly fill in multiple-choice answers; the chances are you'll get too many wrong and lose a quarter of a point for each wrong answer.

Q. SHOULD I DO THE MULTIPLE-CHOICE PASSAGES IN THE ORDER THEY APPEAR ON THE EXAM?

A. Many students choose to answer the multiple-choice passages in the order they appear on the exam, as it is a very systematic and logical approach. However, be sure to pace yourself and do not let one passage eat up too much of your time, subsequently causing you to slight your time on the last passage(s). Overall, remember that your score is determined by the total number of questions you answer correctly, minus a quarter point for wrong answers.

Q. WHAT SCORE WILL I GET FOR A RIGHT ANSWER, A WRONG ANSWER, AND NO ANSWER IN THE MULTIPLE-CHOICE SECTION?

A. For each correct response, you receive one point; a wrong answer deducts .25 from your score, and an omitted answer earns zero. If you get every multiple-choice answer correct, the total score will equal 45% of 150, or 67.5 points. You will find more explanation on converting raw scores to scaled scores on page 9.

Q. IS ONE OF THE THREE ESSAYS COUNTED MORE HEAVILY THAN THE OTHERS?

A. No, all three essays are counted equally. Since the essay portion of the test is 55% of your total score, each essay equals 18.3% of your essay score.

Q. DO I HAVE TO PLAN MY ESSAY IN ADVANCE?

A. In general, yes, this is a good strategy. An outline is never required and will never be seen by the readers anyway, but clear and logical organization is indeed an important criterion on which your essay is scored. You need to at least know what points you intend to make and the order in which you plan to present them.

Q. HOW MANY PARAGRAPHS SHOULD I WRITE FOR EACH ESSAY?

A. As many paragraphs as you need to fully develop and present your ideas. While the introduction-body-conclusion format is most frequently used, the number of body paragraphs presented varies from student to student and topic to topic. An introductory paragraph that contains a thesis is understandably an appropriate beginning, but do not worry if you don't get to the conclusion. Read more about essay organization and development in the Introduction to the Essay Section.

Q. HOW MANY PAGES SHOULD EACH ESSAY BE?

A. No set length is required; however, most high-scoring essays are approximately one and a half pages long. Naturally, some essays are shorter and some are longer. Instead of worrying about length, concentrate on addressing all of the tasks of the topic and developing your ideas thoroughly. Be aware that very short essays, such as those that are only about half a page in length, are considered "unacceptably brief" and score very low; they simply do not demonstrate enough development of their ideas to receive a passing score. You can read student sample essays in the Introduction to the Essay Section and get a feel for length.

Q. SHOULD I WORRY ABOUT GRAMMAR AND SPELLING?

A. Good news! You don't have to worry too much about your spelling. If you can spell reasonably well, no reader will dock your score. When you read any of the scoring guides for essays, you will notice that the word "spelling" is never mentioned. The readers are remarkably tolerant; they want to read your words. Grammar and punctuation can be another issue, though. The readers are always willing to overlook what they call "minor errors" or "honest mistakes" that are made under timed pressure. They understand that what you have produced is a first draft that is likely to have a few flaws. However, if your errors are persistent and serious, the reader will have to lower your score. In fact, the scoring guide states that no essay that is particularly poorly written, one with errors so severe that they distract the reader's attention from the student's ideas, may receive a score higher than a two.

Q. SHOULD I WRITE MY ESSAYS IN CURSIVE OR SHOULD I PRINT?

A. You need to write as legibly as you can, so use whatever method is easiest to read. I stress again that the readers want to be able to reward you for your essay; to do so they have to read the words. Please don't forget to use a nice black or blue pen; avoid ones that "bleed through" paper, as you'll want to write on the back of the page.

Q. DO THE ESSAYS NEED A TITLE?

A. Not at all. It will never affect your score. I can guarantee that readers are bored by dull titles anyway. Why not just get started on the essay itself?

Q. MAY I BE CREATIVE IN MY ESSAY WRITING?

A. The number-one rule is that you must address the essay question; if you can do so in a creative fashion, you may be rewarded, as long as it works well. Again, once you read some sample scoring guides, you'll notice that creativity is never mentioned as a specific criterion for scoring. The basic tenants are that your essay must be focused on the topic, organized and well-developed. Do all that in a creative style and the reader may be pleasantly surprised. I've read creative essays that received a nine because they covered all the necessary points and presented ideas in such a refreshing style.

Q. HOW MUCH OF THE ESSAY PASSAGE SHOULD I QUOTE?

A. No set, formulaic answer exists. Yes, you do need to refer to the passage appropriately in order to support your ideas, and many of those examples can take the form of quotations. However, a string of irrelevant quotations, glued together with a few of your own words will not help your score at all. Read the many sample essays in this text to get a feel for what's appropriate.

Q. CAN I PASS THE TEST IF I DON'T FINISH AN ESSAY?

A. Of course! Understandably, a radically unfinished essay will receive a very low score, so try to pace yourself accordingly, devoting approximately 40 minutes to each essay. Doing so should allow you time to finish each essay. Also, practice your pacing many times before the test. I also advise practicing the planning period over and over. If, within approximately 10–12 minutes, you can organize what you're going to say and the order in which you're going to present it, you should have enough time to actually write the words and sentences. Finally, if you find yourself in a time crunch on the day of the test, remember that body paragraphs are much more important than concluding paragraphs — especially conclusions that merely summarize — and you should devote your time to getting your ideas down on paper. The readers' constant motto is "reward the writers for what they do well."

Q. CAN YOU TELL ME HOW TO APPROXIMATE MY SCORE FROM MY PRACTICE TESTS INTO AN AP SCALED SCORE OF ONE-THROUGH-FIVE?

A. Approximating your score is a bit more complicated than merely counting your numbers right and numbers wrong, but follow these directions and use the chart that follows. Additionally, you will find a sample scoring worksheet located in this text after each full-length sample exam (on the page before the answers and explanations).

The total score on the exam is 150. Since the essay and multiple-choice parts are weighted 55% to 45%, there are 82.5 points for the essays and 67.5 for the multiple-choice questions. Since the three essays are graded on a nine-point scale (plus zero), each point on your essay raw score would be multiplied by 3.055. Three nines would total 27×3.055, which would total 82.5. If there are 55 multiple-choice questions, each point in the raw score would be multiplied by 1.227 to equal 67.5, Remember that the raw score in the multiple-choice section is determined by the number of correct answers less one-quarter point for each wrong answer. A test with 30 right, 20 wrong, and 5 omitted would have a raw score of $30 - 5$, or 25. This raw score converts to a total of 30.675 (25×1.227).

The total number of points required for a final score of 5, 4, or 3 is different each year, but a very reasonable assumption is 100–150 for a score of 5, 86–99 for a score of 4, and 67–85 for a score of 3. The following chart gives you an idea of the combined scores you need on the essay and the multiple-choice sections in order to receive final scores of 3, 4, or 5. The chart assumes that there are 55 multiple-choice questions and three essay questions graded from 0–9.

If a student received fives on all three essays, in order to receive a final score of three, he or she would need a raw score (the number correct less one-quarter times the number wrong) of at least eighteen on the multiple-choice section. To receive a final score of 5, that student would need a raw score of at least 46 in the multiple-choice section.

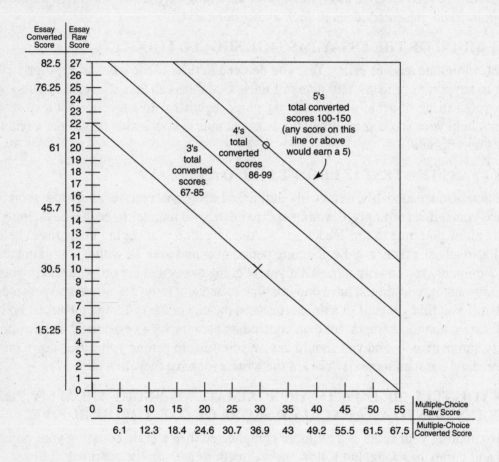

Some Successful Testing Strategies

1. **Increase your awareness of the test structure;** Know how many questions you'll be asked, how much time you'll have, what basic skills you need, and so forth. Of course, these preliminaries are all covered in this book.

2. **Understand the thought process behind the exam.** If you understand what the test makers have in mind when they write questions and answers, you'll avoid fighting the test, and your elimination of wrong answers will go faster.

3. **Read the test directions carefully!** Become familiar with the wording of the directions in advance so that you'll be as comfortable as possible on the day of your AP exam.

4. **Mark your answer sheet carefully.** If you skip an answer, mark it *in your test book* and then check to make sure that the next answer has been correctly entered on your answer sheet.

5. **Practice your pacing and timing skills.** For multiple-choice questions, complete the easiest ones first; in essay writing, follow your preplanned strategy.

6. **Overall, be prepared!** Become familiar with the test. Remember that increased comfort builds confidence and relieves anxiety. These skills can all be improved by practicing *frequently.*

PART II

ANALYSIS OF EXAM AREAS

This section is designed to introduce you to each AP area by carefully reviewing the

1. ability tested
2. basic skills necessary
3. directions
4. analysis of directions
5. suggested approaches and strategies

Introduction to the Multiple-Choice Section

The multiple-choice section is normally 60 minutes long and consists of about 55 questions. You should expect four reading passages that represent a variety of rhetorical modes (for example, narration, argumentation, persuasion, description). The passages may vary in length from about 300 to about 800 words. Each passage is followed by 10 to 15 questions based on its content. These questions are not ordered by level of difficulty. Occasionally, a multiple-choice section of the exam may have five passages, rather than four, with fewer questions per passage. You will, however, always have the same approximate number of total questions on every exam.

Remember that you're not expected to be familiar with the passage or its specific content. Consider this section to be akin to a scavenger hunt; the passage will give you everything you need, it's just up to you to find it and think about it accurately. Any technical information crucial to comprehending the passage, as well as unusual or foreign phrases, will be defined for you.

You will be more comfortable with both the essay and multiple-choice sections if you are adept at reading works from many genres and time periods. For instance, the test can cover works from autobiographies or biographies, historical writing, essays and literature criticism, journalism, political writing, nature writing, and scientific writing. The test passages can be up to about 400 years old, so you'll need to practice comprehending and appreciating the style of older pieces as well as contemporary ones. A student who only practices with modern-day authors will not be as relaxed during the exam reading as one who has been exposed to Milton or Dr. Johnson.

Ability Tested

This section tests your ability to analyze the linguistic and rhetorical choices of an author. You are expected to show an awareness of the stylistic effects created by specific word choices. These questions also test your ability to examine prose passages critically, to understand the author's meaning and purpose, to comprehend structural organization, to recognize rhetorical modes, and to analyze syntax, figurative language, style, and tone. The level of difficulty reflects college-level study.

Basic Skills Necessary

In general, you need an adequate background in grammar and in literary analysis. Although the questions don't specifically ask for definitions of terms (such as "subordinate clause" or "syntax"), you should be familiar with terms that may show up in the question stems or as answer choices. See the Glossary of Important Terms for a review of the terms you're likely to encounter on the test; you must understand *how* the terms create meaning. In addition, you need to have developed proficiency in careful reading for your analysis and interpretation of the passages. You can gain this proficiency by active, visual reading.

Directions

Directions: This section contains selections from prose works and questions on their content, form, and style. Read each selection carefully. Choose one of the best answers of the five choices.

Questions 1– . Read the following passage carefully before you begin to answer the questions.

Analysis of Directions

- **Use self-discipline to manage your time effectively during the test.** You can develop this skill through practice. You should divide your time for each passage accordingly. Do *not* let yourself fall further and further behind as the test progresses.

- **Answer all the questions to the best of your ability before going on to the next passage.** This strategy avoids your having to return to any given passage at the end of the test just to answer a few skipped questions. If you put yourself in the position of returning to a passage, you'll have to reread it and that process is too time consuming.

- **Read each passage carefully and critically.** First, paraphrase the author's ideas as you read; then, concentrate on effective word choice. Avoid getting bogged down in diction, whether it's a word you don't know or the structure of a sentence that's confusing. Simply keep trying to get the main point and then let the questions guide what you need to know.

- **Read all the answer choices.** Remember that the directions call for the *best* answer choice, which means there can be more than one reasonable choice for each question. Eliminate wrong answer choices. Never forget that the wrong answer is wrong for a reason. The correct response will not have a single wrong word in it. You can become more proficient at eliminating wrong answers by practicing spotting the wrong word or phrase in the incorrect responses.

Suggested Strategies for Reading Passages and Questions

1. **First, skim the question to find out what you should concentrate on.** Doing so as you read the passage helps you focus on what the test writers found important. Skimming involves a very fast reading speed — approximately 1000 words per minute — so be aware that during this skimming, you are really just glancing at the questions. Ignore any "generic" questions, such as ones that ask you the author's main purpose or main point; instead try to find approximately five specific ideas that you can look for while you read the passage. Do not try to memorize the questions; you're just glancing at them to help you focus.

   This technique works well when you practice frequently enough before the test for it to become second nature. You should look for the specific content of each question. For example, don't merely note that a question asks you to draw an inference. You must also focus upon the specific content included in the inference. Prior practice is essential for you to become comfortable with the strategy of skimming the questions prior to reading the passage.

2. **Read each passage *actively* and *visually*.** *Active reading* means that you should underline and mark key words and ideas (just the few most important ones) as you read. Don't sit passively and merely let your eyes move across the page. Scientific studies support the idea that active readers gain higher immediate retention than do passive readers, and immediate retention is all you need in this case. You'll not be concerned at all with long-term memory on the day of the exam.

   Visual reading means that you should picture any action of the passage in your mind; create a movie, if you will. Visual reading is a most valuable tool for eliminating distractions while reading. It gives your brain a task to perform and helps keep your mind on the content of the passage. Most people are visual learners; they remember more after they have "seen" something, even if it's in their imagination Both of these strategies enhance your immediate retention and concentration — just what you need the most on this test. Practice these skills daily and watch them become more effective with continued use.

3. **Paraphrase while you're reading.** This technique also helps your immediate retention and understanding of the author's ideas. By definition, paraphrasing means that you can articulate the author's ideas in *your own words*. This is an essential skill for comprehension, and, like visual reading, gives your brain "something to do" that is on task while you read. Every question that asks about a passage's main ideas or an author's point can be answered correctly if you paraphrase accurately. For any given passage, paraphrase each paragraph as a unit, and then paraphrase the author's overall point that covers all of the paragraphs. Practice by *writing down* your concise statement of an author's point immediately after reading a paragraph or a whole passage. Later, you can develop this skill to the point that it's internalized, and you can paraphrase very quickly. You'll find that eventually you can paraphrase effectively *while* you're reading.

4. **Read the question carefully after you've read the passage.** Don't assume from an earlier skimming that you know each question well. You must understand exactly what you're being asked. Students who frequently choose the wrong answer have misread the question by either reading too quickly or by not being sure what's actually being asked.

5. **Read all the answer choices carefully.** Eliminate a wrong-answer choice as you read it and cross out that letter *in the test book.* Never waste time rereading the wrong answers. Make sure that your answer choice is accurate according to the passage and that it answers the question.

6. **Leave the most difficult questions until the end of each section.** From your practice on the test, you can learn to recognize which questions are harder for you and which ones you can do accurately and quickly. Then use this knowledge as part of your personal strategy to get the most correct answers you possibly can. Remember to treat each passage as a unit and try to answer all the questions you can for that passage within your time limit before going on to the next passage.

7. **One way to increase your score is to always analyze the questions that you get wrong on the practice tests.** Try to find out why you selected each incorrect answer choice. Did you misread the question? Did you misread the answer? Did you work too quickly? Try to detect any trends; for example, a certain question type may always be the hardest for you. Then you can study, analyze, and understand why the correct answer is better than your choice. This analysis will help you to stop repeating the same mistakes.

8. **Practice!** With extensive practice, you'll increase your familiarity with the question types. Thus, you'll begin to think like the test makers, not the test takers, and your score will improve.

Reasons Answers May Be Wrong

Understanding how to eliminate incorrect answer choices saves time and increases accuracy. Of course the test writers are trying to "trick" you. If you understand the tricks they frequently throw at you, you'll work faster to eliminate wrong answers and you'll be less likely to be deceived by them. When trying to eliminate wrong answers remember to think like a test writer, not a test taker. Remember to cross out each wrong answer in the test booklet; don't waste time rereading these wrong answers. Wrong answers can be:

1. **Contradictory to the passage.** If you read the passage carefully, and paraphrase accurately you won't be tricked into the time-consuming process of rereading it to find what the author really said.

2. **Irrelevant or not addressed in the passage.** Again, poor readers are tricked into rereading to look for ideas that weren't there in the first place. Readers who are accurate at paraphrasing can quickly eliminate the irrelevant or "never addressed" answer choice.

3. **Unreasonable.** If the answer makes you shake your head and ask, "Where did they get that idea?" it's unreasonable. You should be able to spot unreasonable answer choices quickly.

4. **Too general or too specific for the question.** Understand the degree of specificity that you need for a correct answer. For instance, if the question asks for the best title of a passage, you need a general answer, one that encompasses the content of the entire essay. On the other hand, if you're asked about the author's use of a certain quotation, the correct answer is likely to be quite specific.

Finally, never forget that the wrong answer is wrong for a specific reason and *will* always have an inaccurate word or phrase. Practice crossing out the exact word or phrase that is wrong and you'll find you can perform faster and with greater confidence. The correct answer will not have a single word that is inaccurate.

Question Categories to Expect

In general, the test questions tend to fall into just a few categories. By becoming familiar with these areas, you can more quickly understand what you're being asked. Also, you'll be more comfortable with the test format and able to work faster. As with all testing strategies, your practice in recognizing the question types *before* the test is essential.

A brief analysis of these questions types follows.

Questions about Rhetoric

The majority of the questions on the test are of this type and test your ability to understand *how* language works in each passage. These questions ask you to analyze the syntax (word order and word choice), point of view, and figurative language and its effects. Your mere recognition of these elements is not enough; you must be able to understand precisely how and why the devices of rhetoric produce particular effects.

Some of the ways this question type may be worded on the test are

- The shift in point of view has the effect of . . .
- The syntax of lines _____ to _____ serves to . . .
- Which of the following choices best describes what "_____" symbolizes?
- The second sentence is unified by metaphorical references to . . .
- As lines _____ and _____ are constructed, "_____" is parallel to which of the following?
- The antecedent for "_____" is . . .
- The third sentence remains coherent because of the use of . . .
- The phrase "_____" has the effect of . . .
- The style of the passage can best be characterized as . . .
- The sentence "_____" is chiefly remarkable for its . . .

Questions about the Author's Meaning and Purpose

These question types also appear frequently on the test. They measure your ability to interpret the author's theme, meaning, or purpose. As with the rhetorical questions, these questions are closely tied to specific word choices; however, now you must determine *why* the author chooses the wording, not what effect it produces. These questions demonstrate the understanding of the author's thematic reason for choosing certain phrases. Some of the ways this question type may be worded are

- Which of the following best identifies the meaning of "_____"?
- Which of the following best describes the author's purpose in the last sentence?
- The main purpose of "_____" is to make clear . . .
- The author emphasizes "_____" in order to . . .
- The sympathy referred to in line _____ is called "_____" because it . . .
- What is the function of _____?
- By "_____," the author most probably means . . .
- In context, which of the following meanings are contained in "_____"?

Questions about the Main Idea

These questions also appear quite frequently; they test your understanding of the author's ideas, attitude, and tone. To prepare for these questions, paraphrase everything that you read. First, make yourself practice this skill in writing — literally write down an author's point in a sentence or two. After such practice, you'll be able to do it internally while you read, and you'll have greater comprehension.

Some of the ways these questions may be worded are

- The theme of the second paragraph is . . .
- The speaker's attitude is best described as one of . . .
- The speaker interests the audience by stressing the idea that . . .
- It can be inferred from the description of _____ that which of the following qualities are valued by the author?
- In context, the sentence "_____" is best interpreted as which of the following?
- The atmosphere is one of . . .
- Which of the following would the author be LEAST likely to encourage?
- Which of the following is true about the various assertions made in the passage?
- All of the following ideas may be found in the passage EXCEPT . . .

Questions about Organization and Structure

Appearing less frequently than the first three question types, these questions test your ability to perceive how the passage is organized. For example, you need to know if the passage follows a comparison/contrast structure or if it gives a definition followed by examples. Other passages may be organized around descriptive statements that then lead to a generalization. These are just a few of the methods an author may use to organize ideas. You also need to understand how the structure of the passage works. For example, you must know how one paragraph relates to another paragraph or how a single sentence works within a paragraph.

Some of the ways this question type may be worded are

- The quotation "_____" signals a shift from . . .
- The speaker's mention of "_____" is appropriate to the development of her argument by . . .
- The type of argument employed by the author is most similar to which of the following?
- The speaker describes _____ in an order best described as moving from . . .
- The relationship between _____ and _____ is explained primarily by the use of which of the following?
- The author's discussion depends on which of the following structures?
- Which of the following best describes the function of the third paragraph in relation to the preceding two?

Questions about Rhetorical Modes

You should expect only a few questions of this type on the test. These questions ask you to identify and recognize the various rhetorical modes that authors use. You must know the difference between narration, description, argumentation, and exposition. Understanding *why* a particular mode is effective for the author's ideas is also helpful.

Some of the ways these questions may be worded are

- The pattern of exposition exemplified in the passage can best be described as . . .
- The author's use of description is appropriate because . . .
- Which of the following best describes the author's method?
- Because the author uses expository format, he is able to . . .

Other Possibilities

Be aware that the question types listed above do not constitute a complete list. You will encounter questions that don't seem to fit into a category. However, by understanding what question types are asked most frequently, you will increase your familiarity with the test and improve your understanding of how to find correct answers. Don't be thrown off balance by questions that don't seem to fall into set categories.

Examples of Multiple-Choice Passages and Questions

This section contains two passages that are typical of the ones chosen for the multiple choice section of the exam, followed by sample questions. Read the passage(s) carefully, and attempt to find the correct answer to each question. The answers and their explanations follow.

Sample Multiple-Choice Passages, Questions, Answers, and Explanations

Set 1

Directions: The following excerpt, from the twentieth-century writer Ellen Meloy, is typical of the difficulty of the passages you will encounter on the actual AP Exam. Read it carefully and then answer the 15 multiple-choice questions that follow. Choose the *best* answer of the five options. Answers and explanations for the questions immediately follow. Then, you will find another sample passage with its questions, answers, and explanations.

The morning sun, already burning an eighty-degree day, tops a cliff cut with fine strata of red rock and broken at its foot by emerald cottonwoods and a silt-
(5) gold river. I don a khaki uniform shirt, shorts, ninety-seven-cent hot pink thongs and, clipboard in hand, walk from the trailer to a boat ramp plunked down in nearly a million acres of
(10) sparsely inhabited desert. This is an act of courage. Courage to face the violation of isolation rather than isolation itself, for I savor the remoteness and the rare times I'm alone on this muscular river in
(15) southern Utah, a precious ribbon of wild water between reservoirs and the suck holes of industry and agriculture.

Officially, I'm here to have my peace disturbed. Floaters must have a permit to
(20) run this stretch of river. During the peak season a ranger checks lottery-drawn launch dates and a short list of gear related to safety and environmental protection. The permit system allows the

(25) federal agency in charge to hold numbers of floaters to a maximum of about 10,000 a year, set in 1979, when use increased 250 percent in just three seasons. Each year since, the actual number
(30) of people down the river has hovered close to this ceiling, which the agency believes is the river's capacity for a "quality wilderness experience." Socially, if not physically, however,
(35) "wilderness experience" seems to have become an illusion if not irrelevant. Right now I'm the voluntary ranger managing both the illusion and the irrelevance.

(40) Most people accept the permit system as a panacea for the explosion in numbers of river runners and the consequences for a fragile riparian corridor. Others find regulation about as painless
(45) as an IRS audit.

They see the Southwest as a region of federally neutered rivers where a person is no longer free to kill himself in a

(50) four-foot rubber ducky pulling an inner tube piled with beans, testosterone, and a small machete. Instead, some geek rangerette at the put-in asks to see his bilge pump.

(55) The boat ramp is swarming with people and vehicles to be shuttled to the take-out. Someone's dog is throwing up what appears to be rabbit parts. I'm approached by a pickup driven by a man waving a spray nozzle and hose hooked (60) to a large barrel of allegedly lethal chemicals. He's from county weed control, he says. Have I seen the loathsome pepperweed? Not a leaf, I lie.

Cheerfully I sign the permit of the (65) outfitter who specializes in theme river trips—stress management seminars, outings for the crystal fondlers or fingernail technicians of East Jesus, New Jersey, overcoming, at last, their irra-(70) tional fear of Nature. Today's load is priests troubled by a lapsed faith—pale, anxious, overweight fellows in the early stages of heatstroke. I also check gear and answer questions about bugs, (75) snakes, scorpions, camps, rapids and Indians (one side of the river is reservation land). Do I live here full-time? they ask. No, I respond, except for an occasional shift at the put-in, I'm on (80) the river eight days out of sixteen, six months a year.

Would I please call their mother in Provo to tell her they forgot to turn off the oven? Am I afraid of being alone (85) when the ax murderer shows up? Did Ed Abbey live in that trailer over there. Some rafts look as if they barely survived World War II.

Others are outfitted with turbody-(90) namic chrome-plated throw lines, heat-welded vinyl dry-bags, cargo nets spun from the fibers of dew-fed arachnids from Borneo, horseshoes, volleyball sets, sauna tents, coffin-sized coolers (95) stuffed with sushi, a small fleet of squirt boats, whining packs of androgynous progeny who prefer to be at home fulfilling their needs electronically. All of this gear is color-coordinated with SPF 14 (100) sunscreen and owned by business majors in Styrofoam pith helmets and Lycra body gloves, in which they were placed at birth. Once loaded, their boats are pieces of personal architecture, stun-(105) ning but nevertheless stuck on the sandbar six feet out from the boat ramp after a dramatic send-off.

1. The speaker of the passage is best described as a

   A. chronicler of events of the past.

   B. dispassionate eyewitness of the scene.

   C. commentator on contemporary American mores.

   D. concerned and angry ecologist.

   E. fictional persona describing imaginary events.

23

2. In the first paragraph, the author uses the reference to her "ninety-seven cent hot pink thongs" in order to

   I. set a tone of casual and humorous informality.

   II. show the speaker's unconcern for the expected ranger uniform.

   III. exemplify man's desecration of the natural world.

   A. I only

   B. I and II only

   C. I and III only

   D. II and III only

   E. I, II, and III

3. The move from the first paragraph (lines 1–17) to the second (lines 18–39) can best be described as a shift from

   A. personal reminiscence to impersonal inquiry.

   B. poetic description to dispassionate reasoning.

   C. philosophical meditation to satiric argument.

   D. minute description to explanatory generalization.

   E. personal expression to objective exposition.

4. In line 33, the author puts the phrase "quality wilderness experience" in quotation marks in order to

   A. draw special attention to a phrase that sums up the meaning of the whole passage.

   B. give proper credit for a felicitous phrase that is not her own.

   C. help the reader to remember the phrase.

   D. disassociate herself from the language of the federal agency.

   E. encourage wider participation in "wilderness experience."

5. The third paragraph of the passage (lines 40–45) employs all of the following EXCEPT

   A. pun

   B. simile

   C. metaphor

   D. hyperbole

   E. slang

6. All of the following words or phrases are examples of the author's use of colloquialism EXCEPT

   A. "plunked down," lines 8–9.

   B. "muscular river," line 14.

   C. "rubber ducky," line 49.

   D. "geek rangerette," lines 51–52.

   E. "East Jesus, New Jersey," lines 68–69.

7. In the fifth and sixth paragraphs (lines 54–81), the author characterizes the rafters by describing all of the following EXCEPT their

   A. possessions

   B. physical appearance

   C. occupations

   D. responses to nature

   E. dialogue

8. In the final paragraph, all of the following are probably fanciful comic details EXCEPT

   A. "turbodynamic chrome-plated throw lines," lines 89–90.

   B. "heat-welded vinyl dry-bags," lines 90–91.

   C. "the fibers of dew-fed arachnids from Borneo," lines 92–93.

   D. "sauna tents," line 94.

   E. "progeny who prefer to be at home," line 97.

9. In lines 96–98, the phrase "androgynous progeny who prefer to be at home fulfilling their needs electronically" refers to

   A. discontented house-pets unaccustomed to outdoor life.

   B. children who would rather be watching television.

   C. elaborate radio equipment carried by the rafters.

   D. expensive refrigeration units that are slowly defrosting.

   E. electric motors for propelling the river-rafts.

10. The effect of the last sentence of the passage (lines 103–107) can be best described as a(n)

    A. comic anti-climax.

    B. resolution of an argument.

    C. symbolic metaphor.

    D. deliberate understatement.

    E. allegorical conclusion.

11. In the course of the passage, the speaker suggests her disapproval of all of the following EXCEPT

    A. rafters hostile to government regulations.

    B. industry and agriculture.

    C. stress-management seminars.

    D. conspicuous consumers.

    E. government regulation of the wild rivers.

12. In which paragraph is the speaker's feeling for the landscape revealed most clearly?

    A. the first

    B. the second

    C. the third

    D. the fourth

    E. the sixth

13. A primary rhetorical strategy in the passage is to

    A. use the experience of an individual's life to generalize about life in general.

    B. stimulate the reader's interest by withholding important information.

    C. convince the reader of the speaker's objectivity by presenting an opposing viewpoint.

    D. make its point by an accumulation of carefully observed details.

    E. imply support of a position that is later to be withdrawn.

14. In the course of the passage, the speaker uses all of the following tones of voice EXCEPT

   A. amused

   B. annoyed

   C. arrogant

   D. satiric

   E. cheerful

15. Which of the following best describes the primary purpose of the passage?

   A. to describe an idyllic scene in nature.

   B. to protest against the loss of the isolated wilderness.

   C. to comment upon a popular misconception.

   D. to satirize aspects of the back-to nature movement.

   E. to reveal the personality of the speaker.

Answers and Explanations for Set 1

This passage is from Ellen Meloy's essay "Communiqué from the Vortex of Gravity Sports."

1. C. The passage is written in the present tense, and describes events of the present time. Though it sometimes employs overstatement for comic effect, the passage is apparently a factual, not a fictional account. Though the speaker is mindful of ecology, she is neither angry nor dispassionate; she is an amused and amusing commentator on this scene that reveals some contemporary American mores.

2. B. The speaker's hot-pink thongs reveal her humorous informality and her unconventional notion of a uniform. To read a "desecration" of the natural world into this detail is to miss the tone, to take the passage far too seriously. Since it is the speaker who is wearing the thongs, it is unlikely that they carry such dire significance.

3. E. The first paragraph places the speaker in the scene, and tells us something of her feelings. The second paragraph gives an explanation of why she is here. Of the five answers, E, if not ideal, is the best choice, as it avoids the outright errors of "reminiscence" and "inquiry," of "reasoning," of "meditation" and "argument," and of "minute description" and "generalization."

4. D. Since the speaker has serious doubts about the accuracy of this phrase, she disassociates herself from it by using quotation marks. It may be that she objects to the trite and ungrammatical use of "quality" as an adjective; she certainly questions the use of the word "wilderness" to describe this situation.

5. A. The paragraph does not use a pun, but it does employ a simile ("painless as an IRS audit"), metaphor ("explosion," "neutered"), hyperbole or overstatement ("four-foot rubber ducky") and slang ("geek").

6. B. The phrase "muscular river" is figurative, a personification of the river, but it is not colloquial diction. The other four phrases are examples of the effective use of colloquialism in the passage.

7. D. The paragraphs describe the rafters' equipment and appearance, the jobs of some of them, and, in indirect discourse, their dialogue. We are not told about their responses to nature.

8. E. The "progeny who prefer to be at home" are, no doubt, all too real. The other details are more likely to be comic inventions.

9. B. The phrase is a circumlocutionary way of describing the children who prefer television to wild rivers.

10. A. Words and phrases like "architecture," "stunning," and "dramatic send-off" suggest some big event, but the reality is the anti-climax of "stuck on the sandbar six feet out from the boat ramp."

11. E. The second and third paragraphs suggest that the speaker approves of government regulation of the rivers as a way to protect the "fragile riparian corridor." Her disapproval of the macho rafters who object to the permit system is behind the comedy of the third paragraph. Paragraphs five and six make fun of trendy stress-management seminars and the conspicuous consumption of the too-well-equipped rafters, while the first paragraph speaks of the "precious ribbon of wild water between reservoirs and the suck holes of industry and agriculture."

12. A. The speaker reveals her own feelings about the wilderness in the first paragraph of the passage.

13. D. Of the five rhetorical strategies proposed, only the use of observed details is relevant to this prose.

14. C. At one time or another, the speaker sounds amused, annoyed, satiric, and cheerful, but she is never arrogant.

15. D. Though the passage does reveal the speaker's regret at the loss of isolated wilderness in the first paragraph, the subject is not developed. Most of the passage is concerned with the presentation of the rafters seeking a "quality wilderness experience."

Set 2

Directions: This second sample passage was written by Frederick Douglass. Read it carefully and answer the 11 questions that follow. As always, find the *best* answer choice.

Very soon after I went to live with Mr. and Mrs. Auld, she very kindly commenced to teach me the A,B,Cs. After I had learned this, she assisted me in
(5) learning to spell words of three or four letters. Just at this point of my progress, Mr. Auld found out what was going on, and at once forbade Mrs. Auld to instruct me further, telling her, among
(10) other things, that it was unlawful, as well as unsafe, to teach a slave to read. It would forever unfit him to be a slave. He would at once become unmanageable, and of no value to his master. As to him-
(15) self, it could do him no good, but a great deal of harm. It would make him discontented and unhappy. These words sank deep into my heart, stirred up sentiments within that lay slumbering, and called
(20) into existence an entirely new train of

thought. It was a new and special revelation, explaining dark and mysterious things, with which my youthful understanding had struggled, but struggled in (25) vain. I now understood what had been to me a most perplexing difficulty — to wit, the white man's power to enslave the black man. It was a grand achievement, and I prized it highly. From that (30) moment, I understood the pathway from slavery to freedom. It was just what I wanted, and I got it at a time when I least expected it. Whilst I was saddened by the thought of losing the aid of my (35) kind mistress, I was gladdened by the invaluable instruction which, by the merest accident, I had gained from my master. Though conscious of the difficulty of learning without a teacher, I set (40) out with high hope, and a fixed purpose, at whatever cost of trouble, to learn how to read.

The very decided manner with which he spoke, and strove to impress his wife (45) with the evil consequences of giving me instruction, served to convince me that he was deeply sensible of the truths he was uttering. It gave me the best assurance that I might rely with the utmost (50) confidence on the results which, he said, would flow from teaching me how to read. What he most dreaded, that I most desired. What he most loved, that I most hated. That which to him was a great (55) evil, to be carefully shunned, was to me a great good, to be diligently sought; and the argument which he so warmly urged, against my learning to read, only served to inspire me with a desire and determi- (60) nation to learn. In learning to read, I owe almost as much to the bitter opposition of my master, as to the kindly aid of my mistress. I acknowledge the benefit of both.

1. From its content, we can infer that the passage was written by

   A. a nineteenth-century white narrator hostile to slavery.

   B. a modern historian.

   C. an ex-slave looking back on his past.

   D. a modern autobiographer.

   E. a white narrator sympathetic to slavery.

2. From the report of Mr. Auld's words in lines 10–16, we can infer that he believed that the illiterate slave was

   I. a valuable legal property.

   II. one incapable of learning.

   III. one content with his or her position.

   A. III only

   B. I and II only

   C. I and III only

   D. II and III only

   E. I, II, and III

3. Of the following, which are figurative rather than literal?

   I. "sentiments within that lay slumbering," lines 18–19

   II. "an entirely new train of thought," lines 20–21

   III. "the pathway from slavery to freedom," lines 30–31

   A. I only

   B. I and II only

   C. I and III only

   D. II and III only

   E. I, II, and III

4. In lines 15 and 16, if the pronouns "it" have a single word as their antecedent, they refer to

    A. "revelation," line 21.

    B. "things," line 23.

    C. "understanding," line 23.

    D. "difficulty," line 26.

    E. "power," line 27.

5. In line 43, the word "decided" can be best defined as

    A. judgmental

    B. definite

    C. inclusive

    D. stentorian

    E. patriarchal

6. In lines 52–54 (" What he most . . . I most hated."), the author employs

    I. two sentences in a parallel structure.

    II. a parallel structure in the first sentence (lines 52–53).

    III. a parallel structure in the second sentence (line 53–54).

    A. I only

    B. I and II only

    C. I and III only

    D. II and III only

    E. I, II, and III

7. In lines 54–56 ("That which to him . . . to be diligently sought"), all of the following are balanced against each other EXCEPT

    A. "that which" — "was to him"

    B. "him" — "me"

    C. "great" — "great"

    D. "evil" — "good"

    E. "carefully" — "diligently"

8. In line 63, if the word "benefit" which can mean "a kindly act" or "anything contributing to improvement" is used to denote the first of these meanings, the final line of the passage is an example of

    A. paradox

    B. overstatement

    C. metaphor

    D. irony

    E. personification

9. The passage could be used to support effectively a general argument about

    A. the kinder treatment of slaves by women than by men.

    B. the importance of motivation to learning.

    C. the physical cruelty in the treatment of slaves.

    D. the dangers of education.

    E. the corruption that results from power.

10. All of the following describe the style of the passage EXCEPT

    A. the use of carefully balanced sentences.

    B. the occasional use of short loose sentences.

    C. the use of the first person pronoun.

    D. the use of original metaphors and similes.

    E. the use of indirect discourse.

11. The passage illustrates the truth of the paradox that

    A. learning may be power.

    B. slavery may be freedom.

    C. a foe may be an ally.

    D. poverty may be wealth.

    E. a falsehood may be truth.

Answers and Explanations for Set 2

The passage is from the autobiography, *Narrative of the Life of Frederick Douglass, an American Slave* (1845).

1. C. The first 20 lines of the passage reveal that the speaker had been a slave, and that he learned that literacy is the "pathway from slavery to freedom." The passage itself is evidence of achievement of that literacy.

2. C. We can infer the value of the illiterate slave from the slave owner's fear that the literate slave will have "no value." We see his willed belief in the contentedness of the slave from his saying the literate slave would be "discontented and unhappy." Since Mr. Auld takes pains to withhold education from his slave, he cannot believe that they are incapable of learning.

3. C. The first quotation personifies "sentiments," and the third compares literacy and a "pathway." The word "train" has as one of it several literal meanings "series" or "sequence" and the use of the word here is literal, not a reference to Amtrak.

4. A. It is tempting to see the whole clause "I now understood . . . the most perplexing difficulty" as the antecedent of "it;" if the pronouns refer to a single word, it must be "revelation" (line 21) rather than "understanding" (line 23) since this "understanding" is "in vain." The antecedent must be an "achievement" of the speaker.

5. B. As it is used here, "decided" is an adjective meaning "definite" or "unhesitatingly."

6. E. There are three parallels here. Both short sentences balance the "What he . . ." clause with the "that I . . ." clause, and the two sentences use the same parallel structures.

7. A. The "that which" is not repeated or balanced. It is the subject of both parts of this compound sentence.

8. D. If "benefit" is used with its associations of kindness, it is ironic in this context, since Mr. Auld's real purpose was to maintain his power over his slave. That his attempt to prevent his slave from learning to read motivates him to do so is also an example of dramatic irony.

9. **B.** The passage is essentially about Frederick Douglass's learning to read, and he gives much of the credit for this achievement to his motivation, his "fixed purpose, at whatever cost or trouble." The other topics are perhaps true, but none is really an issue in this passage.

10. **D.** There are no similes and only a few commonplace metaphors in the passage. Lines 33–38 are carefully balanced. The last sentence of the passage is a good example of a short, simple sentence. Lines 10–14 use indirect discourse, and the whole passage employs a first person speaker.

11. **C.** The paradox central to the passage is Mr. Auld's double role of oppressor and benefactor.

A Successful Approach to the Multiple-Choice Section

Many who take the AP exam don't get their best score because they spend too much time dwelling on hard questions, leaving insufficient time to answer the easy questions they can get right. Don't let this happen to you. Use the following system to mark your answer sheet:

For each passage and its set of questions

1. Answer easy questions immediately.

2. On more difficult questions, take advantage of being able to mark in your test booklet. As you eliminate an incorrect answer choice from consideration, mark it out in your question booklet as follows:

Notice that some choices are marked with question marks, signifying that they may be possible answers. This technique will help you avoid reconsidering those choices you've already eliminated and will help you narrow down your possible answers. If you've managed to eliminate two or more answers from consideration but still are not sure of the answer, mark a guess answer at this point. If you wish to reconsider these guess answers before you go on to the next set, you'll be able to identify them from the marks you've made eliminating wrong answers.

3. On questions you find very difficult — those on which you cannot eliminate wrong answers, leave the answer blank (but be careful to place your next answer in the right place on the answer sheet), put a check mark in the margin next to the question, and go on. Sometimes, consideration of other questions in the set suddenly sheds light on the questions you left blank, and you can then quickly return to it and choose an answer.

Note: You don't have to erase the marks you make in your *test booklet*. However, don't make extraneous marks on your *answer sheet* because in machine scoring, such marks can be counted as wrong answers.

A Patterned Plan of Attack

Multiple-Choice Section

Follow this procedure for each passage and set of questions.

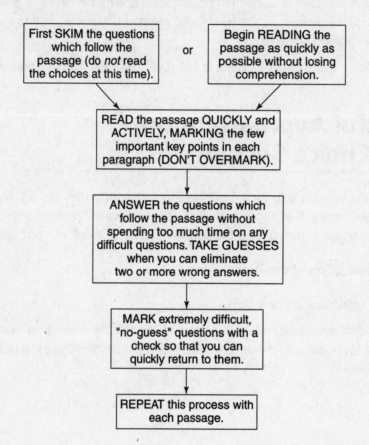

First SKIM the questions which follow the passage (do *not* read the choices at this time).

or

Begin READING the passage as quickly as possible without losing comprehension.

READ the passage QUICKLY and ACTIVELY, MARKING the few important key points in each paragraph (DON'T OVERMARK).

ANSWER the questions which follow the passage without spending too much time on any difficult questions. TAKE GUESSES when you can eliminate two or more wrong answers.

MARK extremely difficult, "no-guess" questions with a check so that you can quickly return to them.

REPEAT this process with each passage.

Introduction to the Essay Section

Sometimes called the free-response questions, this section of the AP exam requires that you write three essays. This essay section is normally two hours long. The suggested time for each essay is forty minutes. You must write your three essays in this time period, and you must write an essay on each of the three topics given; there are no alternative choices. You should expect one topic to be based on a fiction or nonfiction reading passage and to call for an analysis of style. A second topic, also based on a reading passage, calls for an argumentative essay. A third question may deal with a general topic related to language, or it may approach a passage from an angle different from that of the first question. For example, it may ask for a discussion of rhetorical purpose rather than an analysis of style. Remember that each of the three essays equals one-third of the total essay score and that the total for the essay portion equals 55 percent of the entire AP test score. A more detailed explanation of the essay scoring follows. You will be given an essay-writing booklet in which to write your essays; the test booklet includes blank space in which to plan your essays.

Ability Tested

This section tests your ability to demonstrate an understanding of *how* language works while simultaneously demonstrating your ability to communicate intelligent ideas in essay form. You should read the prose passages very carefully and then quickly articulate ideas because each essay should be written in thirty-five to forty minutes. Your discussion of such literary aspects as tone, attitude, and persuasion is essential to obtaining a good score.

Basic Skills Necessary

The basic skill necessary for the essay section is the ability to articulate and prove a thesis through concrete examples. You must be able to write on any assigned subject. Your paragraphs should be well developed, your overall essay organization should make sense, and your writing should demonstrate college-level thinking and style. The basic writing format of introduction, body, and conclusion is helpful, but to achieve a high score, you *must* demonstrate *how* language creates an effect. Analysis of diction, sentence style, and paragraph structure are vital tools in proving how a piece of writing works. Overall, you must show that you can read the question (and any subsequent passage) carefully, plan an intelligent thesis, organize and present valid and sufficient evidence while connecting such evidence to the thesis, and use college-level skill with your own language.

Directions

Each essay topic has its own wording and therefore its own directions, but general instructions similar to the following are printed on the cover of the essay booklet:

Directions: Three essay questions are printed in this booklet. Use this booklet to make your notes. You will be told when to open the essay-writing booklet and begin. Suggested writing time is given for each question.

Analysis of Directions

Although each essay topic has its own specific requirements, use these general suggestions for all of your essays.

- Use the test booklet to plan your essay. A poorly planned or an unplanned essay frequently reveals problems in organization and development.

- Practice frequently so that you're comfortable with the timing.

- Become familiar with the types of topics and comfortable with writing in a variety of modes.

- Organize your ideas logically, and be careful to stay on the topic.

- Write as legibly as possible; the readers have to be able to read your essay.

Suggested Strategies for Essays

Remember the following as you practice writing the essay.

- Consider using the standard format: introduction-body-conclusion.

- Clearly divide ideas into separate paragraphs; clearly indent the paragraphs.

- Stay on the topic; avoid irrelevant comments or ideas.

- Use sophisticated language and sentences with syntactic variety.

- Be organized and logical in your presentation.

- Be sure to address *all* of the tasks the essay question requires.

Essay Scoring

Each of the three essays equals one-third of the total essay score, and the entire essay (free-response) section equals 55 percent of the total AP score.

Each essay is read by experienced, well-trained high school AP teachers or college professors. The essay is given a holistic score from one to nine. (A score of zero is recorded for a student who writes completely off the topic — for example, "Why I think this test is a waste of money." A student who doesn't even attempt an essay, who leaves a blank page, also receives a zero.) The reader assigns a score based on the essay's merits as a whole, on what the paper does well; the readers don't simply count errors. Although each essay topic has its own scoring rubric (scoring guide) based on that topic's specific information, a general sample breakdown of the scoring for a style-analysis question is as follows:

High Score (8–9)

This essay clearly demonstrates a significant understanding of the passage, its style, and the essay question. The author of this essay shows a significant comprehension of how the language in a passage creates an effect. For a top-scoring essay, the language should be sophisticated; the sentences should have syntactic variety. Overall, this essay has intelligent ideas, that are thoroughly developed, sound organization, strong evidence, and articulate diction. While a top scoring essay may have a few flaws, they will be minor and infrequent.

Medium-High Score (6–7)

This essay completes the task of the essay topic well — it shows some insights but usually with less precision and clarity than the high-score papers. Some of the observations the author makes may be obvious instead of deeply insightful, or the observations may not be as fully substantiated as those of the top-scoring essays; in other words, they are not as thoroughly developed. There may be lapses in correct diction or sophisticated language, but the essay is generally well written.

Medium Score (5)

The medium-score paper completes the essay, but with no special insights; the analysis lacks depth, and it merely states the obvious. Because of these weaknesses, the ideas are predictable and the paragraphs weak. The writer does not demonstrate thorough understanding of the effects of rhetorical devices; he or she only observes that they are present in the passage. Language in the medium-score essay is usually acceptable but fairly simple, and sentences are frequently of the same length and pattern.

Medium-Low Score (3–4)

This paper is weaker than the "5" score because its author misses important ideas in the passage. This essay summarizes the passage's ideas instead of analyzing them; it makes assertions without supporting them with evidence; it pays little attention to rhetorical devices. Any essay that merely paraphrases the passage will earn no score higher than a "3."

Low Score (1–2)

This low-scoring, weak essay demonstrates minimal understanding of the topic or the passage. Perhaps unfinished, this essay has no analysis and little clarity. Usually little or no evidence is offered as a basis for the writer's ideas. Incorrect assertions may be made about the passage. Stylistically, the paper may show consistent grammatical problems, and sentence structure is usually simple and unimaginative.

Types of Essay Topics

Although the wording varies, there are only six categories of essay questions. When you've become familiar with these, your planning should go much faster on the day of the test; this knowledge will also help you to stay on the topic.

1. **Agree or disagree.** This common question type can also be considered part of the general-statement category listed below. You can expect either a short sentence or two that have built-in controversy or a longer reading passage for which you are asked to evaluate the validity of the author's ideas. Persuasive writing is essential for this category.

2. **Author's attitude, tone, or point of view.** Common in recent AP tests, this question type is based on a reading passage in which you must read between the lines — in other words, read inferentially — to understand the author's attitude toward the subject. Literary analysis is the thrust of this essay type.

3. **Analyze effect.** There's a good chance that this type of question will be asked on your AP exam. Like questions on author attitude, these require an analytical essay based on a reading passage. However, here you must understand *how* word choice, diction, syntax, and rhetoric work together to produce an effect in a passage. Be sure that you understand the effect produced before you begin writing. Uncertainty results in muddled ideas.

4. **Author's purpose.** Appearing only occasionally, these questions ask you to discuss *why* an author writes what he or she does. You may, for instance, be asked to explain why a political speech is written as it is or why an author describes the physical world as he or she does.

5. **General statement about society or human nature.** This topic is rarely based on a reading passage. Frequently, it's placed as the final essay question. For example, you may be asked to describe a favorite location from the perspective of two times in your life, to compare the dialects of different groups of people to comment on humanity after reading a one-sentence aphorism, or to explain what importance knowledge has in your life. These topics are designed to let you use your own experience and observations as evidence while reflecting on all humankind.

6. **Comparison/contrast.** Although not often used, this type of topic shows up occasionally. These questions are frequently based on two reading passages — perhaps two authors on the same subject, two descriptions of a location, or two drafts of the same work from one author. If you get a comparison/contrast topic, be sure to read it carefully and analyze beyond the obvious similarities of and differences between the passages.

Pacing the Essay

With an average time of only forty minutes per essay, you should divide your time as follows:

Spend about ten minutes reading the topic and the passage carefully and planning your essay.

This organizational time is crucial to producing a high-scoring essay. In the first ten minutes, you need to follow these steps. Do it efficiently, and you'll know what you want to write and the order in which you'll present your ideas.

1. Read the topic's question carefully so that you know exactly *what* you're being asked to do.

2. Read the passage carefully, noting what evidence and rhetorical devices are relevant to the essay question.

3. Conceive your thesis statement, which will go in your introductory paragraph.

4. Organize your body paragraphs, deciding what evidence from the passage to use and what relevant remarks to make about the evidence.

The importance of this planning phase cannot be overemphasized. When your essay has been well planned, your writing flows faster, the essay is on the topic and well organized, and the paragraphs are well developed. You must practice this essential planning step several times before you take the actual AP exam.

Take about twenty-five minutes to write the essay.

If you've planned well, your writing should be fluent and continuous; avoid stopping to reread what you've written. Twenty-five minutes is sufficient time to produce all of the writing needed.

Save about five minutes to proofread your essay.

Reserving a few minutes allows you time to catch the "honest mistakes" that can be easily corrected, such as a misspelled word or punctuation error. In addition, it lets you set the essay to rest, knowing what you've written, so that you can go on to the next topic and give it your full attention.

Planning the Essay

Your planning and organizing should be done in the test booklet, which provides space for that purpose. Begin by reading the essay question carefully. Underline the key words and phrases of the prompt so that you *thoroughly* understand what your tasks are. Then read any accompanying passage analytically, always keeping the essay question in mind. As you read, underline important ideas and phrases that relate to the topic. Your goals while reading are to

- understand the author's point
- relate the passage to the essay question
- begin gathering evidence to support the points of your essay
- look for nuances of diction and syntax

After you've read both the question and the passage carefully, you're ready to plan and organize your essay. Again, use the space provided in the test booklet. Organize your thoughts using whatever method you're most comfortable with — outlining, clustering, listing, and so forth. Planning at this stage is crucial to producing a well-written essay and should provide the following:

1. your thesis statement
2. a list of supporting evidence
3. the order of presentation of that evidence
4. a list of logical paragraph units
5. notes on analysis or commentary to be added regarding the evidence (analysis which connects your evidence both to your thesis and to the essay question)

Be careful to manage your time during the planning stage. If you overplan, you may run out of time to commit all your ideas to paper; if you fail to plan sufficiently, you're likely to produce an unorganized essay or one that's not as thorough as it should be. Remember that you do *not* have time to write out full sentences for everything that is in the list above, with the possible exception of the thesis. Simply jot down phrases and ideas quickly. Your goal here is only to *plan* the essay; if you do that well, your writing will go much faster. You'll then need only to put it all down on paper, in complete sentences, and you'll have produced a well-written essay.

Writing the Essay

A convenient format for essay writing uses the standard structure of introduction, body, and conclusion. The body should be made up of several paragraphs, but the introduction and conclusion require only one paragraph each.

In your introduction, make sure that you include a strong, analytical thesis statement, a sentence that explains your paper's idea and defines the scope of your essay. Also, be sure that the introduction lets the reader know that you're on topic; use key phrases from the question if necessary. The introductory paragraph should be brief, as only a few sentences are necessary to state your thesis. Definitely try to avoid merely repeating the topic in your thesis; instead let the thesis present what it is that you will specifically analyze. Imagine, for instance, that the topic asks you to "analyze the ways in which the author recreates his experience, perhaps considering such devices as diction, imagery, pacing, and contrast." A bland, repetitive thesis might read, "The author uses diction, imagery and contrast to recreate his experience." A more effective thesis might state, "The author's terrifying experience is vividly reconstructed through fast-paced diction, darkly menacing imagery, and stark contrasts in pacing." While this second thesis still uses the structure of the topic, it at least identifies the thrust of the student writer's ideas.

The body paragraphs are the heart of the essay. Each should be guided by a topic sentence that is a relevant part of the introductory thesis statement. Always supply a *great deal* of relevant evidence from the passage to support your ideas; feel free to quote the passage liberally. However, be sure to connect your ideas to the thesis. Explain exactly how the evidence presented leads to your thesis. Avoid obvious commentary. A medium-low-scoring paper merely reports what's in the passage. A high-scoring paper makes relevant, insightful, analytical points about the passage. Remember to stay on the topic.

Your conclusion, like your introduction, shouldn't be longwinded or elaborate. Do attempt, however, to provide more than mere summary; try to make a point beyond the obvious, which will indicate your essay's superiority. In other words, try to address the essay's greater importance in your conclusion. As one AP reader remarked, "I ask my students to get *global and noble.*" Of course, you should also keep in mind that a conclusion is not absolutely necessary in order to receive a high score. Never forget that your body paragraphs are more important than the conclusion so do not slight them merely to add a conclusion.

Remember to save a few minutes to proofread and to correct misspelled words, revise punctuation errors, and replace an occasional word or phrase with a more dynamic one. Do not make major editing changes at this time. Trust your original planning of organization and ideas, and only correct any obvious errors that you spot.

Some Suggestions about Style

On the actual exam, you won't have enough time during your proofreading to make major adjustments of style. However, as you practice, you can experiment with some stylistic devices that you can easily incorporate into your writing. Remember that top-scoring essays are stylistically mature and that your goal is to produce college-level writing. By answering the following questions and then practicing these suggestions, you'll improve your writing.

- **How long are your sentences?** You should try for some variety in sentence length. Remember that the occasional concise, simple sentence can "pack a punch" and grab a reader's attention when it's placed among a series of longer sentences. If an essay's sentences are all of the same length, none of them stand out.

- **What words do you use to begin your sentences?** Again, variety, is desirable. Try to avoid "there is" or "there are" (or any other dull wording). Also avoid beginning every sentence with the subject. For variety, try such grammatical constructions as a participial phrase, adverbial clause, etc.

- **Does every word you use help your essay?** Some bland, vague words to avoid include "a lot," "a little," "things," "much," and "very." Additionally, phrases like "I think," "I believe," "I feel," "in my opinion," "so as you can see," and "in conclusion," are unnecessary.

- **How many linking verbs do you use?** The linking verb (to be) has no action, is vastly overused, and produces unimaginative prose. Replace as many of these as possible with action verbs.

- **What sentence patterns do you use?** Again, you should aim for variety; avoid using the same pattern over and over. Also, try inverting the normal order; for example, try putting a direct object at the beginning of the sentence for emphasis.

- **Are all your compound sentences joined in the same way?** The usual method is to use a comma and a coordinating conjunction (such as "and," "but," or "yet"). Try experimenting with the semicolon and the dash to add emphasis and variety (but be sure you're using these more sophisticated punctuation devices correctly).

- **How many prepositional phrases do you see?** Eliminate as many as possible, especially the possessive prepositional phrase. Change "the words of Homer" to "Homer's words."

- **Do you use any parallel construction?** Develop your ability to produce parallelisms and your writing will appear more polished and memorable. Parallel construction also adds a delightful, sophisticated rhythm to your sentences. You can find examples of parallelism in the Glossary of Important Terms.

- **Do you use any figures of speech?** If you practice incorporating the occasional use of alliteration, repetition, imagery, and other figures of speech, your writing will be more vivid and engaging.

- **What does your essay sound like?** Have a friend read your essay aloud to you and listen to how it sounds.

Finally, a word about vocabulary. Of course, the use of sophisticated language is one of your goals, but do *not* use words you're unfamiliar with. In your practice, *look up* new words in a dictionary before you use them, especially if you find them in a thesaurus. Of course, you are not permitted to use a dictionary or thesaurus during the actual exam. Variety in word choice is as essential as variety in sentences, so don't try to overload an essay with fancy, multisyllabic words. Use succinct words that specifically fit your purpose.

Sample Topics with Student Essays

Now let's examine some sample essays that were written by AP students under timed conditions. They are reproduced here as they were written, including some misused words and spelling and punctuation errors. You'll find a topic, scoring guide, and high- and medium-scoring essays with analysis for each of the two following passages.

Question 1

Directions: The following passage is from George Elliot's novel *The Mill on the Floss*. After reading it carefully, write an essay that clearly defines the author's attitude and assumptions about human nature. Analyze the use of language to convince the reader of the author's assertions.

It was one of their happy mornings. They trotted along and sat down together, with no thought that life would ever change much for them: they would only get bigger and not go to school, and it would always be like the holidays; they would always live together and be fond of each other. And the mill with its booming — the great chestnut-tree under which they played at houses — their own little river, the Ripple, where the banks seemed like home, and Tom was always seeing the water-rats, while Maggie gathered the purple plumy tops of the reeds, which she forgot and dropped afterwards . . . these things would always be just the same to them.

Life did change for Tom and Maggie; and yet they were not wrong in believing that the thoughts and loves of those first years would always make part of their lives. We could never have loved the earth so well if we had had no childhood in it, — if it were not the earth where the same flowers come up again every spring that we used to gather with our tiny fingers as we sat lisping to ourselves on the grass — the same hips and haws on the autumn hedgerows — the same redbreasts that we used to call "God's birds," because they did no harm to the precious crops. What novelty is worth that sweet monotony where everything is known and *loved* because it is known?

The wood I walk in on this mild May day, with the young yellow-brown foliage of the oaks between me and the blue sky, the white star-flowers and the blue-eyed speedwell and the ground ivy at my feet — what grove of tropic palms, what strange ferns or splendid broad-petalled blossoms, could ever thrill such deep and delicate fibers within me as this home-scene? These familiar flowers, these well-remembered bird-notes, this sky, with its fitful brightness, these furrowed and grassy fields, each with a sort of personality given to it by the capricious hedgerows — such things as these are the mother tongue of our imagination, the language that is laden with all the subtle inextricable associations the fleeting hours of our childhood left behind them. Our delight in the sunshine on the deep-bladed grass to-day, might be no more than the faint perception of wearied souls, if it were not for the sunshine and the grass in the far-off years which still live in us, and transform our perception into love.

Scoring Guide for Question 1 (George Eliot)

8–9 In a well-written essay, this writer clearly demonstrates an understanding of the author's attitude and underlying assumptions about humankind while also demonstrating how the author's language conveys that attitude. The writer presents a clear, relevant thesis backed up with strong evidence from the passage. Analysis of the evidence and how it demonstrates the author's attitude about human nature is insightful. Not necessarily without flaws, the essay shows maturity in its use of language and sentence structure.

6–7 Well presented, this essay accurately describes Eliot's attitude about human nature but perhaps in a less explicit manner than that of the high-scoring essay. Discussion of the author's techniques may be less thorough, and evidence presented may be less specific.

Connection between the evidence and the thesis may be less insightful. Overall, the essay shows satisfactory control over format and language, although some errors may be present.

5 The writer of the average paper recognizes the author's attitude about human nature but may be imprecise in discussing that attitude. Attempts to analyze the author's language may be simplistic, and evidence offered may be insufficient to prove the thesis adequately. Organization may be clear but not as sophisticated as that in the better-written paper. Inconsistencies in the command of language may be present.

3–4 This essay attempts to address the essay question but may fail to accurately address the author's attitude. It may not complete all of the tasks of the question. Inadequate evidence for the writer's ideas may be a problem. Insights may be inaccurate or superficial. The essay may convey ideas, but weak control over language may distract the reader's attention. Frequent errors in mechanics may be present.

1–2 This essay fails to respond sufficiently to the question or the passage. It may fail to recognize the author's attitude and may misread the passage so as to distort it. With little or no evidence offered, the essay may fail to persuade the reader, and the connection between the evidence and the thesis may be shallow or nonexistent. Persistent weaknesses may be evident in the basic elements of composition or writing skills.

High-Scoring Essay

George Eliot's passage from <u>The Mill on the Floss</u> paints an appealing portrait of country life and a sunny picture of the human disposition. Eloquent yet readable, enthralling and complex, her assertions about temperament and perception strike a chord of familiarity in the reader without turning to tragedy or exploring the darker elements of human nature. Eliot uses loving, nostalgic descriptions of the natural world as seen through the eyes of a child to illustrate man's affection for that which is safe and known. She demonstrates that the perceptions formed in our childhood stay with us and influence our adult lives, convincing the reader of her assertions through skillful images of childhood harmony and the subsequent mature joy in those remembered fragments of youth.

Eliot first takes a nostalgic look at the carefree days of childhood. She explores the happy innocence of Maggie and Tom, assured that their lives will never change. She first makes the reader want to accept the notion that our childhoods form our futures, by making the scene idyllic and happy. The children "trot along" and "sit down together," content in their companionship, and happy to play in nature. With adult reflection, Eliot uses similar imagery later in the passage, placing the narrator in a splendid natural setting that is reminiscent of the childhood scene from earlier. This technique helps to <u>show</u> readers that adult life has many of the same elements of childhood, rather than simply telling them.

When young, the only change the children foresee is positive: they won't have to go to school any more; every day will be a holiday. Eliot implies that these expectations never fully die, even in adults. Unrealistic as they know it to be, adults do want every day to be a holiday, and they do wish, however faintly, that adult life could be more like an extended summer vacation, that "these things would always be just the same." These notions reinforce Eliot's assumption that humanity desires some degree of permanence in life, some memories that will remain peaceful and calm.

By tapping into subconscious childlike desires and recognizing the near universal optimism of childhood, Eliot wins readers over to her side. Few readers will be able to resist or deny her later assertion that "the thoughts and loves of those first years would always make a part of their lives" as she looks back from adulthood. She leads readers to believe that childhood is continually alive and well, coloring a view on the world, because she has discovered a self-fulfilling prophecy of human nature. Readers believe it to be true because they want it to be true, because they have no other option than to believe. If they cannot return to childlike openness from time to time in their adult lives, where is there hope in the world?

The Mill on the Floss takes the converse of Thomas Wolfe's position. Perhaps you can't go home again. But maybe home can come to you . . .indeed, perhaps home never really leaves us, even as we travel our distances and believe that our lives have changed beyond recognition. Through her resoundingly positive, almost archetypal images — of grass, sunshine, of blue sky, of oak trees — Eliot seeks to reassure us that life has much goodness. After all, if the enormous eyes of childhood wonder shape each individual's paradigm, must not mankind be essentially good? Eliot has prepared a proscenium for Hope.

Analysis of the High-Scoring Essay

This high-scoring essay is well presented, with effective wording to match its insightful comments. The first paragraph introduces Eliot's assertions about human nature, which are developed in greater detail in the later paragraphs. This student also includes a very nicely written statement about how fond memories of youth can bring "subsequent mature joy" to adults. The universal appeal is relaxing and comforting.

The student proceeds to explore Eliot's ideas on childhood memories and adult reflection on those memories, referring to appropriate sections in the text for example. The student also acknowledges the effect of credibility that comes with placing the narrator in a natural scene for reflection as opposed to simply telling the reader an insight. In the next paragraph, the student further clarifies Eliot's assumptions about human nature by explaining that humans desire something to hold on to, some permanent harmony in a somewhat chaotic world. The student shows skill in incorporating quotations into the essay so that they are integrated, not distracting.

The student realizes that one of Eliot's most effective techniques is "tapping into subconscious childlike desires" in all readers and then continues the discussion by doing the same. This handling is forceful; who hasn't wished, at some time, that summer idyll could last forever? This student demonstrates a coherent understanding of the effect of Eliot's diction by inducing the same effect in the essay's reader.

The essay concludes with a nice allusion to Thomas Wolfe, showing that the student is well read. The last paragraph reinforces the concept that both the student and Eliot present so coherently — that there is something warm and comfortable in the memories of youth, and reflecting on them, we can maintain hope for our future. This conclusion does much more than merely end the essay. It provides insight and optimism. This essay deserves a high score.

Medium-Scoring Essay

The attitude of George Eliot about human nature is that people don't want the world to change very much. They like the way things are when they are children and they hope it will blissfully stay the same when they are adults. The problem with this is that they don't always stay the same. George Eliot discusses this in his passage from The Mill on the Floss.

The children think that they won't have to go to school, that all the good things of their childhood will remain constant. This is common with children, and Eliot defends this idea about human nature with his antidote about the children enjoying a happy morning, confident about their future. Later, when they are adults, they will appreciate what they see in nature because of the pleasant experiences they had when they were children.

Eliot uses a lot of pleasant descriptions of nature — trees, rivers, rats, flowers — to describe why they like things that are the same as when they were young. He uses diction to persuade the reader that this is something that all people share. He talks about exotic, tropical scenes as not being exciting after awhile because they are not as thrilling as home. But normal remembrances do last longer because they are comfortable and familiar. People like to have the same things and experiences again because it makes them feel safe.

The whole world may be changing, but not all of it. Some things in nature like "white star-flowers" and "yellow-brown foliage" don't change, and these things make his characters feel good. Eliot assumes that humanity needs the comfort and security of permanence.

So Eliot convinces the reader with his descriptive writing and his diction that childhood is an important time and the nature of children we should understand. We all have to change because that's what make's the world go round. So his attitude in writing The Mill on the Floss helps to convince us that's true. While we can still daydream, still reflect on the joyous days of youth.

Analysis of the Medium-Scoring Essay

This essay attempts to address the essay question; in a simplistic way, the first sentence provides a summation of Eliot's philosophy. It has no strong thesis, but the first paragraph is basically on topic. However, pronoun problems begin to appear in this first section; an example is the ambiguous word "they" in the third sentence. Additionally, the student mistakenly identifies George Eliot as a male, but students are not expected to be familiar with all authors from English literature.

The second paragraph reiterates the idea of permanence and also vaguely ties in the children's happy morning that begins the passage. Unfortunately, the student misuses the word "antidote" for "anecdote," probably a mistake made under time pressure.

The third paragraph discusses more of Eliot's ideas, still on topic, but it does not present substantial evidence to convince the reader. Phrases like "He uses diction" are not supported by examples or with any mention of how that diction affects the work.

The short fourth paragraph is repetitive; no new points are presented. It appears as if the student was determined to use a few quotations and tried to build a paragraph around these two phrases. There is no connection between these quotations and the thesis, and one wonders why the student thinks the flowers will never change. This paragraph suffers from poor development.

The conclusion merely summarizes the passage. Overall, this paper is hardly convincing, although it is adequate in its presentation. It needs more analysis and evidence and a proofreading for mechanical errors in order to achieve a higher score.

Question 2

Directions: The following essay comes from Sir Thomas More's *Utopia* (1516). Read the passage carefully, and then write an essay that evaluates the validity of the speaker's ideas in light of contemporary standards. Use evidence from your own experience, reading, or observation to develop your essay and convince the reader of your ideas.

On Communal Property

By this I am persuaded that unless private property is entirely done away with, there can be no fair distribution of goods, nor can the world be happily governed. As long as private property remains, the largest and far the best part of mankind will be oppressed with an inescapable load of cares and anxieties. This load, I admit, may be lightened somewhat, but cannot be entirely removed. Laws might be made that no one should own more than a certain amount of land nor possess more than a certain sum of money. Or laws might be passed to prevent the prince from growing too powerful and the populace from becoming too strong. It might be made unlawful for public offices to be solicited, or sold, or made burdensome for the officeholder by great expense. Otherwise officeholders are tempted to reimburse themselves by dishonesty and force, and it becomes necessary to find rich men for those offices which ought rather be held by wise men. Such laws, I say, may have as much effect as good nursing has on men who are dangerously sick. Social evils may be allayed and mitigated, but so long as private property remains, there is no hope at all that they may be healed and society restored to good health. While you try to cure one part, you aggravate the disease in other parts. In redressing one evil another is committed, since you cannot give something to one man without taking the same thing from another.

Scoring Guide for Question 2 (Thomas More)

8–9 This well-written essay clearly takes a stand concerning More's ideas on communal property and substantially supports that stand. The thesis is articulate and relevant to the topic. The paper provides strong and relevant evidence intelligently connected to the thesis. The paper demonstrates an understanding of the needs of the essay. Although it need not be without errors, the paper shows a mature command of style and language.

6–7 This essay contemplates More's ideas on communal property but produces a less explicit thesis. Perhaps less relevant or insufficient evidence is offered, and the reader may not be as thoroughly convinced as with a top-scoring paper. Although well written, it may demonstrate some errors while still showing satisfactory control over diction and the essay requirements.

5 The adequate presentation in this essay includes a thesis, but one that is perhaps not as well thought out as in higher-scoring essays. The ideas may be too hastily conceived after a cursory reading of More's concepts. Overall, the argument may not be as strong or convincing. It may appear more opinionated without sufficient evidence to support the opinions. Acceptable organization may be evident, but the style may not be as sophisticated as in higher-scoring essays.

3–4 This low-scoring essay fails to convince the reader. The weak presentation in this essay may include an unsupported or unsubstantiated thesis, weak paragraph development, and/or poor organization. The paper may exhibit confusion in ideas and superficial thinking and evidence. Frequent mechanical errors may persist.

1–2 This poorly written essay lacks clarity and coherence. It may have an overly obvious thesis or no thesis at all. It may contain little or no evidence, and the connection between the evidence and the thesis may be shallow or nonexistent. The paper may be unusually short and exhibit poor essay skills. Weak sentence construction and persistent weaknesses in command of the language may be present.

High-Scoring Essay

Sir Thomas More's Utopia discusses ideas and conflicts still relevant to society today. He manages to perceptively express the nature of wealth and material goods; and although written over 400 years ago, his essay still reveals essential truths about the attitudes in our contemporary society.

More primarily addresses the issue of ownership of private property and its hindrance upon the fair distribution of wealth. More points out that ownership of private wealth hurts those who have little or none themselves, which makes up the majority of the population. More perceives that "As long as private property remains, the largest and far the best part of mankind will be oppressed with an inescapable load of cares and anxieties." In today's society, More's idea still holds true. The majority of the population does control less than their fair amount of wealth and goods. This is evident not just in America, but also among competing nations of the world. Each day, in countries like Mexico, the poor struggle to keep from getting poorer, while the wealth of many of the rich grows more opulent. Because of this unfair distribution of wealth, the poor have little opportunity to change their worsening situations.

More's concerns also go beyond the poor and encompass another major realm of controversy: politics. More correctly predicts the nature of politics which exists in a society where not everyone is of the same economic class. He suggests that "it might be made unlawful for public offices to be solicited, or sold, or made burdensome for the officeholder by great expense. Otherwise officeholders are tempted to reimburse themselves by dishonesty and force, and it becomes necessary to find rich men for those offices which ought rather be held by wise men." This prediction has certainly come true in contemporary America, where the vast number of politicians tend to come from the upper echelons of society; conversely, one would be hard-pressed to name a top office-holder who rose from the ranks of the poor under-class. In addition, just as Plato saw the needs for wise, rational men to fill the position of philosopher-king, More also realizes the danger of public offices held by rich men rather than wise men, an event fostered by a society in which unequal distribution of goods exists. Both Plato and More have made a valid point here, and the voting public should be constantly cautioned to question a potential leader's wisdom and rational thinking before they vote.

While More's essays define the evils that burden a private property owning society, More fails to see some of the problems that would follow with completely eradicating the system. More suggests several legal reforms to stop and prevent the amassing of goods by citizens. When this is stopped, however, all incentive to work is taken away. People rarely have the time, the energy, or the interest to work solely for the merit of working. In contemporary society, human nature drives people to work to earn something tangible — be it wealth, or goods, or love. More's reforms

are also unfair. While upon a first glance they may sound fair and equal, in reality they are not. This system would be unfair to hard workers who do deserve a reward, and unfair to lazy workers who don't earn what they receive. Instead of promoting equality, this system would promote laziness and remove the incentive to work. In theory this would be a good system. But, in reality, Sir Thomas More's Utopia does not work. The recent breakdown of the Soviet Union alone disproves More's system.

More's essay perceptively observes some of the major injustices and corruptions within a private property owning society. While these are valid, pertinent issues, More overlooks some of the inherent pitfalls within the system of a society which bans the ownership of private property.

Analysis of the High-Scoring Essay

This thoughtful essay immediately addresses the topic in its first sentence. The writer uses contemporary examples to buttress points and also insightfully comments that More addresses more concepts than money and land distribution. The writer's inclusion of Plato in the third paragraph relevantly extends this idea. In the fourth paragraph, the writer acknowledges that More fails to accurately predict all the consequences of his proposals — the problem that the need for reward is inherent in human nature. Showing both advantages and disadvantages of More's proposal demonstrates the skill of close reading and a high degree of maturity in this writer. To improve this essay, the writer could have worked on a stronger thesis that more accurately addresses the writer's points; notice that the thesis does not allude to any criticism of More's ideas. Some of the vague wording could be made more specific. In general, the essay's ideas are more sophisticated than their presentation.

This essay is well organized and the ideas are supported by examples from contemporary society. Overall, this essay deserves a high score for pointing out the validity of More's ideas for today's society as well as their perhaps mistaken assumptions.

Medium-Scoring Essay

Sir Thomas More's Utopia discusses fair government and equal social status within our society, and identifies the need for people to give up their private property. His ideas (as

written about in the essay) are valid in light of contemporary standards.

More's initial position that private property is an unnecessary evil within our society at first appears to be blatantly Communistic. His desires to redistribute wealth and property, and to make laws preventing people from earning too much money seem absurd at first glance. However, on further inspection, the reader realizes that some of More's views are valid and relevant to society. In lines 18–23 More predicts corruption of the government, something that our nation has been experiencing for several decades. This corruption is a result of politicians feeling obligated to remunerate themselves for the great expense they go through as a part of their job. More sums this up very nicely and accurately as he points out that rich men (instead of wise men) take over the offices of government.

Not only do we see the validity of More's views in our current day and age, but personally speaking, I agree with More's beliefs. The greed and self-interest associated with Capitalism are two symptoms of the sickness that comes with private property. It is wrong for a country's government to allow some people to starve on the streets while others are living like kings. More sympathizes for the great majority of people who do not have much private property, as shown in lines 4–7.

Throughout his essay More proposes solutions to the problem of private property. He advocates altruism and his ideas are shown to be relevant to our society. His essay is very valid in light of today's social standards.

Analysis of the Medium-Scoring Essay

This medium-scoring essay attempts to address the topic. The first paragraph produces a thesis that claims that More's ideas are valid for contemporary society, but little else is presented here. The thesis is not highly thought-provoking, and it contains some redundancy ("as written about in the essay").

The student spends almost half of the second paragraph explaining his or her first impression of More, only to reverse it after a deeper analysis. This student should be commended for looking below the surface, but no evidence is offered to support the student's opinions. This paragraph would be stronger if the student were to include some examples of government corruption, rather than merely alluding to them.

The third paragraph becomes a forum for the student's personal beliefs. Once again, the student presents relevant ideas but little evidence for them. The only example included, the idea that the government allows poor people to starve while other live like kings, may indeed be true but is not specific. In addition, the reader must twice return to the More essay to find what statement the student refers to, in "as shown in lines 3–6," for example, making the reader assume the student's task of relating the essay's ideas to More's.

The concluding paragraph merely summarizes the essay's only point, that the writer finds More's ideas valid. There's not much of substance here, and the conclusion doesn't help to convince the reader of the validity of the writer's opinions.

Although this essay does take a stand, it offers only weak support and sometimes simplistic and redundant wording. This essay would be stronger if the student were to include more of More's ideas and test their validity by today's standards. Overall, this essay is adequate, but it is not persuasive enough to merit a higher score.

PART III

DIAGNOSTIC MINI-TEST

The Mini-Test that follows is designed to familiarize you with some of the AP language exam question types. It will also assist you in assessing some of your strengths and weaknesses. This short assessment includes complete answers and explanations, two essays written by AP students, and analysis of those essays.

The format, levels of difficulty, and question structures are similar to those on the actual AP language exam. The actual AP exam is copyrighted and may not be duplicated, and these questions are not taken directly from the actual test.

Answer Sheet for the Mini-Test

(Remove This Sheet and Use It to Mark Your Answers)

Section I
Multiple Choice Questions

1 Ⓐ Ⓑ Ⓒ Ⓓ Ⓔ
2 Ⓐ Ⓑ Ⓒ Ⓓ Ⓔ
3 Ⓐ Ⓑ Ⓒ Ⓓ Ⓔ
4 Ⓐ Ⓑ Ⓒ Ⓓ Ⓔ
5 Ⓐ Ⓑ Ⓒ Ⓓ Ⓔ
6 Ⓐ Ⓑ Ⓒ Ⓓ Ⓔ
7 Ⓐ Ⓑ Ⓒ Ⓓ Ⓔ
8 Ⓐ Ⓑ Ⓒ Ⓓ Ⓔ
9 Ⓐ Ⓑ Ⓒ Ⓓ Ⓔ
10 Ⓐ Ⓑ Ⓒ Ⓓ Ⓔ

CUT HERE

Section I: Multiple-Choice Questions

Time: 12 Minutes

10 Questions

Directions: This section contains a selection from a prose work and questions on its content, style, and form. Read each section carefully. Choose the best answer of the five choices.

Questions 1–10. Read the passage carefully before you begin to answer the questions.

Mini-Test Passage

On Route 301 south of Tampa, billboards advertising Sun City Center crop up every few miles, with pictures of Cesar Romero and slogans that read
(5) FLORIDA'S RETIREMENT COMMUNITY OF THE YEAR, 87 HOLES OF GOLF, THE TOWN TOO BUSY TO RETIRE. According to a real-estate brochure, the town is "sensibly located . . .
(10) comfortably removed from the crowded downtown areas, the highway clutter, the tourists, and the traffic." It is 25 miles from Sarasota, and 11 miles from the nearest beach on the Gulf Coast.
(15) Route 301, an inland route — to be taken in preference to the coast road, with its lines of trucks from the phosphate plants — passes through a lot of swampland, some scraggly pinewoods, and acre
(20) upon acre of strawberry beds covered with sheets of black plastic. There are fields where hairy, tough-looking cattle snatch at the grass between the palmettos. There are aluminum warehouses,
(25) cinder-block stores, and trailer homes in patches of dirt with laundry sailing out behind. There are Pentecostal churches

and run-down cafes and bars with rows of pickup trucks parked out front.
(30) Turn right with the billboards onto Route 674, and there is a green-and-white suburban-looking resort town. Off the main road, white asphalt boulevards with avenues of palm trees give onto
(35) streets that curve pleasingly around golf courses and small lakes. White ranch-style houses sit back from the streets on small, impeccably manicured lawns. A glossy four-color map of the town put
(40) out by a real-estate company shows cartoon figures of golfers on the fairways and boats on the lakes, along with drawings of churches, clubhouses, and curly green trees. The map is a necessity for
(45) the visitor, since the streets curve around in a maze fashion, ending in culs-de-sac or doubling back on themselves. There is no way in or out of Sun City Center except by the main road bisecting the
(50) town. The map, which looks like a child's board game (Snakes and Ladders or Uncle Wiggily), shows a vague area — a kind of no-man's-land — surrounding the town. As the map

(55) suggests, there is nothing natural about Sun City Center. The lakes are artificial, and there is hardly a tree or shrub or blade of grass that has any correspon-dence in the world just beyond it. At the
(60) edges of the development, there are houses under construction, with the seams still showing in the transplanted lawns. From there, you can look out at a flat brown plain that used to be a cattle
(65) ranch. The developer simply scraped the surface off the land and started over again.

Sun City Center is an unincorporated town of about 8,500 people, almost all
(70) of whom are over the age of 60. It is a self-contained community, with stores, banks, restaurants, and doctors' offices. It has the advertised 87 holes of golf; it also has tennis courts, shuffleboard
(75) courts, swimming pools, and lawn-bowling greens. In addition to the regular housing, it has a "life-care facil-ity" — a six-story apartment building with a nursing home in one wing. "It's a
(80) strange town," a clinical psychologist at the University of South Florida, in Tampa, told me before I went. "It's out there in the middle of nowhere. It has a section of private houses, where people
(85) go when they retire. Then it has a sec-tion of condos and apartments, where people go when they can't keep up their houses. Then it has a nursing home. Then it has a cemetery." In fact, there is
(90) no cemetery in Sun City Center, but the doctor was otherwise correct.

Sun City Center has become a world unto itself. Over the years, the town at-tracted a supermarket and all the stores
(95) and services necessary to the mainte-nance of daily life. Now, in addition, it has a golf-cart dealer, two banks, three savings and loan associations, four restaurants, and a brokerage firm. For
(100) visitors, there is the Sun City Center Inn. The town has a post office. Five

churches have been built by the resi-dents and a sixth is under construction. A number of doctors have set up offices
(105) in the town, and a Bradenton hospital re-cently opened a satellite hospital with 112 beds. There is no school, of course. The commercial establishments all front on the state road running through the
(110) center of town, but, because most of them are more expensive than those in the neighboring towns, the people from the surrounding area patronize only the supermarket, the Laundromat, and one
(115) or two others. The local farmers and the migrant workers they employ, many of whom are Mexican, have little relation-ship to golf courses or to dinner dances with organ music. Conversely, Sun
(120) Citians are not the sort of people who would go to bean suppers in the Pentecostal churches or hang out at raunchy bars where gravel-voiced women sing "Satin Sheets and Satin
(125) Pillows." The result is that Sun Citians see very little of their Florida neighbors. They take trips to Tampa, Bradenton, and Sarasota, but otherwise they rarely leave the green-and-white develop-
(130) ments, with their palm-lined avenues and artificial lakes. In the normal course of a week, they rarely see anyone under sixty.

1. In the first paragraph, the author refers to the "fields where hairy, tough-looking cattle snatch at the grass between the palmettos" in order to

   I. deny the area any pastoral attractiveness

   II. underscore the loss when farmland is subdivided for retirement homes

   III. suggest the savagery of the natural world that can be ordered and made beautiful by human projects

A. I only

B. II only

C. I and III only

D. II and III only

E. I, II, and III

2. In the last three sentences of the first paragraph ("There are fields . . . parked out front"), the author uses all of the following EXCEPT

A. parallel structure

B. periodic sentences

C. specific details

D. direct statements

E. subject-verb inversions

3. In the quotation at the end of the third paragraph, the use of two sentences with "where" clauses and three sentences beginning with "Then" has which of the following effect?

I. It provides a rhetorical parallelism for an unspoken chronological progression.

II. It invites the reader to supply the "where" clauses for the last two sentences that begin with "There."

III. It provides a series of transitions that direct the reader's attention to the speaker.

A. II only

B. I and II only

C. I and III only

D. II and III only

E. I, II, and III

4. In the last paragraph, the list of services available in Sun City Center itemized in the sentence in lines 96–99 ("Now, in addition . . . brokerage firm") effectively suggests the residents' concern with

A. avoiding the idea of death

B. physical comforts

C. impressing one another

D. relaxation

E. money

5. Which of the following does NOT accurately describe the sentence in the fourth paragraph "Conversely, Sun Citians are not the sort of people who would go to bean suppers in the Pentecostal churches or hang out at raunchy bars where gravel-voiced women sing 'Satin Sheets and Satin Pillows.'" (lines 124–125)?

A. It reinforces the idea of the preceding sentence.

B. It effectively contrasts the Sun City Center residents and their neighbors.

C. It recalls details of the description at the end of the first paragraph.

D. It attacks the values of the people who live in the area near Sun City Center.

E. It presents an image that is amusing in its incongruity.

6. The effect of the last paragraph of the passage is to call attention to the

   A. age of the Sun City Center's residents

   B. convenience of life in Sun City Center

   C. political indifference of the Sun City Center's residents

   D. isolation of the Sun City Center's residents

   E. wealth of the Sun City Center's residents

7. Which of the following best describes the diction of the passage?

   A. formal and austere

   B. informal and documentary

   C. abstract

   D. artless and colloquial

   E. highly metaphorical

8. Which of the following quotations from the passage best sums up its main idea?

   A. "As the map suggests, there is nothing natural about Sun City Center." (lines 54–56)

   B. "The developer simply scraped the surface off the land and started over again." (lines 65–67)

   C. "Sun City Center is an unincorporated town of about 8,500 people, almost all of whom are over the age of 60." (lines 68–70)

   D. "In fact, there is no cemetery in Sun City Center, but the doctor was otherwise correct." (lines 89–91)

   E. "The result is that Sun Citians see very little of their Florida neighbors." (lines 125–126)

9. A principal rhetorical strategy of the passage as a whole is to

   A. depict a small city by presenting information in a chronological narrative

   B. portray a place by comparison and contrast

   C. raise and then answer questions about the nature of a place

   D. progressively narrow the focus from a larger area to a smaller one and its residents

   E. develop a discussion of a unique location by using multiple points of view

10. All of the following are characteristics of the style of this passage EXCEPT

   A. variety in the length of its sentences

   B. infrequent use of the first person

   C. infrequent use of adjectives

   D. infrequent use of simile

   E. frequent use of specific dates

Section II: Essay Question

Suggested Time: 40 minutes

Directions: The following passage comes from Michel-Guillaume-Jean de Crèvecoeur's *Letters from an American Farmer* (1782). Read the selection carefully, and then write an essay in which you analyze Crèvecoeur's attitude toward Europeans and Americans, concentrating on how his diction reflects his opinions.

In this great American asylum, the poor of Europe have by some means met together, and in consequence of various causes; to what purpose should they ask (5) one another what countrymen they are? Alas, two thirds of them had no country. Can a wretch who wanders about, who works and starves, whose life is a continual scene of sore affliction or pinch- (10) ing penury; can that man call England or any other kingdom his country? A country that had no bread for him, whose fields procured him no harvest, who met with nothing but the frowns of the rich, (15) the severity of the laws, with jails and punishments; who owned not a single foot of extensive surface of this planet? No! Urged by a variety of motives, here they came. Everything has tended to re- (20) generate them; new laws, a new mode of living, a new social system; here they are become men: in Europe they were as so many useless plants, wanting vegetative mold and refreshing showers; they (25) withered, and were mowed down by want, hunger, and war; but now by the power of transplantation, like all other plants they have taken root and flourished! Formerly they were not num- (30) bered in any civil lists of their country, except in those of the poor; here they rank as citizens. By what invisible power has this surprising metamorphosis been performed? By that of the laws (35) and that of their industry. . . .

What then is the American, this new man? He is either a European, or the descendant of a European, hence that strange mixture of blood, which you (40) will find in no other country. I could point out to you a family whose grandfather was an Englishman, whose wife was Dutch, whose son married a French woman, and whose present four sons (45) have now four wives of different nations. *He* is an American, who leaving behind him all his ancient prejudices and manners, receives new ones from the new mode of life he has embraced, (50) the new government he obeys, and the new rank he holds. He becomes an American by being received in the broad lap of our great *Alma Mater.* Here individuals of all nations are melted into a (55) new race of men, whose labors and posterity will one day cause great changes in the world. Americans are the western pilgrims, who are carrying only with them that great mass of arts, sciences, (60) vigor, and industry which began long since in the east; they will finish the great circle.

Answer Key for The Mini-Test

Section I: Multiple-Choice Questions

1. A
2. B
3. B
4. E
5. D
6. D
7. B
8. A
9. D
10. C

Section II: Essay Question

An essay scoring guide, student essays, and analysis appear beginning on page 60.

Answers and Explanations for the Mini-Test

Section I: Multiple-Choice Questions

From *Cities on a Hill* by Frances Fitzgerald

1. **A.** The passage presents the area around Sun City Center as ugly: "scraggly pinewoods" and a "lot of swampland." Although the land is used for cattle ranching, the prose denies it any charm or beauty. The passage has no concern with making a case for the subdivision as ecologically good (**III**) or bad (**II**). In the passage, ecology is not an issue.

2. **B.** These are all loose, not periodic, sentences. Each of the sentences could end after just three or four words. There is parallel structure in the repeated "There are." The sentences are direct statements made up chiefly of specific details. All three sentences place the verbs ("are") before the subjects ("fields," "warehouses," "churches").

3. **B.** The repetition of "it has" and "then it has" is an example of parallel structure, and the chronology progresses from the time when the people first move to Sun City Center to a later time when health begins to fail, to a time of greater weakness, to death (**I**). The two "where" clauses invite us to add two more "where" clauses into the last two sentences, thus mentally completing the implied parallel construction: i.e. "it has a nursing home, *where they go when they can't keep up their condos*" and "it has a cemetery, *where they go when they die*" (**II**). The series does not call attention to the speaker (**III**).

4. **E.** There are five services listed, and three of the five (banks, savings and loan associations, and a brokerage firm) are specifically related to money. A fourth, the golf-cart dealer, is at least tangentially related to affluence. Choices **B, C,** and **D** are plausible, but **E**, although it may seem obvious, is the best choice.

5. **D.** The sentence reinforces the idea of the sentence before — the alienation of the Sun Citians from their neighbors (choices **A** and **B**). The bars and Pentecostal churches were mentioned in the last sentence of the first paragraph (**C**). The notion of a group of middle-class senior citizens sitting in a run-down café listening to country-western music is amusing in its incongruity (**E**). The passage is not satiric. Its point is not that Sun Citians or their neighbors are flawed, but that they have nothing in common.

6. **D.** Although the paragraph begins with an account of the stores and services of Sun City Center, even the first sentence insists on this development as "a world unto itself." And the last two-thirds of the paragraph (beginning with "There is no school, of course") gives evidence to support the notion of the residents' isolation from the rest of the world.

7. **B.** While perhaps not an ideal answer, choice **B** is the best of the five choices here. The passage is not formal and austere, not abstract, not artless (although a few phrases could be called colloquial), and not at all highly metaphorical.

8. **A.** Choices **B, C,** and **D** don't really sum up a central idea of the passage. Both **A** and **E** are good answers, but **A** can include the idea of **E,** while **E** is more narrow. The whole passage is about the unnaturalness of Sun City Center, its oddness in this geographical

area, and the segregation of its residents from their neighbors and from a world where many people are still under 60. "Sun City Center has become a world unto itself" in the last paragraph would also be a good answer.

9. **D.** The best choice here is **D.** The passage begins with the geography of the central west coast of Florida but narrows to Sun City Center ("Turn right onto Route 674"). The second paragraph maps out the town, while the third and fourth describe its residents. The passage is not a chronological narrative (**A**), uses contrast only in the last paragraph (**B**), asks no questions (**C**), and has only one point of view and one additional quoted comment (**D**).

10. **C.** The passage varies its sentence length, uses the first person only once (paragraph three), uses very little figurative language, and uses a large number of specific details. It is very dependent on adjectives and without its adjectives, it would be barren and unrecognizable.

Section II: Essay Question

Scoring Guide for the Essay Question (Michel de Crèvecoeur)

8–9 This well-written essay clearly demonstrates understanding of Crèvecoeur's attitude toward Americans and a thorough comprehension of how his diction reflects his attitude. The thesis is articulate and thoughtful. Strong and relevant evidence from Crèvecoeur's essay is included. Thoroughly convincing, the essay shows a clear command of essay writing skills. Although it need not be without errors, the paper shows a mature style and use of language.

6–7 This essay shows the student's comprehension of Crèvecoeur's ideas, but its thesis may be less explicit than that of the top-scoring essay. The evidence offered may not be as convincing or thorough, making the essay less persuasive. Still, the essay is fairly convincing and shows clear thinking. The connection between the evidence and Crèvecoeur's attitude may not be as clear as in top-scoring essays. Although well written, it may demonstrate some errors while still showing satisfactory control over diction and the essay requirements.

5 This adequately written essay shows some understanding of Crèvecoeur's attitude but may not show clear comprehension of the relationship between his language and his attitude. The thesis may be simplistic and predictable and the evidence offered insufficient to prove the writer's points. Evidence presented for Crèvecoeur's attitude may be too brief or understated. Although the presentation of ideas may be acceptable, the paper as a whole is not strongly convincing. Acceptable organization and development may be evident, but the style may not be as sophisticated as that of higher-scoring essays.

3–4 This low-scoring essay fails to convince the reader. The weak presentation may not demonstrate a clear understanding of Crèvecoeur's ideas. Comprehension of how Crèvecoeur's language communicates his attitude may be lacking. The thesis may be unsubstantiated, paragraph development may be weak, and superficial thinking may be evident. Connection between Crèvecoeur's language and the paper's thesis may be nonexistent or trite. Frequent mechanical errors that distract the reader may be present.

1–2 This poorly written essay lacks coherence and clarity. It may present only a brief synopsis of Crèvecoeur's attitude with no mention of how his language reflects that attitude. The thesis may be overly obvious or missing. Little or no evidence may be offered, and the connection between the evidence and the thesis may be shallow or nonexistent. The paper may be unusually short and exhibit poor fundamental essay skills. Weak sentence construction may persist, and persistent weaknesses in mechanics may be present.

High-Scoring Essay

Many foreigners came to America during the republic's formative years to explore life in the new nation. The writings of de Tocqueville and Charles Dickens commented on the new American character and government in the nineteenth century. Michel-Guillaume-Jean de Crèvecoeur, who wrote *Letters from an American Farmer* in 1782, was not alone in his endeavor, though he was one of the first to visit the new United States. His writing generally reflects a positive image of Americans. While taking note of their humble origins and lack of cultural refinement, he praises the resilience of American citizens. Crèvecoeur's diction, and the positive connotations of the words he uses to describe Americans, clearly present his positive, though occasionally paternal and superior, attitude toward Americans.

Americans are defined by Crèvecoeur largely in terms of the land they left. Their new nation is a haven from a Europe of "severe laws, with jails and punishments." The common folk in England are faced by the "frowns of the rich." The new Americans have left the "refinement" of Europe behind, along with the class system and much else which had restricted them. These images tell as much about Crèvecoeur's attitude toward Europeans as it does toward Americans. The negativity attached to Americans' backgrounds perhaps emphasizes their ultimate determination and drive once they arrived on new soil. Crèvecoeur deliberately uses negative phrases in describing Americans' pasts so that their change in the new country will be even more dramatic.

Crèvecoeur emphasizes the newness of the United States, thus implying a positive impression of the land. While he may look down somewhat on the breeding and manners of the Americans, noting that they come from the lower rungs of European social hierarchy, he certainly believes the new land is good for them. America is a place of "regenerative" powers, with "new laws, a new mode of living, a new social system." Crèvecoeur credits America with encouraging the "flourishing" of the world's poor and unwanted. Might he then be looking down on America, as the "asylum" he describes in the opening sentence, a refuge suitable only for the wretches of sophisticated European life? Perhaps. But he leaves no doubt about the successful attainment of such a goal, lauding it by writing that the "surprising metamorphosis" from wretches to citizens is thanks to American "laws and . . . industry."

Although Crèvecoeur generally presents Americans in laudable terms, a trace of condescension appears in some phrases. America was made up of "wretches" who had previously "wandered about." They had endured lives of "sore affliction or pinching penury." But despite the seeming elitism of Crèvecoeur's description, his word choices elicit sympathy rather than scorn in the attentive reader because he is referring to the Americans' previous lives in Europe. Crèvecoeur makes a careful point of the work ethic of these derelict new countrymen, essentially homeless among the world's nations. Such attention clearly shows that

Crèvecoeur is sensitive to the plight of the new Americans.

Crèvecoeur writes as if America has surpassed his expectations as a melting pot of undesirables. He has an optimistic view of the country's role in the future. Compared to crusaders, the Americans he praises are the "western pilgrims" full of the "great mass of arts, sciences, vigor, and industry" that once issued from the east. It is important to note that Crèvecoeur ends his essay on a positive tone, with phrasing that emphasizes greatness. Here, in his conclusion, Crèvecoeur's attitude toward Americans really shines with enthusiasm. They are the nation of the future he believes, and they will deeply influence the future of the world with their newborn splendor.

Analysis of the High-Scoring Essay

This thorough and well-written essay succeeds both in covering the topic and in convincing the reader. The student demonstrates a clear comprehension of the passage and does not merely present a one-sided view of Crèvecoeur. The first paragraph introduces and relates other foreign authors who also addressed the personality of the new Americans. Ultimately, it presents a thoughtful thesis that shows a full understanding of Crèvecoeur's attitude while also mentioning his diction.

In the second paragraph, the student addresses Crèvecoeur's negative statements about the Americans' background in Europe and does a nice job of placing this negativity in context by pointing out that it will be balanced with the "dramatic" changes that take place once the new citizens have become Americans. This paragraph, like those that follow, is thoughtful and articulate, presenting an ample number of specific examples for the student's points and providing connection to the thesis.

The next paragraph addresses the transformation that took place in the Americans after they arrived in the new country. This unified paragraph uses quotations from the passage well and presents interesting ideas from the student. This writer shows the ability to think about and interpret Crèvecoeur's ideas, not simply to present them.

The fourth paragraph describes the "condescension" in some of Crèvecoeur's phrasing; again the student does an admirable job of presenting Crèvecoeur's attitude while remembering that the topic asks for diction analysis. The student clearly sees that, although Crèvecoeur presents many negative ideas about the Americans' background, essentially, he praises Americans.

The essay ends positively, just as Crèvecoeur's does. The student's wording, like Crèvecoeur's, shows optimism and provides a clean ending to a fairly long essay. Influencing the future with "newborn splendor" sums up both Crèvecoeur's attitude and the student's ideas very nicely. Overall, the essay uses sophisticated wording and contains many intelligent ideas. It reads well because it's clear that the student has ideas of his or her own and is not merely listing Crèvecoeur's.

Medium-Scoring Essay

Crèvecoeur was a French writer who wrote about life in the rural parts of America. He has a partly negative attitude about America, and cuts down the Americans many times in his essay. He also gives them some praise for starting over and doing something new. He also praises them for succeeding at something new.

He uses diction to obtain these results. A careful use of diction shows readers that he sometimes doesn't think much of the American people as a whole. He points out that they were the "poor of Europe" who, as "wretches," lived a life of "sore affliction." He also says that "two thirds of them had no country." This hardly sounds like Crèvecoeur admires the Americans background. He stereotypes Americans to all be like this.

Crèvecoeur continues his diatribe against Americans as he calls them "useless plants" in Europe. But finally, he has something more generous to say about Americans as he claims these plants have "taken root and flourished" here in American soil. So, although these Americans were low-life Europeans, once they became Americans they became "new."

They became "citizens." Crèvecoeur also notices that Americans work hard and have good laws. I find it interesting that even though he has some good things to say about Americans, he still claims negative things; he believes that once the new Americans arrived, they left behind them all their "ancient prejudices . . . receiving new ones . . ." We in America today like to believe that we hold no prejudices; at least that's one of the principles that our country was founded on.

Thus it can be seen that Crèvecoeur seemed to have some good thoughts about Americans, but that he was by no means entirely impressed by them. He uses his diction to present his opinions, and very strong diction at that. His wording is surprisingly harsh at times, considering that he seems to want to praise Americans for what they have accomplished, yet he spends so much time degrading their background. His attitude toward Americans is best described as guarded; he certainly does not show Americans in nothing but glowing terms.

Analysis of the Medium-Scoring Essay

This essay, although well organized, clearly shows the student's problems in both reading and writing skills. It begins by attempting to address the topic, but it does so with such a vague thesis that all it essentially sets forth is the simplistic idea that Crèvecoeur is both positive and negative about Americans. How Crèvecoeur's diction establishes that attitude is not yet addressed.

The student then devotes a paragraph to proving how negatively Crèvecoeur viewed the Americans' backgrounds by supplying a fair amount of evidence from Crèvecoeur's text. The student cites several examples of negative wording but also makes mistakes. First, the student borders on a misreading of the passage. In explaining the despair that Americans felt before coming to this country, Crèvecoeur's purpose seems to be to show how much the Americans had to overcome, thus emphasizing their strength. However, this student concentrates on only the negative European experience and transfers that negativity to the Americans *after* they became Americans. The student's second mistake is failing to address the topic clearly, failing to comment on exactly *how* Crèvecoeur's attitude is presented through his diction. This student simply gives the evidence and leaves it to the reader to make the connection.

The next paragraph tries to establish Crèvecoeur's positive attitude toward Americans, but the evidence presented is weak; the student offers little more than that the country is "new" and that people are now "citizens." The student turns again to a negative reading of the text, focusing on Crèvecoeur's claim that Americans have prejudices. Because of this change in direction, the paragraph lacks unity.

The concluding paragraph finally mentions diction again, but again it makes no connection between Crèvecoeur's word choice and the attitude it reflects. Unfortunately, this paragraph is merely summary. Overall, the essay's weaknesses stem from a cursory reading of the passage, weak presentation of evidence, and a lack of attention to the topic of the thesis. Simplistic thinking and simplistic diction combine here to produce a bland essay that fails to convince the reader.

PART IV

PAST AP ENGLISH LANGUAGE ESSAYS

By examining essay topics from previous exams, you can notice trends and become familiar with the question categories to expect. You will find topics from the last twenty years paraphrased in this part. Read them and become comfortable with the question format. Also be aware of the different writing modes the essays require. Top scoring students can write in a variety of modes.

Past AP English Language Essay Topics

In the following chart you will find a paraphrasing of English Language Essay Topics since 1980. While an exact topic is never reused, when you read this information you should look for trends and patterns in the essay topics. Examine the different modes the essay category requires. For instance, understand the difference between writing a style analysis essay and writing a persuasive essay. Notice that in the "free response" topics you may use examples from your observation, experience, or reading to support your ideas. Finally, be aware that the real test will not be printed like this; it will not tell you that the topic is a "style analysis" one or a "persuasive" one, for example. However, you should be able to understand what category the topic fits into from your practice.

Year	Question Category	Passage/Topic (Title of Passage & Author)
1980	Argumentative	Discuss the grounds on which a group could attack or suppress a work, such as a book, movie, etc., then defend the work.
	Style Analysis	Two eyewitness accounts of two different funerals are given, one from Henry James, the other from Ralph Ellison. Analyze the differences in their perspectives as seen in their rhetoric.
	Free Response	"Querencia" is defined as a "feeling for one's own place"; identify your "own place" and explain its meaning.
1981	Style Analysis	A passage from "The Rattler" by Donald Peattie is given in which he describes coming upon a rattlesnake in the desert. Discuss the passage's effect and how it is created by the author's techniques.
	Style Analysis	A portion of the letter written by George Bernard Shaw after the death of his mother is presented. Describe the author's attitude toward his mother and her cremation; analyze how his language conveys his attitude.
	Persuasive	A short passage from Thomas Szasz is given that discusses the struggle for definition. Agree or disagree with author's position and draw upon your experience, observation, or reading to support your position.
1982	Style/Persuasive	A passage is given in which the author disagrees with the adage "where ignorance is bliss, 'tis folly to be wise." Summarize the passage's reasoning and agree or disagree with the author's opinion.

(continued)

Year	Question Category	Passage/Topic (Title of Passage & Author)
	Style Analysis	The given passage is a statement of veto from Governor Adali E. Stevenson to the state congress. Analyze the Governor's strategies and devices that make his argument effective.
	Free Response	Describe a place so that it conveys a recognizable feeling through specific details without having to state that feeling.
1983	Free Response	Analyze both the good and bad effects of a change in society that has occurred or that you would like to see occur.
	Style Analysis	A passage from Thomas Carlyle's *Past and Present* is given. Define the author's attitude toward work, what assumptions he makes about human nature, and how his language persuades the reader of the validity of his position.
	Free Response	Agree or disagree with the concept that "when everything is superlative, everything is mediocre" while considering the "ethical and social consequences of language inflation."
1984	Free Response	Examine the importance of time, how you keep track of time, and what this reveals about you.
	Argumentative	Two passages are given that have different definitions of freedom. One is by Percy Bysshe Shelley and the other by John Milton. Discuss the concept expressed in each passage and examine the concepts' differences.
	Style Analysis	A passage from Norman Mailer that describes Paret, a Cuban boxer, is given. Analyze the effect of the passage on the reader and how Mailer's style produces that effect.
1985	Style Analysis	Two passages describe the Soviet Union's launching of the first satellite in 1957. Analyze the stylistic and rhetorical differences between the passages.
	Style Analysis	Two drafts from the same writer reflect his thoughts about how war changed his attitude about language. Discuss reasons for the writer's additions and deletions and how the revisions affect the passage.
	Free Response	The passage implies that television should reflect the real world. Defend one or more of the propositions in the passage.
1986	Style Analysis	Two Native American writers, N. S. Momaday and D. Brown, describe similar landscapes. Analyze how their respective styles reveal their different purposes.
	Language	Pairs of words similar in meaning but different in connotation are given, i.e., "religion & cult." Choose one or more pairs and elaborate on their distinctions.

Year	Question Category	Passage/Topic (Title of Passage & Author)
	Free Response	A quote claiming that human nature yearns for patterns, structure, and conformity is given. Agree or disagree with the concept and use your experiences, observations or readings to back up your opinion.
1987	Persuasive	Agree or disagree with E. M. Forester's quotation in which he claims the he would rather betray his country than betray a friend.
	Style Analysis	A passage from Zora Neal Hurston's *Dust Tracks on a Road* is given; analyze how her diction and point of view enhances our view of her childhood.
	Free Response	Examine how the language of a specific group you know well, such as an ethnic or social group, reflects that group. Describe the language (sociolect) of that group and discuss its influences.
1988	Argumentative	A passage from De Tocqueville's *Democracy in America* is given in which he concludes that democracy "throws [man] back forever upon himself alone." Evaluate his ideas.
	Style Analysis	A passage from Frederick Douglass explains how he felt after escaping slavery and arriving in New York in 1838. Analyze how his diverse language presents his various states of mind.
	Free Response	Describe a place that might be of interest or significance to others. Include descriptive detail and your attitude regarding this location.
1989	Argumentative	An announcement from a church bulletin reprinted in a magazine is given; the heading in the magazine implies a criticism of American values. Argue for or against the implied criticism.
	Style Analysis	A passage from Martin Luther King's *Why We Can't Wait* is given; analyze how his style fits his rhetorical purpose.
	Free Response	Describe how one person can be perceived differently at different times or in different situations.
1990	Style Analysis	A passage from Beryl Markham's autobiography is given. Analyze how her style reflects her personality.
	Style Analysis	Two passages describe the Galapagos Islands. Analyze the stylistic and rhetorical differences between them.
	Argumentative	Present an argument for or against the Supreme Court ruling which limited the First Amendment Rights of student newspapers, claiming that a school newspaper is a "laboratory situation" that can be curbed to remain consistent with the school's "basic educational mission."

(continued)

Year	Question Category	Passage/Topic (Title of Passage & Author)
1991	Style Analysis	A passage from the composer Igor Stravinsky is given: analyze how his language choices and rhetorical devices present his point of view.
	Style Analysis	A passage from Richard Rodriguez's autobiography is given; analyze how his rhetoric and style reflect his attitude toward his family and himself.
	Free Response/ Persuasive	A Biblical quote from Ecclesiastes claims that more knowledge brings more sorrow. Agree or disagree and use your experience, observations, or reading to support your position.
1992	Style Analysis	A speech from Queen Elizabeth I to her troops during the war with the Spanish Armada is given. Identify her purpose and analyze how she uses language to achieve that purpose.
	Persuasive	A passage from Joseph Addison's *Spectator* claims that mankind uses ridicule for bad aims instead of using it to achieve good. Defend, challenge or qualify the concept, using your experience, reading, or observation to back up your ideas.
	Style Analysis	A passage from Nancy Mairs about being a "cripple" is given; analyze how she presents herself through language and rhetorical features.
1993	Style Analysis	A passage from Jane Austen and a passage from Charles Dickens are given, each dealing with the subject of marriage. Compare the rhetorical strategies in the passages and the possible effects of each proposal.
	Persuasive	A passage from H. L. Mencken clarifies his view about the relationship between an artist and society. Defend, qualify, or challenge Mencken's view and support your position with references to particular writers, artists, or composers.
	Style Analysis	A passage from E. M. Forster's essay "My Wood" describes his feeling about owning property that he bought from his book royalties. Analyze how his rhetoric and Biblical allusions convey his attitude.
1994	Style Analysis	A passage from Sir George Savile, a member of King Charles II's Privy Council, is given in which he addresses the criticism that the King loves only pleasure. Clarify what attitude Savile wants the reader to adopt and how his rhetorical strategies encourage that attitude.
	Persuasive	A quotation from Barbara Tuchman's *March of Folly* is given, in which she asserts the role that "wooden-headedness" plays in human affairs. Defend, challenge, or qualify her idea, using your reading and/or observation to support your position.

Year	Question Category	Passage/Topic (Title of Passage & Author)
	Style Analysis	A passage from Joan Didion's essay "Los Angeles Notebook" is given in which she describes the Santa Ana winds and their effect on people. Analyze how her style promotes her views.
1995	Persuasive	A passage is used in which John Ruskin claims that precedence should be given to the soldier over the merchant or manufacturer. Evaluate Ruskin's argument.
	Style Analysis	A column by Ellen Goodman called "The Company Man" is given. Analyze how her language and rhetorical technique conveys her attitude.
	Free Response/ Persuasive	A passage from James Baldwin about the importance of language as the "key to identity" and social acceptance is given. Defend, challenge or qualify Baldwin's ideas, using your experience, observation or reading to develop your opinion.
1996	Style Analysis	A letter from Lady Montagu to her daughter is given, regarding the education of her granddaughter. Analyze the rhetorical strategies and stylistic devices she uses to present her ideas about the role that education played in women's lives in the eighteenth century.
	Style Analysis	A passage from Gary Soto's autobiography is presented in which he recounts an experience of stealing a pie at age six. Examine how his style re-creates both the experience and his ensuing guilt.
	Free Response/Persuasive	A passage from Lewis Lapham's *Money and Class in America* is given in which he observes the attitudes of Americans toward wealth. Defend, challenge, or qualify his view, based on your own experience and knowledge.
1997	Style Analysis	A passage from Meena Alexander's autobiography, *Fault Lines*, is given. Analyze how her language represents her "fractured identity."
	Style Analysis	A passage from the autobiography, *Narrative of the Life of Frederick Douglass, an American Slave,* is presented. Analyze how the third paragraph differs stylistically from the rest of the passage and reinforces Douglass' purpose.
	Free Response/Persuasive	A passage from Neil Postman, a contemporary social critic, contrasts the view of the future as presented in Orwell's *1984* and Huxley's *Brave New World*. Postman finds Huxley's ideas more relevant. Agree or disagree with Postman's idea, based on your understanding of modern society.

(continued)

Year	Question Category	Passage/Topic (Title of Passage & Author)
1998	Style Analysis	A letter from Charles Lamb to English romantic poet William Wordsworth is given. Analyze the techniques Lamb uses to reject an invitation by Wordsworth to visit.
	Free Response/ Persuasive	A passage from Henry James's novel *The Portrait of a Lady* is given, in which two conversationalists present differing views about what constitutes the self. Using your experiences, observations, or reading, develop whichever position you feel has greater validity.
	Style Analysis	Two letters are presented that deal with an advertising company's use of the slogan "It's the Real Thing" to promote a book. One letter is from a Coca-Cola Company executive and the second is a reply from the advertiser. Analyze the rhetorical strategies each writer uses and examine which is more successful in its persuasion.
1999	Style Analysis	Two passages describing Florida's Okefenokee Swamp are presented. Analyze how the style of each passage reflects each author's purpose.
	Style Analysis	A passage from Jamaica Kinkaid's essay, "On Seeing England for the First Time" is given. Analyze how her attitude toward England is presented through her rhetoric.
	Free Response/ Persuasive	A quotation from Teiresias in the play *Sophocles* is given in which he observes that "the only crime [in man] is pride." Evaluate the validity of his claim, using your experience, observation, or reading to support your opinion.
2000	Style Analysis	A passage from Eudora Welty's autobiography, *One Writer's Beginnings* is given in which she explains the value that reading books has had on her development as a writer. Analyze how her language explores the power of these experiences.
	Style Analysis	A passage from George Orwell is given that criticizes Gandhi and makes a point for humans being imperfect instead of saints. Analyze how Orwell disapproves of Gandhi and how effective he is in presenting his own opinion.
	Free Response/Persuasive	A quotation is given from the title character in King Lear, which comments on the relationship between wealth and justice. Paraphrase Lear's comment, then defend, challenge, or qualify that assertion with examples from reading, experience, or observation.

PART V

GLOSSARY OF IMPORTANT TERMS FOR THE AP LANGUAGE EXAM

The following glossaries list technical terms, both literary and grammatical, that you should be familiar with before the AP exam. These are not exhaustive lists of every term you might encounter. For example, you won't find parts of speech defined, as it is assumed that AP students are familiar with them. The first glossary includes terms common in both multiple-choice and essay sections. The second includes terms used exclusively in the essay section.

Terms for the Multiple-Choice and Essay Sections

Some of the following terms may be used in the multiple-choice questions and/or answers, or in essay section instructions. You might choose to incorporate others into your essay writing, for example, to help explain the effect of a literary device mentioned in the essay prompt.

ad hominem argument: From the Latin meaning "to or against the man," this is an argument that appeals to emotion rather than reason, to feeling rather than intellect.

allegory: The device of using character and/or story elements symbolically to represent an abstraction in addition to the literal meaning. In some allegories, for example, an author may intend the characters to personify an abstraction like hope or freedom. The allegorical meaning usually deals with moral truth or a generalization about human existence.

alliteration: The repetition of sounds, especially initial consonant sounds in two or more neighboring words (as in "she sells sea shells"). Although the term is not used in the multiple-choice section, you can look for alliteration in any essay passage. The repetition can reinforce meaning, unify ideas, and/or supply a musical sound.

allusion: A direct or indirect reference to something which is presumably commonly known, such as an event, book, myth, place, or work or art. Allusions can be historical, (like referring to Hitler), literary (like referring to Kurtz in *Heart of Darkness*), religious (like referring to Noah and the flood), or mythical (like referring to Atlas). There are, of course, many more possibilities, and a work may simultaneously use multiple layers of allusion.

ambiguity: The multiple meanings, either intentional or unintentional, of a word, phrase, sentence, or passage.

analogy: A similarity or comparison between two different things or the relationship between them. An analogy can explain something unfamiliar by associating it with or pointing out its similarity to something more familiar. Analogies can also make writing more vivid, imaginative, or intellectually engaging.

antecedent: The word, phrase, or clause referred to by a pronoun. The AP language exam occasionally asks for the antecedent of a given pronoun in a long, complex sentence or in a group of sentences.

aphorism: A terse statement of known authorship which expresses a general truth or moral principle. (If the authorship is unknown, the statement is generally considered to be a folk proverb.) An aphorism can be a memorable summation of the author's point.

apostrophe: A figure of speech that directly addresses an absent or imaginary person or personified abstraction, such as liberty or love. The effect may add familiarity or emotional intensity. William Wordsworth addresses John Milton as he writes, "Milton, thou shouldst be living at this hour: England hath need of thee."

atmosphere: The emotional mood created by the entirety of a literary work, established partly by the setting and partly by the author's choice of objects that are described. Even such elements as a description of the weather can contribute to the atmosphere. Frequently, atmosphere foreshadows events. See **mood.**

clause: A grammatical unit that contains both a subject and a verb. An independent, or main, clause expresses a complete thought and can stand alone as a sentence. A dependent, or subordinate, clause cannot stand alone as a sentence and must be accompanied by an independent clause. Examine this sample sentence: "Because I practiced hard, my AP scores were high." In this sentence, the independent clause is "my AP scores were high," and the dependent clause is "Because I practiced hard."

colloquial/colloquialism: The use of slang or informalities in speech or writing. Not generally acceptable for formal writing, colloquialisms give work a conversational, familiar tone. Colloquial expressions in writing include local or regional dialects.

conceit: A fanciful expression, usually in the form of an extended metaphor or surprising analogy between seemingly dissimilar objects. A conceit displays intellectual cleverness due to the unusual comparison being made.

connotation: The nonliteral, associative meaning of a word; the implied, suggested meaning. Connotations may involve ideas, emotions, or attitudes. See **denotation.**

denotation: The strict, literal, dictionary definition of a word, devoid of any emotion, attitude, or color. See **connotation.**

diction: Related to style, diction refers to the writer's word choices, especially with regard to their correctness, clearness, or effectiveness. For the AP exam, you should be able to describe an author's diction (for example, formal or informal, ornate or plain) and understand the ways in which diction can complement the author's purpose. Diction, combined with syntax, figurative language, literary devices, etc., creates an author's style. Note: this term frequently appears in the essay question's wording. In your thesis avoid phrases such as, "The author uses diction . . . ." Since diction, by definition, *is word choice,* this phrase really says, "The author chooses words to write . . ." which is as redundant (and silly) as claiming, "A painter uses paints to paint." At least try to put an adjective in front of the word "diction" to help describe it, such as "stark diction" or "flowery and soft diction." See **syntax.**

didactic: From the Greek, didactic literally means "teaching." Didactic works have the primary aim of teaching or instructing, especially the teaching of moral or ethical principles.

euphemsim: From the Greek for "good speech," euphemisms are a more agreeable or less offensive substitute for generally unpleasant words or concepts. The euphemism may be used to adhere to standards of social or political correctness, or to add humor or ironic understatement. Saying "earthly remains" rather than "corpse" is an example of euphemism.

extended metaphor: A metaphor developed at great length, occurring frequently in or throughout a work. See **metaphor.**

figurative language: Writing or speech that is not intended to carry literal meaning and is usually meant to be imaginative and vivid. See **figure of speech.**

figure of speech: A device used to produce figurative language. Many compare dissimilar things. Figures of speech include, for example, apostrophe, hyperbole, irony, metaphor, metonomy, oxymoron, paradox, personification, simile, synecdoche, and understatement.

generic conventions: This term describes traditions for each genre. These conventions help to define each genre; for example, they differentiate between an essay and journalistic writing or an autobiography and political writing. On the AP language exam, try to distinguish the unique features of a writer's work from those dictated by convention.

genre: The major category into which a literary work fits. The basic divisions of literature are prose, poetry, and drama. However, genre is a flexible term; within these broad boundaries exist many subdivisions that are often called genres themselves. For example, prose can be divided into fiction (novels and short stories) or nonfiction (essays, biographies, autobiographies, etc.). Poetry can be divided into such subcategories as lyric, dramatic, narrative, epic, etc. Drama can be divided into tragedy, comedy, melodrama, farce, etc. On the AP language exam, expect the majority of the passages to be from the following genres: autobiography, biography, diaries, criticism, essays, and journalistic, political, scientific, and nature writing.

homily: This term literally means "sermon," but more informally, it can include any serious talk, speech, or lecture involving moral or spiritual advice.

hyperbole: A figure of speech using deliberate exaggeration or overstatement. Hyperboles often have a comic effect; however, a serious effect is also possible. Often, hyperbole produces irony at the same time.

imagery: The sensory details or figurative language used to describe, arouse emotion, or represent abstractions. On a physical level, imagery uses terms related to the five senses; we refer to visual, auditory, tactile, gustatory, or olfactory imagery. On a broader and deeper level, however, one image can represent more than one thing. For example, a rose may present visual imagery while also representing the color in a woman's cheeks. An author, therefore, may use complex imagery while simultaneously employing other figures of speech, especially metaphor and simile. In addition, this term can apply to the total of all the images in a work. On the AP exam, pay attention to *how* an author creates imagery and to the effect of that imagery.

inference/infer: To draw reasonable conclusion from the information presented. When a multiple-choice question asks for an inference to be drawn from the passage, the most direct, most reasonable inference is the safest answer choice. If an inference is implausible, it's unlikely to be the correct answer. Note that if the answer choice is directly stated, it is *not* inferred and is wrong.

invective: An emotionally violent, verbal denunciation or attack using strong, abusive language.

irony/ironic: The contrast between what is stated explicitly and what is really meant; the difference between what appears to be and what actually is true. In general, there are three major types of irony used in language:

1. In *verbal* irony, the words literally state the opposite of the writer's (or speaker's) true meaning.

2. In *situational* irony, events turn out the opposite of what was expected. What the characters and readers think ought to happen is not what does happen.

3. In *dramatic* irony, facts or events are unknown to a character in a play or piece of fiction but known to the reader, audience, or other characters in the work. Irony is used for many reasons, but frequently, it's used to create poignancy or humor.

loose sentence: A type of sentence in which the main idea (independent clause) comes first, followed by dependent grammatical units such as phrases and clauses. If a period were placed at the end of the independent clause, the clause would be a complete sentence. A work containing many loose sentences often seems informal, relaxed, and conversational. See **periodic sentence.**

metaphor: A figure of speech using implied comparison of seemingly unlike things or the substitution of one for the other, suggesting some similarity. Metaphorical language makes writing more vivid, imaginative, thought provoking, and meaningful. See **simile.**

metonomy: A term from the Greek meaning "changed label" or "substitute name," metonomy is a figure of speech which the name of one object is substituted for that of another closely associated with it. A news release that claims "the White House declared" rather than "the President declared" is using metonomy. This term is unlikely to be used in the multiple-choice section, but you might see examples of metonomy in an essay passage.

mood: This term has two distinct technical meanings in English writing. The first meaning is grammatical and deals with verbal units and a speaker's attitude. The *indicative* mood is used only for factual sentences. For example, "Joe eats too quickly." The *subjunctive* mood is used for a doubtful or conditional attitude. For example, "If I were you, I'd get another job." The *imperative* mood is used for commands. For example, "Shut the door!" The second meaning of mood is literary, meaning the prevailing atmosphere or emotional aura of a work. Setting, tone, and events can affect the mood. In this usage, mood is similar to tone and atmosphere.

narrative: The telling of a story or an account of an event or series of events.

onomatopoeia: A figure of speech in which natural sounds are imitated in the sounds of words. Simple examples include such words as buzz, hiss, hum, crack, whinny, and murmur. This term is not used in the multiple-choice section. If you identify examples of onomatopoeia in an essay passage, note the effect.

oxymoron: From the Greek for "pointedly foolish," an oxymoron is a figure of speech wherein the author groups apparently contradictory terms to suggest a paradox. Simple examples include "jumbo shrimp" and "cruel kindness." This term does not appear in the multiple-choice questions, but there is a slight chance you will see it used by an author in an essay passage or find it useful in your own essay writing.

paradox: A statement that appears to be self-contradictory or opposed to common sense, but upon closer inspection contains some degree of truth or validity. The first scene of *Macbeth,* for example, closes with the witches' cryptic remark "Fair is foul, and foul is fair. . . ."

parallelism: Also referred to as parallel construction or parallel structure, this term comes from Greek roots meaning "beside one another." It refers to the grammatical or rhetorical framing of words, phrases, sentences, or paragraphs to give structural similarity. This can involve, but is not limited to, repetition of a grammatical element such as a preposition or verbal phrase. A famous example of parallelism begins Charles Dickens's novel *A Tale of Two Cities:* "It was the best of times, it was the worst of times, it was the age of wisdom, it was the age of foolishness, it was the epoch of belief, it was the epoch of incredulity . . . ." The effects of parallelism are numerous, but frequently, they act as an organizing force to attract the reader's attention, add emphasis and organization, or simply provide a musical rhythm. Other famous examples include *Julius Caesar's* "I came, I saw, I conquered," or, as Tennyson's poem "Ulysses" claims, "To strive, to seek, to find, and not to yield."

parody: A work that closely imitates the style or content of another with the specific aim of comic effect and/or ridicule. As comedy, parody distorts or exaggerates distinctive features of the original. As ridicule, it mimics the work by repeating and borrowing words, phrases, or characteristics in order to illuminate weaknesses in the original. Well-written parody offers enlightenment about the original, but poorly written parody offers only ineffectual imitation. Usually an audience must grasp literary allusion and understand the work being parodied in order to fully appreciate the nuances of the newer work. Occasionally, however, parodies take on a life of their own and don't require knowledge of the original.

pedantic: An adjective that describes words, phrases, or general tone that is overly scholarly, academic, or bookish.

periodic sentence: A sentence that presents its central meaning in a main clause at the end. This independent clause is preceded by a phrase or clause that cannot stand alone. For example, "Ecstatic with my AP scores, I let out a loud shout of joy!" The effect of a periodic sentence is to add emphasis and structural variety. See **loose sentence.**

personification: A figure of speech in which the author presents or describes concepts, animals, or inanimate objects by endowing them with human attributes or emotions. Personification is used to make these abstractions, animals, or objects appear more vivid to the reader.

point of view: In literature, the perspective from which a story is told. There are two general divisions of point of view and many subdivisions within those.

1. The *first-person narrator* tells the story with the first-person pronoun, "I," and is a character in the story. This narrator can be the protagonist (the hero or heroine), a participant (a character in a secondary role), or an observer (a character who merely watches the action).

2. The *third person narrator* relates the events with the third person pronouns, "he," "she," and "it." There are two main subdivisions to be aware of: *omniscient* and *limited omniscient*. In the "third person omniscient" point of view, the narrator, with godlike knowledge, presents the thoughts and actions of any or all characters. This all-knowing narrator can reveal what each character feels and thinks at any given moment. The "third person limited omniscient" point of view, as its name implies, presents the feelings and thoughts of only one character, presenting only the actions of all remaining characters. This definition applies in questions in the multiple-choice section. However, on the essay portion of the exam, the term "point of view" carries a different meaning. When you're asked to analyze an author's point of view, the appropriate point for you to address is the author's **attitude.**

predicate adjectives: One type of subject complement — an adjective, group of adjectives, or adjective clause that follows a linking verb. It is in the predicate of the sentence, and modifies or describes the subject. For example, in the sentence "My boyfriend is tall, dark, and handsome," the group of predicate adjectives ("tall, dark, and handsome") describes "boyfriend."

predicate nominative: A second type of subject complement — a noun, group of nouns, or noun clause that renames the subject. It, like the predicate adjective, follows a linking verb and is located in the predicate of the sentence. For example, in the sentence "Abe Lincoln was a man of integrity," the predicate nominative is "man of integrity," as it renames Abe Lincoln. Occasionally, this term or the term predicate adjective appears in a multiple-choice question.

prose: One of the major divisions of genre, prose refers to fiction and nonfiction, including all its forms, because they are written in ordinary language and most closely resemble everyday speech. Technically, anything that isn't poetry or drama is prose. Therefore, all passages in the AP language exam are prose. Of course, prose writers often borrow poetic and dramatic elements.

repetition: The duplication, either exact or approximate, of any element of language, such as a sound, word, phrase, clause, sentence, or grammatical pattern. When repetition is poorly done, it bores, but when it's well done, it links and emphasizes ideas while allowing the reader the comfort of recognizing something familiar. See **parallelism.**

rhetoric: From the Greek for "orator," this term describes the principles governing the art of writing effectively, eloquently, and persuasively.

rhetorical modes: This flexible term describes the variety, the conventions, and the purposes of the major kinds of writing. The four most common rhetorical modes and their purposes are as follows:

1. The purpose of *exposition* (or expository writing) is to explain and analyze information by presenting an idea, relevant evidence, and appropriate discussion. The AP language exam essay questions are frequently set up as expository topics.

2. The purpose of *argumentation* is to prove the validity of an idea, or point of view, by presenting sound reasoning, discussion, and argument that thoroughly convince the reader. *Persuasive* writing is a type of argumentation having the additional aim of urging some form of action.

3. The purpose of *description* is to re-create, invent, or visually present a person, place, event, or action so that the reader can picture that being described. Sometimes an author engages all five senses in description; good descriptive writing can be sensuous and picturesque. Descriptive may be straightforward and objective or highly emotional and subjective.

4. The purpose of *narration* is to tell a story or narrate an event or series of events. This writing mode frequently uses the tools of descriptive writing.

These four writing modes are sometimes referred to as modes of discourse.

rhetorical question: A question that is asked merely for effect and does not expect a reply. The answer is assumed.

sarcasm: From the Greek meaning "to tear flesh," sarcasm involves bitter, caustic language that is meant to hurt or ridicule someone or something. It may use irony as a device, but not all ironic statements are sarcastic, that is, intending to ridicule. When well done, sarcasm can be witty and insightful; when poorly done, it's simply cruel.

satire: A work that targets human vices and follies, or social institutions and conventions, for reform or ridicule. Regardless of whether or not the work aims to reform humans or their society, satire is best seen as a style of writing rather than a purpose for writing. It can be recognized by the many devices used effectively by the satirist, such as irony, wit, parody, caricature, hyperbole, understatement, and sarcasm. The effects of satire are varied, depending on the writer's goal, but good satire — often humorous — is thought provoking and insightful about the human condition.

simile: An explicit comparison, normally using *like, as,* or *if.* For example, remember Robbie Burns' famous lines, "O, my love is like a red, red rose / That's newly sprung in June. / O, my love is like a melody, / That's sweetly played in tune." See **metaphor.**

style: The consideration of style has two purposes:

1. An evaluation of the sum of the choices an author makes in blending diction, syntax, figurative language, and other literary devices. Some authors' styles are so idiosyncratic that we can quickly recognize works by the same author (or writer emulating that author's style). Compare, for example, Jonathan Swift to George Orwell, or William Faulkner to Ernest Hemingway. We can analyze and describe an author's personal style and make judgments on how appropriate it is to the author's purpose. Styles can be called flowery, explicit, succinct, rambling, bombastic, commonplace, incisive, or laconic, to name only a few examples.

2. Classification of authors to a group and comparison of an author to similar authors.

By means of such classification and comparison, one can see how an author's style reflects and helps to define a historical period, such as the Renaissance or the Victorian period, or a literary movement, such as the romantic, transcendental, or realist movement.

subject complement: The word (with any accompanying phrases) or clause that follows a linking verb and complements, or completes, the subject of the sentence by either (1) renaming it or (2) describing it. The former is technically called a predicate nominative, the latter a predicate adjective. See *predicate nominate* and *predicate adjective* for examples of sentences. This term is occasionally used in a multiple-choice question.

subordinate clause: Like all clauses, this word group contains both a subject and a verb (plus any accompanying phrases or modifiers), but unlike the independent clause, the subordinate clause cannot stand alone; it does not express a complete thought. Also called a dependent clause, the subordinate clause depends on a main clause, sometimes called an independent clause, to complete its meaning. Easily recognized key words and phrases usually begin these clauses — for example: although, because, unless, if, even though, since, as soon as, while, who, when, where, how, and that.

syllogism: From the Greek for "reckoning together," a syllogism (or syllogistic reasoning) is a deductive system of formal logic that presents two premises — the first one called "major" and the second "minor" — that inevitable lead to a sound conclusion. A frequently cited example proceeds as follows:

- *Major premise:* All men are mortal.
- *Minor premise:* Socrates is a man.
- *Conclusion:* Therefore, Socrates is mortal.

A syllogism's conclusion is valid only if each of the two premises is valid. Syllogisms may also present the specific idea first ("Socrates") and the general idea second ("All men").

symbol/symbolism: Generally, anything that represents or stands for something else. Usually, a symbol is something concrete — such as an object, action, character, or scene — that represents something more abstract. However, symbols and symbolism can be much more complex. One system classifies symbols in three categories:

1. *Natural* symbols use objects and occurrences from nature to represent ideas commonly associated with them (dawn symbolizing hope or a new beginning, a rose symbolizing love, a tree symbolizing knowledge).

2. *Conventional* symbols are those that have been invested with meaning by a group (religious symbols, such as a cross or Star of David; national symbols, such as a flag or an eagle; or group symbols, such as skull and crossbones for pirates or the scales of justice for lawyers).

3. *Literary* symbols are sometimes also conventional in the sense that they are found in a variety of works and are generally recognized. However, a work's symbols may be more complicated as is the whale in *Moby Dick* and the jungle in *Heart of Darkness*. On the AP exam, try to determine what abstraction an object is a symbol for and to what extent it is successful in representing that abstraction.

syntax: The way an author chooses to join words into phrases, clauses, and sentences. Syntax is similar to diction, but you can differentiate the two by thinking of syntax as referring to *groups* of words, while diction refers to individual words. In the multiple-choice section of the AP language exam, expect to be asked some questions about how an author manipulates syntax. In the essay section, you will need to analyze how syntax produces effects. When you are analyzing syntax, consider such elements as the length or brevity of sentences, unusual sentence constructions, the sentence patterns used, and the kinds of sentences the author uses. The writer may use questions, declarations, exclamations, or rhetorical questions; sentences are also classified as periodic or loose, simple, compound, or complex sentences. Syntax can be tricky for students to analyze. First try to classify *what kind* of sentences the author uses, and then try to determine *how* the author's choices amplify meaning, in other words *why they work well* for the author's purpose.

theme: The central idea or message of a work, the insight it offers into life. Usually, theme is unstated in fictional works, but in nonfiction, the theme may be directly stated, especially in expository or argumentative writing.

thesis: In expository writing, the thesis statement is the sentence or group of sentences that directly expresses the author's opinion, purpose, meaning, or proposition. Expository writing is usually judged by analyzing how accurately, effectively, and thoroughly a writer has proven the thesis.

tone: Similar to mood, tone describes the author's attitude toward his or her material, the audience, or both. Tone is easier to determine in spoken language than in written language. Considering how a work would sound if it were read aloud can help in identifying an author's tone. Some words describing tone are playful, serious, businesslike, sarcastic, humorous, formal, ornate, and somber. As with attitude, an author's tone in the exam's passages can rarely be described by one word. Expect that it will be more complex. See **attitude** in the "Terms for the Essay Section" that follows.

transition: A word or phrase that links different ideas. Used especially, although not exclusively, in expository and argumentative writing, transitions effectively signal a shift from one idea to another. A few commonly used transitional words or phrases are furthermore, consequently, nevertheless, for example, in addition, likewise, similarly, and on the contrary.

understatement: The ironic minimalizing of fact, understatement presents something as less significant than it is. The effect can frequently be humorous and emphatic.

Understatement is the opposite of **hyperbole.**

wit: In modern usage, wit is intellectually amusing language that surprises and delights. A witty statement is humorous, while suggesting the speaker's verbal power in creating ingenious and perceptive remarks. Wit usually uses terse language that makes a pointed statement. Historically, wit originally meant basic understanding. Its meaning evolved to include speed of understanding, and finally (in the early seventeenth century), it grew to mean quick perception including creative fancy.

Terms for the Essay Section

The following words and phrases have appeared in recent AP language exam essay topics. While not a comprehensive list of every word or phrase you might encounter, it will help you understand what you're being asked to do for a topic.

attitude: A writer's intellectual position or emotion regarding the subject of the writing. In the essay section, expect to be asked what the writer's attitude is and how his or her language conveys that attitude. Also be aware that, although the singular term "attitude" is used in this definition and on the exam, the passage will rarely have only one attitude. More often than not, the author's attitude will be more complex than that, and the student who presents this complexity — no matter how subtle the differences — will appear to be more astute than the student who only uses one adjective to describe attitude. Of course, don't force an attitude that has no evidence in the passage, but rather understand that an accurate statement of an author's attitude is not likely to be a blatantly obvious idea. If it were that simple, the test committee wouldn't ask you to discuss it.

concrete detail: Strictly defined, "concrete" refers to nouns that name physical objects — a bridge, a book, or a coat. Concrete nouns are the opposite of abstract nouns (which refer to concepts like freedom and love). However, as used in the essay portion of the AP test, this term has a slightly different connotation. The directions may read something like this: "Provide concrete detail that will convince the reader." This means that your essay should include detail in the passage; at times, you'll be asked to provide detail from you own life (reading, observation, experience, and so forth).

descriptive detail: When an essay uses this phrase, look for the writer's sensory description. Descriptive detail appealing to the visual sense is usually the most predominant, but don't overlook other sensory detail. As usual, after you identify a passage's descriptive detail, analyze its effect.

devices: The figures of speech, syntax, diction, and other stylistic elements that collectively produce a particular artistic effect.

language: When you're asked to "analyze the language," concentrate on how the elements of language combine to form a whole — how diction, syntax, figurative language, and sentence structure create a cumulative effect.

narrative devices: This term describes the tools of the storyteller (also used in nonfiction), such as ordering events so that they build to a climactic moment or withholding information until a crucial or appropriate moment when revealing it creates a desired effect. On the essay exam, this term may also apply to biographical and autobiographical writing.

narrative technique: The style of telling the "story," even if the passage is nonfiction. Concentrate on the order of events and on their detail in evaluating a writer's technique.

persuasive devices: When asked to analyze an author's persuasive devices, look for the words in the passage that have strong connotations — words that intensify the emotional effect. In addition, analyze *how* these words complement the writer's argument as it builds logically. Speeches are often used in this context, since they are generally designed to persuade.

persuasive essay: When asked to write a persuasive essay, you should present a coherent argument in which the evidence builds to a logical and relevant conclusion. Strong persuasive essays often appeal to the audience's emotions or ethical standards.

resources of language: This phrase refers to all the devices of composition available to a writer, such as diction, syntax, sentence structure, and figures of speech. The cumulative effect of a work is produced by the resources of language a writer chooses.

rhetorical features: This phrase refers to how a passage is constructed. If asked to consider rhetorical structure, look at the passage's organization and how the writer combines images, details, or arguments to serve his or her purpose.

sentence structure: When an essay question asks you to analyze sentence structure, look at the type of sentences the author uses. Remember that the basic sentence structures are simple, compound, and complex, and variations created with sentence combining. Also consider variation or lack of it in sentence length, any unusual devices in sentence construction, such as repetition or inverted word order, and any unusual word or phrase placement. As with all devices, be prepared to discuss the effect of the sentence structure. For example, a series of short, simple sentences or phrases can produce a feeling of speed and choppiness, which may suit the author's purpose.

stylistic devices: An essay that mentions stylistic devices is asking you to note and analyze all of the elements in language that contribute to style — such as diction, syntax, tone, attitude, figures of speech, connotations, and repetition.

PART VI

FIVE FULL-LENGTH PRACTICE TESTS

This section contains five full-length simulated AP English language exams. The practice tests are followed by complete answers, explanations, and analysis of techniques. In addition, two sample essays written by AP students and analyses of the essays are included for each essay topic.

The format, levels of difficulty, question structures, and number of questions are similar to those found on actual AP language exams. The actual AP exam is copyrighted and may not be duplicated; therefore, these questions are not taken from the actual tests.

When taking these exams, try to simulate test conditions by following the time allotments carefully. Remember, the total testing time for each practice test is three hours. Be aware of the time allotted for each section.

Answer Sheet for Practice Test 1

(Remove This Sheet and Use it to Mark Your Answers)

Section 1
Multiple Choice Questions

PASSAGE 1

1 Ⓐ Ⓑ Ⓒ Ⓓ Ⓔ
2 Ⓐ Ⓑ Ⓒ Ⓓ Ⓔ
3 Ⓐ Ⓑ Ⓒ Ⓓ Ⓔ
4 Ⓐ Ⓑ Ⓒ Ⓓ Ⓔ
5 Ⓐ Ⓑ Ⓒ Ⓓ Ⓔ
6 Ⓐ Ⓑ Ⓒ Ⓓ Ⓔ
7 Ⓐ Ⓑ Ⓒ Ⓓ Ⓔ
8 Ⓐ Ⓑ Ⓒ Ⓓ Ⓔ
9 Ⓐ Ⓑ Ⓒ Ⓓ Ⓔ
10 Ⓐ Ⓑ Ⓒ Ⓓ Ⓔ
11 Ⓐ Ⓑ Ⓒ Ⓓ Ⓔ
12 Ⓐ Ⓑ Ⓒ Ⓓ Ⓔ
13 Ⓐ Ⓑ Ⓒ Ⓓ Ⓔ
14 Ⓐ Ⓑ Ⓒ Ⓓ Ⓔ

PASSAGE 2

15 Ⓐ Ⓑ Ⓒ Ⓓ Ⓔ
16 Ⓐ Ⓑ Ⓒ Ⓓ Ⓔ
17 Ⓐ Ⓑ Ⓒ Ⓓ Ⓔ
18 Ⓐ Ⓑ Ⓒ Ⓓ Ⓔ
19 Ⓐ Ⓑ Ⓒ Ⓓ Ⓔ
20 Ⓐ Ⓑ Ⓒ Ⓓ Ⓔ
21 Ⓐ Ⓑ Ⓒ Ⓓ Ⓔ
22 Ⓐ Ⓑ Ⓒ Ⓓ Ⓔ
23 Ⓐ Ⓑ Ⓒ Ⓓ Ⓔ
24 Ⓐ Ⓑ Ⓒ Ⓓ Ⓔ
25 Ⓐ Ⓑ Ⓒ Ⓓ Ⓔ
26 Ⓐ Ⓑ Ⓒ Ⓓ Ⓔ
27 Ⓐ Ⓑ Ⓒ Ⓓ Ⓔ
28 Ⓐ Ⓑ Ⓒ Ⓓ Ⓔ

PASSAGE 3

29 Ⓐ Ⓑ Ⓒ Ⓓ Ⓔ
30 Ⓐ Ⓑ Ⓒ Ⓓ Ⓔ
31 Ⓐ Ⓑ Ⓒ Ⓓ Ⓔ
32 Ⓐ Ⓑ Ⓒ Ⓓ Ⓔ
33 Ⓐ Ⓑ Ⓒ Ⓓ Ⓔ
34 Ⓐ Ⓑ Ⓒ Ⓓ Ⓔ
35 Ⓐ Ⓑ Ⓒ Ⓓ Ⓔ
36 Ⓐ Ⓑ Ⓒ Ⓓ Ⓔ
37 Ⓐ Ⓑ Ⓒ Ⓓ Ⓔ
38 Ⓐ Ⓑ Ⓒ Ⓓ Ⓔ
39 Ⓐ Ⓑ Ⓒ Ⓓ Ⓔ
40 Ⓐ Ⓑ Ⓒ Ⓓ Ⓔ
41 Ⓐ Ⓑ Ⓒ Ⓓ Ⓔ
42 Ⓐ Ⓑ Ⓒ Ⓓ Ⓔ
43 Ⓐ Ⓑ Ⓒ Ⓓ Ⓔ

PASSAGE 4

44 Ⓐ Ⓑ Ⓒ Ⓓ Ⓔ
45 Ⓐ Ⓑ Ⓒ Ⓓ Ⓔ
46 Ⓐ Ⓑ Ⓒ Ⓓ Ⓔ
47 Ⓐ Ⓑ Ⓒ Ⓓ Ⓔ
48 Ⓐ Ⓑ Ⓒ Ⓓ Ⓔ
49 Ⓐ Ⓑ Ⓒ Ⓓ Ⓔ
50 Ⓐ Ⓑ Ⓒ Ⓓ Ⓔ
51 Ⓐ Ⓑ Ⓒ Ⓓ Ⓔ
52 Ⓐ Ⓑ Ⓒ Ⓓ Ⓔ
53 Ⓐ Ⓑ Ⓒ Ⓓ Ⓔ
54 Ⓐ Ⓑ Ⓒ Ⓓ Ⓔ
55 Ⓐ Ⓑ Ⓒ Ⓓ Ⓔ
56 Ⓐ Ⓑ Ⓒ Ⓓ Ⓔ
57 Ⓐ Ⓑ Ⓒ Ⓓ Ⓔ

CUT HERE

Section I: Multiple-Choice Questions

Time: 60 minutes

57 Questions

Directions: This section consists of selections from prose works and questions on their content, style, and form. Read each selection carefully. Choose the best answer of the five choices.

Questions 1–14. Read the following passage carefully before you begin to answer the questions.

First Passage

The written word is weak. Many people prefer life to it. Life gets your blood going, and it smells good. Writing is mere writing, literature is mere. It ap-
(5) peals only to the subtlest senses — the imagination's vision, and the imagination's hearing — and the moral sense, and the intellect. This writing that you do, that so thrills you, that so racks and
(10) exhilarates you, as if you were dancing next to the band, is barely audible to anyone else. The reader's ear must adjust down from loud life to the subtle, imaginary sounds of the written word. An or-
(15) dinary reader picking up a book can't yet hear a thing; it will take half an hour to pick up the writing's modulations, its ups and downs and louds and softs.

An intriguing entomological experi-
(20) ment shows that a male butterfly will ignore a living female butterfly of his own species in favor of a painted cardboard one, if the cardboard one is big. If the cardboard one is bigger than he is, bigger
(25) than any female butterfly ever could be. He jumps the piece of cardboard. Over and over again, he jumps the piece of cardboard. Nearby, the real, living butterfly opens and closes her wings in vain.

(30) Films and television stimulate the body's senses too, in big ways. A nine-foot handsome face, and its three-foot-wide smile, are irresistible. Look at the long legs on that man, as high as a wall,
(35) and coming straight toward you. The music builds. The moving, lighted screen fills your brain. You do not like filmed car chases? See if you can turn away. Try not to watch. Even knowing
(40) you are manipulated, you are still as helpless as the male butterfly drawn to painted cardboard.

That is the movies. That is their ground. The printed word cannot com-
(45) pete with the movies on their ground, and should not. You can describe beautiful faces, car chases, or valleys full of Indians on horseback until you run out of words, and you will not approach the
(50) movies' spectacle. Novels written with film contracts in mind have a faint but unmistakable, and ruinous, odor. I cannot name what, in the text, alerts the

GO ON TO THE NEXT PAGE

89

(55) reader to suspect the writer of mixed motives; I cannot specify which sentences, in several books, have caused me to read on with increasing dismay, and finally close the books because I smelled a rat. Such books seem uneasy being books; (60) they seem eager to fling off their disguises and jump onto screens.

Why would anyone read a book instead of watching big people move on a screen? Because a book can be litera- (65) ture. It is a subtle thing — poor thing, but our own. In my view, the more literary the book — the more purely verbal, crafted sentence by sentence, the more

imaginative, reasoned, and deep — the (70) more likely people are to read it. The people who read are the people who like literature, after all, whatever that might be. They like, or require what books alone have. If they want to see films that (75) evening, they will find films. If they do not like to read, they will not. People who read are not too lazy to flip on the television; they prefer books. I cannot imagine a sorrier pursuit than struggling (80) for years to write a book that attempts to appeal to people who do not read in the first place.

1. Which of the following terms can be used to describe the imagery of the last sentence in the first paragraph ("An ordinary . . . and softs")?

   I.   Simile

   II. Metaphor

   III. Synthesthetic

   A. I only

   B. II only

   C. I and III only

   D. II and III only

   E. I, II, and III

2. In the second paragraph of the passage, the author employs

   A. a concession to an opposing point of view

   B. a cause and effect relationship

   C. a smile

   D. a metaphor

   E. an extended definition

3. Which of the following best describes how the second and third paragraphs are related?

   A. The second paragraph makes an assertion that is qualified by the third paragraph.

   B. The second paragraph asks a question that is answered by the third paragraph.

   C. The second paragraph describes a situation that is paralleled in the third paragraph.

   D. The second paragraph presents as factual what the third paragraph presents as only a possibility.

   E. There is no clear relationship between the two paragraphs.

4. The "nine-foot handsome face" (lines 31–32) refers to

   A. the female butterfly

   B. literary creativity

   C. a television image

   D. an image in the movies

   E. how the imagination of a reader may see a face

5. In the fourth paragraph, the author argues that

    I.   action scenes are better in films than in books

    II. novels written with an eye on future film adaptation stink

    III. novels specifically written to be adapted into films do not make superior films

    A. II only

    B. I and II only

    C. I and III only

    D. II and III only

    E. I, II, and III

6. The last sentence of the fourth paragraph ("Such books . . . onto screens") contains an example of

    A. personification

    B. understatement

    C. irony

    D. simile

    E. syllogism

7. According to the passage, literature is likely to be characterized by all of the following EXCEPT

    A. colloquial language

    B. imagination

    C. verbal skill

    D. moral sense

    E. intelligence

8. In the last sentence of the last paragraph, the phrase "sorrier pursuit" can be best understood to mean

    A. more regretful chase

    B. poorer occupation

    C. more sympathetic profession

    D. sadder expectation

    E. more pitiful striving

9. In the last paragraph, the phrase "a poor thing, but our own" is adapted from Shakespeare's "a poor . . . thing, sir, but mine own." The change from the singular to the plural pronoun is made in order to

    A. avoid the use of the first person

    B. include all readers of this passage who prefer literature

    C. avoid direct quotation of Shakespeare and the appearance of comparing this work to his

    D. suggest that the number of readers is as great as the number of moviegoers

    E. avoid overpraising literature compared to films, which are more popular

GO ON TO THE NEXT PAGE

10. The sentences "The written word is weak" (line 1), "An ordinary reader . . . a thing" (lines 14–16), and "The printed word . . . should not" (lines 44–46) have in common that they

   A. concede a limitation of the written word

   B. assert the superiority of film to writing

   C. do not represent the genuine feelings of the author

   D. deliberately overstate the author's ideas

   E. are all ironic

11. With which of the following statements would the author of this passage be most likely to disagree?

   A. Life is more exciting than writing.

   B. People who dislike reading should not be forced to read.

   C. Good books will appeal to those who do not like to read as well as to those who do.

   D. The power of film is irresistible.

   E. Novels written for people who hate reading are folly.

12. The passage in its entirety is best described as about the

   A. superiority of the art of writing to the art of film

   B. difficulties of being a writer

   C. differences between writing and film

   D. public's preference of film to literature

   E. similarities and differences of the novel and the film

13. Which of the following best describes the organization of the passage?

   A. A five-paragraph essay in which the first and last paragraphs are general and the second, third, and fourth paragraphs are specific.

   B. A five-paragraph essay in which the first two paragraphs describe writing, the third and fourth paragraphs describe film, and the last paragraph describes both writing and film.

   C. Five paragraphs with the first about literature, the second about butterflies, and the third, fourth, and fifth about the superiority of film.

   D. Five paragraphs with the first and last about writing, the third about film, and the fourth about both film and writing.

   E. Five paragraphs of comparison and contrast, with the comparison in the first and last paragraphs and the contrast in the second, third, and fourth.

14. All of the following rhetorical features appear in the passage EXCEPT

   A. personal anecdote

   B. extended analogy

   C. short sentence

   D. colloquialism

   E. irony

Question 15–28. Read the following passage carefully before you begin to answer the questions.

Second Passage

These are the times that try men's souls. The summer soldier and the sunshine patriot will, in this crisis, shrink from the service of their country; but he (5) that stands it now deserves the love and thanks of man and woman. Tyranny, like hell, is not easily conquered; yet we have this consolation with us, that the harder the conflict, the more glorious (10) the triumph. What we obtain too cheap, we esteem too lightly: it is dearness only that gives everything its value. Heaven knows how to put a proper price upon its goods; and it would be strange indeed if (15) so celestial an article as freedom should not be highly rated. Britain, with an army to enforce her tyranny, has declared that she has a right not only to tax, but "to bind us in all cases whatso- (20) ever," and if being bound in that manner is not slavery, then is there not such a thing as slavery upon earth. Even the expression is impious; for so unlimited a power can belong only to God. . . .

(25) I have as little superstition in me as any man living, but my secret opinion has ever been, and still is, that God Almighty will not give up a people to military destruction, or leave them un- (30) supportedly to perish, who have so earnestly and so repeatedly sought to avoid the calamities of war, by every decent method which wisdom could invent. Neither have I so much of the infidel in (35) me as to suppose that He has relinquished the government of the world, and given us up to the care of devils; and as I do not, I cannot see on what grounds the King of Britain can look up to heaven (40) for help against us: a common murderer, a highwayman, or a housebreaker has as good a pretense as he. . . .

I once felt all that kind of anger, which a man ought to feel, against the (45) mean principles that are held by the tories: a noted one, who kept a tavern at Amboy, was standing at his door, with as pretty a child in his hand, about eight or nine years old, as I ever saw, and after (50) speaking his mind as freely as he thought was prudent, finished with this unfatherly expression, "Well! Give me peace in my day." Not a man lives on the continent but fully believes that a sepa- (55) ration must some time or other finally take place, and a generous parent should have said, "If there must be trouble, let it be in my day, that my children may have peace"; and this single reflection, well (60) applied, is sufficient to awaken every man to duty. Not a place upon earth might be so happy as America. Her situation is remote from all the wrangling world, and she has nothing to do but to (65) trade with them. A man can distinguish himself between temper and principle, and I am as confident, as I am that God governs the world, that America will never be happy till she gets clear of for- (70) eign dominion. Wars, without ceasing, will break out till that period arrives, and the continent must in the end be conqueror; for though the flame of liberty may sometimes cease to shine, the coal (75) can never expire. . . .

The heart that feels not now is dead: the blood of his children will curse his cowardice who shrinks back at a time when a little might have saved the (80) whole, and made them happy. I love the man that can smile in trouble, that can gather strength from distress, and grow brave by reflection. 'Tis the business of

GO ON TO THE NEXT PAGE

little minds to shrink; but he whose heart (85) is firm, and whose conscience approves his conduct, will pursue his principles unto death. My own line of reasoning is to myself as straight and clear as a ray of light. Not all the treasures of the world (90) so far as I believe, could have induced me to support an offensive war, for I think it murder; but if a thief breaks into my house, burns and destroys my property, and kills or threatens to kill me, or (95) those that are in it, and to "bind me in all cases whatsoever" to his absolute will, am I to suffer it? What signifies it to me, whether he who does it is a king or a common man; my countryman or not (100) my countryman; whether it be done by an individual villain, or an army of them? If we reason to the root of things we shall find no difference; neither can any just cause be assigned why we (105) should punish in the one case and pardon in the other.

15. The essay appears to be addressed to

   A. the British government

   B. British citizens

   C. Americans

   D. the American government

   E. all oppressed people

16. When the author addresses the "summer soldier and the sunshine patriot," he is most likely referring to

   A. the American army's reserve soldiers

   B. those citizens who are infidels

   C. the British soldiers stationed in America

   D. those who support the revolution only when convenient

   E. the government's specialized forces

17. The author's style relies on heavy use of

   A. allegory and didactic rhetoric

   B. aphorism and emotional appeal

   C. symbolism and biblical allusion

   D. paradox and invective

   E. historical background and illustration

18. Which of the following does the author NOT group with the others?

   A. Common murderer

   B. Highwayman

   C. Housebreaker

   D. King

   E. Coward

19. The "God" that the author refers to can be characterized as

   A. principled

   B. vexed

   C. indifferent

   D. contemplative

   E. pernicious

20. Which of the following rhetorical devices is NOT one of the author's tools?

   A. Anecdote

   B. Simile

   C. Aphorism

   D. Understatement

   E. Symbolism

21. According to the author, freedom should be considered

   A. that which will vanquish cowards

   B. one of the most valuable commodities in heaven

   C. that which can be achieved quickly

   D. desirable but never attainable

   E. an issue only governments should negotiate

22. The author's purpose in using the phrase "with as pretty a child . . . as I ever saw" (lines 47–49) is most likely to

   A. prove that the tavern owner has a family

   B. display his anger

   C. add emotional appeal to his argument

   D. symbolically increase the tavern owner's evil

   E. dismiss traditional values

23. Which of the following would NOT be considered an aphorism?

   A. "Tyranny, like hell, is not easily conquered" (lines 6–7)

   B. "the harder the conflict, the more glorious the triumph" (lines 8–10)

   C. "What we obtain too cheap, we esteem too lightly" (lines 10–11)

   D. "Not a place upon earth might be so happy as America" (lines 61–62)

   E. "though the flame of liberty may sometimes cease to shine, the coal can never expire" (lines 73–75)

24. As seen in lines 61–75, the author feels that, in an ideal world, America's role in relation to the rest of the world would be

   A. only one of commerce

   B. one of aggressive self-assertion

   C. more exalted than Britain's

   D. sanctified by God

   E. one of complete isolationism

25. The rhetorical mode that the author uses can best be classified as

   A. explanation

   B. description

   C. narration

   D. illustration

   E. persuasion

GO ON TO THE NEXT PAGE

26. Which of the following best describes the author's purpose in the sentence "The heart that feels not now is dead . . ." (lines 76–80)?

    A. To suggest that children should also join the revolution

    B. To plant fear in people's hearts

    C. To plead to the king once again for liberty

    D. To encourage retreat in the face of superior force

    E. To encourage support by an emotional appeal to all men

27. All of the following rhetorical devices are particularly effective in the last paragraph of the essay EXCEPT

    A. aphorism

    B. simile

    C. deliberate ambivalence

    D. parallel construction

    E. analogy

28. The author's main purpose in the essay can best be described as

    A. a summons for peace and rational thinking

    B. overemotional preaching for equality

    C. a series of unwarranted conclusions

    D. a patriotic call to duty and action

    E. a demand for immediate liberty

Questions 29–43. *Read the following passage carefully before you begin to answer the questions.*

Third Passage

It was a hazy sunrise in August. . . . The sun, on account of the mist, had a curious sentient, personal look, demand-ing the masculine pronoun for its ade-
(5) quate expression. His present aspect, coupled with the lack of all human forms in the scene, explained the old-time heli-olatries in a moment. . . . The luminary was a golden-haired, beaming, mild-
(10) eyed, God-like creature, gazing down in the vigour and intentness of youth. . . .

His light, a little later, broke through chinks of cottage shutters, throwing stripes like red-hot pokers upon cup-
(15) boards, chests of drawers, and other fur-niture within; and awakening harvesters who were not already astir.

But of all ruddy things that morning the brightest were two broad arms of
(20) painted wood, which rose from the mar-gin of a yellow cornfield hard by Marlott village. They, with two others below, formed the revolving Maltese cross of the reaping-machine, which had been
(25) brought to the field on the previous evening to be ready for operations this day. The paint with which they were smeared, intensified in hue by the sun-light, imparted to them a look of having
(30) been dipped in liquid fire. . . .

Two groups, one of men and lads, the other of women, had come down the lane just at the hour when the shadows of the eastern hedge-top struck the west
(35) hedge midway, so that the heads of the groups were enjoying sunrise while their feet were still in the dawn. . . .

Presently, there arose from within a tickling like the lovemaking of the
(40) grasshopper. The machine had begun, and a moving concatenation of three horses and the aforesaid long rickety machine was visible over the gate, a dri-ver sitting upon one of the hauling
(45) horses, and an attendant on the seat of the implement. Along one side of the field the whole wain went, the arms of the mechanical reaper revolving slowly, till it passed down the hill quite out of
(50) sight. In a minute it came up on the other side of the field at the same equable pace; the glistening brass star in the forehead of the fore horse first catching the eye as it rose into view over the stub-
(55) ble, then the bright arms, and then the whole machine.

The narrow lane of stubble encom-passing the field grew wider with each circuit, and the standing corn was re-
(60) duced to a smaller area as the morning wore on. Rabbits, hares, snakes, rats, mice, retreated inwards as into a fast-ness, unaware of the ephemeral nature of their refuge, and of the doom that
(65) awaited them later in the day when, their covert shrinking to a more and more horrible narrowness, they were huddled together, friends and foes, till the last few yards of upright wheat fell also un-
(70) der the teeth of the unerring reaper, and they were every one put to death by the sticks and stones of the harvesters.

The reaping machine left the fallen corn behind it in little heaps, . . . and
(75) upon these the active binders in the rear laid their hands — mainly women, but some of them men in print shirts, render-ing useless the two buttons behind, which twinkled and bristled with sun-
(80) beams at every movement of each wearer, as if they were a pair of eyes in the small of his back.

GO ON TO THE NEXT PAGE

But those of the other sex were the most interesting of this company of (85) binders, by reason of the charm which is acquired by woman when she becomes part and parcel of outdoor nature, and is not merely an object set down therein as at ordinary times. A field-man is a per- (90) sonality afield; a field-woman is a portion of the field; she has somehow lost her own margin, imbibed the essence of her surrounding, and assimilated herself with it. . . .

(95) There was one wearing a pale pink jacket, another in a cream-coloured tight-sleeved gown, another in a petticoat as red as the arms of the reaping-machine. . . . This morning the eye (100) returns involuntarily to the girl in the pink cotton jacket, she being the most flexuous and finely-drawn figure of them all. But her bonnet is pulled so far over her brow that none of her face is (105) disclosed while she binds, though her complexion may be guessed from a stray twine or two of dark brown hair which extends below the curtain of her bonnet. Perhaps one reason why she se- (110) duces casual attention is that she never courts it, though the other women often gaze around them.

At intervals she stands up to rest, and to retie her disarranged apron, or to pull (115) her bonnet straight. Then one can see the oval face of a handsome young woman with deep dark eyes and along heavy clinging tresses, which seem to clasp in a beseeching way anything they fall (120) against. The cheeks are paler, the teeth more regular, the red lips thinner than usual in a country-bred girl.

29. In describing the sun, (lines 2–11) the author most frequently employs which of the following rhetorical devices?

A. Apostrophe

B. Personification

C. Onomatopoeia

D. Paradox

E. Parallel clauses

30. Of the following, which best illustrates the time that passes in the passage?

A. "The luminary was a golden-haired, beaming, mild-eyed God-like creature" (lines 8–10)

B. "His light . . . broke through chinks of cottage shutters" (lines 12–13)

C. "awakening harvesters who were not already astir" (lines 16–17)

D. "which rose from the margin of a yellow cornfield" (lines 20–21)

E. "the heads of the groups were enjoying sunrise while their feet were still in the dawn." (lines 35–37)

31. In lines 38–70, the steady movement of the reaping-machine as it cuts the wheat and reduces the animals' territory serves to reinforce the

A. positive aspects of technological progress

B. politicalization of pastoral areas

C. relentless momentum of industrialization

D. alacrity with which the task can be completed

E. comparison between the machine and the sun's movement

32. From the author's description of the "unerring reaper" in the sixth paragraph (lines 57–72), the machine can best be characterized as

A. a genuine improvement for humans

B. a benevolent companion to humans

C. a high-technology device run astray

D. an inevitable aspect of the future

E. a menacing destroyer of natural habitats

33. The effect of moving from a description of the sun to a description of the reaping-machine is to

A. diminish the power of the sun

B. connect the sun to something human

C. emphasize the lifelike quality of both objects

D. suggest the power of the machine

E. comment on the negative aspects of the two

34. Which of the following best explains the author's purpose in describing the animals of the field?

A. To demonstrate the effect of industrialization on nature

B. To illustrate the ruthlessness of the humans who kill them

C. To satirize the animals' flight from the terrifying machine

D. To suggest the senselessness of animals' deaths

E. To reduce any sympathy the reader may have for the animals

35. In context, "the ephemeral nature of their refuge" (lines 63–64) most probably means the

A. sturdiness of their burrows

B. universality of their fear

C. human-like quality of their thoughts

D. animal instinct common to all creatures

E. transitory character of their environment

36. The description of the two buttons on the men's trousers has the effect of

A. metaphorical seriousness

B. humorous visual appeal

C. symbolizing the men's self-consciousness around women

D. superfluous detail

E. ironic hyperbole

37. According to the passage, the women and men in the field differ from each other because

A. the men take more care with their work

B. society's attitude inadvertently inhibits the women's productivity

C. it is one place where the women can excel over men

D. the women become a component of the field

E. the women's individual personalities become stronger

GO ON TO THE NEXT PAGE

38. It can be inferred that the beauty of the girl in the pink jacket

    A. is flaunted by the means of her clothing

    B. is impossible to detect

    C. draws unsolicited attention

    D. reveals her aristocratic background

    E. is harmonious with nature

39. Which of the following best describes the tone of the passage?

    A. Engrossed

    B. Condescending

    C. Optimistic

    D. Ironic

    E. Cavalier

40. It can be inferred from the passage that the girl in the pink jacket is

    A. popular with the locals

    B. flirtatious with the field-men

    C. overwhelmingly attractive

    D. more reserved than her coworkers

    E. older than most of the other girls

41. The author's main purpose in describing the girl in the pink jacket is to

    A. demonstrate her kinship to others

    B. reveal how dissimilar she is to the other villagers

    C. concentrate on her composure and dignity

    D. contrast her sophistication with the others' naiveté

    E. explain what a nonconformist she is

42. Which of the following rhetorical devices is NOT present in the essay?

    A. Parallelism

    B. Allegory

    C. Personification

    D. Allusion

    E. Simile

43. The structure of the passage can be described as

    A. becoming increasingly more abstract to humans while providing commentary about humanity

    B. comparing and contrasting animals to humans while providing commentary about humanity

    C. giving specifics to support generalizations about the Industrial Revolution

    D. illustrating the same scene from differing points of view

    E. moving from a visual overview of the village down to specific people

Questions 44–57. Read the following passage carefully before you begin to answer the questions.

Fourth Passage

Studies serve for delight, for ornament, and for ability. Their chief use for delight is in privateness and retiring; for ornament, is in discourse; and for ability, is in the judgment and disposition of business; for expert men can execute, and perhaps judge of particulars, one by one; but the general counsels, and the plots and marshaling of affairs come best from those that are learned. To spend too much time in studies is sloth; to use them too much for ornament is affectation; to make judgment wholly by their rules is the humor of a scholar. They perfect nature, and are perfected by experience; for natural abilities are like natural plants, that need pruning by study; and studies themselves do give forth directions too much at large, except they be bounded in by experience. Crafty men condemn studies, simple men admire them, and wise men use them; for they teach not their own use; but that is a wisdom without them and above them, won by observation. Read not to contradict and confute, nor to believe and take for granted, nor to find talk and discourse, but to weigh and consider. Some books are to be tasted, others to be swallowed, and some few to be chewed and digested; that is, some books are to be read only in parts; others to be read but not curiously; and some few to be read wholly, and with diligence and attention. Some books also may be read by deputy, and extracts made of them by others; but that would be only in the less important arguments and the meaner sort of books; else distilled books are, like common distilled water, flashy things. Reading maketh a full man; conference a ready man; and writing an exact man. And therefore, if a man write little, he had need have a great memory; if he confer little, he had need have a present wit; and if he read little, he had need have much cunning, to seem to know that he doth not. Histories make men wise; poets, witty; the mathematics, subtle; natural philosophy, deep; moral, grave; logic and rhetoric, able to contend: *Abeunt studia in mores!*[1] Nay, there is no stand or impediment in the wit but may be wrought out by fit studies; like as diseases of the body may have appropriate exercises. Bowling is good for the stone and reins, shooting for the lungs and breast, gently walking for the stomach, riding for the head, and the like. So if a man's wit be wandering, let him study the mathematics; for in demonstrations, if his wit be called away never so little, he must begin again. If his wit be not apt to distinguish or find differences, let him study the schoolmen; for they are *cymini sectores!*[2] If he be not apt to beat over matters, and to call up one thing to prove and illustrate another, let him study the lawyers' cases. So every aspect of the mind may have a special receipt.

Notes: (1) "Studies from character." Ovid, (2) Literally, "cutters of cumin seed," or hair splinters

GO ON TO THE NEXT PAGE

44. The audience that might benefit the most from the author's ideas is likely to be those who

A. have returned to university study

B. think studies are unnecessary

C. are poor readers

D. already have university degrees

E. are successful in business

45. The word "humor," (line 14) can be best defined as

A. mirth

B. benefit

C. excuse

D. aspiration

E. temperament

46. According to the passage, reading is beneficial when supplemented by

A. academic necessity

B. literary criticism

C. personal experience

D. brief discussion

E. historical background

47. A prominent stylistic characteristic of the sentence "Read not to . . . weigh and consider" (lines 25–29) is

A. understatement

B. metaphor

C. hyperbole

D. parallel construction

E. analogy

48. The sentence "They perfect nature . . . by experience" (lines 15–20) most probably means that

A. professor should emphasize reading over personal experience

B. the message in some books is too complex to be understood by the common person

C. the ideas in books are readily accessible to one who reads widely

D. people misspend valuable time in the pursuit of evasive knowledge

E. that everything one learns in books cannot necessarily be applied directly to real-life situations

49. In context, the word "observation" (line 25) is analogous to

A. "experience" (line 16)

B. "directions" (line 19)

C. "studies" (line 21)

D. "wisdom" (line 24)

E. "believe" (lines 26–27)

50. According to the passage, which of the following are reasonable uses for one's studies?

I. For private enjoyment

II. For intelligent conversation

III. For sound judgment

A. I only

B. II only

C. III only

D. II and III only

E. I, II, and III

51. What paradox about studies does the author present?

    A. Crafty men may be tempted to ignore studies.

    B. Those who are too consumed by studies become indolent.

    C. Some books can never be completely understood.

    D. Not all books are approached the same way.

    E. Some "defects of the mind" can never be remedied.

52. Which of the following does the author imply is the greatest error a reader can commit?

    A. Reading voraciously

    B. Reading only excerpts

    C. Reading only what professors recommend

    D. Reading without thinking

    E. Reading only for pleasure

53. Which of the following phrases may be seen as rhetorically similar to "Some books are to be tasted . . . chewed and digested" (lines 29–31)?

    I. "natural abilities . . . need pruning by study (lines 16–18)

    II. "Some books also may be read . . . by others" (lines 35–37)

    III. "like as diseases . . . have appropriate exercises" (lines 55–56)

    A. I only

    B. II only

    C. II and III only

    D. I and III only

    E. I, II, and III

54. In context, the phrase "not curiously" (line 33) means

    A. with questions in mind

    B. with great interest

    C. without much scrutiny

    D. without strong background

    E. with personal interpretation

55. Stylistically, the sentence "Reading maketh a full man . . . writing an exact man" (lines 41–43) is closest in structure to

    A. "To spend too much time . . . the humor of a scholar." (lines 10–14)

    B. "They perfect nature, and are perfected by experience . . . bounded in by experience." (lines 15–20)

    C. "Some books also may be read by deputy . . . flashy things." (lines 35–41)

    D. "Nay, there is no stand or impediment . . . exercises." (lines 53–56)

    E. "So if a man's wit be wandering . . . begin again." (lines 60–64)

56. The word "wit," as it is used in line 60, can be interpreted to mean

    A. wisdom, intuition

    B. mind, intelligence

    C. humor, caprice

    D. opinion, sentiment

    E. geniality, jocundity

GO ON TO THE NEXT PAGE

57. Which of the following ideas is contradicted in the essay?

    A. Specific ailments have specific cures.

    B. Reading should be adjusted to suit one's purpose.

    C. An educated man makes sound business decisions.

    D. All books should be read in the same manner.

    E. Excessive studying can be counterproductive.

IF YOU FINISH BEFORE TIME IS CALLED, CHECK YOUR WORK ON THIS SECTION ONLY. DO NOT WORK ON ANY OTHER SECTION IN THE TEST.

STOP

Section II: Essay Questions

Time: 2 Hours

3 Questions

Question 1

(Suggested time — 40 minutes. This question counts one-third of the total essay section score.)

In the following two passages, Virginia Woolf describes two different meals that she was served during a university visit; the first meal was served at the men's college, while the second meal was served at the women's college.

Directions: Read the two passages carefully; then write an essay in which you analyze Woolf's underlying attitude toward women's place in society as she describes the two meals. Discuss how such elements as narrative structure, manipulation of language, selection of detail, and tone contribute to the effect of the passage.

Passage I

It is a curious fact that novelists have a way of making us believe that luncheon parties are invariably memorable for something very witty that was said, or for something very wise that was done. But they seldom spare a word for what was eaten. It is part of the novelist's convention not to mention soup and salmon and ducklings, as if soup and a salmon and ducklings were of no importance whatsoever, as if nobody ever smoked a cigar or drank a glass of wine. Here, however, I shall take the liberty to defy that convention and to tell you that the lunch on this occasion began with soles, sunk in a deep dish, over which the college cook had spread a counterpane of the whitest cream, save that it was branded here and there with brown spots like the spots on the flanks of a doe. After that, came the partridges, but if this suggests a couple of bald, brown birds on a plate you are mistaken. The partridges, many and various, came with all their retinue of sauces and salads, the sharp and the sweet, each in its order; their potatoes, thin as coins but not so hard; their sprouts, foliated as rosebuds but more succulent. And no sooner had the roast and its retinue been done with than the silent serving-man, the Beadle himself perhaps in a milder manifestation, set before us, wreathed in napkins, a confection which rose all sugar from the waves. To call it pudding and so relate it to rice and tapioca would be an insult. Meanwhile the wineglasses had flushed yellow and flushed crimson; had been emptied; had been filled. And thus by degrees was lit, halfway down the spine, which is the seat of the soul, not that hard little electric light which we call brilliance, as it pops in and out upon our lips, but the more profound, subtle and subterranean glow, which is the rich yellow flame of rational intercourse. No need to hurry. No need to sparkle. No need to be

GO ON TO THE NEXT PAGE

anybody but oneself. We are all going to heaven . . . in other words, how good life seemed, how sweet its rewards, how trivial this grudge or that grievance, how admirable friendship and the society of one's kind, as, lighting a good cigarette, one sunk among the cushions in the window-seat.

Passage II

Here was my soup. Dinner was being served in the great dining-hall. Far from being spring it was in fact an evening in October. Everybody was assembled in the big dining-room. Dinner was ready. Here was the soup. It was a plain gravy soup. There was nothing to stir the fancy in that. One could have seen through the transparent liquid any pattern that there might have been on the plate itself. But there was no pattern. The plate was plain. Next came beef with its attendant greens and potatoes — a homely trinity, suggesting the rumps of cattle in a muddy market, and sprouts curled and yellowed at the edge, and bargaining and cheapening, and women with string bags on Monday morning. There was no reason to complain of human nature's daily food, seeing that the supply was sufficient and coal-miners doubtless were sitting down to less. Prunes and custard followed. And if any one complains that prunes, even when mitigated by custard, are an uncharitable vegetable (fruit they are not), stringy as a miser's heart and exuding a fluid such as might run in miser's veins who have denied themselves wine and warmth for eighty years and yet not given to the poor, he should reflect that there are people whose charity embraces even the prune. Biscuits and cheese came next, and here the water-jug was liberally passed round, for it is the nature of biscuits to be dry, and these were biscuits to the core. That was all. The meal was over. Everybody scraped their chairs back; the swing-doors swung violently to and fro; soon the hall was emptied of every sign of food and made ready no doubt for breakfast next morning.

Question 2

(Suggested time — 40 minutes. This question counts one-third of the total essay section score.)

Directions: Read the following excerpt from Ralph Waldo Emerson's speech, "The American Scholar," which was delivered at Cambridge on August 31, 1837. Then write a well-reasoned essay that defends, challenges, or qualifies Emerson's ideas about books and their usefulness. Use evidence from your own experience, reading, or observation to develop your essay.

The theory of books is noble. The scholar of the first age received into him the world around; brooded thereon; gave it the new arrangement of his own mind, and uttered it again. It came into him — life; it went out from him — truth. It came to him — short-lived actions; it went out from him — immortal thoughts. It came to him — business; it went from him — poetry. It was — dead fact; now, it is quick thought. It can stand, and it can go. It now endures, it now flies, it now inspires. Precisely in proportion to the depth of mind from which it issued, so high does it soar, so long does it sing.

Or, I might say, it depends on how far the process had gone, of transmuting life into truth. In proportion to the completeness of the distillation, so will the purity and imperishableness of the product be. But none is quite perfect. . . . Each age, it is found, must write its own books; or rather, each generation for the next succeeding. The books of an older period will not fit this.

Yet hence arises a grave mischief. The sacredness which attaches to the act of creation — the act of thought — is instantly transferred to the record. The poet chanting, was felt to be a divine man. Henceforth the chant is divine also. The writer was a just and wise spirit. Henceforth it is settled, the book is perfect; as love of the hero corrupts into worship of his statue. Instantly, the book becomes noxious. The guide is a tyrant. . . . The sluggish and perverted mind of the multitude, always slow to open to the incursions of Reason, having once so opened, having once received this book, stands upon it, and makes an outcry, if it is disparaged. Colleges are built on it. Books are written on it by thinkers, not by Man Thinking; by men of talent, that is, who start wrong, who set out from accepted dogmas, not from their own sight of principles. Meek young men grow up in libraries, believing it their duty to accept the views which Cicero, which Locke, which Bacon, have given, forgetful that Cicero, Locke, and Bacon were only young men in libraries when they wrote these books.

Hence, instead of Man Thinking, we have the book-worm. . . .

Books are the best of things, well used; abused, among the worst.

GO ON TO THE NEXT PAGE

Question 3

(Suggested time — 40 minutes. This question counts one-third of the total essay section score.)

Samuel Johnson wrote, "Our desires increase with our possessions. The knowledge that something remains yet unenjoyed impairs our enjoyment of the good before us."

Directions: Write a persuasive essay that either qualifies, agrees with, or disagrees with Johnson's assertion. Use personal experience, reading, or observation to develop your ideas.

IF YOU FINISH BEFORE TIME IS CALLED, CHECK YOUR WORK ON THIS
SECTION ONLY. DO NOT WORK ON ANY OTHER SECTION IN THE TEST.

Answer Key for Practice Test 1

Section I: Multiple-Choice Questions

First Passage	**Second Passage**
1. D	**15.** C
2. B	**16.** D
3. C	**17.** B
4. D	**18.** E
5. B	**19.** A
6. A	**20.** D
7. A	**21.** B
8. B	**22.** C
9. B	**23.** D
10. A	**24.** A
11. C	**25.** E
12. C	**26.** E
13. D	**27.** C
14. E	**28.** D

Third Passage

29. B

30. E

31. C

32. E

33. D

34. A

35. E

36. B

37. D

38. C

39. A

40. D

41. B

42. B

43. E

Fourth Passage

44. B

45. E

46. C

47. D

48. E

49. A

50. E

51. B

52. D

53. D

54. C

55. A

56. B

57. D

Section II: Essay Questions

Essay scoring guides, student essays, and analyses appear beginning on page 120.

Practice Test 1 Scoring Worksheet

Use the following worksheet to arrive at a probable final AP grade on Practice Test 1. While it is sometimes difficult to be objective enough to score your own essay, you can use the sample essay answers that follow to approximate an essay score for yourself. You might also give your essays (along with the sample essays) to a friend or relative to score if you feel confident that the individual has the knowledge necessary to make such a judgment and that he or she will feel comfortable in doing so.

Section I: Multiple-Choice Questions

$$\underset{\substack{\text{right} \\ \text{answers}}}{\rule{2cm}{0.4pt}} - (\tfrac{1}{4} \text{ or } .25 \times \underset{\substack{\text{wrong} \\ \text{answers}}}{\rule{2cm}{0.4pt}}) = \underset{\substack{\text{multiple-choice} \\ \text{raw score}}}{\rule{3cm}{0.4pt}}$$

$$\underset{\substack{\text{multiple-choice} \\ \text{raw score}}}{\rule{3cm}{0.4pt}} \times 1.18 = \underset{\substack{\text{multiple-choice} \\ \text{converted score}}}{\rule{3cm}{0.4pt}} \text{ (of possible } 67.5\,)$$

Section II: Essay Questions

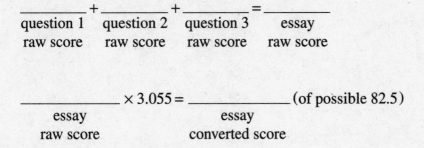

$$\underset{\substack{\text{question 1} \\ \text{raw score}}}{\rule{2cm}{0.4pt}} + \underset{\substack{\text{question 2} \\ \text{raw score}}}{\rule{2cm}{0.4pt}} + \underset{\substack{\text{question 3} \\ \text{raw score}}}{\rule{2cm}{0.4pt}} = \underset{\substack{\text{essay} \\ \text{raw score}}}{\rule{2cm}{0.4pt}}$$

$$\underset{\substack{\text{essay} \\ \text{raw score}}}{\rule{3cm}{0.4pt}} \times 3.055 = \underset{\substack{\text{essay} \\ \text{converted score}}}{\rule{3cm}{0.4pt}} \text{ (of possible } 82.5\,)$$

Final Score

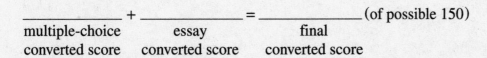

$$\underset{\substack{\text{multiple-choice} \\ \text{converted score}}}{\rule{3cm}{0.4pt}} + \underset{\substack{\text{essay} \\ \text{converted score}}}{\rule{3cm}{0.4pt}} = \underset{\substack{\text{final} \\ \text{converted score}}}{\rule{3cm}{0.4pt}} \text{ (of possible } 150\,)$$

111

Probable Final AP Score

Final Converted Score	Probable AP Score
150–104	5
103–92	4
91–76	3
75–50	2
49–0	1

Answers and Explanations for Practice Test 1

Section I: Multiple-Choice Questions

First Passage

From *The Writing Life* by Annie Dillard.

1. D. The figure is a metaphor, not a simile. Synesthetic imagery moves from the stimulation of one sense to a response by another sense, as a certain odor induces the visualization of a certain color. Here, the act of reading, a visual stimulus, produces sounds.

2. B. The paragraph describes a cause (the large cardboard butterfly) and its effect ("He jumps the piece of cardboard"). The paragraph does not contain any metaphors, similes, extended definitions, or concessions to an opposing view. The paragraph is used to compare the butterfly's and the human response to size, but the comparison is not made in this paragraph.

3. C. The first sentence of the third paragraph makes clear the relevance of the second. As the butterfly automatically responds to size, so humans respond to the larger stimuli of films. The last sentence makes the comparison explicit with its simile. The third paragraph doesn't qualify the second (**A** and **D**). The second paragraph doesn't ask why butterflies behave as they do (**B**).

4. D. The nine-foot handsome face with its three-foot-wide smile is an image on the movie screen to which we cannot help responding. Since the point of the paragraph is the irresistible appeal of size, the reference is to the larger-than-life film rather than to the television set.

5. B. Although the author claims she can recognize and will dislike a book when written with an eye on film adaptation, she makes no comment on the quality of the films these books may become. The first four sentences of the paragraph assert the superiority of films in depicting spectacle and scenes of action. Her dissatisfaction with novels written for film adaptation is expressed twice in terms of smell: "a faint but unmistakable, and ruinous odor" and "I smelled a rat."

6. A. The figure here is personification. The metaphor compares books to people (who can be "uneasy," "eager," and wear "disguises"). The figure is neither understood nor ironic. It is a metaphor, not a simile or a syllogism.

7. A. The question uses the phrase "according to the passage," and although the writer uses colloquial language ("smell a rat"), she doesn't call it a characteristic of literature. These qualities are cited in the first paragraph ("the imagination's vision . . . the moral sense . . . the intellect") and the last ("the more purely verbal, crafted sentence by sentence, the more imaginative").

8. B. The phrase means something like "a greater waste of time." The best of the five choices here is "poorer occupation." "Sorry" here means "sad" or "pathetic" (a sorry excuse), and "pursuit" means "occupation," not "chase."

9. B. Choice **A** can't be right, since "our" is the first person plural possessive pronoun. The phrase, like most of the passage, makes only modest claims for literature, based upon the greater subtlety of the verbal appeal. The move from the first person singular ("I") of the fourth paragraph to the plural here seems intended to assert a solidarity with the people "who like literature." Choice **E** explains the phrase "a poor thing," but the question asks about the plural "our." Choice **D** is untrue and **C** most unlikely. Many readers won't notice the allusion at all, and if they do, they won't see that it is an oblique form of self-promotion.

10. A. Throughout the passage, the author frankly admits the limitations of the written word and concedes to the film advantages in certain areas. All three of these sentences admit that writing is not powerful, or not immediately so, or not so effective in some areas as other forms of expression. The first two don't deal with film (**B**). Choices **C, D,** and **E** are all untrue. The passage is genuine and doesn't employ overstatement of irony.

11. C. The first paragraph supports the idea that life is more exciting than writing. The whole passage suggests that reading is a special taste that some people have acquired, but it makes no case for forcing literature upon those who prefer film or television. In fact, the last sentence contends that the attempt to win over nonreaders is foolish (**E**). The third paragraph calls film "irresistible." The passage makes no claim of universal appeal for even the best books (**C**). Literature, it calmly argues, will appeal to those who like literature.

12. C. The focus of the passage is on the nature of writing and film and their differences. The only mention of the novel is of the book written to be made into film (**E**). The passage ignores the difficulties of being a writer (**B**). Although the author may agree with the ideas of **A** and **C,** neither is the central concern of this passage.

13. D. The first and last paragraphs are primarily about writing. The second paragraph, about the butterfly, is an analogy for the appeal of the big — the film as opposed to literature — and the third and fourth paragraphs are about films and novels written to become films. Choice **E** misrepresents the first, second, and final paragraphs. Choice **A** misrepresents the entire passage.

14. E. The passage doesn't employ irony. There is a personal anecdote in the description of the author's reading novels written for film (paragraph four), an extended analogy in paragraphs two (the butterfly) and three (the film), short sentences throughout the passage, and colloquialism in a phrase like "I smelled a rat."

Second Passage

From *The American Crisis* by Thomas Paine.

15. **C.** It is the author's intent that American citizens will read this essay and thus become inspired to support the revolution. There is no indication that he is speaking of the government of either Great Britain or America, choices **A** and **D**. British citizens, choice **B,** is an unreasonable answer, unsupported by the essay. Choice **E** is far too general; the author is speaking only to the oppressed people of America, not of all the world.

16. **D.** The "summer soldier" and the "sunshine patriot" serve their country only when conditions are favorable to themselves, a behavior akin to that of the proverbial "fair-weather friend." These conditionally patriotic citizens, who want to get involved only on their own terms, are the target of the author's criticism in this sentence. Choices **A** and **E** are unreasonable; neither army reserves nor special forces existed at this time. Choice **B** also makes no sense; while the word "infidel" is used in the second paragraph, it has nothing to do with the quotation given. Choice **C** is contradictory to the meaning of the quotation given; if the professional British soldiers were instead "summer soldiers," the revolution would be easier to accomplish.

17. **B.** The essay is filled with aphorisms — brief, witty sayings — and emotional appeals. Examples of aphorisms here are "the harder the conflict, the more glorious the triumph" (lines 9–10) and "What we obtain too cheap, we esteem too lightly" (lines 10–11). The author appeals to emotions in his claim that a man's children will curse his cowardice if he fails to act now. Answer **A** is inaccurate because, although it can be argued that parts of the essay are allegorical, it does not use didactic rhetoric. The author's purpose is clearly to persuade, not to teach, and the rhetoric is too highly charged with emotion to be described as didactic. Choice **C** is only partially correct. An argument can be made that the essay uses symbolism; for example, the man who runs the tavern at Amboy may be a symbol for all that the author considers to be wrong with American citizens. But this lone example does not constitute "heavy use." Although "God" is mentioned in three of the four paragraphs, those mentions are not technically biblical allusion. The author does not use paradox and invective (**D**) or historical background and illustration (**E**).

18. **E.** The author groups the King of Britain with muderers, highwaymen, and housebreakers (lines 39–41) but not with cowards. The line "the blood of his children will curse his cowardice" (lines 77–78) refers to Americans who fail to support the revolution, not to the king.

19. **A.** God, as characterized here, is a just and principled deity who will not let a people perish through military destruction because they have "earnestly and so repeatedly sought to avoid the calamities of war" (lines 31–32). Nor, the author suggests, will this God abandon humans, giving them up "to the care of devils" (line 37). None of the references to God are negative, so "vexed" (angry), "indifferent," and "pernicious" (extremely destructive) are inappropriate answers. Choice (**D**) "contemplative," implies merely that God meditates, but the author suggests a more active God.

20. D. The author's forceful language is nearly the opposite of understatement. He uses anecdote (the story of the tavern owner), simile (for example, "clear as a ray of light" — lines 88–89), aphorisms (for example, "What we obtain too cheap, we esteem too lightly" — lines 10–11), and symbolism (for example, the story of the tavern owner).

21. B. In lines 12–16, the author claims that "Heaven knows how to put a proper price upon its goods; and it would be strange indeed if so celestial an article as freedom should not be highly rated." Choice **A** is inaccurate because the author never addresses the relationship between freedom and cowardice. **C** contradicts the essay. The author states strongly that freedom does not come easily. **D** also contradicts the essay; the author hopes that one day Americans will know true freedom. **E** is not addressed in the essay.

22. C. The picture of the tavern owner holding the hand of his child is likely designed to increase the emotional appeal of this essay, appealing to every man's desire to protect his family, even if he has to fight in order to save it. As the author says, it is "sufficient to awaken every man to duty." Choice **A** is too simplistic. True, the mention of the child shows that this man has a family, but introducing that fact is not the purpose of the reference. Answer **B** is incorrect because it isn't the image of the *child* that provokes the author's anger, but the image of the child's complacent *father*. The author *may* feel that the tavern owner is "evil," but the child's image doesn't symbolically increase the evil (**D**). Choice **E** contradicts the passage. The author appeals to the traditional values of family and freedom.

23. D. Since aphorisms are short, proverbial sayings of general truth, choice **D** doesn't fit the definition but rather may be more accurately considered a cliché.

24. A. The author states that America's "situation is remote from all the wrangling world, and she has nothing to do but <u>to trade with them</u>" (lines 62–65). The author does picture America as the "conqueror" but only with regard to winning its freedom from Britain, which makes choice **B** too strong a statement to be correct. The author never implies that America should be greater than Britain (**C**) or sanctified by God (**D**). Choice **E** contradicts the passage; if a country conducts trade, its stance is not one of "complete isolationism."

25. E. The author hopes to encourage his readers to take action, and he writes persuasively to achieve that aim.

26. E. There is a strong emotional appeal as the author warns men that their children will think them cowards and, as he claims, that the heart of a reader who does not feel as he does is "dead." Choice **A** has no support in the essay. Choice **B** isn't his *purpose*, the outcome he desires. He wants men to join the revolution, to take action, not simply to be afraid. **C** is inaccurate because the sentence quoted in this question is not directed to the king, but to American citizens. There is no mention of the superiority of either American or British forces and no mention of the advisability of retreat (**D**).

27. C. The author demonstrates no ambivalence in this paragraph. He takes a strong stand without vacillation. The paragraph does include the other devices listed. For example, aphorism — "Tis the business of little minds to shrink" (lines 83–84), simile — "My own line of reasoning is . . . as straight and clear as a ray of light" (lines 87–89), parallel construction — "What signifies it to me . . . an army of them?" (lines 97–102), and analogy — the comparison of the king to common thieves (line 92 to end).

28. D. Clearly, this author hopes his readers will feel that it is their patriotic duty toward America to join in supporting the revolution. While the author might value "peace and rational thinking," he also clearly suggests that revolution now is necessary to produce later peace. The negative "overemotional" and "unwarranted" in choices **B** and **C** should alert you to the fact that these are not likely answers. The essay contradicts choice **E**. The author suggests that "Tyranny, like hell, is not easily conquered," that is, freedom will *not* come immediately. In addition, the essay's primary purpose is to persuade Americans to join in the struggle to win their liberty, not simply to demand that the British government grant it to them.

Third Passage

From *Tess of the D'Urbervilles* by Thomas Hardy.

29. B. The author uses personification several times as he describes the sun. For example, the sun had a "curious sentient, personal look," demands a "masculine pronoun," and is a "golden-haired, beaming, mild-eyed, God-like creature."

30. E. The passage begins at dawn and moves toward midmorning. Choice **E** best shows this progression. The other choices occur early in the morning and don't suggest the passage of time.

31. C. The key phrase of the question, "steady movement," reinforces " restless momentum" in choice **C**. Choice **A** is incorrect because the author implies no "positive aspects" of progress; in fact, the destruction of the animals' environment suggests a negative attitude. "Alacrity" (**D**), which means cheerful readiness or promptness, is not suggested in the passage.

32. E. The reaping-machine is responsible for the destruction of the animals' homes in the field. It mows down the wheat ("corn" here is a general term for grain of any kind), leaving the homeless animals to await death at the hands of the field crews. Choices **A, B, C,** and **D** are not addressed in the passage. While the machine may *possibly* be an improvement for humans — an inevitable aspect of the future, or a benevolent companion — the author doesn't address these possibilities.

33. D. The sun is described in powerful terms, with its "vigour and intentness of youth" and light that "broke . . . like red-hot pokers." Because the machine's description immediately follows that of the sun, it is also seen as powerful, with phrases that subtly compare the machine to the sun, such as "brightest . . . intensified . . . by the sunlight" and "having been dipped in liquid fire." Choice **B** is incorrect; while the passage suggests a connection between the sun and the machine, the machine is not human. Choice **C** is incorrect because, even though the sun is personified, the machine is not. Choice **E** is also incorrect. Although there is negativity here concerning the reaping-machine, there is none concerning the sun.

34. A. Industrialization, exemplified by the reaping-machine, is shown to have a strong effect on nature. The author doesn't characterize the humans, who must kill the animals, as "ruthless" (**B**), but rather comments on the occurrence matter-of-factly. There is no evidence of satire in the passage (**C**) or comment about the senselessness of the animals' death (**D**).

35. E. "Ephemeral" means transitory or temporary, and "refuge" means shelter (the field of wheat).

36. B. Visually, the description of the buttons on the men's trousers is humorous. One pictures these hard-working field men whose buttons on their backsides "twinkled . . . at every movement . . . as if they were a pair of eyes." There is no metaphor (**A**) or evidence of self-consciousness around women (**C**). Although some reader might feel that the detail is superfluous (**D**), that is not the *effect* of the description. And although some exaggeration (hyperbole) may exist here, there is no irony (**E**).

37. D. The author claims that a woman becomes a "portion of the field" (a component of it), that she has "assimilated herself with it."

38. C. The "eye returns involuntarily" to the girl, and although she "seduces casual attention," she "never courts it." It is obvious, then, that she doesn't "flaunt" her beauty (**A**), and there is no evidence that she is "aristocratic" (**D**). Choice **B** is incorrect because the girl's beauty *is* possible to detect: she is a "handsome young woman with deep dark eyes." While choice **E** is an inference one could possibly draw, it is not a certain one.

39. A. The author's tone is engrossed, occupied with his subject. The fine attention to detail — from the sun, to the machine, to the girl — demonstrates the author's interest.

40. D. The girl in the pink jacket doesn't talk to the other workers and keeps her head down as she works, supporting the idea that she is reserved, quiet. It can be inferred that the others are less reserved because, while the girl "never courts [attention], the other women often gaze around them." There is no evidence in the passage to support choices **A** or **E**, and choice **B** contradicts the passage as you've seen. Choice **C** is incorrect because, although the girl is obviously attractive, "overwhelmingly" is an exaggeration.

41. B. The girl in the pink jacket has paler cheeks, more regular teeth, and thinner lips than do the other country-bred girls. The author sets this girl apart from the other villagers. In the passage, no kinship to others (**A**) or sophistication (**D**) is suggested. The author does not concentrate on her dignity (**C**), but on her appearance and behavior as she works in the field. The word "noncomformist" (**E**) implies an intentional failure to conform, and there is no evidence of such intent in the passage.

42. B. The passage is not allegorical; the characters are literal country villagers, not representative of abstract qualities. The passage uses hyperbole (in the description of the sun, the machine, and the buttons on men's trousers), personification (also in the description of the sun), allusion (in the comparison of the machine's arms to a Maltese cross), and simile (in phrases such as "like red-hot pokers").

43. E. The passage begins in the sky with the sun, moves down to earth into the village, and finally to specific villagers as they wake and begin their day.

Fourth Passage

From "Of Studies" by Francis Bacon.

44. B. Most of these comments explain the benefits of studies (for pleasure, discussion, business, and so forth). Thus, the audience that would most benefit from this essay's message is likely to be those who think they don't need studies. Choices **A, D,** and **E** name audiences who are probably already aware of the benefits of studies. Poor readers (**C**) don't necessarily need to be convinced of the benefits of studies but rather may need to improve their reading skills.

45. E. The author explains how students may focus on their studies incorrectly. One may spend too much time in studies and thus be guilty of sloth, or one may use them only to impress others (displaying affectation). Also, one may make judgments based solely upon studies, failing to consider real-life experience. The author uses the term "humor," while modern writers might label the scholars' tendency temperament, or disposition.

46. C. The author claims, in lines 15–16, that studies "are perfect by <u>experience</u>" and in line 20, that they are "bounded in by <u>experience.</u>"

47. D. Parallel construction is evident — "to contradict and confute," "to believe and take," "to find talk and discourse," "to weigh and consider."

48. E. The author, in this sentence, discusses how people need to "prune" their natural abilities by study. At the same time, however, studies need to be "bounded in by experience." The message is one of moderation and inclusion — neither studies nor experiences should be relied on exclusively or predominantly.

49. A. The wisdom "won by observation" is analogous to that "perfected by experience" (lines 15–16). In both instances, the author recommends reading to gain knowledge but also incorporating life's observations and experiences to obtain wisdom.

50. E. The author suggests all three of these uses in the second sentence. Personal reading brings "delight" (enjoyment), contributes to "discourse" (intelligent conversation), and aids in the "disposition of business" (sound judgment).

51. B. "To spend too much time in studies is sloth" (lines 10–11) paradoxically suggests that too much work on studies can lead to laziness and lack of work. In other words, overemphasis on studies avoids work in the outside world. Choices **A, D,** and **E** are not paradoxes. While choice **C** might have paradoxical elements, it is not mentioned in the essay.

52. D. In lines 26–29, the author claims that one should read "not to contradict and confute, nor to believe and take for granted, nor to find talk and discourse, but to <u>weigh and consider.</u>" A reader should think. Reading voraciously or only for pleasure, choices **A** and **E,** are not necessarily "errors." Choices **B** and **C** are perhaps reading mistakes, but the non-thinking reader is presented as the greater problem.

53. D. The sentence in this question uses analogy, comparing reading to eating. In choice **I,** reading is compared to pruning a plant. In choice **III,** a third analogy compares "impediments" in understanding to physical diseases of the body. There is no analogy in choice **II.**

54. C. This sentence discusses how readers might adapt their reading style to the subject matter and their purpose. By reading "not curiously," the author means reading without great care or scrutiny, reading cursorily. Choices **A, B,** and **E** directly contradict the idea of reading without considerable scrutiny.

55. A. The sentence in the question contains parallel construction in which three ideas make up the sentence. Choice **A** uses the same structure, presenting three similarly phrased ideas which make up the sentence.

56. B. By "wit," the author means one's mind, one's intelligence, which can be focused through specific types of reading. Choice **A** may appear to be correct, but the author never addresses intuition. In addition, if a person has already attained wisdom, his or her mind is not likely to need the remedies proposed by the author.

57. D. The eating analogy in lines 29–35 suggests that books should be consumed in different manners and for different purposes.

Section II: Essay Questions

Question I

Scoring Guide for Question 1 (Virginia Woolf)

8–9 In a well-written essay, this writer clearly demonstrates an understanding of Woolf's attitude about women in society, while also analyzing how the author's structure, diction, tone and detail convey that attitude. The writer presents a clear, relevant thesis supported by strong evidence from the passage. Analysis of the evidence and how it reflects the author's attitude about women in society is insightful. Not necessarily without flaw, the essay still shows maturity in its use of language and sentence structure.

6–7 Well presented, this essay accurately describes Woolf's attitude about women in society, but perhaps less explicitly than does the high-scoring essay. Discussion of the author's techniques may be less thorough, or evidence presented may be less specific. Connection between the evidence and the thesis may be less insightful. Although some errors may be present, the essay, overall, shows satisfactory control of format and language.

5 The writer of the average paper may recognize the author's attitude about women in society but may be less precise in discussing that attitude. Attempts to analyze the author's language may be simplistic; or evidence offered may be insufficient to prove the thesis adequately. Organization may be clear but not as effective as that of the better-written paper. Inconsistencies in the command of language may be present.

3–4 This essay attempts to address the essay question but may fail to accurately address the author's attitude. It may not complete all of the tasks of the question. Inadequate evidence for the writer's ideas may be a problem. Insights may be inaccurate or superficial. The essay may convey ideas, but weak control over language may distract the reader's attention. Frequent errors in mechanics may be present.

1–2 This essay fails to respond sufficiently to the question or the passage. It may fail to recognize the author's attitude or may misread the passage so as to distort it. With little or no evidence offered, the essay may fail to persuade the reader, and the connection between the evidence and the thesis may be shallow or nonexistent. Persistent weaknesses may be evident in the basic elements of composition or writing skills.

High-Scoring Essay

The differences between men's and women's colleges were considerable in Virginia Woolf's day. Rather than assert this in a pedestrian, expository way, Woolf uses the respective meals served at each college to illustrate the discrepancies between the schools. The meals are a metaphorical device, akin to a poetic conceit; Woolf makes a far more forceful, profound distinction between the male and female schools through such juxtaposition than if she had merely enumerated their inconsistencies. Woolf details the relative poverty of the women's school, and therefore women's position in society, through varied sentence structure, diction and imagery between the descriptions of the meals.

Fundamentally different premises underlie each meal. The men's meal is a luxury to be enjoyed, the women's a metabolic necessity to be endured. Woolf, in describing the men's meal, dismisses the notion that " . . . soup and salmon and ducklings were of no importance whatsoever, as if nobody ever smoked a cigar or drank a glass of wine." She offers a breathless explanation of the sensual joy the meal affords. Diction and sensory detail showcase the piquant pleasure to be taken in foods "spread . . . of the whitest cream," "Sharp and sweet . . . succulent." The men's meal is a catalyst for the "profound, subtle and subterranean glow . . . of rational intercourse." Of course, no similar premium is put on rational intercourse among women, judging by the amenities of the women's meal. They drink not wine "flushed crimson," but rather eat "transparent . . . plain gravy soup." Dry biscuits and water replace partridges, and such victuals provide no stimulus for enlightened conversation; when the eating is done, the women rise and that is all.

Woolf describes the women's meal in plain language, in blunt, staccato, repetitive bursts: "Here was my soup . . . Dinner was ready. Here was the soup. It was plain gravy soup . . . The plate was plain." All the eloquent wordiness has vanished. The images are those of poverty and ugliness, and the meal is only justified as being superior to that of a coal miner. The prunes are " . . . stringy as a miser's heart and exuding a fluid such as might run in misers' veins . . . " In contrast, the other meal's imagery is that of opulence. The potatoes are like coins, the sprouts "foliated as rosebuds." This is a meal fit for kings, and the diction is suggestive of royalty: "The partridges . . . came with all their retinue . . ." The men are reassured by the meal that they are all going to heaven; the women's meal is a hurried "homely trinity."

As a metaphor for the chasm separating male and female education, and society as a whole, Woolf's piece is mordantly effective. Her point is made with more economy and vivacity through anecdote than it would be through explanation or a propounding of evidence about the inferiority of female schools. By painting the male university as lavish and its female counterpart as lowly, Woolf succeeds in crystalizing her attitude for readers.

Analysis of the High-Scoring Essay

This writer addresses the question; he or she also demonstrates a deep understanding of the subtle differences between the two passages. This writer's thesis is relevant and on topic. The body paragraphs provide ample evidence for ideas, and the quotations are used effectively to prove this writer's points. This paper does not merely dwell on the obvious aspects of the passage, but probes more deeply into the ramifications of the two meals. Especially effective is the section in which the writer demonstrates how Woolf's diction suggests the meaning of each meal. For example, reread the end of the fourth paragraph as this writer connects the word "retinue" with royalty and goes on to suggest what that royal meal does for the men; it reassure them that they are going to heaven. This type of thinking demonstrates the level of analysis necessary for a high score; the writer understands *how* the language of the essay helps to create an effect.

The vocabulary and sentence structure are also very sophisticated, as they should be in all top-scoring essays. The phrasing is creative and pleasing. Wording such as "akin to a poetic conceit," "a metabolic necessity," "piquant pleasure," and "mordantly effective" are just a few of the phrases that sing to the reader's ear. In addition, this writer demonstrates a keen sense of sentence structure and thus adds sufficient variety in both sentence pattern and length.

Although very well written, this essay could be improved by providing a stronger connection between ideas, evidence, and thesis. Also, a more profound point could be made about the deeper issues involved in the "chasm separating male and female education." In addition, the writer could concentrate more on Woolf's attitude *as* he or she presents the evidence.

Medium-Scoring Essay

Meals are important, but they are often ignored or not thought of much. People often eat in a hurry, and often they don't pay much attention to the details of what they are actually eating.

Virginia Woolf calls readers' attention to this in the selection about two meals which she had when she was at the university. She had one of these at the men's college and the other at the women's college. They were very different in the food but also in the whole atmosphere of the place where she ate.

Woolf says that though people don't often notice it, the food we eat tells us important things about where we are. She compares the two parts of the university with the different meals. She uses narrative structure, details and tone to present her attitude about the two meals and inform readers of which one she likes better, and why.

The first meal she describes, which is at the men's college, is the one which Woolf likes better. The reasons become obvious for this, because the food is far more appetizing and the atmosphere is just nicer generally. Woolf uses lots of details and metaphors to describe this meal, and often her descriptions are full of imagery. It is all very fancy, with a uniformed waiter serving roast, and Woolf drinks a lot of wine, which sends a glow down her spine. She comments that all the other eaters were very friendly and everything seemed nice and happy after the meal. "We are all going to heaven" she says after the meal. It is almost a religious experience for them.

The second meal is at the women's college, and Woolf's attitude toward it is not as positive. That is understandable, but the food is not even close to as good. Woolf uses lots of metaphors to make the food seem gross and very repulsive. The beef is like "the rumps of cattle in a muddy market, and sprouts curled and yellowed at the edge" she says. The prunes are stringy and miserly, and instead of the good pudding that she ate at the men's college, she has to eat custard that is not nearly so good. The biscuits are dry and unappetizing, which makes for a meal that is not very appealing. She doesn't talk about friends or smoking at this meal, which makes it far less homely than the men's meal.

Thus, through her metaphors and affective descriptions of the food at the two meals, Woolf compares them and strongly shows her attitude to the readers. She makes one realize that even though we don't often think about meals, they are important. The differences are something to realize, and Woolf's excellent description helps you do just that.

Analysis of the Medium-Scoring Essay

This essay earns a medium score because it recognizes some of the differences between the two meals. However, it doesn't merit a higher score because it fails to address Woolf's attitudes as displayed through her description of the meals. The introductory remarks go on far too long (for three paragraphs). When the thesis is finally stated, it's bland and obvious, as is the entire essay. This writer mentions that Woolf presents her attitudes but never clarifies what he or she thinks these attitudes are; basically, the thesis merely restates portions of the question.

This writer has chosen to discuss the two meals separately, in two paragraphs, a technique which doesn't allow for strong comparison. This writer does accurately present some evidence, but in many cases, it is not sufficient. For example, where are the metaphors referred to? Since they aren't included in the essay, the reader is left guessing. The writer does see some interesting description in the passages but fails to make an intelligent point about it, and the analysis offered is shallow and obvious. Also, no connection is made between the evidence presented and the major topic of Woolf's attitude.

In addition, this essay demonstrates some stylistic and grammatical problems and is not helped by the use of unsophisticated words and phrases such as "things," "a lot," and "not as good." Some awkward sentences tend to distract the reader's attention from this writer's ideas. Incorrect word choices, such as "affective" instead of "effective," show that this writer doesn't have a strong command of the language. This difficulty is further demonstrated by pronoun problems such as the use of "you" in the last sentence and "them" at the end of the fourth paragraph.

The positive aspects of this essay are few; it does try to make a point, and it follows many of the conventions of proper writing style. However, the numerous errors and its uninteresting, obvious ideas keep it from achieving a higher score.

Question 2

Scoring Guide for Question 2 (Ralph Waldo Emerson)

8–9 This well-written essay clearly takes a stand concerning Emerson's ideas about the usefulness of books and substantially supports it. The thesis is well thought out and relevant to the topic. The paper provides ample evidence to prove the writer's ideas and clearly connects the evidence to the thesis. Thoroughly convincing, the paper demonstrates a significant understanding of the needs of the essay. Although it need not be without errors, the paper shows a mature command of style and language.

6–7 This essay demonstrates understanding of Emerson's ideas but produces a less explicit thesis than that of higher-scoring essays. Perhaps less relevant evidence is offered, making the essay less persuasive. Still, it is fairly convincing and shows clear thinking. The connection between the evidence and the thesis may not be as articulate as in top-scoring essays. Although well written, this essay may demonstrate some errors while still showing satisfactory control over diction and the essay requirements.

5 This adequately written essay shows some understanding of Emerson's ideas but produces a thesis that may be weak or predictable. The opinions may be too hastily conceived after a cursory reading of Emerson's concepts. Overall, the argument, although acceptable, may not be persuasive or thought provoking. It may appear opinionated without sufficient evidence to support the opinions. Acceptable organization may be evident, but the style may not be as sophisticated as that of higher-scoring essays.

3–4 This low-scoring essay fails to convince the reader. The weak presentation may show an unsubstantiated thesis or no thesis at all, weak paragraph development and/or weak organization, insufficient evidence for points made, or superficial thinking. Confusion about Emerson's ideas may be evident, and frequent mechanical errors may be present.

1–2 This poorly written essay lacks coherence and clarity. The thesis may be overly obvious or absent. Little or no evidence may be offered for the thesis, and connection between the evidence and the thesis may be shallow or nonexistent. The paper may be unusually short and exhibit poor fundamental essay skills. Weak sentence construction may persist, and persistent weaknesses in command of the language may be present.

High-Scoring Essay

Ralph Waldo Emerson is perhaps overly strident in his speech, "The American Scholar." But such zeal serves to make a trenchant point about the tendency toward rigid reverence of "Great Works," as if each were the Holy Grail itself. He asserts: "Books are the best of things, well used; abused, among the worst." Emerson delivers a stinging indictment of "bookworms." He argues that even the greatest thinkers were once humble students. The danger, Emerson claims, is that of transferring our respect from the venerable acts of creation, of thought, to that endeavor's imperfect product. He believes scholars must not so prostrate themselves before the majesty of profound works, that they forget their creators, whom they should emulate in creative thought. They should not idolize the books themselves in a sort of cult of inferiority, Emerson says, but rather write their own books, their own truths, undertake their own sacred acts of creation.

In a strict sense, these points are valid. But Emerson goes beyond these points; he overstates his case. He is treading the ground between the good scholar and the singular genius. Perhaps, given his own stature, it is only fitting that he should hold us to such lofty standards. Nevertheless, his warnings against showing too much respect for books, are not altogether true. Such arguments, about the paramount importance of individual thought, can readily be misused to justify a dismissal of the past. Often such self-indulgent, arrogant, arguments are used by those less gifted than Emerson as an excuse to disregard the wisdom that has come before them.

A social critic recently said, "It's fine to learn how to think, but what's the point if you have nothing to think about?" The modern education system has sought to shoulder the burden of "teaching students how to think," often elevating such a subjective goal to status superior to teaching facts and sharing insights about past generations. In short, they focus more on method and process than what students actually learn.

Some students graduate from American high schools ignorant of when the Civil War occurred or the difference between the Preamble and the Constitution and Das Kapital. Reading and digesting the thoughts of the past is as essential as learning the rules of grammar so as to intelligently violate them. In light of today's high illiteracy rate, society's problems hardly include too many people being "bookworms" or attempting to follow the doctrines of Plato or John Locke or Mahatma Gandhi.

We as Americans share a heritage of ideas. Common assumptions must be examined so that we understand where such "conventional wisdom" came from, for it is only then that we may change the portions of it which may be unjust or clouded by bias. Certainly great books should not be locked away, immune from criticism. Neither, however, should they be lambasted out of visceral ignorance, in the name of "individuality."

Studying and learning from the works of the past, and creating new original writing and thought in the present are not mutually exclusive propositions. Most scholars lack Emerson's genius, but they will be hard-pressed to find a spark of creativity by meditating in the dark.

Emerson implies that ideas are not great in and of themselves. But ideas can be great. Proof resides in the overwhelming numbers of anonymous poems that fill anthology books. How many aphorisms are repeated daily by speakers who know not whether they generated from the tongue of William Churchill or Will Rogers? This is not to suggest that great ideas cannot be proved wrong.

That Emerson denies perfection to any ideas is hardly a danger. Since no writer, however brilliant, is perfect, it is perfectly safe to acknowledge certain ideas as great, without granting them perfection and immunity.

When people do not know the past, they face the peril of perpetually re-inventing the wheel — blissfully ignorant of their tendency toward trite alliteration or insipid cliches.

Analysis of the High-Scoring Essay

This thorough, thoughtful, and well-written essay deserves a high score. It begins with the topic and promptly takes a relevant position on the issue of studying from books and ideas of the past. The student shows a clear understanding of Emerson's ideas by restating and elaborating on the major points.

The student then points out a major dilemma inherent in a facile acceptance of Emerson's ideas — that of dismissing the past and wisdom that has come before.

The student's essay proceeds with a two-paragraph discussion of the state of education today, pointing out the dual needs of teaching both facts and the thinking process. These paragraphs are particularly relevant to the topic, and the student's examples are presented with insight.

The student also acknowledges our American heritage and the necessity of using books to understand that heritage so that the country's great ideas are not hidden away.

The next paragraph counters Emerson's position with optimism — the student claims that we can have it all; we can learn from the past and still become clear, independent thinkers who create new ideas.

The essay points out that great new ideas do exist and cites contemporary, anonymous poems as examples of these new ideas. The student also acknowledges that ideas can be great while being imperfect and that such imperfection is no reason to dismiss them entirely.

The student completes the essay with a brief conclusion reminding the reader that humans may be doomed to repeat their mistakes and to reinvent the wheel unless they learn from the great ideas of the past. Overall, this essay's points are valid, and without dismissing Emerson lightly, the student intelligently discusses his concepts.

Medium-Scoring Essay

The process of finding meaningful things in life is not always clear. It is not simple to discover what is true and what is just fancy rhetoric or skirting of the issues. Ralph Waldo Emerson, considered one of our best writers and speakers, gave a speech in Cambridge in 1837, where he talked about books and how they can help us to find the truth which we are seeking in our life.

Emerson said in his speech that books are noble and age-old scholars gave arrangement to the life they saw and organized it. Then they put it into the books that they wrote, and produced a new truth for people to refer to. But he also says that each new generation of Americans has to write their own books. They have to discover their own versions of the truth, and what that truth actually means to them.

He was right. He was also right when he said that we can't just go by what was said then, because the ones who wrote the books that fill our libraries were just young and naïve when they authored those books. How can we be sure they are right, just because they are old? Why are they elevated to the status of classics as if they are perfect?

He says you shouldn't spend all your time in the library, however, I know some people who do just this. The result is that instead of having their own ideas, they just listen to all the old ones, and their creativity is stifled. I agree that it is more important to be a thinking man than one who just accepts everything. You need to have the freedom to have your own ideas, to let them flow without being influenced by principles and underlying ideas already presented in books. These ideas might be right, but if everyone only reads them without thinking for themselves, the country will be full of brainwashed people.

They might be well educated, but what will be the price of that education?

He said that books can be best if they are used well, but among the worst of things if they are abused. What this actually encourages is for one to be intelligent about reading and not to believe everything that you read. Also, he says that we should not be bookworms, so caught up in the details of what people said in the past that we don't bother to think our own thoughts about the present or concerning issues of the future that are important to our society. This is the centerpiece of his speech. He means that books have a noble "theory." He also means that in practice we must live up to that theory. We must live up to that theory by not being blind or gullible. Instead, we must be <u>Thinking Men</u> and not <u>thinkers only</u>. He talked about how what we observe has to be filtered in to the truth by our own original ideas. We have to use books wisely, Emerson believed, and I agree wholeheartedly.

Analysis of the Medium-Scoring Essay

This essay would score at the low end of the medium range. It begins with a vague introduction that essentially restates a few points from Emerson's speech. The student does not yet state a thesis or take a position.

The second paragraph continues this trend, merely paraphrasing Emerson's speech without critical thinking about those ideas. An essay that *only* paraphrases the passage will score no higher than a three.

Eventually, in the third paragraph, the student presents an opinion and takes a position, although it is repetitively worded. The student seems to have finally started thinking as he or she questions the validity of older books and the pedestal upon which the classics have been placed.

The fourth paragraph is probably the best in this student's essay and saves the score from sinking even lower. The student uses personal experience as an example, citing other students who have become "stifled" in their creativity by spending too much time in the library, consuming old books and old ideas without thinking while they read. The writer apparently understands the need for every student to become an individual thinker, an analyzer of ideas.

However, the next paragraph reverts to simple paraphrasing. It offers no additional commentary from the student.

The essay reaches an adequate conclusion, explaining the need to read wisely and not be gullible. Ultimately, the student writer manages to insert enough of his or her own commentary about Emerson's concepts to salvage the score. However, this essay could be greatly improved by reducing the paraphrasing and including much more analysis and evidence. Remember that this topic specifically directs students to "use evidence from your own experience, reading, or observation to develop your essay." This writer has barely accomplished that goal, and thus, the score suffers.

Question 3

Scoring Guide for Question 3 (Samuel Johnson)

8–9 This well-written essay clearly takes a stand concerning Johnson's ideas on possessions and substantially supports it. The thesis is articulate and relevant to the topic. The paper provides strong and relevant evidence intelligently connected to the thesis and demonstrates an understanding of the needs of the essay. Although it need not be without errors, the paper shows mature command of style and language.

6–7 This essay contemplates Johnson's ideas on possessions but produces a less explicit thesis. Perhaps less relevant or insufficient evidence is offered, and the reader may not be as thoroughly convinced as with a top-scoring paper. Although well-written, the essay may demonstrate some errors while still showing satisfactory control over diction and the essay requirements.

5 The adequate presentation in this essay includes a thesis but one that is perhaps not as well thought out as in higher-scoring essays. The ideas may be too hastily conceived. Overall, the argument may not be as strong or convincing as in a higher-scoring paper. It may appear more opinionated without sufficient evidence to support the opinions. Acceptable organization may be evident, but the style may not be as sophisticated as that in higher-scoring papers.

3–4 This low-scoring essay fails to convince the reader. The weak presentation may include an unsupported or unsubstantiated thesis, weak paragraph development, and/or poor organization. Confusion may be present in the paper's ideas. Superficial thinking and evidence may be present. Frequent mechanical errors may persist.

1–2 This poorly written essay lacks clarity and coherence. It may have an overly obvious thesis or no thesis at all. Little or no evidence may be a problem, and the connection between the evidence and the thesis may be shallow or nonexistent. The paper may be unusually short and exhibit poor fundamental essay skills. Weak sentence construction may persist, and persistent weaknesses in command of the language may be present.

High-Scoring Essay

There are as many different motivations and convictions which serve to "make people tick" as there are people to experience such impulses. Beyond the broad abstractions, each of us may have a unique force driving us toward happiness — toward the degree of success or self-fulfillment we desire. Nevertheless, the American Dream of financial security and independence, of building a comfortable life, is widespread if not universal.

The poor must struggle for the rudimentary elements of sustenance. The rich are at times perceived as avaricious, striving continually like Philistines for material rewards. Yet such characteristics tend to oversimplify the issues. The truth of the inverse relation Samuel Johnson describes — "Our desires increase with our possessions" — depends closely on his wording.

Desires may increase with our possessions, in the sense that they will numerically increase. Desire, however, the drive and will to succeed, tends to stay constant with each individual, whether poor or wealthy. A person who has worked relentlessly from humble beginnings will likely not abandon that work ethic simply because he has reached some nebulous, ill-defined level of attainment that others term "success." Conversely, Johnson's statement may not apply to the stereotypical "happy-go-lucky" person who desires nothing more than an average home and job, and who may be completely satisfied with his life, once having attained these possessions. Some people simply do not want to improve their place in society, nor do they want to increase their possessions.

Johnson's second statement is more unequivocally true. He writes, "The knowledge that something remains yet unenjoyed impairs our enjoyment of the good before us." Consistent with many a common aphorism — a bird in the hand is worth two in the bush, the grass is always greener on the other side, ad infinitum — Johnson is correctly attesting that many possessions and concrete rewards tend to numb and dull our perceptions, to make us less cognizant of the simple things which enrich our lives more than any amount of gold or stock certificates ever can.

The trick to correctly evaluating the veracity of Johnson's assertion is to avoid blanket generalizations, i.e. "all rich are greedy" or "all poor people are easily pleased." Discerning readers will be able to point to instances in which Johnson is proved correct, and others which contradict his thesis. Nevertheless, it would not be unfair to say that he makes a reasonable statement.

Analysis of the High-Scoring Essay

The first paragraph, although it doesn't directly address Samuel Johnson's concepts, indirectly qualifies them. The student seems to feel that Johnson's remarks don't universally apply, that people have "different motivations."

The second paragraph deals with Johnson's ideas more overtly and states the student's opinion more clearly — that to accept Johnson's generalities is to "oversimplify" the issues.

The third paragraph offers a more philosophical discussion of Johnson's notion regarding desire. The student makes a distinction between "desires" and "desire," defining "desire" as the "drive and will to succeed" and asserting that people possess this quality in varying degrees. The writer provides hypothetical examples: the person who has a diligent work ethic and doesn't abandon it, even after achieving success, and one who has earned some possessions, such as a home, and desires no more. These examples provide support to the student's opinion that the first half of Johnson's statement should be qualified.

The fourth paragraph examines Johnson's second assertion and agrees that humans are not always happy with what they have (an idea the student supports by citing two aphorisms, although the first incorrectly suggests a point of view opposite to that of Johnson and the student writer). The writer asserts that we are "less cognizant" of the simple pleasures of life which "enrich our lives more" than material objects ever can.

The student's conclusion restates his or her opinion that Johnson's statement, although partially true, cannot be universally applied. The essay, on the whole, is well-written and insightful.

Medium-Scoring Essay

Most people want to have money and attain success. But then what happens when you achieve that goal, and move from poor to rich? Many Americans just become greedy. They already have a lot, but they just want more. Their thirst for money cannot be satisfied, like a man in the desert.

Samuel Johnson addressed this problem. He wrote, "Our desires increase with our possessions. The knowledge that something remains yet unenjoyed impairs our enjoyment of the good before us." I agree that this usually true, and it can be seen in all classes of society. Even poor people prove this point, because they need to first get a house and food for their family. Once they do that, they can feel that the house is no longer good enough and they want to move up. So this family works harder to get a newer house and more possessions, but they forget to appreciate what they have at the time, always thinking that they need more. It's like the unsatisfied family in D. H. Lawrence's "Rocking Horse Winner" that knows "there must be more money!"

This is also the usual attitude that rich people have about money. They are usually less humble about money because they are rich. It is like a game to these rich people, to see how much more money they can get. They are usually more likely to be greedy than the poor or middle class people who just want food, a place to live, and maybe an entertaining evening on occasion; these people think like the lead actor in the movie "Wall Street" who said that "Greed is good."

Rich people are greedier. They usually want to have yachts and fly all over the world to visit ancient ruins or walk the streets of Paris. But poor and middle class people, whether they admit it or not, would probably like the same things, or at least they would like the opportunity for the same things. People just forget to enjoy what they have and always think of what else they need, what else they can buy. Samuel Johnson was correct years ago; his ideas are even more true in modern times.

Analysis of the Medium-Scoring Essay

This essay would likely receive a score near the lower end of the medium range. The introductory paragraph seems to agree with Johnson but is not clear on the agreement.

The second paragraph states the student's opinion — that he or she does agree with Johnson — and continues with the theoretical example of a poor family that wants more possessions even after basic needs have been met. The student includes a pertinent quotation from D. H. Lawrence, but the presentation is not sophisticated, with the quotation seeming to be appended as an afterthought.

The third paragraph addresses the rich and their attitudes toward money. As previously, the student doesn't substantiate opinions with convincing discussion or specific evidence. The quotation from the movie *Wall Street,* while superficially related to the subject, provides no strong evidence.

The conclusion restates the student's opinion once again and continues to make generalities about human nature that need additional support in order to convince a reader. The student *is* to be commended for integrating Johnson's ideas throughout the essay and for good organization. However, these positive points are offset by the negative: an overly opinionated tone, a lack of both adequate discussion and convincing examples, and faults in style and command of language, both of which are simplistic.

Answer Sheet for Practice Test 2

(Remove This Sheet and Use it to Mark Your Answers)

Section I
Multiple-Choice Questions

PASSAGE 1

1 Ⓐ Ⓑ Ⓒ Ⓓ Ⓔ
2 Ⓐ Ⓑ Ⓒ Ⓓ Ⓔ
3 Ⓐ Ⓑ Ⓒ Ⓓ Ⓔ
4 Ⓐ Ⓑ Ⓒ Ⓓ Ⓔ
5 Ⓐ Ⓑ Ⓒ Ⓓ Ⓔ
6 Ⓐ Ⓑ Ⓒ Ⓓ Ⓔ
7 Ⓐ Ⓑ Ⓒ Ⓓ Ⓔ
8 Ⓐ Ⓑ Ⓒ Ⓓ Ⓔ
9 Ⓐ Ⓑ Ⓒ Ⓓ Ⓔ
10 Ⓐ Ⓑ Ⓒ Ⓓ Ⓔ
11 Ⓐ Ⓑ Ⓒ Ⓓ Ⓔ
12 Ⓐ Ⓑ Ⓒ Ⓓ Ⓔ
13 Ⓐ Ⓑ Ⓒ Ⓓ Ⓔ
14 Ⓐ Ⓑ Ⓒ Ⓓ Ⓔ

PASSAGE 2

15 Ⓐ Ⓑ Ⓒ Ⓓ Ⓔ
16 Ⓐ Ⓑ Ⓒ Ⓓ Ⓔ
17 Ⓐ Ⓑ Ⓒ Ⓓ Ⓔ
18 Ⓐ Ⓑ Ⓒ Ⓓ Ⓔ
19 Ⓐ Ⓑ Ⓒ Ⓓ Ⓔ
20 Ⓐ Ⓑ Ⓒ Ⓓ Ⓔ
21 Ⓐ Ⓑ Ⓒ Ⓓ Ⓔ
22 Ⓐ Ⓑ Ⓒ Ⓓ Ⓔ
23 Ⓐ Ⓑ Ⓒ Ⓓ Ⓔ
24 Ⓐ Ⓑ Ⓒ Ⓓ Ⓔ
25 Ⓐ Ⓑ Ⓒ Ⓓ Ⓔ
26 Ⓐ Ⓑ Ⓒ Ⓓ Ⓔ

PASSAGE 3

27 Ⓐ Ⓑ Ⓒ Ⓓ Ⓔ
28 Ⓐ Ⓑ Ⓒ Ⓓ Ⓔ
29 Ⓐ Ⓑ Ⓒ Ⓓ Ⓔ
30 Ⓐ Ⓑ Ⓒ Ⓓ Ⓔ
31 Ⓐ Ⓑ Ⓒ Ⓓ Ⓔ
32 Ⓐ Ⓑ Ⓒ Ⓓ Ⓔ
33 Ⓐ Ⓑ Ⓒ Ⓓ Ⓔ
34 Ⓐ Ⓑ Ⓒ Ⓓ Ⓔ
35 Ⓐ Ⓑ Ⓒ Ⓓ Ⓔ
36 Ⓐ Ⓑ Ⓒ Ⓓ Ⓔ
37 Ⓐ Ⓑ Ⓒ Ⓓ Ⓔ
38 Ⓐ Ⓑ Ⓒ Ⓓ Ⓔ
39 Ⓐ Ⓑ Ⓒ Ⓓ Ⓔ
40 Ⓐ Ⓑ Ⓒ Ⓓ Ⓔ
41 Ⓐ Ⓑ Ⓒ Ⓓ Ⓔ

PASSAGE 4

42 Ⓐ Ⓑ Ⓒ Ⓓ Ⓔ
43 Ⓐ Ⓑ Ⓒ Ⓓ Ⓔ
44 Ⓐ Ⓑ Ⓒ Ⓓ Ⓔ
45 Ⓐ Ⓑ Ⓒ Ⓓ Ⓔ
46 Ⓐ Ⓑ Ⓒ Ⓓ Ⓔ
47 Ⓐ Ⓑ Ⓒ Ⓓ Ⓔ
48 Ⓐ Ⓑ Ⓒ Ⓓ Ⓔ
49 Ⓐ Ⓑ Ⓒ Ⓓ Ⓔ
50 Ⓐ Ⓑ Ⓒ Ⓓ Ⓔ
51 Ⓐ Ⓑ Ⓒ Ⓓ Ⓔ
52 Ⓐ Ⓑ Ⓒ Ⓓ Ⓔ
53 Ⓐ Ⓑ Ⓒ Ⓓ Ⓔ
54 Ⓐ Ⓑ Ⓒ Ⓓ Ⓔ
55 Ⓐ Ⓑ Ⓒ Ⓓ Ⓔ
56 Ⓐ Ⓑ Ⓒ Ⓓ Ⓔ

Section I: Multiple-Choice Questions

Time 60 minutes

56 questions

Directions: This section consists of selections from prose works and questions on their content, form, and style. Read each selection carefully. Choose the best answer of the five choices.

Questions 1–14. Read the following passage carefully before you begin to answer the questsions.

First Passage

Here then was I (call me Mary Beton, Mary Seton, or Mary Carmichael or by any name you please — it is not a matter of any importance) sitting on the banks
(5) of a river a week or two ago in fine October weather, lost in thought. That collar I have spoken of, women and fiction, the need of coming to some conclusion on a subject that raises all sorts of
(10) prejudices and passions, bowed my head to the ground. To the right and left bushes of some sort, golden and crimson, glowed with the colour, even it seemed burnt with the heat, of fire. On
(15) the further bank the willows wept in perpetual lamentation, their hair about their shoulders. The river reflected whatever it chose of sky and bridge and burning tree, and when the undergraduate had
(20) oared his boat through the reflections they closed again, completely, as if he had never been. There one might have sat the clock round lost in thought. Thought — to call it by a prouder name
(25) than it deserved — had let its line down

into the stream. It swayed, minute after minute, hither and thither among the reflections and weeds, letting the water lift it and sink it, until — you know the little
(30) tug — the sudden conglomeration of an idea at the end of one's line: and then the cautious hauling of it in, and the careful laying of it out? Alas, laid on the grass how small, how insignificant this
(35) thought of mine looked; the sort of fish that a good fisherman puts back into the water so that it may grow fatter and be one day worth cooking and eating. I will not trouble you with that thought now,
(40) though if you look carefully you may find it for yourselves. . . .

But however small it was, it had, nevertheless, the mysterious property of its kind — put back into the mind, it be-
(45) came at once very exciting and important; and as it darted and sank, and flashed hither and thither, set up such a wash and tumult of ideas that it was impossible to sit still. It was thus that I
(50) found myself walking with extreme

GO ON TO THE NEXT PAGE

rapidity across a grass plot. Instantly a man's figure rose to intercept me. Nor did I at first understand that the gesticulations of a curious-looking object, in a (55) cut-away coat and evening shirt, were aimed at me. His face expressed horror and indignation. Instinct rather than reason came to my help; he was a Beadle; I was a woman. This was the turf; there (60) was the path. Only the Fellows and Scholars are allowed here; the gravel is the place for me. Such thoughts were the work of a moment. As I regained the path the arms of the Beadle sank, his (65) face assumed its usual repose, and thought turf is better walking than gravel, no very great harm was done. The only charge I could bring against the Fellows and scholars of whatever the (70) college might happen to be was that in protection of their turf, which has been rolled for 300 years in succession, they had sent my little fish into hiding.

What an idea it had been that had sent (75) me so audaciously trespassing I could not now remember. The spirit of peace descended like a cloud from heaven, for if the spirit of peace dwells anywhere, it is in the courts and quadrangles of (80) Oxbridge on a fine October morning. Strolling through those colleges past those ancient halls the roughness of the present seemed smoothed away; the body seemed contained in a miraculous (85) glass cabinet through which no sound could penetrate, and the mind, freed from any contact with facts (unless one trespassed on the turf again), was at liberty to settle down upon whatever medi- (90) tation was in harmony with the moment.

As chance would have it, some stray memory of some old essay about revisiting Oxbridge in the long vacation brought Charles Lamb to mind. . . . (95) Indeed, among all the dead . . . Lamb is one of the most congenial. . . . For his essays are superior . . . because of that wild flash of imagination that lightning crack of genius in the middle of them which (100) leaves them flawed and imperfect, but starred with poetry. . . . It then occurred to me that the very manuscript itself which Lamb had looked at was only a few hundred yards away, so that one (105) could follow Lamb's footsteps across the quadrangle to that famous library where the treasure is kept. Moreover, I recollected, as I put this plan into execution, it is in this famous library that the (110) manuscript of Thackeray's *Esmond* is also preserved . . . but here I was actually at the door which leads to the library itself. I must have opened it, for instantly there issued, like a guardian angel bar- (115) ring the way with a flutter of black gown instead of white wings, a deprecating, silvery, kindly gentleman, who regretted in a low voice as he waved me back that ladies are only admitted to the library if (120) accompanied by a Fellow of the College or furnished with a letter of introduction.

That a famous library has been cursed by a woman is a matter of complete indifference to a famous library. Venerable (125) and calm, with all its treasures safe locked within its breast, it sleeps forever. Never will I wake those echoes, never will I ask for that hospitality again.

1. According to the passage, the narrator uses several names (lines 1–2) in order to

   A. make a universal statement about all humankind

   B. deemphasize her personal identity

   C. introduce her many pseudonyms as an author

   D. attempt to impress the reader with her literacy

   E. mask her true identity from the reader

2. The literary device used to describe the speaker's thought "Thought . . . eating." (lines 24–38) is

   A. a simile

   B. a metaphor

   C. personification

   D. an apostrophe

   E. hyperbole

3. In the phrase "you know the little tug" (lines 29–30), the speaker abstractly refers to

   A. a fish's pull on a fishing line

   B. the Beadle's insisting she move off the lawn

   C. the annoying loss of a thought

   D. the sudden awareness of an idea

   E. the pull of her guilty conscience

4. The effect that the Beadle has on the narrator is to

   A. encourage her pursuit of knowledge

   B. cause her thoughts to retreat

   C. assure her of correct directions

   D. condemn the women's movement

   E. inquire if she needs additional assistance

5. It can be inferred that the narrator realizes that she cannot remember her thought because

   A. it passes so quickly

   B. the student rowing by interrupts it

   C. it is not important enough

   D. it does not compare to great author's ideas

   E. it is so carefully and slowly thought out

6. The lawn and library serve the purpose of

   A. symbolizing the obstacles that women face

   B. reminding readers of the rigors of university study

   C. contrasting relaxation with research

   D. introducing the existence of equality for women

   E. minimizing the author's point about women's roles

GO ON TO THE NEXT PAGE

7. The passage contains all of the following rhetorical devices EXCEPT

   A. personification

   B. metaphor

   C. simile

   D. literary allusion

   E. allegory

8. The author's purpose in the passage is to

   A. explain her anger at the Beadle

   B. personify nature's splendor

   C. illustrate how men can inhibit women's intellectual pursuits

   D. recall the enticing glory of university study

   E. preach her beliefs about women's roles in society

9. The organization of the passage could be best characterized as

   A. stream of consciousness mixed with narration of specific events

   B. comparison and contrast of two incidents

   C. exposition of the women's movement and the author's opinions

   D. description of both external reality and the author's thoughts

   E. flowing smoothly from general ideas to specific statements

10. The pacing of the sentence "But however small it was . . . it was impossible to sit still" (lines 42–49)

   A. reflects the acceleration of her thoughts

   B. represents a continuation of the pace of the description of the river

   C. contrasts with the fish metaphor

   D. suggests a sluggishness before the Beadle's interruption

   E. parallels that of the description of the library doorman

11. The speaker's description of the Beadle and the library doorman serves to

   A. confirm the horror of what she has done

   B. frighten women away from universities

   C. encourage women to rebel against men

   D. contrast the men's manners

   E. satirize the petty men who enforce the rules

12. The phrase "for instantly there issued . . . waved me back" (lines 114–119) can best be characterized as containing

   A. obvious confusion from the doorman

   B. metaphorical reference to a jailer

   C. awed wonder at the man's position

   D. humorous yet realistic description

   E. matter-of-fact narration

13. At the time of the occurrences she describes, the speaker probably felt all of the following EXCEPT

   A. indignation

   B. bewilderment

   C. delight

   D. exasperation

   E. repression

14. The pattern of the passage can best be described as

   A. alternating between a description of external reality and internal commentary

   B. the presentation of a social problem followed by its resolution

   C. general statements followed by illustrative detail

   D. presentation of theory followed by exceptions to that theory

   E. comparison and contrast of great authors' ideas

Questions 15–26. Read the following passage carefully before you begin to answer the questions.

Second Passage

[Alexander Pope] professed to have learned his poetry from Dryden, whom, whenever an opportunity was presented, he praised through his whole life with
(5) unvaried liberality; and perhaps his character may receive some illustration if he be compared with his master.

Integrity of understanding and nicety of discernment were not allotted in a
(10) less proportion to Dryden than to Pope. The rectitude of Dryden's mind was sufficiently shown by the dismission of his poetical prejudices, and then rejection of unnatural thoughts and rugged numbers.
(15) But Dryden never desired to apply all the judgment that he had. He wrote, and professed to write, merely for the people, and when he pleased others, he contented himself. He spent no time in
(20) struggles to rouse latent powers; he never attempted to make that better which was already good, nor often to mend what he must have known to be faulty. He wrote, as he tells us, with very
(25) little consideration; when occasion or necessity called upon him, he poured out what the present moment happened to supply, and, when once it had passed the press, ejected it from his mind: for
(30) when he had no pecuniary interest, he had no further solicitude.

Pope was not content to satisfy; he desired to excel, and therefore always endeavored to do his best: he did not
(35) court the candor, but dared the judgment of his reader, and, expecting no indulgence from others, he showed none to himself. He examined lines and words with minute and punctilious observa-
(40) tion, and retouched every part with indefatigable diligence, till he had left nothing to be forgiven. . . .

His declaration that his care for his works ceased at their publication was

GO ON TO THE NEXT PAGE

(45) not strictly true. His paternal attention never abandoned them; what he found amiss in the first edition, he silently corrected in those that followed. He appears to have revised the *Iliad,* and freed it (50) from some of its imperfections, and the *Essay on Criticism* received many improvements after its first appearance. It will seldom be found that he altered without adding clearness, elegance, or (55) vigor. Pope had perhaps the judgment of Dryden; but Dryden certainly wanted the diligence of Pope.

In acquired knowledge, the superiority must be allowed to Dryden, whose (60) education was more scholastic, and who before he became an author had been allowed more time for study, with better means of information. His mind has a larger range, and he collects his images (65) and illustrations from a more extensive circumference of science. Dryden knew more of man in his general nature, and Pope in his local manners. The notions of Dryden were formed by comprehen- (70) sive speculation, and those of Pope by minute attention. There is more dignity in the knowledge of Dryden, and more certainty in that of Pope.

Poetry was not the sole praise of ei- (75) ther; for both excelled likewise in prose; but Pope did not borrow his prose from his predecessor. The style of Dryden is capricious and varied; that of Pope is cautious and uniform. Dryden obeys the (80) motions of his own mind; Pope constrains his mind to his own rules of composition. Dryden is sometimes vehement and rapid; Pope is always smooth, uniform, and gentle. Dryden's page is a

(85) natural field, rising into inequalities, and diversified by the varied exuberance of abundant vegetation; Pope's is a velvet lawn, shaven by the scythe, and leveled by the roller.

(90) Of genius, that power which constitutes a poet; that quality without which judgment is cold, and knowledge is inert, that energy which collects, combines, amplifies, and animates; the (95) superiority must, with some hesitation, be allowed to Dryden. It is not to be inferred that of this poetical vigor Pope had only a little, because Dryden had more; for every other writer since (100) Milton must give place to Pope; and even of Dryden it must be said, that, if he has brighter paragraphs, he has not better poems. Dryden's performances were always hasty, either excited by (105) some external occasion, or extorted by domestic necessity; he composed without consideration, and published without correction. What his mind could supply at call, or gather in one excursion, was (110) all that he sought, and all that he gave. The dilatory caution of Pope enabled him to condense his sentiments, to multiply his images, and to accumulate all that study might produce or chance (115) might supply. If the flights of Dryden therefore are higher, Pope continues longer on the wing. If of Dryden's fire the blaze is brighter, of Pope's the heat is more regular and constant. Dryden often (120) surpasses expectation, and Pope never falls below it. Dryden is read with frequent astonishment, and Pope with perpetual delight.

15. The essay's organization could best be described as

A. exposition of a thesis followed by illustrations

B. chronological presentation of each author's works

C. presenting ideas based on their order of importance

D. basing each paragraph on a different argument

E. comparison of and contrast between the two writers

16. In context, "candor" (line 35) can be interpreted to mean

A. kindness

B. criticism

C. excellence

D. sincerity

E. indifference

17. In each of the following pairs of words, the first refers to Dryden, the second to Pope. Which pair best describes their prose style?

A. Dignified vs. simplistic

B. Passionate vs. lyrical

C. Unsystematic vs. harmonious

D. Punctilious vs. careless

E. Pedantic vs. impetuous

18. Which of the following best describes Pope's attitude toward his own writing?

A. "[he] dared the judgment of his reader" (lines 35–36)

B. "His parental attention never abandoned them" (lines 45–46)

C. "It will seldom be found that he altered without adding clearness" (lines 52–54)

D. "Pope is cautious and uniform" (lines 78–79)

E. "Pope continues longer on the wing" (lines 116–117)

19. The passage's points could be more convincing if the writer were to offer

A. less emphasis on Pope's writing and editing diligence

B. more direct language to present his ideas about the authors

C. more discussion of Dryden's editing theories

D. more point-by-point comparisons of each author's prose

E. specific examples from each poet's work to support his opinions

20. Which of the following is NOT found in the essay?

A. For Pope, good writing meant rewriting.

B. Both authors were productive.

C. Dryden is the superior prose writer.

D. Dryden follows his own mind more than Pope does.

E. Pope's writing is like a manicured lawn.

GO ON TO THE NEXT PAGE

21. Which of the following best characterizes Dryden's method of writing?

 A. "he never attempted to make better that which was already good" (lines 20–22)

 B. "he poured out what the present moment happened to supply" (lines 26–28)

 C. "when he had no pecuniary interest, he had no further solicitude" (lines 30–31)

 D. "His mind has a larger range" (lines 63–64)

 E. "the superiority must, with some hesitation, be allowed to Dryden" (lines 94–96)

22. Although Pope did not have as strong a scholastic background as did Dryden, the writer implies that Pope

 A. chose subjects unrelated to Dryden's

 B. had great familiarity with his subject matter

 C. feigned completing university study

 D. compensated by emulating Dryden

 E. undermined any effort on his behalf

23. According to the passage, genius can invigorate which of the following in an author?

 I. Judgment

 II. Knowledge

 III. Power

 A. I only

 B. III only

 C. I and II only

 D. II and III only

 E. I, II, and III

24. What does the writer suggest as the main reason that Dryden's writing style labels him as genius?

 A. The apparent effortlessness of his writing

 B. He "continues longer on the wing" (lines 116–117)

 C. That his prose is a "natural field"

 D. That his academic studies prepare him so well

 E. That the age he lived in was noted for intelligence

25. In lines 84–89 ("Dryden's page . . . roller"), which of the following literary devices is used to summarize the differences between Dryden's and Pope's prose?

 A. Syllogism

 B. Personification

 C. Understatement

 D. Metaphor

 E. Simile

26. Of the following, which is NOT a major distinction the writer draws between Dryden and Pope?

 A. Their educational foundation

 B. Their prose style

 C. Their skill in writing

 D. Their vigor in writing

 E. Their editing practice

Questions 27–41. Read the following passage carefully before you begin to answer the questions.

Third Passage

It is remarkable that there is little or nothing to be remembered written on the subject of getting a living; how to make getting a living not merely honest and
(5) honorable, but altogether inviting and glorious; for if *getting* a living is not so, then living is not. One would think, from looking at literature, that this question had never disturbed a solitary individ-
(10) ual's musings. Is it that men are too much disgusted with their experience to speak of it? The lesson of value which money teaches, which the Author of the Universe has taken so much pains to
(15) teach us, we are inclined to skip altogether. As for the means of living, it is wonderful how indifferent men of all classes are about it, even reformers, so called, — whether they inherit, or earn,
(20) or steal it. I think that Society has done nothing for us in this respect, or at least has undone what she has done. Cold and hunger seem more friendly to my nature than those methods which men have
(25) adopted and advise to ward them off.

The title *wise* is, for the most part, falsely applied. How can one be a wise man, if he does not know any better how to live than other men? — if he is only
(30) more cunning and intellectually subtle? Does Wisdom work in a tread-mill? or does she teach how to succeed *by her example?* Is there any such thing as wisdom not applied to life? Is she merely
(35) the miller who grinds the finest logic? Is it pertinent to ask if Plato got his *living* in a better way or more successfully than his contemporaries, — or did he succumb to the difficulties of life like
(40) other men? Did he seem to prevail over

some of them merely by indifference, or by assuming grand airs? Or find it easier to live, because his aunt remembers him in her will? The ways in which most
(45) men get their living, that is, live, are mere makeshifts, and a shirking of the real business of live, — chiefly because they do not know, but partly because they do not mean, any better.

(50) The rush to California, for instance, and the attitude, not merely of merchants, but of philosophers and prophets, so called, in relation to it, reflect the greatest disgrace on mankind.
(55) That so many are ready to live by luck, and so get the means of commanding the labor of others less lucky, without contributing any value to society! And that is called enterprise! I know of no more
(60) startling development of the immorality of trade, and all the common modes of getting a living. The philosophy and poetry and religion of such a mankind are not worth the dust of a puffball. The hog
(65) that gets his living by rooting, stirring up the soil so, would be ashamed of such company. If I could command the wealth of all the world by lifting my finger, I would not pay *such* a price for it.
(70) Even Mahomet knew that God did not make this world in jest. It makes God to be a moneyed gentleman who scatters a handful of pennies in order to see mankind scramble for them. The world's
(75) raffle! A subsistence in the domains of Nature a thing to be raffled for! What a comment, what a satire, on our institutions! The conclusion will be, that mankind will hang itself upon a tree.
(80) And have all the precepts in all the

GO ON TO THE NEXT PAGE

Bibles taught men only this? and is the last and most admirable invention of the human race only an improved much-
(85) rake? Is this the ground on which Orientals and Occidentals meet? Did God direct us so to get our living, digging where we never planted, — and He would, perchance, reward us with lumps
(90) of gold? God gave the righteous man a certificate entitling him to food and raiment, but the unrighteous man found a facsimile of the same in God's coffers, and appropriated it, and obtained food
(95) and raiment like the former. It is one of the most extensive systems of counterfeiting that the world has ever seen. I did not know that mankind was suffering for want of gold. I have seen a little of it. I
(100) know that it is very malleable, but not so malleable as wit. A grain of gold will gild a great surface, but not so much as a grain of wisdom.

The gold-digger in the ravines of the
(105) mountains is as much a gambler as his fellow in the saloons of San Francisco. What difference does it make whether you shake dirt or shake dice? If you win, society is the loser. The gold-digger is
(110) the enemy of the honest laborer, whatever checks and compensations there may be. It is not enough to tell me that you worked hard to get your gold. So does the Devil work hard. The way of
(115) transgressors may be hard in many respects. The humblest observer who goes to the mines sees and says that gold-digging is of the character of a lottery; the gold thus obtained is not the same thing
(120) with the wages of honest toil. But, practically, he forgets what he has seen, for he sees only the fact, not the principle, and goes into trade there, that is, buys a ticket in what commonly proves another
(125) lottery, where the fact is not so obvious.

27. The author believes that "getting a living" must be both

A. moral and pious

B. ethical and admirable

C. accessible and sensible

D. desirable and attainable

E. humble and profitable

28. According to the author, although man must earn money, he is indifferent to

A. religion

B. society

C. cold and hunger

D. lessons of value

E. laborers

29. The author asserts that

A. we have forgotten the proper value of money

B. good, hard work will save mankind

C. the world operates solely on luck

D. religion fails to address the merit of labor

E. gold-digging is acceptable under certain conditions

30. The "Author of the Universe" (lines 13–14) can be interpreted as

A. symbol for cosmic consciousness

B. metaphor for a contemporary writer

C. symbol for judgment

D. metaphor for all artists

E. metaphor for God

31. The author's purpose in referring to Plato seems to be to

    A. make the point about gold-digging more universal and timeless

    B. qualify the assertions about gold-digging and their luck

    C. question whether ancient philosophers faced the same dilemmas that others do

    D. consider the ancient philosopher's premises about morality in society

    E. create an authoritative tone to lend credence to the argument

32. What is the antecedent for "it" (line 69)?

    A. "immorality" (line 60)

    B. "philosophy" (line 62)

    C. "hog" (line 64)

    D. "wealth" (line 68)

    E. "world" (line 68)

33. Which of the following is the best example of aphorism?

    A. "The ways in which most men . . . any better." (lines 44–49)

    B. "Nature a thing to be raffled for!" (line 76)

    C. "A grain of gold . . . a grain of wisdom." (lines 101–103)

    D. "What difference does it make . . . shake dice?" (lines 107–108)

    E. "So does the Devil work hard." (lines 118–119)

34. An unstated assumption of the author is that

    A. philosophers should work harder to apply their teachings

    B. a pig would be mortified by some men

    C. society is gradually improving

    D. true wisdom comes only though hard work

    E. what appears honest to one can be harmful to society

35. The author's comments about the California gold rush serve the purpose of

    A. comparing gold-diggers to the ancient Greeks

    B. illustrating how immorally men are earning a living

    C. explaining the relationship of Orientals to Occidentals

    D. sensationalizing a topical and popular occupation

    E. criticizing those who think gold-digging romantic

36. Which of the following negative phrases is, in context, a qualified negative?

    A. "men are . . . disgusted with their experience" (lines 10–11)

    B. "Cold and hunger" (lines 22–23)

    C. "the greatest disgrace on mankind" (line 54)

    D. "the unrighteous man" (line 92)

    E. "society is the loser" (line 109)

GO ON TO THE NEXT PAGE

37. The essay contains all of the following devices EXCEPT

   A. simile

   B. historical allusion

   C. rhetorical question

   D. syllogistic reasoning

   E. religious reference

38. The sentence "A grain of gold . . . a grain of wisdom" (lines 101–103) can best be restated as

   A. knowledge is more valuable than gold

   B. gold-diggers must work harder than philosophers

   C. gold will last longer than knowledge

   D. erudition takes longer to achieve than money

   E. money has no practical purpose

39. The tone of the essay can best be described as

   A. condescending

   B. skeptical

   C. worrisome

   D. indignant

   E. pedestrian

40. Which of the following is NOT part of the author's argument against gold-digging?

   A. "The hog . . . would be ashamed of such company." (lines 64–67)

   B. "digging where we never planted" (lines 87–88)

   C. "I know that it is very malleable" (lines 99–100)

   D. "the enemy of the honest laborer" (line 110)

   E. "of the character of a lottery" (line 123)

41. Which of the following is NOT discussed in the passage?

   A. Man can learn to improve his lot in life.

   B. Authors have not addressed "getting a living."

   C. Gamblers have damaged society.

   D. The title "wise" may be misapplied.

   E. Men are easily lured by monetary rewards.

Questions 42–56. Read the following passage carefully before you begin to answer the questions.

Fourth Passage

The object of this essay is to assert one very simple principle, as entitled to govern absolutely the dealings of society with the individual in the way of
(5) compulsion and control, whether the means used be physical force in the form of legal penalties or the moral coercion of public opinion. That principal is that the sole end for which mankind
(10) are warranted, individually or collectively, in interfering with the liberty of action of any of their number is self-protection. That the only purpose for which power can be rightfully exercised over
(15) any member of civilized community, against his will, is to prevent harm to others. His own good, either physical or moral, is not sufficient warrant. He cannot rightfully be compelled to do or for-
(20) bear because it will be better for him to do so, because it will make him happier, because, in the opinions of others, to do so would be wise or even right. These are good reasons for remonstrating with
(25) him, or reasoning with him, or persuading him, or entreating him, but not for compelling him or visiting him with any evil in case he do otherwise. To justify that, the conduct from which it is desired
(30) to deter him must be calculated to produce evil to someone else. The only part of the conduct of anyone for which he is amenable to society is that which concerns others. In the part which merely
(35) concerns himself, his independence is, of right, absolute. Over himself, over his won body and mind, the individual is sovereign.

It is, perhaps, hardly necessary to say
(40) that this doctrine is meant to apply only to human beings in the maturity of their faculties. We are not speaking of children or of young persons below the age which the law may fix as that of man-
(45) hood or womanhood. Those who are still in a state to require being taken care of by others must be protected against their own actions as well as against external injury. For the same reason we
(50) may leave out of consideration those backward states of society in which the race itself may be considered as in its nonage. The early difficulties in the way of spontaneous progress are so great that
(55) there is seldom any choice of means for overcoming them; and a ruler full of the spirit of improvement is warranted in the use of any expedients that will attain an end perhaps otherwise unattainable.
(60) Despotism is a legitimate mode of government in dealing with barbarians, provided the end be their improvement and the means justified by actually effecting that end. Liberty, as a principle, has no
(65) application to any state of things anterior to the time when mankind have become capable of being improved by free and equal discussion. Until then, there is nothing for them but implicit obedience
(70) to an Akbar or a Charlemagne, if they are so fortunate as to find one. But as soon as mankind have attained the capacity of being guided to their own improvement by conviction or persuasion
(75) (a period long since reached in all nations with whom we need here concern ourselves), compulsion, either in the direct form or in that of pains and penalties for noncompliance, is no longer
(80) admissible as a means to their own good, and justifiable only for the security of others.

GO ON TO THE NEXT PAGE

42. The "one very simple principle" (line 2) is that

   A.   the individual should comply with the government's principles under all conditions

   B.   a domineering government is an effective government

   C.   the government should coerce an individual only when that individual's actions will harm others

   D.   individuals have the right to ignore the government's wishes

   E.   children do not have sovereignty

43. The predicate nominative that complements "That principal," the subject of the second sentence (lines 8–13), is

   A.   "sole end"

   B.   "warranted"

   C.   "liberty of action"

   D.   "self-protection"

   E.   "that the sole end . . . self-protection"

44. According to the passage, which of the following may society compel to act correctly?

   A.   Those who act selfishly

   B.   Those who harm only themselves

   C.   Those who demonstrate personal corruption

   D.   Those who harm others

   E.   Those who protect against despotism

45. The sentence "These are good reasons . . . otherwise" (lines 23–28) is effective because of its

   A.   abstract meaning

   B.   parallel syntax

   C.   metaphorical references

   D.   ironic understatement

   E.   personification of government

46. The principle embodied in the phrase "the individual is sovereign" (lines 37–38) is limited to actions that

   A.   adversely affect all society

   B.   are legal

   C.   affect only the individual

   D.   society generally ignores

   E.   are directed at political enemies

47. According to the passage, which of the following groups may be forced to act in a particular way?

   I.   Children

   II.   Adults

   III. Immature societies

   A.   I only

   B.   II only

   C.   I and II only

   D.   I and III only

   E.   I, II, and III

48. It can be inferred from the passage that despotism is NOT acceptable when

    A. the government's actions do not produce the necessary improvement in its citizens

    B. barbarians are allowed to do as they wish

    C. the government's actions harm children

    D. society in general is insecure and unsafe

    E. the people voice opinions against the despot

49. Which of the following are given as allowable methods for preventing member of society from harming other individuals?

    I.   Physical force
    II. Moral coercion of public opinion
    III. Legal penalties

    A. I only
    B. II only
    C. I and II only
    D. II and III only
    E. I, II, and III

50. Which of the following does the passage imply the author values most highly?

    A. Unlimited individual freedom
    B. Protection of the members of society
    C. Law and order in society
    D. Despotism by the leaders
    E. The sovereignty of children

51. The second paragraph relates to the first paragraph in that it

    A. gives exceptions to the principle of individual sovereignty discussed in the first paragraph

    B. illustrates the actions a government can take in controlling its citizens

    C. lists evidence supporting the assertions made in the first paragraph

    D. gives concrete examples of effective governments

    E. provides anecdotal evidence of individuals acting in self-protection

52. With which of the following would the author most likely agree?

    A. Children should be allowed sovereignty.

    B. Charlemagne would make a good ruler in a society able to be "guided" to its "own improvement."

    C. Forced obedience will always be necessary for mankind.

    D. The only appropriate reason to inhibit a citizen having mature faculties is to prevent harm to others.

    E. Despots will always exist.

53. Which term best describes the tone of the essay?

    A. Sarcastic
    B. Cynical
    C. Optimistic
    D. Matter of fact
    E. Pessimistic

GO ON TO THE NEXT PAGE

54. Which of the following would the author be LEAST likely to encourage?

  A. Despotism for barbarians

  B. Control over children

  C. Absolute freedom of action

  D. Reasoning and persuasion

  E. Self-destructive actions

55. Which of the following rhetorical devices can be found in the essay?

  A. Metaphor

  B. Personification

  C. Syllogistic reasoning

  D. Simile

  E. Historical allusion

56. A major purpose of the passage is to

  A. preach against despotism

  B. clarify the conditions under which a government may coerce citizens to act a certain way

  C. alert society to the potential harm of individual rights

  D. explain why a government should allow individual freedoms

  E. assert the sovereign rights of every individual

IF YOU FINISH BEFORE TIME IS CALLED, CHECK YOUR WORK ON THIS SECTION ONLY. DO NOT WORK ON ANY OTHER SECTION IN THE TEST.

STOP

Section II: Essay Questions

Time: 2 hours

3 questions

Question 1

(Suggested time – 40 minutes. This question counts one-third of the total essay section score.)

Directions: The following passages are comments on two places, M. F. K. Fisher on the French port of Marseille and Maya Angelou on the small town of Stamps, Arkansas. Read both carefully and write an essay on how the two passages are similar and different in their effect and in their authors' handling of the resources of language.

Passage I

One of the many tantalizing things about Marseille is that most people who describe it, whether or not they know much about either the place or the languages they are supposedly using, write the same things. For centuries this has been so, and a typically modern opinion could have been given in 1550 as well as 1977.

Not long ago I read one, mercifully unsigned, in a San Francisco paper. It was full of logistical errors, faulty syntax, misspelled French words, but it hewed true to the familiar line that Marseille is doing its best to live up to a legendary reputation as world capital for "dope, whores, and street violence." It then went on to discuss, often erroneously, the essential ingredients of a true bouillabaisse! The familiar pitch had been made, and idle readers dreaming of a great seaport dedicated to heroin, prostitution, and rioting could easily skip the clumsy details of marketing for fresh fish. . . .

"Feature articles" like this one make it seem probable that many big newspapers, especially in English-reading countries, keep a few such mild shockers on hand in a back drawer, in case a few columns need filling on a rainy Sunday. Apparently people like to glance one more time at the same old words: evil, filthy, dangerous.

Sometimes such journalese is almost worth reading for its precociously obsolete views of a society too easy to forget. In 1929, for instance, shortly before the Wall Street Crash, a popular travel writer named Basil Woon published *A Guide to the Gay World of France: From Deauville to Monte Carlo* (Horace Liveright, New York). (By now even his use of the word "gay" is quaintly naïve enough for a small chuckle. . . .)

Of course Mr. Woon was most interested in the Côte d'Azur, in those far days teeming and staggering with rich English and even richer Americans, but while he could not actively recommend staying in Marseille, he did remain true to his journalistic background with an expectedly titillating mention of it.

***

If you are interested in how the other side of the world lives, a trip through old Marseilles — by daylight — cannot fail to thrill, but it is not wise to venture into this

GO ON TO THE NEXT PAGE

151

district at night unless dressed like a stevedore and well armed. Thieves, cutthroats, and other undesirables throng the narrow alleys, and sisters of scarlet sit in the doorways of their places of business, catching you by the sleeve as you pass by. The dregs of the world are here, unsifted. It is Port Said, Shanghai, Barcelona, and Sidney combined. Now that San Francisco has reformed, Marseilles is the world's wickedest port.

Passage II

There is a much-loved region in the American fantasy where pale white women float eternally under black magnolia trees, and white men with soft hands brush wisps of wisteria from the creamy shoulders of their lady loves. Harmonious black music drifts like perfume through this precious air, and nothing of a threatening nature intrudes.

The South I returned to, however, was flesh-real and swollen-belly poor. Stamps, Arkansas, a small hamlet, had subsisted for hundreds of years on the returns from cotton plantations, and until World War I, a creaking lumbermill. The town was halved by railroad tracks, the swift Red River and racial prejudice. Whites lived on the town's small rise (it couldn't be called a hill), while blacks lived in what had been known since slavery as "the Quarters. . . ."

In my memory, Stamps is a place of light, shadow, sounds and entrancing odors. The earth smell was pungent, spiced with the odor of cattle manure, the yellowish acid of ponds and rivers, the deep pots of greens and beans cooking for hours with smoked or cured pork. Flowers added their heavy aroma. And above all, the atmosphere was pressed down with the smell of old fears, and hates, and guilt.

On this hot and moist landscape, passions clanged with the ferocity of armored knights colliding. Until I moved to California at thirteen I had known the town, and there had been no need to examine it. I took its being for granted and now, five years later, I was returning, expecting to find the shield of anonymity I had known as a child.

Question 2

(Suggested time – 40 minutes. This question counts one-third of the total essay section score.)

Directions: Read the following excerpt from William Hazlitt's *Lectures on the English Comic Writers* (1819). Then write a well-developed essay analyzing the author's purpose by examining tone, point of view, and stylistic devices.

Man is the only animal that laughs and weeps; for he is the only animal that is struck with the difference between what things are, and what they ought to be. We weep at what thwarts or exceeds our desires in serious matters: we laugh at what only disappoints our expectations in trifles. We shed tears from sympathy with real and necessary distress; as we burst into laughter from want of sympathy with that which is unreasonable and unnecessary, the absurdity of which provokes our spleen or mirth, rather than any serious reflections on it.

To explain the nature of laughter and tears, is to account for the condition of human life; for it is in a manner compounded of these two! It is a tragedy or a comedy — sad or merry, as it happens. The crimes and misfortunes that are inseparable from it, shock and wound the mind when they once seize upon it, and when the pressure can no longer be borne, seek relief in tears: the follies and absurdities that men commit, or the odd accidents that befall them, afford us amusement from the very rejection of these false claims upon our sympathy, and end in laughter. If every thing that went wrong, if every vanity or weakness in another gave us a sensible pang, it would be hard indeed: but as long as the disagreeableness of the consequences of a sudden disaster is kept out of sight by the immediate oddity of the circumstances, and the absurdity or unaccountableness of a foolish action is the most striking thing in it, the ludicrous prevails over the pathetic, and we receive pleasure instead of pain from the farce of life which is played before us, and which discomposes our gravity as often as it fails to move our anger or our pity!

GO ON TO THE NEXT PAGE

Question 3

(Suggested time – 40 minutes. This question counts one-third of the total essay section score.)

Directions: The following excerpt is taken from Benjamin Franklin's *Autobiography*. Read the passage carefully and develop an essay that evaluates the validity of Franklin's assertions about the ability to justify one's actions through reasoning. Use evidence from your reading or experience to make your argument convincing.

I believe I have omitted mentioning that in my first voyage from Boston, being becalmed off Block Island, our people set about catching cod and hauled up a great many. Hitherto I had stuck to my resolution of not eating animal food; and on this occasion I considered with my Master Tryon, the taking of every fish as a kind of unprovoked murder, since none of them had or ever could do us any injury that might justify the slaughter. All this seemed very reasonable. But I had formerly been a great lover of fish, and when this came hot out of the frying pan, it smelled admirably well. I balanced some time between principle and inclination: till I recollected, that when fish were opened, I saw smaller fish taken out of their stomachs: Then, thought I, if you eat one another, I don't see why we mayn't eat you. So I dined upon cod very heartily and continued to eat with other people, returning only now and then occasionally to a vegetable diet. So convenient a thing it is to be a *reasonable creature,* since it enables one to find or make a reason for everything one has a mind to do.

IF YOU FINISH BEFORE TIME IS CALLED, CHECK YOUR WORK ON THIS
SECTION ONLY. DO NOT WORK ON ANY OTHER SECTION IN THE TEST.

Answer Key for Practice Test 2

Section I: Multiple-Choice Questions

First Passage

1. B
2. B
3. D
4. B
5. C
6. A
7. E
8. C
9. D
10. A
11. E
12. D
13. C
14. A

Second Passage

15. E
16. A
17. C
18. B
19. E
20. C
21. B
22. B
23. C
24. A
25. D
26. C

Third Passage

27. B
28. D
29. A
30. E
31. C
32. D
33. C
34. E
35. B
36. B
37. D
38. A
39. D
40. C
41. A

Fourth Passage

42. C
43. E
44. D
45. B
46. C
47. D
48. A
49. E
50. B
51. A
52. D
53. D
54. C
55. E
56. B

Section II: Essay Questions

Essay scoring guides, student essays, and analysis appear beginning on page 165.

Practice Test 2 Scoring Worksheet

Use the following worksheet to arrive at a probable final AP grade on Practice Test 2. Because it is sometimes difficult to be objective enough to figure your own essay score, you might give your essays (along with the sample essays) to a friend or relative to score if you feel confident that the individual has the knowledge necessary to make such a judgment and that he or she will feel comfortable doing so.

Section I: Multiple-Choice Questions

$$\underline{\hspace{2cm}} - (^1/_4 \text{ or } .25 \times \underline{\hspace{2cm}}) = \underline{\hspace{2cm}}$$

| right answers | wrong answers | multiple-choice raw score |

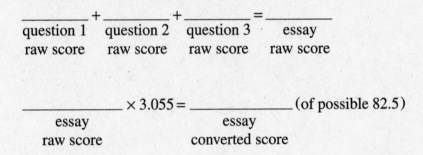

$$\underline{\hspace{3cm}} \times 1.18 = \underline{\hspace{3cm}} \text{ (of possible 67.5)}$$

multiple-choice raw score   multiple-choice converted score

Section II: Essay Questions

$$\underline{\hspace{2cm}} + \underline{\hspace{2cm}} + \underline{\hspace{2cm}} = \underline{\hspace{2cm}}$$

question 1 raw score   question 2 raw score   question 3 raw score   essay raw score

$$\underline{\hspace{3cm}} \times 3.055 = \underline{\hspace{3cm}} \text{ (of possible 82.5)}$$

essay raw score   essay converted score

Final Score

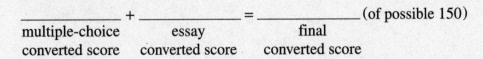

$$\underline{\hspace{3cm}} + \underline{\hspace{3cm}} = \underline{\hspace{3cm}} \text{ (of possible 150)}$$

multiple-choice converted score   essay converted score   final converted score

Probable Final AP Score

Final Converted Score	Probable AP Score
150–104	5
103–92	4
91–76	3
75–50	2
49–0	1

Answers and Explanations for Practice Test 2

Section I: Multiple-Choice Questions

First Passage

From Virginia Woolf's *A Room of One's Own*.

1. **B.** The phrase that follows the list of names explains this answer: "call me . . . by any name you please — it is <u>not a matter of any importance</u>."

2. **B.** The speaker uses a metaphor as she describes her thought, imagining it to be on a fishing line that "swayed . . . among the reflections." The thought becomes a metaphorical fish that she hauls to shore on the line. The device is not personification (**C**) because here an abstract is given animal characteristics rather than human (her thought is compared to a *fish* caught on a line). The remaining choices are not used in this part of the passage.

3. **D.** The phrase that follows the quotation clearly identifies the answer: "the sudden conglomeration of an idea at the end of one's line." Choice **A** names not the abstract meaning but the literal meaning on which the metaphor is based. Choices **B** and **C** mention later occurrences unrelated to this "tug." There is no suggestion that the author has a guilty conscience (**E**).

4. **B.** Being made aware that she is in an area in which only "Fellows and Scholars" are allowed to walk sends her metaphorical "fish into hiding." The Beadle doesn't encourage, direct, or ask her questions — **A, C,** and **E.** The women's movement (**D**) is not addressed in the passage.

5. **C.** In the fish metaphor, the author points out "how small, how insignificant" her thought is when examined. There is no evidence that the thought passes very quickly (**A**) or is carefully thought out (**E**) or that either has to do with her forgetting. Notice of the rower (**B**) occurs before mention of the thought and does not cause her to forget.

6. **A.** The lawn that the author may not walk on and the library that she may not enter are symbols of the obstructions all women face. Choice **D** contradicts the purpose of the passage — to point out *inequality*. Choice **E** is incorrect because these two symbols reinforce, not distract from, the author's point.

7. **E.** There is no allegory, the use of characters to symbolize truths about humanity, in this passage. The passage does use personification ("willows wept in perpetual lamentation"), metaphor (the "fish" sequence"), simile ("like a guardian angel"), and literary allusion (to *Esmond*).

8. C. The vignettes demonstrate how men have told women where they may and may not go; on a deeper level, they suggest that men's attitudes inhibit women in their intellectual pursuits. The author *is* angry (**A**) and touches on nature (**B**), but neither fact names the purpose of the essay. Choice **D** contradicts the passage; women have been *kept away* from university study. Choice **E** overstates. The author neither preaches nor discusses society and women's roles in general.

9. D. The passage presents external reality, such as the descriptions of the environs of the university and the actions of the Beadle and the doorman, while interspersing the author's thoughts about the events. The passage is too logical and grammatical to be classified as a stream of consciousness (**A**) (which is a narrative technique not a structural element). The passage doesn't compare or contrast the two events (**B**) or address the women's movement (**C**). While choice **E** might be a method of organization, it is not used here.

10. A. The sentence accelerates as do her thoughts — "it became at once very exciting, and important; . . . it darted and sank . . . flashed hither and thither . . . tumult of ideas . . . impossible to sit still."

11. E. The description of the men, of their pompous behavior and dress, satirically emphasizes how trifling are the author's supposed crimes, walking on the grass and attempting to enter the library, and how foolish is the men's self-important enforcement of discriminating rules. Choices **A** and **B** contradict the passage. The author doesn't consider what she's done a "horror" nor would she intend to frighten women away from universities. Choice **C** is not addressed. Choice **D** is incorrect because the men's manners are similar, not contrasting.

12. D. The description of the gentleman is realistic but also takes a humorous turn in describing a simple doorman as "like a guardian angel barring the way with a flutter of black gown instead of white wings . . . deprecating" as he bars the author from entering the library. The doorman is not confused (**A**), and the reference is not to a jailer (**B**), but to a guardian angel.

13. C. It is highly unlikely that the events described produced a feeling of delight.

14. A. The author blends a presentation of her thoughts as she walks with description of external reality, such as the Beadle and the library doorman. Choice **B** is incorrect because there is no resolution to her problem. Choices **C, D,** and **E** are not accurate descriptions of the passage's pattern.

Second Passage

From *The Lives of the English Poets* by Samuel Johnson.

15. E. The essay compares and contrasts the two authors, Dryden and Pope. Johnson begins by explaining that Dryden was a strong influence on Pope. Hence, Johnson sets out to "compare [Pope] with his master." The second paragraph explains Dryden's method of writing; the two following paragraphs discuss the care Pope took in writing and editing. The fifth paragraph explains the differences in the author's educational backgrounds, and the sixth compares their prose skills. The essay's concluding paragraph continues to draw comparisons and contrasts, ultimately calling Dryden the better poet, while acknowledging both men's strengths. The essay is primarily one of opinion. There is no thesis given and no extensive use of illustrations (**A**) (other than mention of the *Iliad* and the *Essay on Criticism*). Both choices **B** and **C** are inaccurate. Johnson does not present a different argument in each paragraph (**D**) or strictly present *arguments* at all. The passage is an *analysis* of their styles.

16. **A.** In the eighteenth century, the word "candor" meant kindness, a meaning that fits in context here. Pope did not court his readers' kindness, but "dared [their] judgment." Because the sentence sets up an opposition, "criticism," "excellence," "sincerity" (the modern meaning of "candor"), and "indifference" make little sense, as they are not good opposites of "judgment."

17. **C.** In the sixth paragraph (lines 74–89), Dryden's prose style is described as "capricious," obeying the motions of his own mind," sometimes "vehement and rapid," producing prose that is a "natural field, rising into inequalities . . . diversified" — that is, unsystematic, written quickly and without a preconceived order. Pope's prose, on the other hand, is described as "uniform," while he "constrains his mind to . . . rules of composition." Pope's prose is "smooth, uniform, and gentle," a "velvet lawn." If you check the first word of each answer pair, you will see that choices **A, D,** and **E** can be quickly eliminated as they are not suggested or inappropriate to refer to Dryden's prose. Finally, you can eliminate choice **B.** While Dryden might be considered passionate, there is no suggestion that Pope is lyrical. (Note: In answering questions of this sort, you can also begin by checking the second term of each pair.)

18. **B.** Pope's *attitude* toward his own writing is best seen in "His parental attention never abandoned them," which suggests a nurturing attitude toward his work. Choice **A** shows not so much an attitude toward his writing as it does an attitude toward his audience. While a possible answer, choice **C** deals with the outcome of Pope's editing and is not as clearly an *attitude* as is choice **B.** Choices **D** and **E** are primarily Johnson's opinions of Pope's work.

19. **E.** A reader might be more convinced that Johnson's opinions are valid if presented with some evidence, some examples. He mentions Pope's editing of the *Iliad* but never explains exactly what was changed. He calls Dryden's prose "vehement and rapid" but, again, offers no proof. A reader might be left to wonder what Johnson had read of Pope's and Dryden's works that led him to reach these conclusions, and some examples would help. Choice **A** is incorrect because *less* emphasis would hardly provide a *more* convincing argument. The language of the passage is direct (**B**), and point-by-point comparisons (**D**) are made; more of the same is unlikely to more thoroughly convince the reader. Dryden, it seems, did little editing (**C**), so additional discussion here would not be helpful either.

20. **C.** Johnson makes no definitive claim about the superiority of either author's prose. In the sixth paragraph, they are presented as different in style but not necessarily in quality. It is Dryden's poetry that Johnson says is superior (although with some hesitation).

21. **B.** Johnson explains how quickly Dryden wrote: "He spent no time in struggles to rouse latent powers," and "He wrote, as he tells us, with very little consideration." Choice **A** deals with Dryden's *lack* of rewriting, not his method of writing — what he did not do rather than what he did.

22. **B.** Johnson claims that even though Pope did not have the same education opportunities that Dryden enjoyed, Pope gave his subjects his "minute attention"; he had "more certainty" than Dryden, suggesting that Pope knew his subjects well.

23. **C.** Genius invigorates judgments (without which it is cold) and knowledge (without which it is inert). Genius is not said to invigorate power, rather it *is* power.

24. **A.** The author suggests Dryden's ease in writing as a component of his genius. The fact that Dryden could produce great poetry and admirable prose so quickly and without laborious rewriting and editing attests to Dryden's genius. The quotation given in choice **B** refers to Pope, not to Dryden. Choice **C** may be an apt description of Dryden's prose, but Johnson claims Dryden is genius in his *poetry*. Although Dryden had a strong educational foundation (**D**), Johnson does not address Dryden's education in relation to his genius.

25. **D.** Johnson uses an effective pair of metaphors to summarize his opinion of the two authors' prose: Dryden's is a "natural field," while Pope's is a "velvet lawn." The remaining choices are not used in this sentence.

26. **C.** Johnson clearly acknowledges that both authors are gifted, skillful, and talented and levels little criticism of either writer. All other distinctions given are addressed in the essay.

Third Passage

From Henry David Thoreau's "Life Without Principle."

27. **B.** Thoreau insists that "getting a living" should be "not merely honest and honorable" (ethical), "but altogether inviting and glorious" (admirable).

28. **D.** Thoreau explains that "the lesson of value which money teaches . . . we are inclined to skip altogether" (lines 12–16).

29. **A.** A major assertion of the essay is that people no longer understand the proper value of money. The author claims that people get money in the wrong way and use it based on the wrong principles. Thoreau never addresses what will "save mankind" (**B**). And while he acknowledges that gold-digging may be "hard work," "gold thus obtained is not the same thing with the wages of honest toil" and "society is the loser." Although Thoreau believes that gold-diggers rely on luck to find gold, he doesn't believe that the entire world operates this way (**C**). Neither **D** nor **E** is suggested in the essay.

30. **E.** The "Author of the Universe" to this author is God. None of the other choices is a reasonable answer.

31. **C.** The author wonders if Plato had to face the same dilemmas that others do, if Plato lived his life more admirably than did his contemporaries. The author's points about gold-digging — **A** and **B** — are not addressed in the discussion of Plato. Thoreau doesn't mention Plato's premises about morality (**D**). Mentioning Plato does nothing to change the tone of the essay (**E**), and it is highly unlikely that the author uses Plato merely to impress his readers.

32. **D.** Thoreau claims that he would not raise a finger for all the wealth of the world.

33. **C.** An aphorism, a brief, pointed statement of fundamental truth, is similar to proverb. Choice **C** fits this definition.

34. E. Thoreau suggests that, although gold-digging may appear to be an honest way to earn "food and raiment" to some, it harms society in the same way that gambling does; it "is not the same thing with the wages of honest toil." The author never implies that philosophers should work harder (**A**), that society is improving (**C**), or that hard work produces wisdom (**D**). In fact, he suggests the opposite: hard work can be the "enemy." Choice **B** is not an unstated assumption, but a paraphrase of an explicit statement.

35. B. The California gold rush, which some saw as an example of hard-working men diligently trying to get ahead, is used by this author as an example of immorality, of gambling in life. Thoreau doesn't compare gold-diggers to Greeks (**A**), explore relations of Orientals and Occidentals (**C**) (that relationship is only touched on), sensationalize (**D**), or criticize those who saw the gold rush as romantic (**E**) (he directly criticizes those who participate in the gold-digging).

36. B. Thoreau states that "cold and hunger seem more <u>friendly</u> to my nature." Cold and hunger, generally undesirable states, are here seen as better than man's methods of warding them off.

37. D. There is no syllogistic reasoning in this essay. The author does use simile ("The gold-digger . . . is as much gambler as his fellow in the saloons" — lines 104–106), historical allusion (to Plato and to the gold rush), rhetorical question (for example, "Does Wisdom work in a tread-mill?"), and religious reference (for example, mention of Mahomet and God).

38. A. Knowledge is more valuable than gold; wisdom will gild more surface than gold will.

39. D. The author is angry, indignant at mankind's unseemly pursuit of money.

40. C. This quotation is not part of the argument against gold-digging. It simply states a fact about gold.

41. A. Thoreau doesn't directly address man's improving his lot in life, although one can infer that he probably believes man should do so.

Fourth Passage

From "On Liberty" by John Stuart Mill.

42. C. The author makes this clear distinction in lines 13–17: the "only purpose for which power can be rightfully exercised over any member . . . is to prevent harm to others." Choices **A** and **B** are inaccurate statements of Mill's ideas, and choice **D** is not addressed. Mill does contend that children do not have sovereignty (**E**), but that contention is not the "one very simple principle."

43. E. The predicate nominative is the entire clause "that the sole end . . . self-protection." The clause states precisely what "That principle" is.

44. D. Mill insists that the only justification for controlling the acts of an individual is to prevent harm to others. No other answer choice names such individuals.

45. B. Parallel syntax is evident in the repetition of "or" plus a gerund: "or reasoning . . . or persuading . . . or entreating." None of the other answer choices can be found in this sentence.

46. C. Individuals have complete freedom in actions that affect only themselves — as Mill puts it, "Over himself, over his own body and mind." Choice **A** contradicts the passage, and **B, D,** and **E** are not addressed.

47. D. Children and "those backward states of society in which the race itself may be considered as in its nonage" (immaturity) may be forced to behave in a particular way by parent or government.

48. A. Despotism *is* acceptable "when dealing with barbarians" and when that form of government produces the improvement of its citizens. If this end is *not* achieved, despotism is unacceptable.

49. E. All of the choices, according to Mill, are allowable.

50. B. It can be inferred that, of the choices given, the author values the protection of society most highly. The essay deals primarily with the sovereignty of the individual except in matters of self-protection. But sovereignty of the individual is not among the answer choices. Choice **A** is incorrect because of the word "unlimited." Mill places restriction on individual freedom; it is not absolute.

51. A. The second paragraph gives exceptions to the general principle of individual sovereignty — in the case of children and of "backward states of society." The second paragraph does none of the things listed in choices **B** through **E**.

52. D. This is the major thrust of the essay. Choice **A** contradicts the passage. We have no way to determine Mill's opinion on whether Charlemagne would rule a mature society well (**B**); he is mentioned only as ruling a "backward society." Choices **C** and **E** can be eliminated because of the word "always."

53. D. The passage is presented in a matter-of-fact, analytical tone, without emotional wording. There is no evidence of sarcasm, cynicism, or pessimism. Nor is there any evidence of optimism; by acknowledging that it is at times necessary for a government to interfere in citizens' lives, Mill is more realistic than optimistic.

54. C. As we've seen, Mill does not encourage "absolute" freedom of action. He does not encourage behavior that harms others. While it is unlikely that Mill would strongly encourage people to indulge in "self-destructive" actions, he does assert that an individual should be free to do so, leaving **C** as the best answer.

55. E. Historical allusions are made to the governments of Akbar and Charlemagne. None of the other rhetorical devices is present in the essay.

56. B. The first paragraph is devoted to the assertion that a government may control individuals only to keep others from harm; the second paragraph gives exceptions to this general principle and lists children and barbarians as those who must be kept from harming themselves. Therefore, the purpose of the passage is one of explanation, of clarification. Mill does not preach against despotism (**A**), mention the harm of individual rights (**C**), or assert the sovereign rights of *every* individual (**E**). Choice **D** is incorrect. Mill suggests circumstances in which individual freedoms should be allowed, but he does not discuss "why" that is so.

Section II: Essay Questions

Question 1

Scoring Guide for Question 1
(M. F. K. Fisher and Maya Angelou)

8–9 This well-written essay clearly demonstrates understanding of the similarities of and differences between the effects of the two passages and the authors' handling of the resources of language in producing these effects. The paper supports its points with specific and cogently presented evidence from the passage. While the paper may contain a few minor errors, it demonstrates the ability to communicate effectively and precisely.

6–7 This essay, also well written, accurately identifies the effects of the two passages but perhaps in a less convincing manner than do top-scoring essays. The discussion of the handling of resources of language may be less thorough and specific. Connection between the thesis and the evidence may not be as clear as that found in top-scoring papers. Some errors in mechanics may occur, but overall, this essay shows satisfactory control over organization, development, and use of language.

5 This average essay shows a general understanding of the effects of the passages but may not present as clear a thesis concerning those effects. Its attempts to analyze the handling of resources of language may be simplistic, or evidence offered to support the essay's points may be insufficient and may not be clearly related to the author's use of the resources of language. The essay may be coherently organized but may show inconsistent control of diction.

3–4 This essay attempts to identify and discuss the effects of the passages but does so based on an inaccurate reading or with presentation of inadequate evidence. It may fail to complete all of the tasks given. This paper may simply catalog the devices, the resources of language, without analysis or comment on the connection between effect and language use. Weak control of the essay format and/or language may be evident, and mechanical errors may be frequent.

1–2 This essay fails to sufficiently respond to the question or the passage. It may fail to understand the effects of the passages, misreading them in a way that distorts those effects. Little or no attention may be given to resources of language used in the passages. This essay fails to convince the reader of its points, and its thesis may be shallow or nonexistent. Persistent weaknesses in grammar and organization may be evident.

High-Scoring Essay

Although M. F. K. Fisher's description of Marseille and Maya Angelou's description of Stamps both seek to dispel illusions of their places, they differ in the use of technique, tone, and diction. In the first passage, Fisher uses a satiric style to poke fun of Marseilles' misconceived reputation as "the world's wickedest port." In the other passage, Maya Angelou uses fantastic imagery to also reveal a faulty reputation, this time, of the South. Both authors are attempting to reform mistaken opinions of their places, but they both use extremely different techniques.

In his passage, M. F. K. Fisher seeks only to quell Marseilles' misrepresentation. By wryly examining articles describing Marseilles, Fisher never directly gives his impression of this French port, but instead he reveals the spurious nature of these descriptions. Throughout the passage, a satiric tone is employed. Before introducing Basil Woon's piece on Marseilles, Fisher writes "Some-times such journalese is almost worth reading for its precociously obsolete views." This statement ridicules Woon's work even before it is introduced. Contributing to the tone of his piece, Fisher not only derides the descriptions of Marseille, but also the backgrounds of their writers. Although Woon did not recommend visiting Marseilles, "he did remain true to his journalistic background with an expectedly titillating mention of it." Fisher masks an otherwise intense diatribe with the light-hearted, humorous use of satire.

The use of precise and informal diction also contributes to the effects of the first passage. In describing newspaper descriptions of Marseilles, the words "mile shockers" are used. The concise image formed by these words contributes to the informal mood of the passage. Also, instead of employing the more conservative and respected word "journalism," Fisher chose to use the word "journalese." This simple substitution embodies the essence of the passage. Like the word journalese, the passage continually ridicules writers' misrepresentations of Marseilles.

Using an opposite style of attack, Maya Angelou does not mock the faulty representation of the South. Instead she contrasts both a description of the "American fantasy" of the South with her own vivid impressions. The dream-like tone of the first paragraph is aided by the rich choice of diction. "Women float eternally" among "wisps of wisteria." Like paradise, the word eternally allows this scene of gentle alliteration to last forever.

This fantasy is contrasted in the remaining paragraphs with an intense, passionate tone of life. The descriptions, like smells "spiced with the odor of cattle manure, the yellowish acid of the ponds and rivers, the deep pots of greens and beans," are all concrete. These concrete images sharply contrast the ethereal images of women floating eternally. The misrepresentation of the South is easily dispelled by the reality of Maya Angelou's observations. Furthermore, the choice of diction is superb. Angelou's South was "flesh-real and swollen-belly poor." These words easily bring to mind the harshness of black life in the South. Towards the end of the passage, a metaphor is used to change the direction of the passage from concreteness into memories " . . . passions clanged with the ferocity of armored knights colliding." After erasing the erroneous images of the South, the passage prepares to tell Angelou's story.

Though these passages are similar in their goals, their distinct uses of diction and tone drastically differ their methods of dispelling illusions.

Analysis of the High-Scoring Essay

The paper begins by directly addressing the topic with a relevant comparison of the essays, pointing out that each "seek[s] to dispel illusions" of the perception of a location. This student recognizes that, although the essays have the same purpose, their differences lie in their stylistic choices. Such interesting ideas as these engage the reader.

The next two paragraphs analyze the Fisher passage on Marseille and together demonstrate a clear understanding of Fisher's use of humor and satire to ridicule those who have painted Marseille as the world's "wickedest port." The student supports the point with appropriate quotations from the passage. The second paragraph specifically analyzes and gives evidence for Fisher's purpose — to dispel the myths about Marseille — while the third paragraph explores how the language of the passage contributes to the effect. The student here uses effective organization and sophisticated diction, making this a strong section.

The fourth and fifth paragraphs deal with the Angelou passage, again analyzing the author's effect and the language used to create it. The analysis begins with Angelou's first paragraph, noting its differences from the Fisher passage — specifically, that she "does not mock the faulty representation" as Fisher does and noting that Angelou creates a "dream-like tone" contrasting with her own impressions. The analysis continues with a discussion of diction, noting how effectively Angelou dispels the misrepresentation of the South with her use of concrete images, an exploration of Angelou's use of metaphor, and an explanation of the metaphor's effect in introducing the realistic treatment, which would follow in the work.

The paper concludes with a brief summary of its point — that the authors have similar goals but differing techniques. Although the statement is not itself thought provoking, it is an adequate end to the essay. Overall, this student makes points clearly while demonstrating a competent command of language. The essay prompt asks specifically for a comparison and contrast of the "effect" of the two pieces, and this essay can be faulted because it, to some degree, confuses effect with purpose. The essay also misreads the tone of the Fisher passage as an "intense diatribe" and could benefit from additional evidence from the passages. On the whole, however, the paper is intelligent, articulate, and substantiated with enough evidence to make it an upper-half paper.

Medium-Scoring Essay

Although both passages describe places, their styles are very different. The first passage illustrates how most descriptions of Marseilles treat this city unfairly. This is accomplished through the author's humiliation of these articles. The second passage shows how most people's description of the South is wrong. But rather than through satire, this is accomplished through the use of imagery. Thus both pieces are similar in their effect, but are different in their author's handling of the resources of language.

The first piece by M. F. K. Fisher about the French port of Marseille succeeds in showing that writers about this place only tell the wrong side of the story. Although Marseille like all cities has its attractions and its good points, these writers unfairly give it "A legendary reputation as a world capital for 'dope, whores, and street violence.'" Thus this piece humiliates and satirizes those writers. The tone of this piece is very light and humorous, but it hides the meaning of the author's words.

For instance, "The familiar pitch had been made, and idle readers dreaming of a great seaport dedicated to heroin, prostitution, and rioting could easily skip the clumsy detail of marketing for fresh fish." By including the talk of fresh fish in the sentence, this passage is making a parody of the article where dope, whores, and street violence are combined with how to make a true boullabaisse. The other article that this passage also talks about says "Marseilles is the world's wickedest port." The passage ridicules this piece with the satiric sentence "Sometimes such journalese is almost worth reading for its precociously obsolete views of a society too easy to forget." This piece is sarcastically saying that readers should read this article because it is a great example of something bad. Therefore, this passage is able to use sarcasm, satire, and humiliation to show how Marseille is improperly represented by writers.

The second piece by Maya Angelou about the small town of Stamps, Arkansas tries to show how this place is also improperly represented. This is done by using imagery. First, that passage describes the South as "a much-loved region in the American fantasy where pale white women float eternally under black magnolia trees." These images who that the American fantasy is a peaceful, relaxed South where white people linger around. In fact, this image is wrong. In the next part of the passage, the south is shown in the harsh light reality. "The South I returned to, however, was flesh-real and swollen-belly poor." These images succeed in showing the harshness of life the African Americans led in the South. This sentence also shows this point. "And above all, the atmosphere was pressed down with the smell of old fears, and hates, and guilt. " The use of atmosphere adds to the depressingly real tone created by these images. Also a metaphor is used "passions clanged with the ferocity of armored knights colliding." This adds to the electrical atmosphere of the passage. By using such strong images to create the electrical atmosphere or the passage, the illusion of the first paragraph is shown for with it truly is. Therefore, this passage is able to use images, words, and atmosphere to show how Stamps, Arkansas is improperly represented by the American Fantasy of the South. The style of this passage is different from the other which humiliates the improper representation. Therefore, both passages use their author's handling of the resources of language in a different way to talk about the same effect.

Analysis of the Medium-Scoring Essay

The essay's introduction accurately addresses the topic. However, the student's writing style and depth of thought do not demonstrate the sophistication needed for a high-scoring essay. To claim merely that the two passages are "similar in effect, but . . . different" in their use of language only touches on the topic.

The second paragraph concentrates on Fisher's article and points out that Fisher humiliates (an inaccurate word in this context) and satirizes the authors who had presented Marseille as the "wickedest port." The student seems to recognize Fisher's effect but doesn't extend the observation, merely stating that Fisher is "making a parody" through use of sarcasm. Some examples from the passage are included but are treated perfunctorily and obviously, without depth or strong analysis.

The last paragraph also is accurate in its discussion but presents its points simplistically and uninterestingly. For example, "This sentence also shows the point" fails to connect the two examples effectively, and the claim that the use of metaphor creates an "electrical atmosphere" doesn't explain in what way "armored knights colliding" does so. This paragraph, as do those preceding, makes valid points but doesn't explore them in enough depth to engage or convince the reader. This essay could be greatly improved with the use of deeper analysis and more sophisticated presentation.

Question 2

Scoring Guide for Question 2 (William Hazlitt)

8–9 This well-written essay clearly demonstrates an understanding of Hazlitt's purpose in his discussion of comedy and its nature. In addition, it demonstrates a thorough comprehension of how Hazlitt's tone, point of view, and use of stylistic devices reflect that purpose. The thesis is thoughtful and articulate. Strong and relevant evidence from Hazlitt's essay supports intelligent insights concerning Hazlitt's purpose. Thoroughly convincing, this essay shows a clear command of essay-writing skills. Although it need not be without errors, the paper shows a mature style and use of language.

6–7 This essay comprehends Hazlitt's purpose, but its thesis may be less explicit than that of the top-scoring essay. The evidence offered may be less convincing, but the paper still demonstrates clear thinking. The connection between the evidence and Hazlitt's purpose may not be as clear as in the top-scoring essays. Although well written, the essay may show some errors while maintaining satisfactory control over diction and the essay's requirements.

5 This adequately written essay shows some understanding of Hazlitt's purpose but may not clearly comprehend the relationship between his language and that purpose. The writer may merely list the devices Hazlitt uses without relating them to his purpose. The thesis may be simplistic and the evidence insufficient to prove the writer's assertions. Acceptable organization and development may be evident, but the style may not be as sophisticated as that of higher-scoring essays.

3–4 This low-scoring essay fails to convince the reader. The weak presentation may not demonstrate a clear understanding of Hazlitt's purpose. Comprehension of how Hazlitt's manipulation of language reflects his purpose may be lacking. The thesis may be unsubstantiated, paragraph development may be weak and superficial thinking may be evident. Frequent errors in composition that distract the reader may be present.

1–2 This poorly written essay lacks coherence and clarity. It may attempt to state Hazlitt's purpose without any mention of how his language reflects his purpose. The thesis may be overly obvious or absent. Little or no evidence may be offered, and any connection between the evidence and the thesis may be shallow or nonexistent. The paper may be unusually short, and persistent grammatical problems may exist.

High-Scoring Essay

Two masks symbolize the theater, the one merry, joyful, the other weeping and forlorn. In its turn, the theater acts as a microcosm of life, its twin emblems representative of life's paramount elements: comedy coupled with tragedy.

William Hazlitt explores the relationship of comedy and tragedy, tears and laughter, in Lectures on the English Comic Writers. Hazlitt proposes that, like love and hate, mirth and sadness are not really the opposites that some assume them to be. Apathy is perhaps the true opposite of all four emotions. Both comedy and tragedy are intensely concerned with the human condition. Responses to comedy and tragedy are perhaps our most profound reflexive reactions to the world around us, so it is instructive to examine, as Hazlitt does, the similar foundations of the two.

Hazlitt's enthusiastic tone fits his purpose of persuasion. He writes as if he has just made an amazing discovery, and cannot wait to tell readers about his find. Exploring the nature of the two responses, comedy and tragedy, to the world, Hazlitt writes that both are spurred by man's perception of possibilities, and disappointment or joy results when these are not met, depending on the gravity or ludicrousness of the situation. Indeed comedy often issues from the wellsprings of tragedy and hurt. Laughter can be a defense mechanism, a protective response to the realities of the world and an opportunity to mock the frightening rather than cower before it.

Hazlitt's point of view has arguably become a part of the conventional wisdom these days. Comedy and tragedy are two sides of the same coin, he asserts. Comedy is made up of trifling tragedies. Not serious enough to wound, they instead inspire ridicule and heckling. Confusion can exist between the emotions: People often cry tears of joy on happy occasions or laugh inappropriately in the face of despair. Hazlitt successfully persuades readers of the inexorable relationship between the emotions.

Hazlitt's prose is brisk, almost breathless. Even though compounded with prepositional phrases and the like, the first paragraph of his essay speeds along with emphasized repetition: "We weep . . . we laugh . . . we shed tears . . . we burst into laughter." Hazlitt keeps the reader to a relentless pace with a series of phrases and clauses separated by commas and semicolons, filling long complex sentences. His last sentence in the essay effectively uses technique as it builds to a crescendo. The eureka tone of amazed discovery is in part achieved by a liberal smattering of exclamation points throughout the essay, such as "it is in a manner compounded of these two!" and "it fails to move our anger or our pity!" The gee whiz! tone which these literary techniques help to create does aid in persuading the reader that Hazlitt's conclusions are valid.

Hazlitt's skillful, rhythmic writing seems capable of lulling readers into believing anything he asserts. He accomplishes his purpose with an enthusiastic passage that clearly demonstrates the inseparable connection between laughter and tears. Understand that, and we are well on our way to understanding life.

Analysis of the High-Scoring Essay

This well-written essay begins with two paragraphs that immediately spark the reader's interest, mentioning the comic and tragic masks of the theater and then effectively relating the theater, as a "microcosm of life," to the essay's content and to the topic question. There is no thesis statement, but that isn't an absolute requirement. This student is definitely on the right track, addressing the issue of Hazlitt's purpose and his means of achieving it.

The next two paragraphs explore Hazlitt's point of view and his success in achieving his purpose and his perception of comedy and tragedy, relating that perception to contemporary society's. No strong evidence is presented in these paragraphs, but none is required in paragraphs that serve primarily to discuss Hazlitt's ideas.

The fifth paragraph presents an analysis of Hazlitt's technique and style, noting the use of repetition and aptly describing the essay's pace as "breathless . . . relentless." The student also notes that Hazlitt's use of exclamation points produces a "tone of amazed discovery." This writer demonstrates an accurate understanding of how a writer's technique can produce a specific effect on the reader.

The concluding paragraph reiterates the relationship of Hazlitt's "rhythmic writing" to his purpose but doesn't stop at mere summary. It points to the essay's wider implication — that through understanding laughter and tears, we can broaden our understanding of life. This student, like Hazlitt, demonstrates both lively style and discriminating diction.

Medium-Scoring Essay

William Hazlitt begins by describing the differences between humans and animals. He writes that man has the emotions of humor and sadness that animals don't because men see that things aren't always as good as they could be.

Sometimes people laugh, and sometimes people cry about life, depending on the situation. Through Hazlitt's use of tone and stylistic devices he achieves his purpose to convince the reader that comedy and tragedy spring from the same well of emotion and essentially help mankind to cope with the vicissitudes of life. People just react to life in different ways.

Depending on people and situations, this can be true. "It is a tragedy or a comedy — sad or merry, as it happens," Hazlitt wrote, showing that people can and do react in a different way to the same event. One of Hazlitt's reasons for writing is to prove that mankind needs different reactions; it is part of man's defense mechanism.

Hazlitt's tone tries to educate people about laughing and crying. Perhaps this is so people can feel less self conscious and work together better in the future without worrying whether their response is right or not, since there isn't a lot of difference between comedy and tragedy. So where one person might see one thing as tragic, the other person may not.

Hazlitt uses many literary devices so readers can picture the differing details of comedy and sadness he discusses. He says tragedy can "shock and wound the mind." He describes tears of relief about comedy or happy times without tragedy. He also uses repetition and exclamation to achieve his purpose. Readers now understand the relationship of comedy and tragedy, and agree with his conclusions.

Analysis of the Medium-Scoring Essay

This essay clearly demonstrates areas in which a student writing under time pressure can make mistakes. This paper has a variety of problems in coherence, organization, diction, and proof.

The first paragraph fails to elicit much excitement. A good AP essay doesn't necessarily have to grab attention, but this one is particularly uninteresting, merely paraphrasing Hazlitt's opening comment on humans and animals. The second paragraph improves. The student attempts to identify Hazlitt's purpose. But while the statement is well worded, it does not yet deal with one of the assigned tasks, a discussion of Hazlitt's technique.

The third and fourth paragraphs discuss Hazlitt's contentions, but perfunctorily and without great insight. Although Hazlitt's tone is mentioned at the beginning of the fourth paragraph, no analysis or examples follow. Weaknesses of this sort usually arise from inadequacies in planning and organization.

The last paragraph finally addresses literary devices and lists "repetition and exclamation," but once again, no evidence follows proving the connection between literary devices and purpose. Here, the student seems to be grasping for ideas and unsure of his or her point.

While this essay shows some understanding of Hazlitt's purpose, which is to be commended, attempts at proof, analysis, and discussion produce confused sentences with murky ideas. In addition, the student's language, while occasionally sophisticated, is more often than not simplistic. Cumulatively, the essay fails to convince the reader.

Question 3

Scoring Guide for Question 3 (Benjamin Franklin)

8–9 This well-written essay demonstrates clear ideas substantially supported by thoughtful, relevant evidence. It illustrates a sound awareness of the logical requirements of an argumentative essay. Stylistically, this essay is mature, using sophisticated sentence structure and diction. The writing need not be error-free, but it clearly shows the writer's ability to construct an effective essay through a combined command of language and logic.

7–6 This essay advances a thesis but may provide weaker evidence for it, although the writer's assertions are clear and well presented. The essay's style is appropriate to the task, but perhaps with less maturity than that of the top-scoring papers. Some errors in diction or syntax may be present, but the writer demonstrates satisfactory control over the conventions of writing and presents his or her ideas distinctly.

5 This essay may be tentative in its assertion of a thesis and may not provide sufficient evidence or discussion to thoroughly convince the reader. It may be adequately written but without control of the full range of elements of composition. Organization may be evident but not entirely effective.

3–4 This essay takes the initial steps toward a thesis but falls short in the details necessary to convince a reader. It attempts to convey a point of view but demonstrates weak control over diction, syntax, development, or organization. This essay may have frequent grammatical or spelling errors.

1–2 This essay lacks the clarity and persuasive force required for effective presentation of an argument. Some attempt may be made to address the issue, but with little or no evidence, the paper fails to satisfy the reader. It may be exceptionally short and poorly written on several counts. Organization and paragraph development may be particularly weak. Persistent weaknesses in grammar and spelling may distract the reader.

High-Scoring Essay

It is his reason that separates man from the creatures of the wild. Reason also fathers conscience, to act as a counterweight to the volatile animal passions of which his sentience has suddenly made him aware. If this were the only function of reason, to launch conscience, the world could theoretically be a better place. Imagine a society where a criminal, about to rob a hapless victim, stops as his mind reasons out the consequences. Reaching the reasonable conclusion that any punishment would be longer lasting and worse than the immediate benefits of his crime, the robber stops. Unfortunately, in reality, the human mind just does not work this way. Reason is not entirely an agent of good, of conscience. Reason can enter Promethean combat with the conscience it creates and shrewdly invent a means for its owner to justify some of his baser impulses.

Ben Franklin addresses man's propensity to justify and explain away his actions through reasoning, to allow caprices and animal impulses to persist. His Autobiography makes the valid point that once someone has his mind set on doing something, reason frequently acts as a tool to circumvent conscience rather than as an agent of that conscience.

Indeed, virtually any action can be justified through some semblance of reason, no matter how faulty the logic, how heinous the crime. For every violence, for every deceit, a dozen specious premises rise to the task of denying any wrongdoing by the criminal. For example, study the logic which convinced looters during any recent riots in American inner cities that they were justified in robbing innocent storekeepers. This kind of reasoning, sadly, occurs daily in the minds of humanity.

Empirical approaches to life, from the Socratic method to Hegelian philosophy, have relied on reason to explain both the natural world and the human response to that world. Moral relativism and "situational ethics" depend on reason of a sort. Proponents of such philosophies insist that man must abandon preconceptions, that he must judge each situation as it happens, and use reason to determine what is morally correct under each set of specific circumstances which arise. But it is not only relativists who look to reason as a means of understanding and reacting to the world. Strict, Draconian moral codes find their justification in reason as well. Man's actions, whether representing the "rule of law," or the most liberal definitions of right and wrong, are always defended with arguments paying homage to Reason. This holds as true for the Supreme Court justice as for the urban pickpocket . . . whether the subject feels he is doing the will of God and country, or knows he is shrewdly evading responsibility. Reason is the tool of man's shell game with his conscience.

Franklin, then, is essentially correct. After a moment of balancing "between principle and inclination," man seizes upon the "convenience" of being a "<u>reasonable creature</u>, since it enables one to find or make a reason for everything one has a mind to do." What one has a mind to do may be quixotic or craven, vainglorious or altruistic, but whatever the case man can use reason to nullify the conscience that is its offspring.

Analysis of the High-Scoring Essay

This high-scoring essay begins with a relevant discussion of reason and its function. Initiating the idea that "reason fathers conscience," the student provides a hypothetical example of a robber who stops in midcrime because his reason has convinced him the punishment would exceed the gain. The student's thesis follows, with the interesting concept that reason can engage in "Promethean combat" with the conscience to justify any human action.

The next paragraph acknowledges Ben Franklin as the inspiration for this topic and capsulizes Franklin's remarks about reason. This paragraph serves as direct tie to the essay question.

The third paragraph suggests that humans use reason to justify any kind of action, even immoral ones, and provides another relevant example, looters during recent riots who feel justified in their unlawful actions.

The fourth paragraph includes an intelligent review of several philosophies and "empirical approaches" that use reason as a way of determining one's actions. This paragraph notes that all those taking positions, from Supreme Court justices to common thieves, use reason to justify actions. The paragraph ends with a somewhat mixed but still effective metaphor — "reason is the tool of man's shell game with his conscience."

The concluding paragraph mentions again Franklin's insight, that humans will always find a reasonable way to explain any action. The student once more uses sophisticated style and diction with phrasing like "quixotic or craven, vainglorious or altruistic." This writer possesses the command of language evidenced only in top-scoring essays. This essay might be improved if it recognized Franklin's obviously playful tone and responded in kind, at least to some extent. But, overall, the paper is on topic, philosophically insightful, and intelligently presented and provides sufficient convincing examples from real-life situations.

Medium-Scoring Essay

Ben Franklin is one of our most important Founding Fourfathers. Like Alexander Hamilton and others who never achieved the presidency, he still had a profound impact on the U.S. His importance is shown in his autobiography, where he discusses vegetarianism and the morality of eating fish among other topics.

Ben Franklin contemplates how people can change their mind about things, such as whether it's O.K. to eat animals that have been alive (like fish). He acknowledges that sometimes people are tempted to do something they might think wrong, just as he was tempted by the delightful smell of fish cooking when he was on a boat trip. Franklin also explains that people use reason to approve their actions. His ideas about reason are right. Man frequently employs reason to back up his deeds, whether they are right or wrong. It seems that everyone can find a way to defend their actions. I have personally seen this trait at work, both in myself and my friends.

By using reason, Franklin proved that eating the fish, even though he believed in vegetarianism before, wasn't wrong after all. In the end, Ben Franklin says that it is a good thing that he is a reasonable creature. He means that he was reasonable enough to be open-minded about eating fish; he changed his mind accordingly after listening to his reason. I think Franklin was correct in this point too. It's important to be open-minded about things and not to eliminate what you're willing to try. Like Franklin, we shouldn't be scared to try something new if our reason can explain it to us.

Thus, Ben Franklin shows that reason is a valid tool in helping man to defend his actions, because without reason his actions might be stuck in the same old ways He would never try some thing new. And Benjamin Franklin, as he was a great man of our country, is someone to whom that was important.

Analysis of the Medium-Scoring Essay

This poorly written essay would score at the bottom of the medium range. The first paragraph is ineffective. It fails to address the question of the validity of Franklin's assertions on justifying one's actions through reasoning. The paragraph lacks a thesis and includes such irrelevant information as the reference to Alexander Hamilton. The student also demonstrates weak command of language, misusing words such as "Founding Fourfathers."

The second paragraph improves a bit and approaches the topic. Beginning with a paraphrase of Franklin's fish-eating experience, the student gives an opinion on the validity of using reason. But this thesis is especially weak, merely claiming that Franklin was "right." The writer offers no evidence to convince the reader, but rather claims only to have personally seen some examples.

The next paragraph discusses the need for one to be reasonable in order to try new things. The writer is on shaky ground once again, exhibiting simplistic ideas with no support.

The conclusion merely summarizes the essay and still avoids the topic. This essay deserves a low score because it offers no proof for its assertions, its treatment of the topic is superficial, and its presentation is riddled with errors and unsophisticated diction.

Answer Sheet for Practice Test 3

(Remove This Sheet and Use it to Mark Your Answers)

Section I
Multiple-Choice Questions

PASSAGE 1

1 Ⓐ Ⓑ Ⓒ Ⓓ Ⓔ
2 Ⓐ Ⓑ Ⓒ Ⓓ Ⓔ
3 Ⓐ Ⓑ Ⓒ Ⓓ Ⓔ
4 Ⓐ Ⓑ Ⓒ Ⓓ Ⓔ
5 Ⓐ Ⓑ Ⓒ Ⓓ Ⓔ
6 Ⓐ Ⓑ Ⓒ Ⓓ Ⓔ
7 Ⓐ Ⓑ Ⓒ Ⓓ Ⓔ
8 Ⓐ Ⓑ Ⓒ Ⓓ Ⓔ
9 Ⓐ Ⓑ Ⓒ Ⓓ Ⓔ
10 Ⓐ Ⓑ Ⓒ Ⓓ Ⓔ
11 Ⓐ Ⓑ Ⓒ Ⓓ Ⓔ
12 Ⓐ Ⓑ Ⓒ Ⓓ Ⓔ
13 Ⓐ Ⓑ Ⓒ Ⓓ Ⓔ
14 Ⓐ Ⓑ Ⓒ Ⓓ Ⓔ
15 Ⓐ Ⓑ Ⓒ Ⓓ Ⓔ

PASSAGE 2

16 Ⓐ Ⓑ Ⓒ Ⓓ Ⓔ
17 Ⓐ Ⓑ Ⓒ Ⓓ Ⓔ
18 Ⓐ Ⓑ Ⓒ Ⓓ Ⓔ
19 Ⓐ Ⓑ Ⓒ Ⓓ Ⓔ
20 Ⓐ Ⓑ Ⓒ Ⓓ Ⓔ
21 Ⓐ Ⓑ Ⓒ Ⓓ Ⓔ
22 Ⓐ Ⓑ Ⓒ Ⓓ Ⓔ
23 Ⓐ Ⓑ Ⓒ Ⓓ Ⓔ
24 Ⓐ Ⓑ Ⓒ Ⓓ Ⓔ
25 Ⓐ Ⓑ Ⓒ Ⓓ Ⓔ
26 Ⓐ Ⓑ Ⓒ Ⓓ Ⓔ
27 Ⓐ Ⓑ Ⓒ Ⓓ Ⓔ
28 Ⓐ Ⓑ Ⓒ Ⓓ Ⓔ

PASSAGE 3

29 Ⓐ Ⓑ Ⓒ Ⓓ Ⓔ
30 Ⓐ Ⓑ Ⓒ Ⓓ Ⓔ
31 Ⓐ Ⓑ Ⓒ Ⓓ Ⓔ
32 Ⓐ Ⓑ Ⓒ Ⓓ Ⓔ
33 Ⓐ Ⓑ Ⓒ Ⓓ Ⓔ
34 Ⓐ Ⓑ Ⓒ Ⓓ Ⓔ
35 Ⓐ Ⓑ Ⓒ Ⓓ Ⓔ
36 Ⓐ Ⓑ Ⓒ Ⓓ Ⓔ
37 Ⓐ Ⓑ Ⓒ Ⓓ Ⓔ
38 Ⓐ Ⓑ Ⓒ Ⓓ Ⓔ
39 Ⓐ Ⓑ Ⓒ Ⓓ Ⓔ
40 Ⓐ Ⓑ Ⓒ Ⓓ Ⓔ
41 Ⓐ Ⓑ Ⓒ Ⓓ Ⓔ
42 Ⓐ Ⓑ Ⓒ Ⓓ Ⓔ

PASSAGE 4

43 Ⓐ Ⓑ Ⓒ Ⓓ Ⓔ
44 Ⓐ Ⓑ Ⓒ Ⓓ Ⓔ
45 Ⓐ Ⓑ Ⓒ Ⓓ Ⓔ
46 Ⓐ Ⓑ Ⓒ Ⓓ Ⓔ
47 Ⓐ Ⓑ Ⓒ Ⓓ Ⓔ
48 Ⓐ Ⓑ Ⓒ Ⓓ Ⓔ
49 Ⓐ Ⓑ Ⓒ Ⓓ Ⓔ
50 Ⓐ Ⓑ Ⓒ Ⓓ Ⓔ
51 Ⓐ Ⓑ Ⓒ Ⓓ Ⓔ
52 Ⓐ Ⓑ Ⓒ Ⓓ Ⓔ
53 Ⓐ Ⓑ Ⓒ Ⓓ Ⓔ
54 Ⓐ Ⓑ Ⓒ Ⓓ Ⓔ
55 Ⓐ Ⓑ Ⓒ Ⓓ Ⓔ
56 Ⓐ Ⓑ Ⓒ Ⓓ Ⓔ

Practice Test 3

Section I: Multiple-Choices Questions

Time: 60 minutes

56 Questions

Directions: This section consists of selections from prose works and questions on their content, form, and style. Read each selection carefully. Choose the best answer of the five choices.

Questions 1–15. Read the following passage carefully before you begin to answer the questions.

First Passage

At Oxford in 1850 the contemporaries of young Robert Cecil agreed that he would end as Prime Minister either because or in spite of his remorselessly un-
(5) compromising opinions. Throughout life he never bothered to restrain them. His youthful speeches were remarkable for their virulence and insolence; he was not, said Disraeli, "a man who measures
(10) his phrases." A "salisbury" became a synonym for a political imprudence. He once compared the Irish in their incapacity for self-government to Hottentots and spoke of an Indian candidate for
(15) Parliament as "that black man." In the opinion of Lord Morley his speeches were always a pleasure to read because "they were sure to contain one blazing indiscretion which it is a delight to re-
(20) member." Whether these were altogether accidental is open to question, for though Lord Salisbury delivered his speeches without notes, they were worked out in his head beforehand and
(25) emerged clear and perfect in sentence structure. In that time the art of oratory was considered part of the equipment of a statesman and anyone reading from a written speech would have been re-
(30) garded as pitiable. When Lord Salisbury spoke, "every sentence," said a fellow member, "seemed essential, as articulate, as vital to the argument as the members of his body an athlete."
(35) Appearing in public before an audience about whom he cared nothing, Salisbury was awkward; but in the Upper House, where he addressed his equals, he was perfectly and strikingly at
(40) home. He spoke sonorously, with an occasional change of tone to icy mockery or withering sarcasm. When a recently ennobled Whig took the floor to lecture the House of Lords in high-flown and
(45) solemn Whig sentiments, Salisbury asked a neighbor who the speaker was and on hearing the whispered identification, replied perfectly audibly, "I

GO ON TO THE NEXT PAGE

thought he was dead." When he listened (50) to others he could become easily bored, revealed by a telltale wagging of his leg which seemed to one observer to be saying, "When will all this be over?" Or sometimes, raising his heels off the (55) floor, he would set up a sustained quivering of his knees and legs which could last for half an hour at a time. At home, when made restless by visitors, it shook the floor and made the furniture rattle, (60) and in the House his colleagues on the front bench complained it made them seasick. If his legs were at rest his long fingers would be in motion, incessantly twisting and turning a paper knife or (65) beating a tattoo on his knee or on the arm of his chair. . . .

Mr. Gladstone, though, in political philosophy his bitterest antagonist, acknowledged him "a great gentleman in (70) private society." In private life he was delightful and sympathetic and a complete contrast to his public self. In public acclaim, Salisbury was uninterested, for — since the populace was unin- (75) structed — its opinions, as far as he was concerned, were worthless. He ignored the public and neither possessed nor tried to cultivate the personal touch that makes a political leader a recognizable (80) personality to the man in the street and earns him a nickname like "Pam" or "Dizzy" or the "Grand Old Man." Not in the press, not even in *Punch,* was Lord Salisbury ever called anything but Lord (85) Salisbury. He made no attempt to conceal his dislike for mobs of all kinds, "not excluding the House of Commons." After moving to the Lords, he never

returned to the Commons to listen to its (90) debates from the Peers Gallery or chat with members in the Lobby, and if compelled to allude to them in his own House, would use a tone of airy contempt, to the amusement of visitors from (95) the Commons who came to hear him. But this was merely an outward pose designed to underline his deep inner sense of the patrician. He was not rank-conscious; he was indifferent to honors or (100) any other form of recognition. It was simply that as a Cecil, and a superior one, he was born with a consciousness in his bones and brain cells of ability to rule and saw no reason to make any con- (105) cessions of this prescriptive right to anyone whatever.

Having entered the House of Commons in the customary manner for peers' sons, from a family-controlled (110) borough in an uncontested election at the age of twenty-three, and, during his fifteen years in the House of Commons, having been returned unopposed five times from the same borough, and hav- (115) ing for the last twenty-seven years sat in the House of Lords, he had little personal experience of vote-getting. He regarded himself not as responsible *to* the people but as responsible *for* them. They (120) were in his care. What reverence he felt for anyone was directed not down but up — to the monarchy. He revered Queen Victoria, who was some ten years his senior, both as her subject and, with (125) chivalry toward her womanhood, as a man. For her he softened his brusqueness even if at Balmoral he could not conceal his boredom.

1. In relation to the passage as a whole, the first sentence of the first paragraph presents

   A. a paradox that reveals a dominant characteristic of Lord Salisbury's character

   B. a criticism of Lord Salisbury that the rest of the passage will withdraw

   C. a definition of the principles upon which Lord Salisbury was to base his life

   D. an exception to the ideas that make up the rest of the passage

   E. an amusing comment with no important relevance to the development of the rest of the passage

2. Disraeli's description of Lord Salisbury as not "a man who measure his phrases" (lines 9–10) is an example of

   A. simile

   B. understatement

   C. indirect discourse

   D. *ad hominem* argument

   E. diatribe

3. Compared to the second, third, and fourth paragraphs, the first paragraph makes more extensive use of

   A. direct quotations from Lord Salisbury himself

   B. direct quotations from Lord Salisbury's contemporaries

   C. cause-and-effect reasoning

   D. *ad hominem* argument

   E. abstract generalizations

4. Which of the following best describes the function of the second paragraph of the passage?

   A. It makes an assertion that is proven in the third paragraph.

   B. It defines more clearly the flaws of Lord Salisbury's character.

   C. It develops the ideas of Lord Salisbury's "political imprudence."

   D. It enlarges the characterization begun in the first paragraph.

   E. It refutes a common misconception about Lord Salisbury.

5. We can infer that Salisbury was awkward before an audience he cared little about (paragraph two) because he

   A. was speaking without notes

   B. lacked public-speaking skills

   C. had not bothered to prepare

   D. was nervous about appearing before an audience that he feared was unsympathetic to his ideas

   E. feared he would betray his real feelings of contempt

6. In line 65, the word "tattoo" can be best defined as a

   A. rhythm

   B. continuous drumming

   C. picture on the skin

   D. forbidden activity

   E. percussion instrument

GO ON TO THE NEXT PAGE

7. In the first sentence of the third paragraph, the author cites Gladstone's words about Lord Salisbury because

   I. they have the special authority of words of praise from a political opponent

   II. they introduce a favorable presentation of Lord Salisbury's private life

   III. it would especially embarrass Lord Salisbury to be praised by a political enemy

   A. II only

   B. I and II only

   C. I and III only

   D. II and III only

   E. I, II, and III

8. From the phrase in the third paragraph "not in the press, not even in *Punch,* was Lord Salisbury ever called anything but Lord Salisbury," we can infer that *Punch* was probably a

   A. contemporary novel

   B. political report

   C. conservative magazine

   D. satirical publication

   E. daily newspaper

9. In the last sentence of the third paragraph, all of the following words or phrases function as intensifiers and could be omitted EXCEPT

   A. "simply"

   B. "and brain cells"

   C. "no reason"

   D. "any"

   E. "whatever"

10. Which of the following accurately describe(s) the long sentence which begins the last paragraph of the passage ("Having entered . . . vote-getting")?

   I. It is a sentence containing more than ten prepositional phrases.

   II. It is a sentence using parallel participial phrases.

   III. It is a periodic sentence.

   A. I only

   B. I and II only

   C. I and III only

   D. II and III only

   E. I, II, and III

11. To which of the following would Lord Salisbury have been most likely to have shown deference?

   A. the Prince of Wales

   B. the President of the United States

   C. the elderly female newspaper-seller

   D. the British Prime Minister

   E. a Scottish knight

12. The speaker of the passage may be best described as

   A. a skeptical biographer

   B. a political supporter

   C. a sympathetic observer

   D. a mordant satirist

   E. an objective commentator

13. In its presentation of the character of Lord Salisbury, the passage overtly employs all of the following sources EXCEPT the

    A. words of contemporary politicians

    B. author's interpretation of Lord Salisbury's actions

    C. words of Lord Salisbury himself

    D. judgments of other modern historians

    E. words of unnamed contemporaries of Lord Salisbury

14. Which of the following does the passage present as central to an understanding of Lord Salisbury?

    A. His deep-seated fear of the possibility of major social change

    B. His intense consciousness of his social rank

    C. His hypocrisy

    D. His genuine respect for men and women of all classes

    E. His firm belief in the native superiority of his family

15. The passage reveals all of the following biographical facts about Lord Salisbury EXCEPT that he

    A. served in the House of Commons

    B. was a contemporary of Queen Victoria and of Gladstone

    C. disapproved of home rule for Ireland

    D. served in the House of Lords

    E. became Prime Minister late in the nineteenth century

Questions 16–28. Read the following passage carefully before you begin to answer the questions.

Second Passage: Of Democracy

The Power that makes the laws knows better than any other person how they ought to be executed and how inter-preted. It seems from this that the best (5) constitution would be that where the legislative and executive powers are united: but that very union is the thing which renders this government to unsat-isfactory in certain respects, because (10) those things which ought to be distin-guished are not, and because the prince and the Sovereign, then the same, form in a manner a government without a government.

(15) It is not good for the power that makes the laws to execute them; neither would it be proper that the body of the people should turn their eyes from gen-eral views to fix them on particular ob-(20) jects. Nothing is more dangerous than private interest having any influence on public affairs, and the abuse of the laws by the government is a lesser evil than the corruption of the legislator, which (25) is an infallible consequence of such private views. In such a case, the very substance of the State is changed, and all reformation becomes impossible.

GO ON TO THE NEXT PAGE

A people who never abused the powers (30) of government would never abuse independence; a people who always governed well would have no need to be governed.

Taking the word "democracy" in its (35) strict sense, perhaps there never did, and never will, exist such a government. It is against the natural order that the greater number should govern, and the smaller number be governed. It cannot be imag- (40) ined that the chief part of the people should be always assembled for the discharge of public affairs, and it is evident that commissioners cannot be appointed to govern without the form or adminis- (45) tration changing.

In fact, I believe it may be laid down as a principle that, when the function of government are divided among a number of tribunals, the fewer in number (50) will sooner or later acquire the greatest authority, if it were for no other reason than because affairs will be transacted with greatest ease and expedition in fewest hands, which naturally brings (55) them control of affairs.

Besides, how many circumstances must conspire to make such government possible! First, the State must be a very small one, where the people can easily (60) assemble, and where each citizen can easily know all the others; there must, in the second place, be great simplicity of manners to prevent a multiplicity of affairs and those tedious discussions (65) which are the consequence of them; and there must also be much equality in the rank and fortunes of all the citizens, or there will not be equality of rights and authority for long; finally there must be (70) little or no luxury, for whether luxury be considered as the effect of riches, or as the incitement to covet them, it corrupts

at once both the wealthy and the poor, the one by its possession, the other by (75) the desire of possessing; it betrays a nation into effeminate softness, and debases it by vanity; and it takes away all the citizens from the State by making them subservient to each other, and all (80) the slaves of opinion.

This is the reason why a celebrated author[1] has made virtue the principle on which a republic must be founded; because all these circumstances could (85) never subsist without her ruling influence. But this fine genius has not only omitted making the necessary distinctions, but he is not always exact, and sometimes obscure, and he did not per- (90) ceive that, the sovereign authority being everywhere the same, the same principle must prevail in every well-formed State, though in a greater or less degree, according to its form of government.

(95) I must yet add that there is no government so subject to civil wars and internal agitations as the democratic or popular one, because there is not one which has so strong and so continual a tendency to (100) change its form, or which needs more vigilance and courage to maintain it. This is the constitution which, more than any other, requires the citizen to arm himself with strength and constancy, and (105) to repeat every day of his life what a virtuous Palatine[2] said in the Diet of Poland: *Mal Pericolosam Libertatem Quam Quietum Servitum.[3]*

If there were a nation of gods they (110) might be governed by a democracy. So perfect a government will not agree with men.

Notes: (1) Montesquieu, from *The Spirit of Laws*, Book III, chapter 3., (2) The Palatine of Posen, father of the King of Poland., (3) "Better liberty with danger than peace with slavery."

16. Which of the following does the author cite as possibly a major danger to democracy?

    A. Overcrowded courts

    B. Ineffective committees

    C. Power-hungry leaders

    D. Organized religion

    E. Private enterprise

17. According to the author, which of the following tribunals would be most efficient?

    A. One that represents all socioeconomic levels

    B. One with the fewest members

    C. One of all legislators

    D. One with an equal number of legislators and private interest groups

    E. One made up of experts on the issue

18. Adding to the coherency of the second sentence in the fifth paragraph (lines 58–80) is

    A. heavy use of extended metaphor

    B. persuasive and argumentative tone

    C. complex use of parallel structure

    D. biting condemnation of democracy

    E. use of ironic hyperbole

19. The fifth paragraph (lines 56–80) differs from the other paragraphs in that it

    A. defines how a democracy could be possible

    B. criticizes present democracies

    C. ridicules those who believe in democracy

    D. suggests the ease of implementing a democracy

    E. hypothesizes the traits of a good leader

20. According to the passage, which of the following groups is most likely to function smoothly under a democracy?

    A. Perfect, godlike people

    B. Lawmakers

    C. Minorities

    D. Political leaders

    E. Private business owners

21. It can be inferred from the passage that the foremost obstacle to democracy is

    A. civil war

    B. seditious legislators

    C. avaricious capitalists

    D. the natural order

    E. inequality among citizens

GO ON TO THE NEXT PAGE

22. According to the author, which of the following conditions is/are necessary for an efficient democracy?

    I. Financial equality

    II. Enthusiastic obedience

    III. Simple, uncomplicated lifestyle

    A. I only

    B. I and II only

    C. I and III only

    D. II and III only

    E. I, II, and III

23. The organization of each of the essay's body paragraphs can best be described as presenting

    A. a further discussion of previous tangents

    B. an aspect of democracy and discussion of the aspect

    C. comparison and contrast

    D. strong, persuasive arguments

    E. specific examples illustrating suppositions

24. Which of the following best represents the paradox the author sees in democracy?

    A. "the best constitution . . . so unsatisfactory" (lines 4–9)

    B. "the prince and the Sovereign . . . government without a government" (lines 11–14)

    C. "Nothing is more dangerous than . . . public affairs" (lines 20–22)

    D. "a people who always . . . no need to be governed" (lines 29–33)

    E. "Taking the word . . . such a government." (lines 34–36)

25. The essay may best be characterized as

    A. exposition

    B. argumentation

    C. description

    D. narration

    E. demonstration

26. Of the following phrases, which demonstrates the most condescending attitude?

    A. "a government without a government" (lines 13–14)

    B. "infallible consequence" (line 25)

    C. "those tedious discussions" (line 64)

    D. "needs more vigilance and courage" (lines 100–101)

    E. "will not agree with men" (lines 111–112)

27. Which of the following, if present, would best strengthen the author's argument?

    A. A comparison of democracy with monarchy

    B. Other expert opinions

    C. A historical background of democracies

    D. Examples of more efficient forms of government

    E. Examples of incompetent laws

28. The author's overall attitude toward democracy may best be described as

A. aggressive

B. vituperative

C. moderate

D. skeptical

E. sanguine

Third Passage

This single stick, which you now behold ingloriously lying in that neglected corner, I once knew in a flourishing state in a forest; it was full of sap, full of
(5) leaves, and full of boughs; but now, in vain, does the busy art of man pretend to vie with nature, by tying that withered bundle of twigs to its sapless trunk; 'tis now, at best, but the reverse of what it
(10) was, a tree turned upside down, the branches on the earth, and the root in the air; 'tis now handled by every dirty wench, condemned to do her drudgery, and, by a capricious kind of fate, des-
(15) tined to make other things clean, and be nasty itself; at length, worn to the stumps in the service of the maids, either thrown out of doors, or condemned to the last use, of kindling a fire. When I
(20) beheld this, I sighed, and said within myself: *Surely Man is a Broomstick!* Nature sent him into the world strong and lusty, in a thriving condition, wearing his own hair on his head, the proper
(25) branches of this reasoning vegetable, until the axe of intemperance has lopped off his green boughs, and left him a withered trunk; he then flies to art, and puts on a periwig, valuing himself upon
(30) an unnatural bundle of hairs (all covered with powder) that never grew on his head; but now should this our broomstick pretend to enter the scene, proud of all those birchen spoils it never bore,
(35) and all covered with dust, though the sweepings of the finest lady's chamber, we should be apt to ridicule and despise its vanity. Partial judges that we are of our own excellences, and other men's
(40) defaults!

But a broomstick, perhaps you will say, is an emblem of a tree standing on its head; and pray, what is a man but a topsy-turvy creature, his animal facul-
(45) ties perpetually mounted on his rational, his head where his heels should be, groveling on the earth! And yet, with all his faults, he sets up to be a universal reformer and corrector of abuses, a re-
(50) mover of grievances, rakes into every slut's corner of nature, bringing hidden corruption to the light, and raises a mighty dust where there was none before; sharing deeply all the while in the
(55) very same pollutions he pretends to sweep away; his last days are spent in slavery to women, and generally the least deserving; till, worn out to the stumps, like his brother broom, he is ei-
(60) ther kicked out of doors, or made use of to kindle flames for others to warm themselves by.

GO ON TO THE NEXT PAGE

29. All of the following are present in the opening sentence of the passage EXCEPT

- **A.** syntactically complex structure
- **B.** parallel construction
- **C.** a pedantic tone
- **D.** the narrative of a broomstick's life
- **E.** subordinate clauses

30. According to the author, both a broomstick and a man

- **A.** cleanse the world
- **B.** become corrupted by the evil in society
- **C.** can be proud of their humble accomplishments
- **D.** symbolize integrity in the world
- **E.** were untainted in their natural state

31. Which of the following does the author imply?

  I. Man has the ability to return to a better state.

 II. Man in his youthful, natural state is closer to perfection than when he is older.

III. Man misuses nature for his own needs.

- **A.** I only
- **B.** II only
- **C.** I and II only
- **D.** II and III only
- **E.** I, II, and III

32. According to the passage, the broomstick symbolizes

- **A.** society's corruption of the youth
- **B.** the goodness in nature that man uses and discards
- **C.** the triumph of nature over man's evil tendencies
- **D.** the evil inherent in man's soul
- **E.** the tremendous power of nature that man fears

33. The "axe of intemperance" (line 26) can be interpreted as

- **A.** an understatement of man's dominance over nature
- **B.** a metaphor for nature's nourishing elements
- **C.** a simile comparing man and tree
- **D.** a hyperbole describing man's destruction
- **E.** a metaphor for man's excesses

34. The author's attitude toward mankind can best be described as

- **A.** disillusionment at man's deeds
- **B.** perplexed concern for man's future
- **C.** guarded optimism for man's soul
- **D.** anger at the society man has created
- **E.** sincere praise for man's use of nature

35. Which of the following does NOT demonstrate a negative attitude by this author?

    A. "a flourishing state in a forest" (lines 3–4)

    B. "the axe of intemperance" (line 26)

    C. "an unnatural bundle of hairs" (line 30)

    D. "sweepings of the finest lady's chamber" (line 36)

    E. "sharing . . . the very same pollutions he pretends to sweep away" (lines 54–56)

36. According to the author, which of the following is NOT a similarity between man and the broomstick?

    A. Both endure the same fate.

    B. Both began life in a healthy state.

    C. Both are turned "topsy-turvy."

    D. Both accomplish magnificent achievements.

    E. Both attempt to cleanse while being dirty.

37. The word referred to by the phrase "this reasoning vegetable" (line 25) is

    A. *"Man"* (line 21)

    B. "hair" (line 24)

    C. "head" (line 24)

    D. "branches" (line 25)

    E. "green boughs" (line 27)

38. In the essay, the author uses all of the following literary devices EXCEPT

    A. metaphor

    B. parallel syntax

    C. oxymoron

    D. analogy

    E. symbolism

39. In context, "this our broomstick" (lines 32–33) is a

    A. symbol for the thriving forest

    B. metaphor for man's pretentious character

    C. link between nature and society

    D. demonstration of nature's control

    E. representation of man's intelligence

40. What does the author imply about man's ability to be a "corrector of abuses" (line 49)?

    A. Man easily solves his own problems.

    B. Man effectively improves society.

    C. Man can act as a fair arbitrator in disputes.

    D. Man readily accepts his role as a social reformer.

    E. Man causes problems where none previously existed.

GO ON TO THE NEXT PAGE

41. The tone of the passage can best be
described as

A. neutral toward society

B. condescending toward nature

C. cynical toward mankind

D. bellicose toward mankind

E. dogmatic toward society

42. Which of the following represents the
strongest statement of the author's
theme?

A. "condemned to do her drudgery"
(line 13)

B. "destined to make other things
clean" (lines 14–15)

C. "the axe of intemperance has
lopped off his green boughs"
(lines 26–27)

D. "Partial judges that we are of our
own excellences" (lines 38–39)

E. "his last days are spent in slavery"
(lines 56–57)

*Questions 43–56. Read the following passage carefully before you begin to answer the
questions*

Fourth Passage

The time is coming, I hope, when
each new author, each new artist, will be
considered, not in his proportion to any
other author or artist, but in his relation
(5) to the human nature, known to us all,
which is his privilege, his high duty, to
interpret. "The true standard of the artist
is in every man's power" already, as
[Edmund] Burke says; Michelangelo's
(10) "light of the piazza," the glance of the
common eye, is and always was the best
light on a statue; . . . but hitherto the
mass of common men have been afraid
to apply their own simplicity, natural-
(15) ness, and honesty to the appreciation of
the beautiful. They have always cast
about for the instruction of some one
who professed to know better, and who
browbeat wholesome common-sense
(20) into the self-distrust that ends in sophistication . . . They have been taught to
compare what they see and what they
read, not with the things that they have

observed and known, but with the things
(25) that some other artist or writer has done.
Especially if they have themselves the
artistic impulse in any direction they are
taught to form themselves, not upon life,
but upon the masters who became mas-
(30) ters only by forming themselves upon
life. The seeds of death are planted in
them, and they can only produce the
still-born, the academic. They are not
told to take their work into the public
(35) square and see if it seems true to the
chance passer, but to test it by the work
of the very men who refused and decried
any other test of their won work. The
young writer who attempts to report the
(40) phrase and carriage of every-day life,
who tries to tell just how he has heard
men talk and seen them look, is made to
feel guilty of something low and unwor-
thy by the stupid people who would like
(45) to have him show how Shakespeare's
men talked and looked, or Scott's,

or Thackeray's, or Balzac's, or Hawthorne's, or Dickens's; he is in-
structed to idealize his personages, that
(50) is, to take the life-likeness out of them,
and put the book-likeness into them. He
is approached in the spirit of the
wretched pedantry into which learning . . .
always decays when it withdraws itself
(55) and stands apart from experience in an
attitude of imagined superiority, and
which would say with the same confidence to the scientist: "I see that you are
looking at a grasshopper there which
(60) you have found in the grass, and I suppose you intend to describe it. Now
don't waste your time and sin against
culture in that way. I've got a grasshopper here, which has been evolved at con-
(65) siderable pains and expense out of the
grasshopper in general; in fact, it's a
type. It's made up of wire and cardboard, very prettily painted in a conventional tint, and it's perfectly
(70) indestructible. It isn't very much like a
real grasshopper, but it's a great deal
nicer, and it's served to represent the notion of a grasshopper ever since man
emerged from barbarianism. You may
(75) say that it's artificial. Well, it is artificial;
but then it's ideal too; and what you
want to do is to cultivate the ideal. You'll
find the books full of my kind of
grasshopper, and scarcely a trace of
(80) yours in any of them. The thing that you
are proposing to do is commonplace; but
if you say that it isn't commonplace, for
the very reason that it hasn't been done
before, you'll have to admit that it's
(85) photographic."

I hope the time is coming when not
only the artist, but the common, average
man, who always "has the standard of
the arts in his power," will have also the
(90) courage to apply it, and will reject the
ideal grasshopper wherever he finds it,
in science, in literature, in art, because it
is not "simple, natural, and honest," because it is not like a real grasshopper.
(95) But . . . I think the time is yet far off, and
that the people who have been brought
up on the ideal grasshopper, the heroic
grasshopper, the impassioned grasshopper, the self-devoted, adventureful, good
(100) old romantic cardboard grasshopper,
must die out before the simple, honest,
and natural grasshopper can have a fair
field. I am in no haste to compass the
end of these good people, whom I find
(105) in the meantime very amusing. It is delightful to meet one of them, either in
print or out of it some sweet elderly
lady or excellent gentleman whose
youth was pastured on the literature of
(110) thirty or forty years ago — and to wit-
ness the confidence with which they
preach their favorite authors as all the
law and the prophets. They have commonly read little or nothing since or, if
(115) they have, they have judged it by a standard taken from these authors, and never
dreamed of judging it by nature; they are
destitute of the documents in the case of
the later writers; they suppose that
(120) Balzac was the beginning of realism,
and that Zola is its wicked end; they are
quite ignorant, but they are ready to talk
you down, if you differ from them, with
an assumption of knowledge sufficient
(125) for any occasion. The horror, the resentment, with which they receive any question of their literary saints is genuine;
you descend at once very far in the
moral and social scale, anything short of
(130) offensive personality is too good for
you; it is expressed to you that you are
one to be avoided, and put down even a
little lower than you have naturally
fallen.

GO ON TO THE NEXT PAGE

43. The tone of the passage could best be described as

    A. somber

    B. ornate

    C. didactic

    D. critical

    E. formal

44. The author feels common people make which of the following mistakes?

    A. Judging a work of art too quickly

    B. Letting their own interpretation interfere with their reading

    C. Letting authorities tell them how to interpret literature

    D. Basing their judgments on appearances only

    E. Not modeling their tastes after their neighbors'

45. The phrase "The seeds of death" (line 31) is a

    A. metaphor for imitative art

    B. symbol for the destruction of art

    C. metaphor for the art of an older age

    D. reference to Michelangelo's art

    E. symbol of artistic immaturity

46. In context, which of the following does NOT represent an object of the author's criticism?

    A. "some one . . . who browbeat wholesome common-sense" (lines 17–19)

    B. "are taught to form themselves, not upon life" (line 27–28)

    C. "he is instructed to idealize his personages" (lines 48–49)

    D. "put the book-likeness into them" (line 51)

    E. "will reject the ideal grasshopper" (lines 90-91)

47. The author's criticism of those who read only older literature is tempered by the fact that he

    A. is certain their ideas will die out quickly

    B. finds them entertaining and delightful

    C. dismiss them as unimportant

    D. alleges they do little harm to the average reader

    E. acknowledges that they have great knowledge

48. The idealized grasshopper is a symbol for

    A. the quest to merge art and science

    B. the human search for perfection

    C. art that lasts through the ages

    D. artificial rather than realistic art

    E. the scientist's folly in trying to describe nature

49. According to the author, the irony of the idealized grasshopper is that

    A. it ceases to be realistic

    B. scientists will find it useful

    C. it blends science and art into one

    D. it cannot be distinguished from a real grasshopper

    E. it has not been created

50. Which of the following types of grasshopper does the author feel will be the slowest to become integrated into mainstream literature?

    A. The heroic grasshopper

    B. The ideal grasshopper

    C. The simple, honest, natural grasshopper

    D. The impassioned grasshopper

    E. The good old romantic cardboard grasshopper

51. Which of the following would the author recommend for modern readers?

    I.   Read only classical literature.

    II. Read literature from all ages.

    III. Read with your own interpretation.

    A. I only

    B. II only

    C. III only

    D. I and II only

    E. II and III only

52. The story of the grasshopper contains

    A. hidden hyperbole

    B. satiric humor

    C. overstated oxymoron

    D. ruthless criticism

    E. remarkable realism

53. In context, which of the following best represents the author's main idea about art appreciation?

    A. "simplicity, naturalness, and honesty" (lines 14–15)

    B. "people who would like to have him show how Shakespeare's men talked" (lines 44–46)

    C. "an attitude of imagined superiority" (line 56)

    D. "it is artificial; but then it's ideal too" (lines 76–77)

    E. "witness the confidence with which they preach their favorite authors" (lines 110–112)

54. What similarity is suggested between the scientist and artist who discuss the grasshopper?

    A. The models of their studies will both be artificial.

    B. They both love to observe nature.

    C. They both look to old masters for inspiration.

    D. Both of their methods will become obsolete.

    E. They both spend too much time on research.

55. Which of the following devices is NOT used in the passage?

    A. Irony

    B. Metaphor

    C. Motif

    D. Allusion

    E. Analogy

GO ON TO THE NEXT PAGE

56. The "sweet elderly lady or excellent gentleman" (lines 107–108) represents a stereotype of

    A. current literary critics

    B. the well-rounded literary audience

    C. those who reject new artistic representations

    D. those who read carelessly

    E. middle-class readers

IF YOU FINISH BEFORE TIME IS CALLED, CHECK YOUR WORK ON THIS SECTION ONLY. DO NOT WORK ON ANY OTHER SECTION IN THE TEST.

Section II: Essay Questions

Time: 2 hours

3 Questions

Question 1

(Suggested time – 40 minutes. This question counts one-third of the total essay section score.)

The following excerpt is from Henry James's short story "The Jolly Corner," in which the author tells of a man who returns to his native New York City after living in Europe for thirty-three years. As the passage begins, the main character has reintroduced himself to an old friend, Alice Staverton.

Directions: Read the passage carefully; then write an essay in which you analyze how the author's style effectively implies his attitude toward the past and present. Examine how such elements as narrative structure, manipulation of language, sentence complexity, selection of detail, and overall tone reflect this attitude.

. . . nothing was now likely, he knew, ever to make [Alice Staverton] better-off than she found herself, in the afternoon of life, as the delicately frugal possessor
(5) and tenant of the small house in Irving Place to which she had subtly managed to cling through her almost unbroken New York career. If he knew the way to it now better than to any other address
(10) among the dreadful multiplied number-ings which seemed to him to reduce the whole place to some vast ledger-page, overgrown, fantastic, of ruled and criss-crossed lines and figures if he had
(15) formed, for his consolation, that habit, it was really not a little because of the charm of his having encountered and recognized, in the vast wilderness of the wholesale, breaking through the mere
(20) gross generalization of wealth and force and success, a small still scene where items and shades, all delicate things, kept the sharpness of the notes of a high voice perfectly trained, and where econ-
(25) omy hung about like the scent of a garden.

His old friend with one maid and herself dusted her relics and trimmed her lamps and polished her silver; she stood off, in the awful modern crush, when she
(30) could, but she sallied forth and did battle when the challenge was really to "spirit," the spirit she after all confessed to, proudly and a little shyly, as to that of the better time, that of *their* common,
(35) their quite far-away and antediluvian so-cial period and order. She made use of the street-cars when need be, the terrible things that people scrambled for as the panic stricken at sea scramble for the
(40) boats; she affronted, inscrutably, under stress, all the public concussions and or-deals; and yet, with that slim mystifying grace of her appearance, which defied you to say if she were a fair young
(45) woman who looked older through trou-ble, or a fine smooth older one who looked young through successful indif-ference; with her precious reference, above all, to memories and histories into
(50) which he could enter, she was as exquisite

GO ON TO THE NEXT PAGE

for him as some pale pressed flower (a rarity to begin with), and, failing other sweetnesses, she was a sufficient reward of his effort. They had communities of (55) knowledge, "their" knowledge (this discrimination possessive was always on her lips) of presences of the other age, presences all overlaid, in his case, by the experience of a man and the freedom of (60) a wanderer, overlaid by pleasure, by infidelity, by passages of life that were strange and dim to her, just by "Europe" in short, but still unobscured, still exposed and cherished, under the pious (65) visitation of the spirit from which she had never been diverted.

Question 2

(Suggested time –40 minutes. This question counts one-third of the total essay section score.)

Directions: The following passage is the opening of Susan Sontag's book *Illness as Metaphor.* Read the passage carefully, and write a cohesive essay in which you discuss Sontag's attitudes toward and use of metaphor in this excerpt.

Illness is the night-side effect of life, a more onerous citizenship. Everyone who is born holds dual citizenship, in the kingdom of the well and in the king- (5) dom of the sick. Although we all prefer to use only the good passport, sooner or later each of us is obliged, at least for a spell, to identify ourselves as citizens of that other place.

(10) I want to describe, not what it is really like to emigrate to the kingdom of the ill and live there, but the punitive or sentimental fantasies concocted about that situation: not real geography, but stereo- (15) types of national character. My subject is not physical illness itself but the uses of illness as a figure of metaphor. My point is that illness is *not* a metaphor, and that the most truthful way of regard- (20) ing illness — and the healthiest way of being ill — is one most purified of, most resistant to, metaphoric thinking. Yet it is hardly possible to take up one's residence in the kingdom of the ill unpreju- (25) diced by the lurid metaphors with which it has been landscaped. It is toward an elucidation of those metaphors, and a liberation from them, that I dedicate this enquiry.

Question 3

(Suggested time — 40 minutes. This question counts one-third of the total essay section score.)

Henry David Thoreau wrote, "Many men go fishing all of their lives without knowing that it is not fish they are after."

Directions: In a well thought out essay, examine the accuracy of this aphorism in modern society. Concentrate on examples from your observations, reading, and experiences to develop your ideas.

IF YOU FINISH BEFORE TIME IS CALLED, CHECK YOUR WORK ON THIS SECTION ONLY. DO NOT WORK ON ANY OTHER SECTION IN THE TEST.

Answer Key for Practice Test 3

Section I: Multiple-Choice Questions

First Passage

1. A
2. B
3. B
4. D
5. C
6. B
7. B
8. D
9. C
10. E
11. A
12. E
13. D
14. E
15. E

Second Passage

16. E
17. B
18. C
19. A
20. A
21. D
22. C
23. B
24. D
25. B
26. C
27. C
28. D

Third Passage

29. C
30. E
31. D
32. B
33. E
34. A
35. A
36. D
37. A
38. C
39. B
40. E
41. C
42. D

Fourth Passage

43. D
44. C
45. A
46. E
47. B
48. D
49. A
50. C
51. E
52. B
53. A
54. A
55. C
56. C

Section II : Essay Questions

Essay scoring guides, student essays, and analysis appear beginning on page 207.

Practice Test 3 Scoring Worksheet

Use the following worksheet to arrive at a probable final AP grade on Practice Test 3. While it is sometimes difficult to be objective enough to score your own essay, you can use the sample essay answers that follow to approximate an essay score for yourself. You might also give your essays (along with the sample essays) to a friend or relative to score if you feel confident that the individual has the knowledge necessary to make such judgment and that he or she will feel comfortable in doing do.

Section I: Multiple-Choice Questions

$$\underline{\hspace{2cm}} - (1/4 \text{ or } .25 \times \underline{\hspace{2cm}}) = \underline{\hspace{2cm}}$$
$$\text{right} \qquad\qquad \text{wrong} \qquad \text{multiple-choice}$$
$$\text{answers} \qquad\qquad \text{answers} \qquad \text{raw score}$$

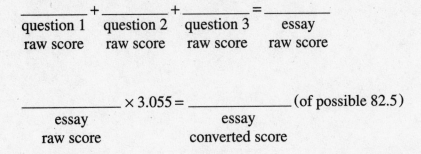

$$\underline{\hspace{3cm}} \times 1.18 = \underline{\hspace{3cm}} \text{ (of possible 67.5)}$$
$$\text{multiple-choice} \qquad\qquad \text{multiple-choice}$$
$$\text{raw score} \qquad\qquad \text{converted score}$$

Section II: Essay Questions

$$\underline{\hspace{1.5cm}} + \underline{\hspace{1.5cm}} + \underline{\hspace{1.5cm}} = \underline{\hspace{1.5cm}}$$
$$\text{question 1} \quad \text{question 2} \quad \text{question 3} \quad \text{essay}$$
$$\text{raw score} \quad\; \text{raw score} \quad\; \text{raw score} \quad\; \text{raw score}$$

$$\underline{\hspace{3cm}} \times 3.055 = \underline{\hspace{3cm}} \text{ (of possible 82.5)}$$
$$\text{essay} \qquad\qquad\qquad \text{essay}$$
$$\text{raw score} \qquad\qquad \text{converted score}$$

Final Score

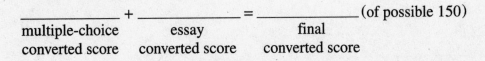

$$\underline{\hspace{3cm}} + \underline{\hspace{3cm}} = \underline{\hspace{3cm}} \text{ (of possible 150)}$$
$$\text{multiple-choice} \qquad \text{essay} \qquad\qquad \text{final}$$
$$\text{converted score} \quad \text{converted score} \quad \text{converted score}$$

Probable Final AP Score

Final Converted Score	Probable AP Score
150–104	5
103–92	4
91–76	3
75–50	2
49–0	1

Answers and Explanations for Practice Test 3

Section I: Multiple-Choice Questions

First Passage

From *The Proud Tower* by Barbara Tuchman

1. **A.** The first sentence speaks of the "remorselessly uncompromising opinions" of Robert Cecil (Lord Salisbury), which paradoxically are to be the means of making him Prime Minister or the obstacle that must be overcome. The freedom with which Lord Salisbury will express and act on his opinions is a central issue in the rest of the passage. The notion is not retracted (**B** or **D**), and although the comment is amusing, it is also relevant (**E**).

2. **B.** The remark is an understatement expressed by using the negative and, in the restraint of its expression, at odds with a phrase like "remarkable for their virulence and insolence." Disraeli's phrase could be called a metaphor ("measure") but not a simile (**A**). It is directly quoted (**C**). Although the remark is "to the man" (*ad hominem*), that is, a personal comment, it is not an *ad hominem* argument (**D**) or diatribe (**E**), an abusive attack.

3. **B.** There are direct quotations from Disraeli, Lord Morley, and an unnamed fellow member in the first paragraph. The later paragraphs have fewer quotations, although at least one can be found in each of the two following paragraphs. Neither the first paragraph nor the rest of the passage makes noteworthy use of cause-and-effect reasoning, *ad hominem* arguments, or abstract generalizations.

4. **D.** The second paragraph and the rest of the passage enlarge the characterization of Lord Salisbury. The second paragraph provides examples of his rudeness and his short attention span but also discusses his attitudes toward the public and his oratorical skills, so **B** and **C** are not quite as accurate as **D**. Choices **A** and **E** are untrue.

5. **C.** Although he spoke without notes, we know from the first paragraph that his speeches could be "clear and perfect." Choices **A** and **B** cannot be correct. The characterization of Lord Salisbury makes it clear that he didn't fear any audience and wasn't at all reluctant to reveal his real feelings. If his speeches in public were awkward, they were so because he was indifferent to what the public thought and didn't, as he saw it, waste his time in preparation for them.

6. **B.** As it is used here, a "tattoo" is a continuous drumming, not the picture on the skin. A student who chooses answer **D,** probably has the word "taboo" in mind.

7. **B.** The praise of an enemy is praise that is untainted by prejudice so I is certainly true. The paragraph goes on to discuss Lord Salisbury's "sympathetic" private self (II). Given Lord Salisbury's indifference to the opinions of others, especially those of the opposing political party, it is far more likely that Salisbury would be equally unconcerned by Gladstone's praise or blame.

8. **D.** Since the phrase says "not in the press," there would be no point in adding "not even in *Punch*" even if *Punch* were the press (**E**). We can infer that *Punch* must be some kind of publication even more likely to take liberties with a public figure than the press, pointing to a satirical publication rather than a conservative one.

9. **C.** The sentence is loaded with intensifiers: "simple," "in his bones and brain cells," "any," "anyone whatever." If the phrase "no reason" were omitted, the sentence would lack a direct object and make no sense.

10. **E.** The sentence contains twelve prepositional phrases. It uses three parallel participial phrases ("having entered . . . ," "having been returned . . . ," and "having . . . sat . . . "). The sentence is periodic, reaching its subject, verb, and object only at the end.

11. **A.** The last paragraph says that Lord Salisbury revered "up — to the monarchy." The only member of the royal family among these choices is the Prince of Wales, the son of the king or queen.

12. **E.** The speaker or author here is a biographer but not a skeptical one. She is not a political supporter or a mordant satirist, the latter phrase being far too strong. The adjective "objective" is more appropriate than "sympathetic," since the passage presents both the strengths and the limitations of its subject.

13. **D.** There is no overt use of the judgments of other modern historians, although the author, no doubt, has studied them. An example of answer choice **A** can be found in the Disraeli quotation; answer **C** can be found in the Gladstone quotation in the second paragraph; and an example of answer choice **E** is in the last sentence in the first paragraph. The conclusion of the third paragraph demonstrates a good example of **B**.

14. **E.** There is no mention of Lord Salisbury's fearing social change (**A**). He is anything but a hypocrite (**C**), and although "he was not rank-conscious," he was uninterested in the general populace. The final sentence of the third paragraph insists upon the importance of his consciousness of himself as a Cecil, a distinguished family for centuries.

15. **E.** Although the passage implies that Lord Salisbury became Prime Minister and implies that this happened sometime after 1850, it doesn't place the event late in the nineteenth century. The other options can be easily demonstrated by closely reading the passage.

Second Passage

From Jean Jacques Rousseau's "On Democracy"

16. **E.** Rousseau claims that "nothing is more dangerous than private interest having any influence on public affairs" (lines 20–22). Choices **A, C,** and **D** are not addressed. Choice **B** is indirectly addressed as the author discusses the number of people who work efficiently together, but *ineffective* committees are not specifically addressed.

17. B. The fourth paragraph asserts that "affairs will be transacted with the greatest ease and expedition in <u>fewest hands</u>" (lines 52–54). Choices **A** and **E** are not addressed. Legislators and private interest groups, **C** and **D,** are discussed but are not related to the efficiency of tribunals.

18. C. This long, complex sentence uses parallel structure to increase its coherence, listing the "circumstances" that "conspire" against democracy. The sentence includes no extended metaphor (**A**), irony, or hyperbole (**E**). Whether the tone is persuasive or argumentative is irrelevant to the *coherence* of the sentence (**B**). Choice **D** is inaccurate for the same reason (irrelevance) and contradicts the sense of the essay.

19. A. All the paragraphs except the fifth suggest reasons that a democracy may not work, but this paragraph outlines what *is* necessary for a democracy. Although Rousseau implies that these conditions are nearly impossible to achieve, he here outlines how a democracy could be possible. "Present democracies" (**B**) and "traits of a good leader" (**E**) are not addressed, and there is no use of ridicule (**C**). Choice **D** is inaccurate because of the word "ease." Rousseau doesn't suggest that democracy is easy to achieve.

20. A. The last paragraph explains that a democracy would work well in a "nation of gods" but that it will not "agree with men." The other choices list normal people, not the godlike.

21. D. From the third paragraph, you can infer that the nature of humanity will not allow a strict sense of the word, "never did, and never will, exist" because it is "against the natural order" that the greater number of people should govern the smaller number. Civil war (**A**) is addressed, but the author claims only that civil war is a *byproduct* of democracy, not its greatest obstacle. Rousseau doesn't see legislators as a serious obstacle to democracy or claim they are seditious (treasonous) (**B**). Nor does he imply that capitalists are "avaricious" (greedy; **C**). While "inequality among citizens" **E** is a possible answer, it is not the *foremost* obstacle to democracy, since it can perhaps be overcome. Choice **D,** however, addresses that in the human condition which Rousseau suggests cannot be changed.

22. C. The fifth paragraph outlines conditions necessary for a democracy to work. Enthusiastic obedience (**II**) is not addressed.

23. B. Each paragraph discusses an aspect of democracy and is clearly unified by discussion of that aspect. The essay employs no comparison and contrast (**C**). While it may argue strongly and persuasively (**D**), such arguments do not describe the paragraph's organization. Argumentation is a *mode* of rhetoric but not a *method* of organization. Choice **E** is tempting. The fifth paragraph for instance, provides examples of "circumstances" which "conspire." But other paragraphs do not follow this supposition/example format, leaving **B** as the best answer.

24. D. The paradox, or self-contradiction, is that people who inherently act correctly in a society have no need of a government at all; they govern themselves.

25. B. The author provides clear arguments concerning democracy. The essay is more than expository (**A**) because it does more than provide information. It doesn't describe democracy (**C**), narrate a story (**D**), or demonstrate anything (**E**).

26. C. The question asks for an example of the author's condescending attitude, one that demonstrates an air of superiority, of patronization. Choice **C** is the best of those listed because of the word "tedious." Rousseau here speaks of the need for simple manners "to prevent a multiplicity of affairs" and claims that the discussions that ensue concerning these "affairs" would be tedious. The remark can be seen as condescending because the citizens involved in those affairs would not likely think them tedious, but rather meaningful and significant. Rousseau seems to condescendingly imply that he considers these discussions a waste of time.

27. C. A historical background of democracies could strengthen Rousseau's assertions (both about impediments to democracy and possibilities for its survival) by providing evidence rather than simply providing opinion. While expert opinions (**B**) might support Rousseau's contentions, they would not necessarily strengthen them.

28. D. Rousseau is indeed skeptical, saying that "strict" democracy is "against the natural order" and suggesting that democracy of any type faces great obstacles. "Aggressive" (**A**) and "vituperative" (**B**) are too strong. Rousseau's argument is calm and rational. "Moderate" (**C**) is too weak. "Sanguine" (**E**), optimistic, is the opposite of Rousseau's attitude.

Third Passage

From "Meditations upon a Broomstick" by Jonathan Swift.

29. C. The sentence is not pedantic (overly scholarly). All of the remaining answer choices can be found in this sentence.

30. E. The broomstick began life in nature in a "flourishing state . . . full of sap, full of leaves, and full of boughs." Man began life in youth "strong and lusty, in a thriving condition." Choices **A**, **C**, and **D** contradict the passage. **B** is not addressed.

31. D. The author feels that man, as a youth, is closer to perfection. The older a man gets, the more mistakes he makes. The author also believes that man misuses nature, as he misuses the broomstick, out of selfishness. The author does not believe it is likely that man will take a turn for the better.

32. B. The broomstick starts life as a flourishing tree, but after man uses it up, he throws it away or burns it. Choices **C** and **E** contradict the passage. Nature does not triumph over man's evil tendencies, and man does not fear nature, but rather destroys it. The evil inherent in man's soul (**D**) is not addressed.

33. E. Intemperance is a lack of moderation in behavior, and the "axe of intemperance" is a metaphor for those excesses. It is the "axe" that chops man down like a tree. Before that, man had "green boughs"; after, he has but a "withered trunk." The phrase does not refer to "man's dominance over nature" (**A**). Nature is not shown as providing much nourishment (**B**); rather, it is destroyed. "Axe of intemperance" is neither a simile (**C**) nor hyperbole (**D**).

34. A. The author is saddened and disillusioned at man's behavior. Choice **B** is incorrect because man's future is not addressed. Choices **C** and **E** contradict the tone of the passage — there is *no* optimism or praise here. This author is angry with *man* and his nature, not the society man has created (**D**).

35. A. The phrase "a flourishing state in a forest" refers to pure, untouched nature (before man chops down trees) and has positive connotations.

36. D. Swift never suggests that man accomplishes anything magnificent; obviously, a broomstick can't claim such an accomplishment.

37. A. "*Man*" is the antecedent: "man" *is* a reasoning vegetable to this author.

38. C. No oxymorons (the juxtaposition of two contradictory terms) appear. All the other literary devices are used.

39. B. Man *pretends* to solve the problems of the world but only makes them worse. Choice **A** is inaccurate — the broomstick represents decline, not thriving. Choice **C** is also inaccurate; the broomstick is a metaphor for *man*, not society. There is no evidence for choice **D**; nature doesn't exert control in this author's world, man does. **E** is obviously incorrect: the broomstick is an analogy for man's physical state, not his intellectual state.

40. E. It is only man's presentation that allows him to believe that he can correct abuses; in fact, he "raises a mighty dust where there was none before."

41. C. Swift is cynical toward mankind and all of man's works, believing that mankind is motivated wholly by self-interest and therefore not to be trusted. This author takes a strong position, not a neutral one (**A**), and while he may be condescending, the condescension is directed toward *man*, not nature (**B**). "Bellicose" (**D**) means quarrelsome and warlike and is too strong a term to accurately describe the tone here.

42. D. Swift appears to concentrate on how inappropriate it is for man to try to reform nature while thinking of himself in such grand terms and, in reality, being the corrupter of nature.

Fourth Passage

From "Criticism and Fiction" by William Dean Howells.

43. D. The best term is "critical." The author's purpose is to criticize those who do not think for themselves, imitating older works in pursuit of art. Some examples of this critical tone: "men have been afraid to apply their won simplicity," "seeds of death are planted," "spirit of the wretched pedantry," "decays when it withdraws itself," "they are destitute of the documents," "they are quite ignorant," "you descend . . . in the moral social scale," and "you are one to be avoided." "Somber" (**A**) is too strong, as evidenced by the playful grasshopper analogy and fun the author pokes at old readers. The sentences are not complex enough or the diction flamboyant enough to be called "ornate" (**B**). The author's purpose is not "didactic" (**C**), that is, he does not mean to teach, and his diction is not pedantic. Choice **E**, "formal," like "ornate," is too strong. The tone is more conversational than formal.

44. C. Howells feels that the common people don't place enough trust in their own abilities to interpret literature, but rather rely on "some one who professed to know better and who browbeat wholesome common-sense" into them (lines 17–19). Choices **A** and **C** are not mentioned. Choices **B** and **E** contradict the passage. Howells feels that common people *should* attempt to make their own judgments rather than copy anyone's taste.

45. A. "The seeds of death" is a metaphor for imitative art, art formed from studying older masters who themselves imitated the life of their time. According to Howells, this practice produces dead art, imitative art. The author doesn't deal with the *destruction* of art (**B**), but with the *imitation* of art. The "seeds of death" do not represent the art of an older age (**C**), but the tendency to mimic the art.

46. E. Howells hopes the artist and common person will *reject* the ideal grasshopper in favor of a more natural form of art.

47. B. While Howells feels that readers who restrict their reading to older literature are narrow-minded, he also finds them "very amusing . . . delightful." The author claims that these old ideas will die out *slowly*, not quickly (**A**), that "the time is yet far off," and doesn't dismiss these readers as unimportant, suggesting only that they are far too limited in their approach. Howells does attribute harm to them (**D**), in their narrow approach, and characterizes their knowledge as assumed rather than great (**E**).

48. D. The idealized grasshopper, made of cardboard and wire, is symbolic of the artificial. No quest to merge art and science is mentioned (**A**); the passage presents only an artist talking to a scientist, and no reference is made to the search for perfection — the cardboard grasshopper is far from perfection. Although this cardboard grasshopper is said by the artist to be indestructible, it will not last through the ages of *art* (**C**) because it is divorced from reality (although the artist seems to think that it will). Choice **E** is incorrect because the scientist doesn't produce the idealized grasshopper; the artist does.

49. A. In the quest for the ideal, the grasshopper is created out of wire, cardboard, and paint, ironically becoming in the process a lesser thing because it does not resemble reality. Even if true (and there is no evidence that they are), choices **B** and **C** are not ironic. Common sense tells us that everyone can tell a cardboard grasshopper from a real one (**D**), and the passage suggests that the cardboard grasshopper has, indeed, been created (**E**).

50. C. In lines 84–103, Howells claims that the natural, simple grasshopper will eventually be recognized. The remaining choices are types of grasshoppers that he hopes will disappear as the natural one emerges.

51. E. Howells urges his readers to read widely from all literary periods and to reach an individual interpretation that is not based on some pedantic notion. Conversely, he feels that it is a mistake to read *only* classical literature.

52. B. Howells's satire makes fun of those who believe that they can create an idealized copy of nature when, obviously, nature's product is alive, real, and superior. It is also humorous to think of this silly cardboard grasshopper as realistic imitation of life. The other answer choices are either stated too strongly or not evident in the passage.

53. A. The author believes that one should use simplicity, naturalness, and honesty in art and in its appreciation. The remaining answers involve attitudes which Howells criticizes.

54. A. While the artist creates an idealized version of the grasshopper and the scientist's description (version) of the grasshopper will be based on reality, both of their creations remain artificial, both representations rather than reality. It is true that Howells presents the scientist's creation as preferable because it approaches reality more closely, but the fact remains that neither creation is *itself* reality. There is no evidence in the passage for the remaining answer choices.

55. C. A motif is a conventional or recurring element in a narrative, a device not found in the passage. The remaining devices are present. Some examples. Irony: the grasshopper analogy (while the artist professes that the cardboard grasshopper is to be preferred to the real, Howells would have the reader understand that the opposite is true). Metaphor: "The seeds of death" (line 31). Allusion: to Shakespeare, Thackeray, Hawthorne, and others. Analogy: extended analogy in the grasshopper segment.

56. C. The objection to these older readers is that they read and interpret based on only older models. They don't consider contemporary literary representation based on contemporary reality worthy of attention and consequently remain "quite ignorant." Current critics (**A**) and middle-class readers (**E**) are not mentioned in the passage. The lady and gentleman are *not* well-rounded readers (**B**) or careless readers (**D**), but narrow readers.

Section II: Essay Questions

Question 1

Scoring Guide for Question 1 (Henry James)

8–9 This well-written essay shows a clear understanding of how an author's choices, especially in diction and selection of detail, reflect attitude. The writer will have accurately read the passage to identify the author's attitude, and will have written an essay that perceptively analyzes several techniques used to communicate that attitude. The essay presents strong, relevant evidence and thoroughly explains how the evidence conveys the author's attitude toward the past and present. While the writing may contain a few minor errors, the paper demonstrates effective and precise communication.

6–7 This essay, also well-written, accurately describes the author's attitude but usually less explicitly than does a top-scoring essay. Discussion of the author's effective use of literary devices may be less thorough and less specific. The connection between the thesis and the evidence may not be as clear as that of top-scoring essays. Some errors in mechanics may occur, but overall this essay shows satisfactory control of organization, development, and use of language.

5 This average essay demonstrates adequate understanding of the author's attitude but may not present as precise a thesis about that attitude. Attempts to analyze literary techniques may be simplistic, or evidence offered may be insufficient to prove the thesis. The paper may not provide a clear connection between the evidence and the author's attitude. The essay may be clearly organized but may show inconsistent control of language.

3–4 This essay attempts to explain the author's attitudes but does so with insufficient evidence or is based on an inaccurate reading of the passage. It may fail to complete all of the tasks set forth in the essay question. This essay may merely catalog the devices used without providing analysis or connection to the thesis. Weak control of the essay format and/or language may be evident, and mechanical errors may be frequent.

1–2 This essay fails to reasonably respond to the question or the passage. It may fail to recognize the author's attitude or may misread the passage so as to distort that attitude. Because little or no evidence is provided for assertions, this essay fails to convince the reader, and the connection between the evidence and the thesis may be shallow or nonexistent. Persistent weaknesses in grammar and/or the basic elements of essay form may be evident.

High-Scoring Essay

Elements of style such as diction, imagery, figurative language, and sentence structure are used by Henry James in his short story "The Jolly Corner" to express the author's attitudes of comfort and familiarity towards the past, and confusion towards the present.

James opens the story with an image of Alice Staverton, an older woman, friend to the main character, "in the afternoon of life," living separately from the rest of a fast-paced New York. James chooses such words as "delicately" and "subtly" to slowly sketch Alice's character, while describing her lifestyle and the way in which she has managed to maintain a smooth career in a changing world. This image is sharply contrasted, a few sentences later, with the metaphor of the growing city, a "vast ledger-page, overgrown, fantastic, of ruled and criss-crossed lines and figures." This image of the present, seen in the nervous, complex city, is always pressing the reader as James continues to describe pedestrians' scramble for the street-cars and the chaos that always ensues. This haste and constant movement enforces James' presentation of the present as a hustle-bustle of anonymous people, strangers in the streets who are always hurrying to unknown destinations. James describes the changing times as an "awful modern crush," insinuating pressure and tension, complexity and confusion.

It is to this fast-paced, quickly evolving world that the main character returns, after a 33-year stay in Europe. He returns to visit Alice and is both surprised and relieved to find her unchanged. James describes the main character's perception of Alice in his expression "she stood off" which depicts Alice's ability to remove herself from the modern world. While she does stand apart to remove herself from the modern world, James also manages to show Alice as a person well-footed in reality. Alice is not a recluse but "she sailed forth and did battle when the challenge was really to 'spirit,'" showing her acceptance of inevitable change. James' word choice when describing her appearance is very effective as he likens her "slim mystifying grace" to a young troubled-looking woman who also gives the appearance of a "fine smooth older one." In this way James leaves the reader with the impression of a woman who does not age, thus emphasizing a more positive outlook towards the older Alice than the chaotic present-day city. However, throughout the uncertainties of a changing era, Alice represents a stable reminder of a past life, "of the better time." This image of the past is emanated by Alice to the main character, who finds solace in her and her home. This outlook — "her precious reference, above all, to memories and histories into which he could enter" — which holds dear older values from another time and place, allow Alice to remain capable of dealing with change in her world. Her memories and knowledge encompass the main character, helping him to reconcile his own confusion upon returning from Europe. James ends this passage by exemplifying Alice's devotion to the past: "that pious visitation of the spirit from which she had never been diverted."

Word choice, figurative language, imagery and deeper meaning are used by James to express his cherished past and the present to which he is less a part of.

Analysis of the High-Scoring Essay

This essay does an admirable job on a difficult topic. It begins by presenting a relevant thesis that accurately states the author's attitude; his view of the past is seen as positive, one with "comfort and familiarity," but his view of the present is more negative, one with "confusion."

The first body paragraph establishes Alice's character and age, and then contrasts her with the present-day city in which she lives. The student uses language effectively in establishing the author's negative impression of the city through choices like "nervous," "complex," "chaos," and "scramble." The text offers ample evidence for the student's ideas, and gives clear connections to the thesis and essay topic.

The second body paragraph returns to Alice and, through her, reinforces the idea of the author's positive attitude toward the past, toward a comfortable life. However, the student doesn't imply that the author merely paints Alice as a fossil living solely in the past, but rather acknowledges that she may represent an older lifestyle while being "well-footed in reality." By emphasizing the comforting effect that Alice has on the main character, this student accurately discusses the author's positive attitude.

The concluding paragraph appears to have been quickly written and essentially only restates the original thesis. Fortunately, the body paragraphs contain ample insight and enough specific evidence to warrant the high score.

Medium-Scoring Essay

Henry James manages to effectively create a sense of the familiar past and the contemplative present, by his use of tone, diction, and style in his short story, "The Jolly Corner."

James' impresses the image of a familiar, comforting past upon the reader by his diction and sentence structures. The author begins by describing how Alice Staverton, old friend of the main character, has "subtly managed to cling through her almost unbroken New York career." This first glimpse of Alice shows her to be tough, but not tenacious. Wording such as "delicately frugal" add to Alice's characteristics of constancy and endurance. Alice represents an older era now passed by, and to her friend who has just returned from Europe, she is a refreshing, comforting reminder of "their quite far-away and antediluvian social period and order." Alice is an escape for the main character who is subject to a changing world upon his return from a 33-year departure.

James also manages to express the complexities of the modern world, ever growing and changing. His description of the new housing developments which look overgrown and confusing is James' first method by which he shows a distasteful present day. He continues to build this image with diction such as "awful modern crush," and with the simile that likens the scramble for the street cars to the scramble for life boats by people stranded at sea. He refers to any occurrence that happens outside of Alice's haven as "public concussions and ordeals." The author paints a picture of a fast-paced world that forces the main character to find refuge with Alice, away from the complex present, couched within encompassing memories and experiences of the past.

Analysis of the Medium-Scoring Essay

This essay is a clear example of the medium-scoring essay — it makes some points but doesn't expand upon them sufficiently to completely deal with the essay tasks. The student comes close to addressing the author's attitude (but not clearly) and mentions that the past is "familiar" and the present "complicated" but fails to integrate these concepts appropriately in the body of the essay.

The second paragraph offers relevant evidence and attempts to address the topic. The student acknowledges that Alice "represents an older era" while being "refreshing" at the same time, but these insights are not connected to the author's attitude toward the past and present. Unfortunately, this paragraph borders on presenting only simple character analysis rather than an investigation of the author's attitude. The attempt is there, and the student is essentially on the right track, but a high-scoring essay pays closer attention to the essay question tasks.

The third paragraph improves; it directly comments on the negative attitude implied, describing the modern world as "over-grown and confusing" and claiming that the author "shows a distasteful present day. The examples that follow this one are also relevant to the student's point. Once again, however, greater emphasis on the author's attitude would improve this paragraph, although this paragraph is a definite improvement over the previous paragraph.

The essay as a whole makes valid points and uses some clever wording. Its primary failing is that it needs to connect the evidence to the topic more strongly and directly.

Question 2

Scoring Guide for Question 2 (Susan Sontag)

8–9 This well-written essay shows clear understanding of both Sontag's attitudes toward metaphor and use of metaphor. The thesis is thoughtful and articulate. Strong and relevant evidence from the passage combines with intelligent insights connecting the evidence to Sontag's attitudes toward metaphor and use of metaphor. Thoroughly convincing, this essay demonstrates a command of essay-writing skills. Although it need not be without errors, the paper is written with mature style and diction.

6–7 This essay demonstrates comprehension of Sontag's attitudes toward metaphor and use of metaphor, but its thesis may be less explicit than that of the top-scoring essay. The evidence offered may be less convincing, but the paper still demonstrates clear thinking. The connection between the evidence and Sontag's attitudes toward metaphor and use of metaphor may not be as clear as that of the top-scoring essay. Although well written, the paper may show some errors, while maintaining satisfactory control over diction and the essay's requirements.

5 This adequately written essay shows some understanding of Sontag's attitudes toward metaphor and use of metaphor but may not clearly demonstrate the relationship between details of the passage and those attitudes and use. The writer may merely name the attitudes without effectively discussing them or may not effectively deal with the author's use of metaphor. The thesis may be simplistic and the evidence insufficient to prove the writer's points. Acceptable organization and development may be evident, but the style may not be as sophisticated as that of higher-scoring essays.

3–4 This low-scoring essay fails to convince the reader. The weak presentation may not demonstrate a clear understanding of either Sontag's attitudes toward metaphor or her use of metaphor. The thesis may be unsubstantiated, paragraph development may be weak, and superficial thinking may be evident. Frequent errors in composition that distract the reader may be present.

1–2 This poorly written essay lacks coherence and clarity. It may attempt to identify an attitude or attitudes without mention of the use of metaphor in the passage. The thesis may be overly obvious or absent. Little or no evidence may be offered, and any connection between the evidence and the thesis may be shallow or nonexistent. The paper may be unusually short, and persistent grammatical problems may exist.

High-Scoring Essay

In this passage, Sontag uses the metaphor of illness as a nation in which we all must eventually reside. In the face of this inevitability, she suggest that it is best to confront illness face to face rather than through a façade of preconceived ideas. Sontag ironically uses this metaphor to express her dismay with the prevalence of such stereotypes regarding the nature of illness.

The paragraph sequence itself helps to illuminate the insidious nature of the metaphor. The passage begins with such a metaphor, equating illness with a detestable nation. With such descriptions as "the night-side of life" and "onerous citizenship," Sontag firmly implant illness' negative connotations in the reader's mind. Yet the very next paragraph opens up with her intent to describe "not what it is really like to emigrate to the kingdom of the ill . . . but the punitive and sentimental fantasies concocted about that situation: not real geography, but stereotypes of national character." In this statement she establishes of her own opening metaphor in general, and specifically of her own opening metaphor by referring to it as "not real geography." In so doing, Sontag alerts the reader to his or her own unquestioning acceptance of such parallels.

Throughout the passage, she continues the use of the geographical metaphor to ironically and effectively show the suggestive power of this literary tool. In her claim "it is hardly possible to take up one's residence in the kingdom of the ill unprejudiced by the lurid metaphors with which it has been landscaped," she subtly weaves in such irony. Her reference to "the kingdom of the ill" is indeed one of the very same "lurid metaphors" against which she cautions the reader. This technique of interweaving irony is very powerful in that the reader, not expecting an author to contradict herself, is forced to reexamine the sentence in closer detail, only to discover the clever subtlety of the author. This forcefully drives home Sontag's implication that the danger in metaphors lies in their unchallenged acceptance.

Sontag's perception of illness metaphors is effectively revealed in the concluding sentence, "It is toward an elucidation of those metaphors that I dedicate this inquiry." By joining the elucidation of metaphor with the liberation from those metaphors, Sontag suggests that close examination will reveal their inaccuracy, thus allowing them to be abandoned by the newly enlightened and astute reader.

Susan Sontag's suspicion of metaphorical approaches to illness is subtly yet clearly conveyed in this passage through irony and implication. The strongest statements are often written between the lines, as Sontag's work clearly demonstrates.

Analysis of the High-Scoring Essay

The essay's introduction effectively addresses the topic: the analysis of Sontag's attitudes toward and use of the metaphor. The student notes that Sontag uses the metaphor as a tool of irony to "express her dismay" at the use of stereotypes. The student's language is sophisticated, inviting the reader to follow the essay's engaging ideas.

The student then analyzes Sontag's sequence of ideas, noting how she effectively presents the concept of illness as metaphor only to dash it to pieces in her following paragraph. The student's presentation is intelligent, and the writing style is strong. Such paraphrasing as "helps to illuminate the insidious nature" demonstrates a strong command of language. The student also includes relevant and sufficient evidence from Sontag's writing to prove the essay's points.

The essay continues the effective discussion in the next paragraph by analyzing Sontag's use of metaphor, noting that Sontag contradicts herself and explaining the effect of that contradiction on the reader — that it forces the reader to reexamine preconceived notions about both illness and metaphor.

The third paragraph begins the conclusion by analyzing Sontag's last sentence, suggesting that Sontag's real purpose is to reveal the inaccuracy of metaphors and thus to enlighten her readers. While this paragraph is not as well developed as the previous ones, it is necessary as it addresses an important part of the topic: Sontag's attitudes toward metaphor. The paragraph could be improved, however, by mention of more than one attitude (the topic specifies "attitudes," plural, which should suggest to the student writer that there may be some ambivalence).

The essay concludes with a summary statement about Sontag's use of metaphor and includes a perceptive comment that readers must read between the lines in order to glean the meaning of an author's writing. Given the essay's thoughtful analysis and sophisticated presentation, it deserves a high score.

Medium-Scoring Essay

In the introduction to Susan Sontag's book, Illness as Metaphor, she talks about using metaphors to compare illness to something else. She believes that metaphors are too limiting to be used to generalize all illness and that they don't allow for a clear view of sickness itself. This attitude is reflected not only in her direct comments, but also through her own use of metaphor.

Her negative attitude about metaphors for illness is stated at various places in the excerpt. She very strongly states that "illness is not a metaphor, and that the most truthful way of regarding illness . . . is one most purified of, most resistant to, metaphoric thinking." This shows that since illness isn't a metaphor, people shouldn't try to treat it like one. Sontag feels that using a metaphor to define illness is not truthful because it doesn't necessarily reveal the whole story. Another example where her attitude about metaphors can be seen is in her comment that, "It is toward . . . a liberation from them, that I dedicate this inquiry." Her whole purpose in the book, then, is to draw people away from the metaphor. She wants to get people to confront illness as it is, without a confining metaphor, to be "liberated" from it.

Sontag shows her dislike for metaphor indirectly by in fact using one herself. She describes "the kingdom of the sick" as "the night-side of life." This establishes a clearly defined view of illness. Then she later seems to point out the invalidity of her own metaphor, when she implies that the "kingdom" is "not real geography but stereotypes."

This implies that it is not based on reality, but rather ideas. She is referring to metaphors as stereotypes, which expresses her view that they are prejudiced and consequently not very accurate. In a roundabout way, by insulting her own metaphor as a mere stereotype, Susan Sontag conveys the error of metaphors.

In this passage, she claims that metaphors should not be used to describe illness. The reasons she gives are that it is not "the most truthful way" of looking at it, and that they are just stereotypes. She even uses one herself to show you that you can't always trust them to be right. What's true for one person may not necessarily be true for another.

Analysis of the Medium-Scoring Essay

This average-scoring essay demonstrates the same faults as do many essays in the medium-score range: it makes some accurate points but without sufficient analysis. In addition, the presentation lacks the sophistication seen in high-scoring essays. Both the points presented and the style of presentation do not rise above the mundane.

The second paragraph is primarily summary, not analysis. While correct in acknowledging that Sontag has a "negative attitude" toward illness metaphors, the student has nothing more important to say than "since illness isn't a metaphor, people shouldn't treat it like one." The student acknowledges Sontag's purpose (which wasn't asked for in the topic), "to draw people away from the metaphor," but shows no deeper perception and continues to write mere summary.

The third paragraph is more thoughtful but, once again, lacks strong analysis. The student suggests that Sontag herself makes use of a metaphor, that of the kingdom, but sees only that she is trying to "convey the error of metaphors." This essay points out only what is obvious to most readers.

The conclusion summarizes the essay's main points about Sontag's attitude toward and use of metaphor, but unfortunately, no new points are presented. Overall, this essay attempts to address the topic, but its ideas are shallow and its presentation simplistic.

Question 3

Scoring Guide for Question 3 (Henry David Thoreau)

8–9 This well-written essay thoroughly explores the accuracy of Thoreau's aphorism in modern society. It articulately and clearly substantiates its points with relevant evidence from contemporary life, connecting that evidence to the thesis with meaningful insight about human nature. Although the paper may contain a few flaws, it demonstrates a command of language, sentence structure, and conventions of essay form.

6–7 This essay explores Thoreau's aphorism but produces a less explicit thesis than that of top-scoring essays. Evidence offered is perhaps less specific or not as clearly connected to the thesis. The paper's ideas may not be as crisply articulated as those in top-scoring essays. Although there may be some errors, the paper is well written and demonstrates mature style and satisfactory command of language.

5 This adequately presented essay has an acceptable thesis and presents some evidence concerning the applicability of the aphorism in modern society but may exhibit flaws in organization, number of examples, or discussion of ideas. In general, this essay is not as effective or convincing because of a pedestrian treatment of the topic, producing commonplace, predictable reading. Inconsistent control of language and sentence structure may be present.

3–4 This essay fails to convince the reader. Superficial thinking and weak evidence may be combined with an uninteresting or obvious thesis. Confused or contradictory thinking may be present, and the essay may lack adequate support to prove its points. Weak organization and paragraph developments may be present. Frequent grammatical problems may distract the reader.

1–2 This essay frequently lacks coherence and clarity of thought and may produce an unclear thesis concerning the accuracy of the aphorism. Little or no evidence may be presented for the thesis, and the connection between the evidence and the thesis may be shallow or nonexistent. The essay may exhibit poor organization and paragraph development. Weak syntax and persistent grammatical errors may be present.

High-Scoring Essay

Henry David Thoreau aptly described the nature of mankind by expressing man's tendency to become lost in unimportant pursuits in today's society. Using fish as a symbol for what people believe they are searching for, Thoreau describes a problem of human nature which is seen in all of society: the problem of continually searching while not recognizing what one truly desires in life.

This problem is clouded by the confusing mist of appearances. This shroud hangs over what society has taught one to see as success: money, fancy cars, large houses, to name a few. In the pursuit of what society deems symbolic of success, one is trapped in the conflict of appearance versus reality. All too often someone craves a material object, only to find it boring shortly after it was acquired.

This, of course, causes the person to want more possessions, always with the same result. This endless cycle continues, the result being dissatisfaction; as Thoreau might note, this person looks for still more fish, not knowing that fish will not satisfy.

This conflict leads only to the greater problem of getting lost in the race for success and losing sight of life's full meaning. In a society such as America, it is easy to forget that inner happiness cannot to be bought with material goods. With so many opportunities for one to flaunt wealth, it is not difficult to understand how people get caught up in trivial pursuits which do not satisfy their actual desire for success. The necessity to discern between needs and wants then becomes apparent within society. Today this confusion of true desire and false success is seen as the divorce rate increases, as drug abuse rises, as people continue to look for permanent happiness and inner success in temporary feelings and actions. Thoreau was accurate as he used this aphorism to describe human tendencies. Sad yet true, Thoreau's comment is still truthful in regard to the earnest search for false success.

Analysis of the High-Scoring Essay

This essay is articulate in its exploration of Thoreau's aphorism in relation to modern society. It clearly takes a stand and buttresses it with discussion and examples. The student is not sidetracked into irrelevance and keeps the commentary specific.

The second paragraph presents its insights with a nice flair. Phrases like "clouded by the confusing mist of appearance" and the "shroud [that] hangs over" are negative images appropriate to the writer's assertions, and reinforce the theme of the deceit of "success" as our society defines it. By returning to Thoreau's symbol of fish, the student completes the paragraph logically and effectively links it to the topic.

The third paragraph continues the philosophical discussion, adding additional relevant, contemporary examples and expanding the notion that people are never satisfied with what they have. Divorce and drugs are especially apt illustrations. The essay would be stronger if it included more such examples, but those used are convincing.

Overall, the essay deserves a fairly high score because it is clearly on topic, is well organized, shows sufficient paragraph development, and demonstrates maturity in style, even if only sporadically. It would earn a higher score if it offered stronger evidence and used more precise language. The repetition of ideas is a problem but one often seen in writing upon philosophical topics under time pressure.

Medium-Scoring Essay

Thoreau's quote relating to man's futile search for fish is applicable to modern society today. I think this quote especially relates to materialism, which is rampant within our greedy, American, self-centered society. Many values today revolve around selfishness and instant gratification, and the big picture of life isn't really seen. This drive for ownership and power and wealth often materializes itself in the mad rush to buy things. Credit cards only encourage this behavior, and the trip for the fish is not what they need. Materialism is a perfect example of this behavior, since many people feel the need to fill their lives with <u>something</u>, whether it's love or money or things. Thoreau sums up this observation about human nature so well, and this statement related not only to Thoreau's society, but to our society in modern America as well. The difference between needs and wants are easily confused, and those who are consumed by materialism cannot see the forest for the trees. I think Thoreau was reminding people not to forget what the important things in life are, and to express the importance of searching for what really matters in life, not settling for temporary things like material goods.

Analysis of the Medium-Scoring Essay

This essay has some merit: It attempts to discuss the topic. The paragraph is acceptable and the points relevant, but the paper falls short of thoroughly convincing a reader. The student's one-paragraph format leads to a rambling, unfocused result here. It isn't the essay's ideas that lower the score, but the presentation. The writer uses pertinent examples from contemporary life, such as the use of credit cards and "materialism," but lapses into vague terms like "things."

The writer should be commended for trying to connect the essay to Thoreau's "fish" aphorism, but that important connection should be incorporated more smoothly. For example, the sudden jump from "credit cards" to "fish" in the fifth sentence needs a transitional phrase so that the reader can follow the writer's argument. In addition, demonstrating more sophisticated skills in the fundamentals of the essay form and more effective diction would significantly improve this essay.

Answer Sheet for Practice Test 4

(Remove This Sheet and Use it to Mark Your Answers)

Section I
Multiple-Choice Questions

PASSAGE 1

1 Ⓐ Ⓑ Ⓒ Ⓓ Ⓔ
2 Ⓐ Ⓑ Ⓒ Ⓓ Ⓔ
3 Ⓐ Ⓑ Ⓒ Ⓓ Ⓔ
4 Ⓐ Ⓑ Ⓒ Ⓓ Ⓔ
5 Ⓐ Ⓑ Ⓒ Ⓓ Ⓔ
6 Ⓐ Ⓑ Ⓒ Ⓓ Ⓔ
7 Ⓐ Ⓑ Ⓒ Ⓓ Ⓔ
8 Ⓐ Ⓑ Ⓒ Ⓓ Ⓔ
9 Ⓐ Ⓑ Ⓒ Ⓓ Ⓔ
10 Ⓐ Ⓑ Ⓒ Ⓓ Ⓔ
11 Ⓐ Ⓑ Ⓒ Ⓓ Ⓔ
12 Ⓐ Ⓑ Ⓒ Ⓓ Ⓔ
13 Ⓐ Ⓑ Ⓒ Ⓓ Ⓔ
14 Ⓐ Ⓑ Ⓒ Ⓓ Ⓔ
15 Ⓐ Ⓑ Ⓒ Ⓓ Ⓔ

PASSAGE 2

16 Ⓐ Ⓑ Ⓒ Ⓓ Ⓔ
17 Ⓐ Ⓑ Ⓒ Ⓓ Ⓔ
18 Ⓐ Ⓑ Ⓒ Ⓓ Ⓔ
19 Ⓐ Ⓑ Ⓒ Ⓓ Ⓔ
20 Ⓐ Ⓑ Ⓒ Ⓓ Ⓔ
21 Ⓐ Ⓑ Ⓒ Ⓓ Ⓔ
22 Ⓐ Ⓑ Ⓒ Ⓓ Ⓔ
23 Ⓐ Ⓑ Ⓒ Ⓓ Ⓔ
24 Ⓐ Ⓑ Ⓒ Ⓓ Ⓔ
25 Ⓐ Ⓑ Ⓒ Ⓓ Ⓔ
26 Ⓐ Ⓑ Ⓒ Ⓓ Ⓔ
27 Ⓐ Ⓑ Ⓒ Ⓓ Ⓔ
28 Ⓐ Ⓑ Ⓒ Ⓓ Ⓔ

PASSAGE 3

29 Ⓐ Ⓑ Ⓒ Ⓓ Ⓔ
30 Ⓐ Ⓑ Ⓒ Ⓓ Ⓔ
31 Ⓐ Ⓑ Ⓒ Ⓓ Ⓔ
32 Ⓐ Ⓑ Ⓒ Ⓓ Ⓔ
33 Ⓐ Ⓑ Ⓒ Ⓓ Ⓔ
34 Ⓐ Ⓑ Ⓒ Ⓓ Ⓔ
35 Ⓐ Ⓑ Ⓒ Ⓓ Ⓔ
36 Ⓐ Ⓑ Ⓒ Ⓓ Ⓔ
37 Ⓐ Ⓑ Ⓒ Ⓓ Ⓔ
38 Ⓐ Ⓑ Ⓒ Ⓓ Ⓔ
39 Ⓐ Ⓑ Ⓒ Ⓓ Ⓔ
40 Ⓐ Ⓑ Ⓒ Ⓓ Ⓔ
41 Ⓐ Ⓑ Ⓒ Ⓓ Ⓔ
42 Ⓐ Ⓑ Ⓒ Ⓓ Ⓔ

PASSAGE 4

43 Ⓐ Ⓑ Ⓒ Ⓓ Ⓔ
44 Ⓐ Ⓑ Ⓒ Ⓓ Ⓔ
45 Ⓐ Ⓑ Ⓒ Ⓓ Ⓔ
46 Ⓐ Ⓑ Ⓒ Ⓓ Ⓔ
47 Ⓐ Ⓑ Ⓒ Ⓓ Ⓔ
48 Ⓐ Ⓑ Ⓒ Ⓓ Ⓔ
49 Ⓐ Ⓑ Ⓒ Ⓓ Ⓔ
50 Ⓐ Ⓑ Ⓒ Ⓓ Ⓔ
51 Ⓐ Ⓑ Ⓒ Ⓓ Ⓔ
52 Ⓐ Ⓑ Ⓒ Ⓓ Ⓔ
53 Ⓐ Ⓑ Ⓒ Ⓓ Ⓔ
54 Ⓐ Ⓑ Ⓒ Ⓓ Ⓔ
55 Ⓐ Ⓑ Ⓒ Ⓓ Ⓔ

CUT HERE

Section I: Multiple-Choice Questions

Time: 60 Minutes

55 Questions

Directions: This section consists of selections from prose works and questions on their content, style, and form. Read each selection carefully. Choose the best answer of the five choices.

Questions 1–15. *Read the following passage carefully before you begin to answer the questions.*

First Passage

We have met here today to discuss our rights and wrongs, civil and political, and not, as some have supposed, to go into the detail of social life alone. We do
(5) not propose to petition the legislature to make our husbands just, generous, and courteous, to seat every man at the head of a cradle, and to clothe every woman in male attire. None of these points,
(10) however important they may be considered by leading men, will be touched in this convention. As to their costume, the gentlemen need feel no fear of our imitating that, for we think it in violation of
(15) every principle of taste, beauty, and dignity; notwithstanding all the contempt cast upon our loose, flowing garments, we still admire the graceful folds and consider our costume far more artistic
(20) than theirs. Many of the nobler sex seem to agree with us in this opinion, for the bishops, priests, judges, barristers, and lord mayors of the first nation on the globe, and the Pope of Rome, with his
(25) cardinals, too, all wear the loose flowing robes, thus tacitly acknowledging that the male attire is neither dignified nor imposing. No, we shall not molest you in your philosophical experiments with
(30) stocks,[1] pants, high-heeled boots, and Russian belts. Yours be the glory to discover, by personal experience, how long the kneepan can resist the terrible strapping down which you impose, in how
(35) short time the well-developed muscles of the throat can be reduced to mere threads by the constant pressure of the stock,[2] how high the heel of a boot must be to make a short man tall, and how
(40) tight the Russian belt may be drawn and yet have wind enough left to sustain life.

But we are assembled to protest against a form of government existing without the consent of the governed —
(45) to declare our right to be free as man is free, to be represented in the government which we are taxed to support, to have such disgraceful laws as give man the power to chastise and imprison his
(50) wife, to take the wages which she earns,

GO ON TO THE NEXT PAGE

the property which she inherits, and, in case of separation, the children of her love; laws which make her the mere dependent on his bounty. It is to protest (55) against such unjust laws as these that we are assembled today, and to have them, if possible, forever erased from our statute books, deeming them a shame and a disgrace to a Christian republic in (60) the nineteenth century. We have met

To uplift woman's fallen divinity

Upon an even pedestal with man's.

And strange as it may seem to many, we now demand our right to vote according (65) to the declaration of the government under which we live. This right no one pretends to deny. We need not prove ourselves equal to Daniel Webster to enjoy this privilege, for the ignorant (70) Irishman in the ditch has all the civil rights he has. We need not prove our muscular power equal to this same Irishman to enjoy this privilege, for the most tiny, weak, ill-shaped stripling of (75) twenty-one has all the civil rights of the Irishman. We have no objections to discuss the question of equality, for we feel that the weight of argument lies wholly with us, but we wish the question of (80) equality kept distinct from the question of rights, for the proof of the one does not determine the truth of the other. All white men in this country have the same rights, however they may differ in mind, (85) body, or estate.

1. stocks, line 30; 2. stock, line 38: a stock is a wide, stiff, necktie worn by men in the mid-nineteenth century.

1. Which of the following words is used with two meanings?

   A. "rights," (line 2)

   B. "wrongs," (line 2)

   C. "seat," (line 8)

   D. "head," (line 8)

   E. "attire," (line 9)

2. The details of lines 7–9 ('to seat every man at the head of a cradle, and to clothe every woman in male attire") probably derive from

   A. the agenda of feminists seeking the franchise.

   B. the attacks by men on women agitating for the vote.

   C. the creative imagination of the speaker.

   D. the historically observed results of granting women the vote.

   E. the classical ideal of society in which men and women are equal.

3. Lines 22–28 advance the argument that

   A. the sexes achieve greater dignity by cross-dressing.

   B. judges and clergymen wear flowing robes because this form of dress is traditional.

   C. American lawyers and clergymen, as well as members of the Roman Catholic hierarchy, regard women's dress as dignified.

   D. human value should not be judged by manner of dress.

   E. women's clothing is more imposing than men's.

4. In the first paragraph, which of the following phrases is used ironically?

   A. "social life," (line 4)

   B. "male attire," (line 9)

   C. "every principle of taste, beauty, and dignity," (lines 15–16)

   D. "nobler sex," (line 20)

   E. "neither dignified nor imposing," (lines 27–28)

5. In which of the following phrases in the first paragraph does the author use mock-serious diction for satiric effect?

   A. "with his cardinals, too," (lines 24–25)

   B. "thus tacitly acknowledging," (line 26)

   C. "philosophical experiments," (line 29)

   D. "well-developed muscles of the throat," (lines 35–36)

   E. "the constant pressure of the stock," (lines 37–38)

6. In lines 38-39, part of the comedy in the references to the "heel of a boot" and "the Russian belt" is due to the fact that

   A. they are worn by men to appear taller and thinner.

   B. both men and women wear boots and belts.

   C. women are more likely to dress to impress other women than to impress men.

   D. men's clothes are, in fact, more comfortable to wear than women's.

   E. the heels of women's shoes are usually higher than those of men's.

7. The purpose of the first paragraph of the passage is to

   A. introduce with examples the issues that are to discussed in the second paragraph.

   B. introduce lightly issues that will be seriously developed in the second paragraph.

   C. comically present issues that the serious second paragraph will not be concerned with.

   D. raise questions to which the second paragraph will give answers.

   E. grant concessions to the opponents which the second paragraph will retract.

8. In line 68 of the second paragraph, the author refers to Daniel Webster

   A. as a representative of American patriotism.

   B. as an example of a great orator.

   C. as a representative of the injustice of the American voting system.

   D. as an example of the male's superiority to the female.

   E. as a representative of intelligence.

9. Together with lines 67–68 ("We need not prove ourselves . . ."), the argument in lines 71–76 ("We need not prove our . . .")

   A. repeats the idea of the sentence that precedes it.

   B. raises possible objections to the idea of the sentence that precedes it.

   C. appears to concede a point, but, in fact, does not.

   D. demonstrates that the weak as well as the ignorant may vote.

   E. is concerned with the question of rights rather than with the question of equality.

GO ON TO THE NEXT PAGE

10. The speaker wishes to keep "the question of equality distinct from the question of rights"(lines 79–81) because

    A.   women cannot be equal to men until their rights are equal to men's.

    B.   though their equality may be doubted, there can be no doubt about women's being denied their rights.

    C.   the question of the equality of men and women must determine whether or not their civil rights should be the same.

    D.   she believes the question of equality has already been settled, but the question of rights has not.

    E.   she can see no real distinction between the two.

11. The tone of the second paragraph can best be described as

    A.   reasonable and disinterested

    B.   soft spoken and confident

    C.   dry and ironical

    D.   angry and authoritative

    E.   tactful and firm

12. Which of the following best describes the relationship between lines 42–62 (paragraph two) and lines 31–41 (paragraph one)?

    A.   lines 42–62 intensify the irony of lines 31–41.

    B.   lines 42–62 mark an important shift in the tone of the passage.

    C.   lines 42–62 introduce a prose style more dependent on concrete details.

    D.   lines 42–62 echo the tone of lines 31–41, but with greater restraint.

    E.   lines 42–62 present a more personal point of view than lines 31–41.

13. Which of the following are used most frequently in the second paragraph?

    A.   ad hominem arguments

    B.   specialized legal diction

    C.   simile and metaphor

    D.   ironic understatements

    E.   parallel constructions

14. The primary purpose of the speaker of the passage is to

A. reveal the injustice to women in the present laws.

B. report events as objectively as possible.

C. introduce and explain a complex issue.

D. discuss the common humanity of both men and women.

E. appeal to the gender prejudices of the audience.

15. The passage implies that the speaker would oppose any significant political change that would not

A. bring additional political advantages to men as well as women.

B. encourage reverence for the leaders of the church.

C. increase the civil rights of all races to whom rights are now denied.

D. alter the laws that deny women representation in government.

E. assure the establishment of universal suffrage.

Questions 16–28. Read the following passage carefully before you begin to answer the questions.

Second Passage

When I was first aware that I had been laid low by the disease, I felt a need, among other things, to register a strong protest against the word "depression." (5) Depression, most people know, used to be termed "melancholia," a word which appears in English as early as the year 1303 and crops up more than once in Chaucer, who in his usage seemed to be (10) aware of its pathological nuances. "Melancholia" would still appear to be a far more apt and evocative word for the blacker forms of the disorder, but it was usurped by a noun with a bland tonality (15) and lacking any magisterial presence, used indifferently to describe an economic decline or a rut in the ground, a true wimp of a word for such a major illness. It may be that the scientist gener- (20) ally held responsible for its currency in modern times, a Johns Hopkins Medical School faculty member justly venerated — the Swiss-born psychiatrist Adolf Meyer — had a tin ear for the finer (25) rhythms of English and therefore was unaware of the semantic damage he had inflicted by offering "depression" as a descriptive noun for such a dreadful and raging disease. (30) Nonetheless, for over seventy-five years the word has slithered innocuously through the language like a slug, leaving little trace of its intrinsic malevolence and preventing, by its very insipidity, a (35) general awareness of the horrible intensity of the disease when out of control.

As one who has suffered from the malady in extremis yet returned to tell the tale, I would lobby for a truly (40) arresting designation. "Brainstorm," for instance, has unfortunately been preempted to describe somewhat jocularly, intellectual inspiration. But something along these lines is needed. Told that

GO ON TO THE NEXT PAGE

(45) someone's mood disorder has evolved into a storm — a veritable howling tempest in the brain, which is indeed what a clinical depression resembles like nothing else — even the uninformed layman (50) might display sympathy rather than the standard reaction that "depression" evokes, something akin to "So what?" or

"You'll pull out of it" or "We all have bad days." The phrase "nervous break-(55) down" seems to be on its way out, certainly deservedly so, owing to its insinuation of a vague spinelessness, but we still seem destined to be saddled with "depression" until a better, sturdier (60) name is created.

16. For which of the following reasons would the speaker prefer to use the word "melancholia" instead of the word "depression?"

   I.   It has been used to refer to the disease for a much longer time.

   II. Its meaning is limited to its reference to mental condition.

   III. It suggests the severity of the disease more effectively.

   A. II only

   B. I and II only

   C. I and III only

   D. II and III only

   E. I, II, and III

17. In line 16, the word "indifferently" can be best defined as

   A. apathetically.

   B. neither particularly well nor badly.

   C. indiscriminately.

   D. disinterestedly.

   E. with no understanding.

18. The speaker objects to the word "depression" to describe the disease because

   I.   its other meanings are nondescript.

   II. it is too euphemistic.

   III. it has been used for only about seventy-five years.

   A. II only

   B. I and II only

   C. I and III only

   D. II and III only

   E. I, II, and III.

19. The phrases "wimp of a word" (line 18) and "tin ear" (lines 24–25) are examples of

   A. paradox

   B. colloquialism

   C. euphemism

   D. mixed metaphor

   E. parody

20. All of the following words or phrases contribute to creating the same meaning and effect EXCEPT

    A. "semantic damage" (lines 26–27).

    B. "dreadful and raging disease" (line 29).

    C. "intrinsic malevolence" (line 33).

    D. "horrible intensity" (lines 35–36).

    E. "howling tempest in the brain" (line 47).

21. The word "brainstorm" (line 40) can probably not be used to replace the word "depression" because

    I. it does not adequately suggest what depression is like.

    II. it already has another very different meaning.

    III. it has comic overtones.

    A. II only

    B. I and II only

    C. I and III only

    D. II and III only

    E. I, II, and III

22. In the sentence in lines 44–54 ("Told that someone's . . . have bad days."), the author

    I. suggests a possible way of changing the conventional response to a victim of depression.

    II. exaggerates the unsympathetic response in order to increase the sympathy for the mentally ill.

    III. exaggerates the suffering of the victim of depression in order to increase the sympathetic response.

    A. I only

    B. II only

    C. I and II only

    D. I and III only

    E. I, II, and III.

23. In lines 55–60, the author refers to the phrase "nervous breakdown" in order to

    A. suggest that the phrase is more evocative that the word "depression."

    B. give an example of an inadequate phrase that is losing its currency.

    C. offer a second example of a bland and unevocative phrase.

    D. contrast a well-chosen name for mental illness with the ill-chosen word "depression."

    E. show that the uninformed layman is unsympathetic to mental illness.

24. Of the following, which would the author probably prefer to use to describe a man suffering from acute depression?

    A. dispirited

    B. down-at-the-mouth

    C. suicidal

    D. gloomy

    E. low

GO ON TO THE NEXT PAGE

25. The passage makes use of all of the following EXCEPT

   A. metaphor.

   B. direct quotation.

   C. literary citation.

   D. hyperbole.

   E. simile.

26. Of the following, which best describes the speaker's attitude toward the use of the word "depression?"

   A. resigned acceptance

   B. amused disapproval

   C. casual disinterestedness

   D. cool dislike

   E. strong resentment

27. Which of the following best describes the purpose of the passage?

   A. To record the history of the word "depression"

   B. To criticize the inadequacy of the word "depression"

   C. To explain the multiple meanings of the word "depression"

   D. To demonstrate the shortcomings of medical language.

   E. To argue for the use of the word "melancholia" in place of the word "depression"

28. Which of the following is a central idea of this passage?

   A. The connotation of a word may be just as important as its meaning.

   B. The healthy do not properly sympathize with victims of mental illness.

   C. The changes in meaning of words over time are unpredictable.

   D. The scientific understanding of depression is incomplete.

   E. Words are an inadequate means of describing reality.

Questions 29–42. Read the following passage carefully before you begin to answer the questions.

Third Passage

    First, he that hath words of any language, without distinct ideas in his mind to which he applies them, does, so far as he uses them in discourse, only make a
(5) noise without any sense or signification; and how learned soever he may seem by the use of hard words, or learned terms, is not much more advanced thereby in knowledge than he would be in learning,
(10) who had nothing in his study but the bare titles of books, without possessing the contents of them. For all such words, however put into discourse, according to the right construction of grammatical
(15) rules, or the harmony of well turned periods, do yet amount to nothing but bare sounds, and nothing else.

    Secondly, he that has complex ideas, without particular names for them, would
(20) be in no better case than a bookseller,

who had in his warehouse volumes that lay there unbound, and without titles; which he could therefore make known to others only by showing the loose sheets,

(25) and communicating them only by tale. This man is hindered in his discourse for want of words to communicate his complex ideas, which he is therefore forced to make known by an enumeration of the

(30) simple ones that compose them; and so is fain often to use twenty words to express what another man signifies in one.

Thirdly, he that puts not constantly the same sign for the same idea, but uses

(35) the same words sometimes in one, and sometimes in another signification, ought to pass in the schools and conversation for as fair a man as he does in the market and exchange, who sells several

(40) things under the same name.

Fourthly, he that applies the words of any language to ideas different from those to which the common use of that country applies them, however his own

(45) understanding may be filled with truth and light, will not by such words be able to convey much of it to others, without defining his terms. For however the sounds are such as are familiarly known,

(50) and easily enter the ears of those who are accustomed to them; yet standing for other ideas than those they usually are annexed to, and are wont to excite in the mind of the hearers, they cannot make

(55) known the thoughts of him who thus uses them.

Fifthly, he that imagined to himself substances such as never have been, and filled his head with ideas which have not

(60) any correspondence with the real nature of things, to which yet he gives settled and defined names, may fill his discourse, and perhaps another man's head, with the fantastical imaginations of his

(65) own brain, but will be very far from advancing thereby one jot in real and true knowledge.

He that hath names without ideas, wants meaning in his words, and speaks

(70) only empty sounds. He that hath complex ideas without names for them, wants liberty and despatch in his expressions, and is necessitated to use periphrases. He that uses his words loosely

(75) and unsteadily, will either be not minded, or not understood. He that applies his names to ideas different from their common use, wants propriety in his language, and speaks gibberish. And he

(80) that hath the ideas of substances disagreeing with the real existence of things, so far wants the materials of true knowledge in his understanding, and hath instead thereof chimeras.

29. As it used in lines 15–16, the word "periods" may be best defined as

A. conclusions.

B. sentences.

C. musical measures.

D. marks of punctuation.

E. times.

30. In line 30, the word "ones" refers to

A. words.

B. books.

C. ideas.

D. discourse.

E. names.

GO ON TO THE NEXT PAGE

31. In the second paragraph, the shift from the first sentence (lines 18–25) to the second sentence (lines 26–32) can be best described as one from

   A. objective to subjective.

   B. indicative to interrogative.

   C. analytical to discursive.

   D. figurative to literal.

   E. speculative to assertive.

32. The comparison of lines 18–25 likens words to

   A. the pages of a book.

   B. the contents of a warehouse.

   C. complex ideas.

   D. booksellers.

   E. the binding of a book.

33. In the first and second paragraphs, the author supports his arguments by the use of

   A. analogies.

   B. personifications.

   C. understatements.

   D. rhetorical questions.

   E. hyperboles.

34. In line 38, the word "fair" is best understood to mean

   A. equitable.

   B. attractive.

   C. clement.

   D. unblemished.

   E. average.

35. The third paragraph of the passage (lines 33–40) is an example of

   A. an extended metaphor.

   B. a loose sentence.

   C. a periodic sentence.

   D. an antithesis.

   E. an ad hominem argument.

36. In line 58, "substances" are contrasted with

   A. shadows.

   B. ideas.

   C. imaginings.

   D. realities.

   E. names.

37. Which of the following best describes the organization of the first five of the six paragraphs in the passage?

   A. paragraph 1; paragraphs 2 and 3; paragraphs 4 and 5.

   B. paragraph 1; paragraphs 2, 3, and 4; paragraph 5.

   C. paragraphs 1, 2, and 3; paragraphs 4 and 5.

   D. paragraphs 1 and 2; paragraph 3; paragraphs 4 and 5.

   E. paragraphs 1 and 2; paragraphs 3 and 4; paragraph 5.

38. Which of the following best describes the relation of the last paragraph to the rest of the passage?

A. It comments upon and develops the arguments of the first five paragraphs.

B. It calls into question the arguments of the preceding paragraphs.

C. It raises new issues about language that the preceding paragraphs have not addressed.

D. It sums up the contents of the first five paragraphs.

E. It develops the ideas raised in the fourth and fifth paragraphs.

39. Which of the following is the meaning of the word "chimeras" that can be inferred from its use in the last sentence of the passage (line 84)?

A. fabulous monsters

B. oriental potentates

C. religious revelations

D. logical conclusions

E. philosophical distinctions

40. In which paragraph is a person who misunderstands the meaning of the word "refuse" and frequently uses it to mean "agree" described?

A. the first (lines 1–17).

B. the second (lines 18–32).

C. the third (lines 33–40).

D. the fourth (lines 41–56).

E. the fifth (lines 57–67).

41. In which paragraph does the passage deal with a speaker or writer who would use the word "apple" to denote a fruit, an animal, and an article of footwear?

A. the first (lines 1–17).

B. the second (lines 18–32).

C. the third (lines 33–40).

D. the fourth (lines 41–56).

E. the fifth (lines 57–67).

42. Which of the following does the passage use as a synonym for "word"?

I.   term

II. name

III. sign

A. III only

B. I and II only

C. I and III only

D. II and III only

E. I, II, and III

GO ON TO THE NEXT PAGE

Questions 43–55. Read the following passage carefully before you begin to answer the questions.

Fourth Passage

Wyoming has no true cities. Every hundred miles or so there's a small town. Some, like Moneta, Arminto, Emblem, Morton, and Bill, boast populations as
(5) minuscule as five or ten. A boomtown I drove through in the eastern part of the state consists of two trailer houses. One is the cafe-post office, the other is the school. Some Wyoming towns are a
(10) brief miscellany of log buildings whose central focus is the bar. When you walk in, everyone is sure to turn and stare at you. Others have shoals of untended pickups, rusting balers, and new back-
(15) hoes behind which lurk a grocery store and a town hall.

Elsewhere, the environments Americans have fashioned for themselves are aswim in paradox. Being both pragma-
(20) tists and idealists, we've adopted all kinds of high-minded utopian ideas, from the Greek revivalist to the International style, but upended them so completely they now stand for opposite
(25) ideals. Walter Gropius's antibourgeois, socialist housing has been transformed into the icy, machined skyscrapers in which the corporate creme de la creme hold court; the Greek columned portico,
(30) which Jefferson loved because it symbolized human uprightness and dignity within the Greek polis, appeared on the mansions of slave owners and came to symbolize their beleaguered era.

(35) Wyoming has no architectural legacy except for the trapper's cabin and homesteader's shack: dark, smoky, often windowless, and papered with the classifieds from the weekly newspaper. Yet I like to
(40) think that those who landed here during Wyoming's territorial days had been exposed to the ideals of Jefferson and Thoreau. Both men distrusted cities, but Thoreau was disdainful of most social
(45) gatherings while Jefferson promoted a local participatory democracy in which each person had a farmable plot and an active citizenship to go with it. They sought out the opposite kinds of free-
(50) dom. Thoreau's had to do with personal privacy, unencumbered by football games and town meetings, while Jefferson's implied a busyness — citizens having a voice in every proceeding.

(55) Wyoming attracted people of both minds. The first trappers and cattlemen, like Osborne Russell and Henry Lovell, thrived on the expanse and solitude of the state. They claimed territory the way
(60) geographers would — on the basis of water, vegetation, the contour of the land, not by the Jeffersonian grid.

The Mormons stretched Jefferson fair-mindedness into a socialistic regime
(65) under the guidance of Brigham Young. Each "colonist" was allotted a town plot, arranged on streets of specific length and width, while farmland and pasturing of livestock remained communal.

(70) The word "building" is both a noun and a verb and implies two contradictory things Americans love: security and movement. We want a firm tie to a place but to remain footloose and fancy free.
(75) Native American rolled up their skins and followed the game through the seasons (now they go on the powwow circuit in smoky colored vans); trappers and mountain men commuted between cities
(80) like St. Louis and the Tetons, the Wind Rivers, the Absaroka Mountains. Even now, cowboys and sheepherders move

from job to job, ranch to ranch, and it's no wonder so many of the manmade
(85) structures here have a temporary feel.

But back to politics. It's one thing to construct shelter and quite another to announce with the grandness of one's architecture a hierarchical intention. Take
(90) medieval Europe, for example, whose first cities were built out of fear. They started as stone walls behind which herdsmen and their families huddled and

fought off invaders. Temporary walls be-
(95) came permanent. People built houses behind them, and itinerant merchants set up shop there. Then the priests came and the governors, and the buildings they erected became physical signs of their authority.
(100) You can go anywhere in Europe and see how they did this. Castles and churches were built on hills. Everyone else had to use their dirty water.

43. In line 10, the phrase "brief miscellany" is best defined as

A. concise collection of verse.

B. short-lived confusion.

C. small hodgepodge.

D. little circle.

E. short varied street.

44. In the phrase "shoals of untended pickups, rusting balers, and new backhoes" (lines 13–15), the author compares vehicles and farm equipment with

A. shallow places.

B. bundles of grain.

C. large groups of fish.

D. camouflaged soldiers.

E. coral reefs.

45. The third paragraph (lines 35–54) contains an example of

A. overstatement.

B. parallel construction in a periodic sentence.

C. literary allusion.

D. apostrophe.

E. first person commentary.

46. From the third and fourth paragraphs, we can infer that Wyoming would have appealed to Thoreau because of its

A. natural beauty.

B. solitude.

C. fur-bearing animals.

D. natural resources.

E. vegetation.

47. In their context in this passage, the fourth and fifth paragraphs function to

A. introduce a new theory about the settlers of Wyoming.

B. prepare for the definitions of "building" in the sixth paragraph.

C. demonstrate the range of the occupations of early Wyoming settlers.

D. develop two ideas presented in the third paragraph.

E. question traditional ideas about the western expansion.

GO ON TO THE NEXT PAGE

48. The passage suggests that Thoreau rather than Jefferson has more in common with all of the following EXCEPT

A. cowboys.

B. Brigham Young.

C. Osborne Russell.

D. Native American hunters.

E. sheepherders.

49. The effect of the parenthetical remark "now they go on the powwow circuit in smoky colored vans" in lines 77–78 is to

I. comment on the mechanization of twentieth century America.

II. establish the close relationship between the "powwow circuit and the "game" of the nineteenth century.

III. stress the importance of the preservation of ancient customs in Native American culture.

A. I only

B. III only

C. I and III only

D. II and III only

E. I, II, and III

50. The function of the last paragraph of the passage (lines 86–103) is to

A. present the European historical precedent of American architecture.

B. sum up the first six paragraphs of the passage.

C. contrast the ideal (America) with the historical (Europe).

D. introduce another paradox in the history of building.

E. introduce new ideas about the relation of architecture and politics.

51. All of the following could be called examples of what the passage defines as an architecture built with a "hierarchical intention" (line 89) EXCEPT

A. European castles.

B. corporate skyscrapers.

C. the towns of Mormon "colonists."

D. European cathedrals.

E. the Greek revival mansions of the Old South.

52. The passage suggests that all of the following are paradoxical pairs EXCEPT

A. pragmatism and idealism.

B. International style architecture and American corporate executives.

C. the American love of security and of movement.

D. Thomas Jefferson and Brigham Young.

E. "building" as a noun and as a verb.

53. Of the following paragraphs in the passage, which one is NOT concerned with the architecture of Wyoming or its designers?

A. the first (lines 1–16)

B. the second (lines 17–34)

C. the third (lines 35–54)

D. the fourth (lines 55–69)

E. the fifth (63–103)

54. The passage contrasts all of the following EXCEPT

 A. society and solitude.

 B. movement and rootedness.

 C. the Greek polis and the slave-owning South.

 D. freedom and security.

 E. the priests and the rulers of the Middle Ages.

55. Which of the following best describes this passage?

 A. a carefully developed logical argument with a focus on a central point

 B. an examination of the values reflected by the buildings of Wyoming

 C. a discursive discussion of the architecture of Wyoming, America, and Europe

 D. an unresolved questioning of the materialism of American values

 E. a brief survey of American architectural history in the nineteenth and twentieth centuries

IF YOU FINISH BEFORE TIME IS CALLED, CHECK YOUR WORK ON THIS SECTION ONLY. DO NOT WORK ON ANY OTHER SECTION IN THE TEST.

Section II: Essay Questions

Time: 2 Hours

3 Questions

Question 1

Suggested time – 40 minutes. This question counts one-third of the total essay score.

In the following excerpt, John Updike, in his essay titled "The First Kiss," describes the opening of a new baseball season, including reflecting on the past season and the attitude of the fans as the new season begins.

Directions: Read the following narrative carefully. Then, in a well-developed essay, analyze the author's use of metaphor and other rhetorical devices to convey an audience's attitude toward a sporting event.

The many-headed monster called the Fenway Faithful yesterday resumed its romance with twenty-five youngish men in red socks who last year broke its (5) monstrous big heart. Just showing up on so dank an Opening Day was an act of faith. But the wet sky dried to a mottled pewter, the tarpaulin was rolled off the infield and stuffed into a mailing tube, (10) and we Faithful braced for the first kiss of another prolonged entanglement.

Who can forget the ups and downs of last year's fling? First, the Supersox; then, the unravelling. Our eyeballs grew (15) calluses, watching Boomer swing from the heels and Hobson throw to the stars. Dismal nights watching the Royals play pinball with our heroes on that plastic prairie in Kansas City. Dreadful days (20) losing count of Yankee singles in the four-game massacre. Fisk standing ever more erect and stoic at the plate, looking more and more like a Civil War memorial financed with Confederate dollars. (25) The Noble Lost Cause.

In September, the mini-resurrection, Zimmer's last stand, the miraculous last week of no losses, waiting for the Yankees to drop one. Which they did. (30) And then, the cruelest tease, the playoff game surrendered to a shoestring catch and a shortstop's cheap home run. Enough. You'll never get us to care again, Red Sox.

(35) But monsters have short memories, elastic hearts, and very foolable faculties, as many an epic attests. From natty-looking to nasty-looking, the fans turned out. "We Miss Louis and Bill," one large (40) cardboard complained. "Windsor Locks Loves the Sox!" a bedsheet benignly rhymed. Some fellow behind us exhaled a sweetish smell, but the dragon's breath was primarily flavored with malt.

(45) Governor King was booed royally. Power may or may not corrupt, but it does not win friends. A lady from Dedham not only sang all the high notes in "The Star-Spangled Banner" but put (50) in an extra one of her own, taking "free" up and out of the ballpark. We loved it. Monsters love high notes and hoards of gold.

The two teams squared off against each other in a state of statistical virginity. Every man in both lineups was batting .000. On the other hand, both pitchers had earned-run averages of 0.00. And every fielder there had thus (60) far played errorless ball.

Eckersley looked quick. A moment of sun made some of the windows of the Prudential Center sparkle. The new Red Sox uniforms appeared tight as outfits (65) for trapeze artists but otherwise struck the proper conservative note, for a team of millionaires: buttons on the shirt and a single red pinstripe. Eckersley yielded a double and then struck out two. The (70) first nicks in statistical virginity had been taken. The season had begun.

We witnessed a little by-play at the beginning that may tell it all. After the Cleveland lineup had been called out, (75) the Red Sox roll began with Zimmer. Out he trotted, last year's anti-hero, the manager who watched ninety-nine victories be not quite enough, with his lopsided cheeks and squint, like a Popeye (80) who has let the spinach settle to his middle. The many-headed monster booed furiously, and Zimmer laughed, shaking hands with his opposite manager, Torborg.

(85) That laugh said a strange thing. It said, *This is fun.* Baseball is meant to be fun, and not all the solemn money men in fur-collared greatcoats, not all the scruffy media cameramen and sour-(90) faced reporters that crowd around the dugouts can quite smother the exhilarating spaciousness and grace of this impudently relaxed sport, a game of innumerable potential redemptions and (95) curious disappointments. This is fun.

A hard lesson for a hungry monster to master, but he has six months to work on it. So let's play ball.

Question 2

Suggested time – 40 minutes. This question counts one-third of the total essay score.

Directions: Read the following excerpt from Cynthia Ozick's, "Portrait of the Essay as a Warm Body." carefully. Then, in a well-organized essay, examine how the author distinguishes an essay from an article. Analyze how she employs rhetorical strategies (perhaps considering such elements as syntax, diction, irony, and paradox), to convey her opinions.

An essay is a thing of the imagination. If there is information in an essay, it is by-the-by, and if there is an opinion in it, you need not trust it for the long run. A (5) genuine essay has no educational, polemical, or sociopolitical use; it is the movement of a free mind at play. Though it is written in prose, it is closer in kind to poetry than to any other form. (10) Like a poem, a genuine essay is made out of language and character and mood and temperament and pluck and chance.

And if I speak of a genuine essay, it is because fakes abound. Here the old-(15) fashioned term poetaster may apply, if only obliquely. As the poetaster is to the poet — a lesser aspirant — so the article is to the essay: a look-alike knockoff guaranteed not to wear well. An article (20) is gossip. An essay is reflection and insight. An article has the temporary advantage of social heat — what's hot out there right now. An essay's heat is interior. An article is timely, topical,

GO ON TO THE NEXT PAGE

(25) engaged in the issues and personalities of the moment; it is likely to be stale within the month. In five years it will have acquired the quaint aura of a rotary phone. An article is Siamese-twinned to

(30) its date of birth. An essay defies its date of birth, and ours too.

A small historical experiment. Who are the classical essayists who come at once to mind? Montaigne, obviously.

(35) Among the nineteenth-century English masters, the long row of Hazlitt, Lamb, De Quincey, Stevenson, Carlyle, Ruskin, Newman, Martineau, Arnold. Of the Americans, Emerson. It may be

(40) argued that nowadays these are read only by specialists and literature majors, and by the latter only when they are compelled to. However accurate the claim, it is irrelevant to the experiment,

(45) which has to do with beginnings and their disclosures.

So the essay is ancient and various: but this is a commonplace. There is something else, and it is more striking

(50) yet — the essay's power. By "power" I mean precisely the capacity to do what force always does: coerce assent. Never mind that the shape and intent of any essay is against coercion or persuasion, or

(55) that the essay neither proposes nor purposes to get you to think like its author. A genuine essay is not a doctrinaire tract or a propaganda effort or a broadside. Thomas Paine's "Common Sense" and

(60) Emile Zola's "J'Accuse" are heroic landmark writings; but to call them essays, though they may resemble the form, is to misunderstand. The essay is not meant for the barricades; it is a stroll

(65) through someone's mazy mind. All the same, the essay turns out to be a force for agreement. It co-opts agreement; it courts agreement; it seduces agreement.

Question 3

Suggested time – 40 minutes. This question counts as one-third of the total essay score.

In her novel, *Adam Bede*, George Eliot observes

> Our deeds determine us, as much as we determine our deeds; and until we know what has been or will be the peculiar combination of outward with inward facts, which constitute a man's critical actions, it will be better not to think ourselves wise about his character.

Directions: In a well-organized essay, defend, challenge or qualify Eliot's assertions. Use your reading, observation, and/or experience to develop your ideas and persuade the reader.

IF YOU FINISH BEFORE TIME IS CALLED, CHECK YOUR WORK ON THIS SECTION ONLY. DO NOT WORK ON ANY OTHER SECTION IN THE TEST.

Answer Key for Practice Test 4

Section I: Multiple-Choice Questions

First Passage

1. A
2. B
3. E
4. D
5. C
6. A
7. C
8. E
9. D
10. B
11. D
12. B
13. E
14. A
15. D

Second Passage

16. E
17. C
18. B
19. B
20. A
21. D
22. A
23. B
24. C
25. D
26. E
27. B
28. A

Third Passage

29. B

30. A

31. D

32. E

33. A

34. A

35. C

36. D

37. E

38. D

39. A

40. D

41. C

42. E

Fourth Passage

43. C

44. A

45. E

46. B

47. D

48. B

49. A

50. E

51. C

52. D

53. B

54. E

55. C

Section II: Essay Questions

Essay scoring guides, student essays, and analysis appear beginning on page 245.

Practice Test 4 Scoring Worksheet

Use the following worksheet to arrive at a probable final AP grade on Practice Test 4. Because it is sometimes difficult to be objective enough to score your own essay score, you might also give your essays (along with the sample essays) to a friend or relative to score if you feel confident that the individual has the knowledge necessary to make such a judgment and that he or she will feel comfortable doing so.

Section I: Multiple-Choice Questions

$$\underset{\substack{\text{right}\\\text{answers}}}{\underline{\hspace{2cm}}} - (^{1}/_{4}\text{ or }.25 \times \underset{\substack{\text{wrong}\\\text{answers}}}{\underline{\hspace{2cm}}}) = \underset{\substack{\text{multiple-choice}\\\text{raw score}}}{\underline{\hspace{2cm}}}$$

$$\underset{\substack{\text{multiple-choice}\\\text{raw score}}}{\underline{\hspace{2cm}}} \times 1.18 = \underset{\substack{\text{multiple-choice}\\\text{converted score}}}{\underline{\hspace{2cm}}} (\text{of possible } 67.5)$$

Section II: Essay Questions

$$\underset{\substack{\text{question 1}\\\text{raw score}}}{\underline{\hspace{1.5cm}}} + \underset{\substack{\text{question 2}\\\text{raw score}}}{\underline{\hspace{1.5cm}}} + \underset{\substack{\text{question 3}\\\text{raw score}}}{\underline{\hspace{1.5cm}}} = \underset{\substack{\text{essay}\\\text{raw score}}}{\underline{\hspace{1.5cm}}}$$

$$\underset{\substack{\text{essay}\\\text{raw score}}}{\underline{\hspace{2cm}}} \times 3.055 = \underset{\substack{\text{essay}\\\text{converted score}}}{\underline{\hspace{2cm}}} (\text{of possible } 82.5)$$

Final Score

$$\underset{\substack{\text{multiple-choice}\\\text{converted score}}}{\underline{\hspace{2cm}}} + \underset{\substack{\text{essay}\\\text{converted score}}}{\underline{\hspace{2cm}}} = \underset{\substack{\text{final}\\\text{converted score}}}{\underline{\hspace{2cm}}} (\text{of possible } 150)$$

Probable Final AP Score

Final Converted Score	Probable AP Score
150–104	5
103–92	4
91–76	3
75–50	2
49–0	1

Section I: Multiple-Choice Questions

First Passage

The passage is taken from an Address delivered by Elizabeth Cady Stanton to the women's rights convention at Seneca Falls in 1848.

1. **A.** Used as it is in the phrase "rights and wrongs," "rights" means that which is morally good or proper. Modified by "civil and political," "rights" also means privileges.

2. **B.** Stanton here is almost certainly taking up the points repeatedly made by the opponents of women's suffrage (the same kind of objections are raised in this century by opponents of women's rights advocates) and using them to provide a comic opening for her address.

3. **E.** Stanton states that clergymen and men in the legal profession in England ("the first nation on the globe") wear flowing robes and so they must agree with women that this attire is more "dignified and imposing" than men's clothing.

4. **D.** The words and phrases in choices **A, B, C,** and **E** mean what they say, but the phrase "nobler sex," used here to refer to men, is ironic. The passage makes clear that Stanton does not believe men are "nobler" than women.

5. **C.** The question asks about the use of mock-serious diction for satiric effect. Options **D** and **E** are satiric, but the language here is not inflated. The correct answer is **C,** which pompously dignifies men's fashions by calling them "philosophical experiments." Stanton achieves a similar comic effect with the phrase "yours be the glory."

6. **A.** An audience (then or now) accustomed to hear of women over-concerned for their clothes and appearance should be amused by this pointing of the finger at men. Modern readers may be surprised to learn of elevator shoes in the mid-nineteenth century, or the Russian belt which, like a corset, would make the waist appear smaller.

7. **C.** The first paragraph here is a comic turn, but it is not about the real issues of the address. In fact, the whole paragraph is a good example of the rhetorical technique in which the speaker, by saying he will not talk about something, talks about it. ("I will not mention that my opponent in this election has served eight years in jail for mail fraud.")

8. **E.** Stanton refers to Daniel Webster to show that males may vote regardless of their education or intelligence. As males, both Daniel Webster and the ignorant ditch-digger have the vote.

9. **D.** The two parallel sentences make the argument that males may vote regardless of their education and regardless of their strength. The vote cannot be given to males because they are stronger physically than females, since gender alone, not physical strength, determines who may vote.

10. **B.** Stanton wants the question of women's rights kept separate from the question of their equality (that is, are females the mental and physical equals of males?) because there can be no doubt about the fact that women are denied rights which the Constitution guarantees.

11. **D.** All of the options except **D** use words that are not appropriate here. Stanton is not "disinterested," not "soft-spoken," not "dry or ironical" (although the first paragraph is), not "tactful." The word "angry" may seem strong here, but of the five choices, this is the best. Stanton's use of words and phrases like "disgraceful," "unjust," "a shame and disgrace," support the choice.

12. **B.** The tone of the second paragraph is totally unlike that of the first. The first paragraph is witty and ironic; the second is dead serious. Both use concrete details (**C**) and both present the author's point of view (**E**).

13. **E.** An ad hominem argument is one that attacks the opponent rather than dealing with the subject ("Can you believe my opponent will raise income taxes when you know he earns ten million a year?") The second paragraph uses parallel constructions in lines 42–54 (the series of infinitives) and lines 67–76, in which the two sentences are parallel.

14. **A.** Though **E** is the next-best choice (**B, C,** and **D** are simply untrue), the real point here is the injustice to women which is itemized in the second paragraph.

15. **D.** Though the author might approve of **C** and **E,** the passage is about the rights and wrongs of women, and the quest of women for the vote.

Second Passage

The passage is from the American novelist William Styron's *Darkness Visible,* an autobiographical account of his suffering from depression.

16. **E.** The first paragraph of the passage gives all three of these reasons for preferring "melancholia" to the less "apt and evocative" word "depression."

17. **C.** Though "indifferent" can mean "apathetic"(**A**) or "average"(**C**), in this context the word has another of its several meanings, "showing no preference or bias, indiscriminate." The author's point is that a word that can be equally well used to denote a rut or financial hard times should not be used to describe a disease so terrible as depression.

18. **B.** The passage objects to using a word with two other commonplace meanings, and to its "bland tonality," its euphemistic effect; the author believes the word is less expressive, less shocking than is necessary to denote the condition accurately. Since the passage suggests the replacement of depression with another word, the length of time the word has been used cannot be held against it. The seventy-five years are too long rather than too short a time.

19. **B.** Both "wimp" and "tin ear" are colloquialisms, that is, a word, phrase, or idiom used in conversation or informal writing. The phrase "wimp of a word" is metaphorical, the word compared to a type of person, but it is not a mixed metaphor which might compare a word to a person and to a tree at the same time.

20. **A.** The phrases in the last four options all refer to the fierce power of depression, the disease. The phrase "semantic damage" refers to harm done by the use of the word "depression," but not to the effect of the illness.

21. **D.** The passage says that "brainstorm" describes the disease well, but that it cannot be used because it already has a different established meaning, and one with comic ("jocular") overtones.

22. **A.** The sentence argues that a better word than depression might change the conventional response to the illness. The author insists that he is not exaggerating ("veritable," "indeed," "like nothing else") what the victim suffers, and we have no reason to assume his examples of the "standard reaction" are inaccurate.

23. **B.** The author alludes to "nervous breakdown" as a phrase that like "depression" is ill-chosen, but, unlike it, is passing out of use. His objection to "nervous breakdown" is not because it is "bland," but because it appears to blame the victims for their illness.

24. **C.** Since the author presents depression as "dreadful and raging," as horrible and malevolent, we can assume he would chose the most powerful adjective of the five, and reject the four other choices as too weak to describe its "horrible intensity."

25. **D.** The passage uses metaphor ("wimp of a word"), simile ("like a slug"), direct quotation ("So what?"), and literary citation (Chaucer), but does not use hyperbole. Its point is that the word "depression" is too understated, the opposite of hyperbole.

26. **E.** The passage uses the phrase "strong protest" in its first sentence, and this position does not change.

27. **B.** Though the passage does incidentally give the history of the word (**A**) and some of its meanings (**C**), its central idea is to protest the "bland tonality" of "depression." The author does reveal his dislike of the phrase, "nervous breakdown," but the passage is focused on the word "depression," not on the shortcomings of medical language in general.

28. **A.** Though the author would probably agree with **B, C,** and **D,** the real issue here is the misleading connotation of the word "depression," when it refers to the illness. The passage complains about the one word, not about all words. Those who genuinely believe that words are an inadequate means of describing reality (**E**) probably do not become professional writers.

Third Passage

The passage is from John Locke's *An Essay Concerning Human Understanding* (1690).

29. **B.** Any of these five choices can define the word "periods," but in this context, the best choice is "sentences." In most multiple-choice exams, a question calling for the definition of a word will ask about a word with several legitimate meanings, and you must look carefully at the context in the passage to determine your answer.

30. **A.** The antecedent of "ones" is "words" in line 27. The "them" that follows ("that compose them") refers to "ideas."

31. **D.** The first sentence employs a figure of speech (a simile) while the second sentence is literal.

32. **E.** The simile compares the man who lacks the words to express his complex ideas to the bookseller whose books are only loose sheets of paper, with no means of binding them together.

33. **A.** The author uses analogies (comparisons) to support his arguments.

34. **A.** In this context, the word "fair" means equitable or honest.

35. **C.** The paragraph is a single periodic sentence, that is, a sentence that is not grammatically complete until its end.

36. **D.** Here the "substances" are imagined and are contrasted with realities. In other usages, the word "substance" denotes reality as opposed to "shadow."

37. **E.** Paragraphs one and two are related; the first presents the speaker who has words but no ideas, and the second one with ideas but no words. Paragraphs three and four describe two related misuses of words: using one word to mean many things, and using words with meanings different from those that are commonly accepted. The fifth paragraph is about imaginary notions.

38. **D.** The sixth paragraph recapitulates the contents of the first five.

39. **A.** In classical myth, a chimera was a monster with the head of a lion, the body of a goat, and the tail of a serpent. The word has come to mean an impossible fantasy, and the adjective "chimerical" means imaginary, unreal, or absurd.

40. **D.** The fourth paragraph describes the man who uses familiar words to mean something different from what everyone else understands them to mean.

41. **C.** The third paragraph describes the man who uses a word "sometimes in one, sometimes in another signification."

42. **E.** All three of these are used interchangeably for "word."

Fourth Passage

The passage is from "Letters to an Architect," by Gretel Ehrlich.

43. **C.** A "miscellany" (the noun form of the adjective "miscellaneous") can be a collection of verse, but in this context, it has its more familiar meaning, a varied collection or medley.

44. **A.** A "shoal" is a shallow or sandbar in the sea or a river, a place that is difficult to navigate. The word that **B** defines is "sheaves."

45. **E.** In fact, the whole passage as part of a letter, has a first-person speaker, but it is not clear in this excerpt until the writer uses the "I" in line 39.

46. B. The third paragraph refers to Thoreau's search for a freedom with "personal privacy." The fourth paragraph describes men like Thoreau who thrived in the "expanse and solitude of the state."

47. D. The third paragraph suggests some differences between Thoreau and Jefferson. The fourth paragraph describes the settlers who resemble Thoreau, while the fifth paragraph presents those with more in common with Jefferson.

48. B. The fifth paragraph associates Brigham Young with Jeffersonian ideas. The four other options are associated with Thoreau in the fourth paragraph.

49. A. Option **II** is simply untrue, and option **III** is one of those answers that sound good and may make a point that is true in another context, but it has no connection at all with the passage at hand.

50. E. The last paragraph is about architecture, but it is not closely related to what has preceded it. It is about medieval Europe, not the Wyoming of the nineteenth and twentieth centuries.

51. C. The last paragraph refers to priests and governors as building to demonstrate their authority. The same may be said of slave owners and businessmen described in the second paragraph. The Mormons, on the other hand, had a "socialist regime."

52. D. Options **A** and **B** are presented as paradoxical in the second paragraph. The fifth paragraph describes the paradox of options **C** and **E,** and presents Brigham Young as extending Jeffersonian ideals.

53. B. The second paragraph is about the architecture "elsewhere." The last paragraph is also about other places.

54. E. The priests and governors of the Middle Ages are alike in their use of architecture with "hierarchical intentions." The other four pairs are contrasts in the passage.

55. C. Of the five choices, **C** is much the best. The passage is discursive, and not at all a carefully developed argument. It does not survey American architecture, and it does not examine the values reflected by the buildings of Wyoming. The second paragraph glances at American materialism, but this is not the subject of the passage.

Section II: Essay Questions

Question 1

Scoring Guide for Question 1 (John Updike)

8–9 Essays that score at the top perceptively analyze how Updike's metaphors and other rhetorical devices help establish the love-hate relationship an audience has towards sports. These essays appreciate how Updike's language works and wisely use appropriate examples from the text, both direct and indirect, to support the writer's ideas. Top-scoring essays offer thorough development and superior organization. While these essays may have a few minor flaws, the writing demonstrates a suave command of written English and the ability to write with syntactic variety.

6–7 Upper-level essays correctly understand how Updike's metaphors work and explore other rhetorical devices as well, using this understanding in the service of explaining how these devices convey attitude. Characteristically, these essays use the text well, abstractly or concretely, to back up the writer's thoughts, although these ideas may not be as perceptive or as sophisticated as those of the top scoring essays. Usually these essays are well developed and organized. Minor errors in writing may be present, but the writer's meaning is clear and coherent.

5 Essays that score in the middle range attempt to analyze the topic, but frequently do not understand how figurative language connects to meaning. Their insights are quite often obvious, pedestrian. Paraphrasing the excerpt instead of analyzing it may be evident. Development and organization may be too brief, illogical or unfulfilled. While the writing style itself may be adequate to convey meaning, inconsistencies in controlling written English may be present.

3–4 Lower-scoring essays fail to respond well to the topic. They may concentrate solely on what the audience feels during a sporting event, or perhaps only discuss the use of metaphor, without connecting figurative language to the audience's attitude. Paraphrasing is frequently employed, instead, on analysis. Development and organization of ideas is often inconsistent and limited. Although the writing may communicate ideas, the writing may have serious or persistent flaws that distract the reader. Many times, these low-scoring essays offer simple ideas that are presented in a simple manner.

1–2 The lowest-scoring essays demonstrate little or no success at analyzing how Updike's language creates attitude. They may pay scant attention to structural or rhetorical techniques or misunderstand their use. They may simply paraphrase the excerpt without supplying any analysis. Frequently, these lowest-scoring essays are extremely brief in development. Language is often imprecise and mechanics are often unsound.

High-Scoring Essay

In this passage, John Updike's juxtaposition of two central metaphors, combined with his occasional bellicose diction, allows him to emphasize the vicissitudes and the simple grandeur of baseball and the game's ability to reveal our humanity. Symbolic of our life and love, baseball offers prospective liberation along with possible disillusionment.

Both the monster and romance metaphors are used throughout the passage, creating a sense of continuity and allowing the author to thematically connect all the elements — from opening day to the action of the field to the real significance of the passage. Phrases like "its monstrous big heart," "act of faith," and "the first kiss of another prolonged entanglement" sustain imagery that the monster is altogether human and thus forgiving and loving. The contrast of the typical monster and the one portrayed as the "Fenway Faithful" not only adds interest to the piece, but also mirrors the roller coaster ride experienced by the fans. From "Supersox" to "dreadful days," the metaphors' inherent contrasts allow Updike to emphasize the same in the hearts of the fans. The author relies on us to draw upon our own life experiences, as we know romance, too, is full of disagreements and perfect moments, of triumphs and disappointments, truly a "hard lesson for a hungry monster to master." And yet, by the end of the passage, the author recognizes the simple beauty of baseball. Updike implies the innocent joy and magnificence in the way these "twenty-five youngish men" manipulate the hearts of fans. Indeed, it is so much like a romance, with its simplicity and complexity, perfectly summed up in the words, "You'll never get us to care again." However, Updike's voice clearly implies the opposite, that this game of love and hate will continue.

Indeed, the author seems to use the game of baseball as a microcosm of the outside world. His use of warlike diction elevates the game to a near life or death struggle. A four game sweep by the Yankees becomes a "massacre;" a winning streak becomes a "mini-resurrection;" and players seem to be "Civil War memorials" who are fighting for a "Noble Lost Cause" in "Zimmer's last stand."

Interestingly enough, this supposed struggle between life and death that is fought out on the baseball diamond ultimately turns into Updike's commentary on life itself. For, in reality, it is not war, but instead, to quote the manager Zimmer, "This is fun." Ultimately, his metaphors using the monster and romance only seek to simplify the relationship between the game and the fans. Like baseball, life, the author implies, should be fun at its core element, stripped of "solemn money men . . . scruffy media cameramen and sour-faced reporters." It is, in the end, a game of "innumerable potential redemptions and curious disappointments." In our attempts to understand, influence, and record these vicissitudes, perhaps Updike's intention is to leave us with some sense of the here and now. Perhaps it's best that we just jeer, holler, boo, and cheer as we enjoy ourselves in the sun. Perhaps that special moment is a little of what that "many-headed monster" feels that makes it come back again and again.

Analysis of the High-Scoring Essay

This essay does an excellent job of addressing the topic; it thoroughly explores metaphors and the connotation of Updike's "warlike diction," showing in the process how these elements create not only Updike's attitude toward baseball, but toward life itself. The introduction clearly tells the reader what to expect and ends with a graceful statement of how baseball symbolizes life. Updike would agree that this student truly comprehends his point.

The first body paragraph examines the monster and romance metaphors, showing how the two are intricately tied. The student offers ample examples of each and then connects them together with appropriate logic and interesting ideas. The student makes noteworthy points about how Updike relies on his audience to connect his ideas about baseball to their own life experiences, which we will find to be "full of disagreements and perfect moments, of triumphs and disappointments. . . ." The student's poise in using parallelism in this sentence also demonstrates his or her polish as a writer, which an AP reader will certainly notice and appreciate. The student's final idea in this paragraph, that baseball is a "game of love and hate" that "will continue," serves effectively not only as a clinching sentence to this paragraph, but also as a transition to the next paragraph, which explores the author's diction.

The second body paragraph scrutinizes how Updike's diction, especially the references to war, emphasize the "life or death struggle" of the game. The student presents virtually every example of "warlike diction" that the excerpt offers, but does not stop at merely listing them. He or she makes a larger point about how this diction helps establish Updike's attitude: that although it may seem like war on the baseball diamond, it is really just a game played for fun. The student has a good perspective on language analysis and life itself.

Overall, this essay covers the topic very well; it is organized logically and develops ideas substantially. The student also demonstrates a very nice flair for language use, as witnessed in the use of parallelism (notice it not only in the first body paragraph as previously noted, but also in the closing two sentences with the repetition on the word "Perhaps. . . .") The student's sentence structure is varied, vocabulary is sophisticated, and a sense of rhythm is present. This essay indeed deserves a high score.

Medium-Scoring Essay

The author's use of the monster metaphor allows him to paint the fans as having similar hopes and reactions to the Boston Red Sox's at times rocky season.

By incorporating the monster metaphor throughout the passage, the author calls the fans both hopeful and disappointed. He writes that last year's had broken its "monstrous big heart," and that showing up was "an act of faith." Clearly, the fans cannot help but come back and watch the Boston Red Sox, despite the multitude of horrifying disappointments, often at the hands of the Yankees. "Monsters," the author writes, "have short memories, elastic hearts, and very foolable faculties." The fans, interestingly, in all their differences, have a singular attitude and wish that unites them. It is this wish for the Boston Red Sox to win that enables the author to group these people into an entity, what he calls the "many-headed monster." What is the focus of much of the passage, however, is a description of the fundamental essence of the game of baseball.

It is decidedly from a baseball fans point of view. It is focused on the fun of baseball, how little things within the game bring so much enjoyment and pleasure. It is, to this author, more than just a game of baseball, but rather a celebration of life and an atmosphere. As the author writes, "Monsters love high notes and hoards of gold," referring to "The Star-Spangled Banner" performance and the governor's appearance. The fans, represented as a whole by the monster, love everything about the atmosphere of baseball. From the pure essence of "statistical virginity" to the manager, "last year's anti-hero," the fans love the effect it has on their lives. They keep coming back, it makes no difference because of the elevation of baseball to a more important level — a staple of their lives. The author may be saying to us that the wonderfulness of baseball is, in itself, good enough.

Analysis of the Medium-Scoring Essay

This essay essentially attempts to accomplish the topic, but does not do much more than paraphrase the original excerpt. The student recognizes that Updike uses a metaphor, but there is little else in this essay that is praiseworthy. The introduction / thesis is somewhat vague. For example, when the student writes that the fans have "similar hopes and reactions" the reader wonders exactly *what* they are similar to; are they similar to the "rocky season"? A clearer thesis statement would certainly help this essay.

The first body paragraph identifies the monster metaphor and correctly identifies that it represents the baseball audience, but the student offers no strong analysis of that metaphor. Instead, the student paraphrases Updike: yes, the fans are "both hopeful and disappointed"; yes, the fans come back to watch over and over; yes, the fans have a "singular . . . wish that unites them," but the student merely lists these ideas and never analyzes *how* Updike's metaphor establishes his attitude. It is not convincing to merely state the attitude and drop a quotation or two from the author.

The second body paragraph, too, is basically accurate in its paraphrasing of Updike; indeed, to Updike the game *is* a "celebration of life." However, once again, the student offers little more than a string of quotations and examples of the behavior and attitude of fans from the passage. For a stronger essay, the student needs to have a *reason* for presenting all of this information, an analytical point about *how* these examples work in this excerpt.

Also compounding the student's weak analytical skills is his or her weak command of written English. Apostrophe errors abound (i.e. "last year's had broken. . . ." "a baseball fans point of view" to name two), plus run-on sentences ("They keep coming back, it makes no difference. . . .") and weak wording ("things," "the author writes," etc.) do not help demonstrate sophistication in this writer. Top-scoring essays answer the topic, have clear organization, develop ideas thoroughly, and demonstrate strong control over written English. This essay simply does not show those traits.

Question 2

Scoring Guide for Question 2 (Cynthia Ozick)

8–9 Essays earning a top score astutely understand the differences between Ozick's attitudes toward essays and articles, while demonstrating a strong appreciation of how her language and style establish those attitudes. These essays are thoroughly developed and refer to the text frequently, demonstrating the ability to explore the subtleties of Ozick's language and syntax. Not necessarily without flaws, these essays still show mastery over the conventions of written English and sophisticated style.

6–7 Well-written, these essays accurately reflect the different attitudes Ozick presents and attempt to connect her style to her attitude. These essays refer to the text and recognize important features of rhetorical development. While these essays might comprehend some of the subtleties of Ozick's language, awareness might not be as far-reaching as the top-scoring essay. Well-developed ideas and clear diction show strong control over the elements of written English, although minor errors may be present.

5 Average essays may not explore the deep differences that the author presents between essays and articles, or may dwell on obvious or superficial differences. Instead of analyzing how the author's style and language create attitude, these essays may rely on paraphrasing the author's points. Development and organization may be clear but not as effective as that of higher-scoring essays. Inconsistencies in the command of language may be present, but the prose in these essays usually is sufficient to convey the writer's ideas.

3–4 These lower-scoring essays may not discuss the author's differences or may only write on Ozick's views of either an essay or an article. They frequently paraphrase without making a connection between the author's point and how her language conveys her attitude. Insights may be inaccurate or trite. The writing may convey some ideas, but weak control over language holds the ideas back. Frequent mechanical errors may be present, suggesting immature control over organization of ideas, diction, or syntax.

1–2 Essays earning a low score fail to respond sufficiently to the topic or the passage. They may try to present a discussion of the author's attitude, but may provide insufficient evidence from the passage, or may misread the passage and present erroneous ideas. Severely limited development hinders the essay. Persistent weaknesses in writing may distract the reader, demonstrating a lack of control of written language.

High-Scoring Essay

Exploiting metaphorical portraitures of the essay, mellifluous syntax, and painstakingly precise paradox, Ozick conveys the intellectual curiosity towards the pulsating, artistically ageless essay, while dismissing the "look-alike knock off" temporary article.

Claiming at first that the essay represents "a thing of the imagination" Ozick's survey of the essay deepens into a three-dimensional, fleshed, elusive body. By first enumerating the metaphorical characteristics of the essay to an artistic perspective, reveling its form akin to poetry, "made out of language and character and mood and temperament and pluck and change," Ozick humanizes the essay's composite personality. Skillfully, the author juxtaposes the ersatz article with the genuine essay to emphasize the inimitable soul of the essay's essence. Indeed, unlike the spurious version, an article, the essay represents a super-mortal, whose blood burns with infinite "reflection and insight," whose skin emanates internal heat, a body whose very being "defies its date of birth." In a sense, Ozick elevates the essay from an ephemeral phantasmagoria to an immortal god, each time tracing its evolution with awe because the essay cannot be hinged or yoked to one static form. Ozick delineates how an essay traverses the landscape of our imagination, piquing in the reader a plaguing sense of direction begot by the various and ancient metaphorical molds assumed by the essay; the lesser article, meanwhile, lies flat, something that "will be stale within the month."

Inculcating the ebb and flow of a harmoniously question-inciting essay upon which it expounds, Ozick's syntax in the second paragraph parallels the challenges posed in a "genuine" essay. Employing imperative adjurations and if-then clauses, the voice carries an edifying, instruction-giving objectivity efficacious in structuring a cohesive conviction that "a genuine essay has no education, polemical or sociopolitical use; it is the movement of a free mind at play." The syntax attempts no moralizing fables, instead bent upon the repetitive construction of contrasting the article with the essay. The Spartan noun-linking verb sequence demonstrates the unaffected, unshielded investigative temerity of "an essay [that] is reflection and insight . . . an essay [whose] heat is interior . . . an essay [that] defies its date of birth" while the article remains merely "gossip" that will last no longer than "a rotary phone." Ozick's disdainful tone when describing an article starkly contrasts with her lofty tone toward essays. Perhaps, Ozick construes, it is the disarming simplicity permeating the essay that renders it captivatingly mysterious. Here is one form, aptly embellished with an armory of rhetorical tricks — such as fragmentation and allusion — to engage the reader into responding to proffered pivotal conjectures like "Who are the classical essayists who come at once to mind?" Curiously enough, despite the segmented nuances of its syntax, the cumulative effect of the essay is to simply "coerce assent."

Paradoxically, the implication of this essay leans toward persuasion. However, like any work of art, the irony herein lies that, as Oscar Wilde noted, "all art is quite useless," and any manifestation of art masquerading with a purpose clearly cannot belong to its high aesthetic class. Thus, Ozick leaves us to question whether the essay can indeed be construed as an artistic form or merely an inveigling penny-tract. Eliminating the possibility that "Paine's 'Common Sense' and Zola's 'J'Accuse'" mirror the essay, Ozick suggests again that the essay is something we cannot conceptualize — a form without formal form. The ultimate paradox that the essay engenders is that, akin to an article, it represents an amorphous form, as well as an art that "co-opts agreement . . . courts agreement . . . seduces agreement."

Analysis of the High-Scoring Essay

This writer addresses the topic in a pleasing fashion. Instead of relying on a traditional format, the writer weaves ideas together skillfully and builds to a last, climactic paragraph. This thought-provoking response succeeds by intelligently articulating the differences between an article and an essay. The thesis is relevant, stimulating and makes a reader want to continue, hoping, to find out what the student will have to discuss about paradox and "mellifluous syntax."

The first body paragraph establishes the vitality of the essay form, surely one of Ozick's strong opinions. By elevating an essay to "artistic perspective" this student shows how Ozick gives animation and sparkle to the concept of an essay. This student's phrasing, for instance in describing an essay as a "super-mortal whose blood burns . . . whose skin emanates . . . heat," unquestionably demonstrates the student's command over figurative language. Then, most appropriately, he or she swiftly classifies an article as something that "lies flat." When discussing an essay, this student's words are as lofty as Ozick's ideas; when discussing an article, this student's words are as simple and concise as Ozick's.

The second body paragraph begins to analyze Ozick's style and syntax in greater detail, aptly exploring Ozick's second paragraph as a way to show the student's understanding of how language works. In evaluating the linking verb pattern, the implied "if . . . then" concepts, and the author's tone, the student quite aptly demonstrates skillful comprehension of Ozick's sentence patterns, artistic choices, and their effect.

The final paragraph analyzes the inherent paradox hidden within Ozick's essay: namely that it actually does "lean toward persuasion" even though Ozick herself claims the contrary. This student demonstrates greater awareness than most, and this paragraph on paradox completes the essay with strong analytical skills; this paragraph truly builds to a crescendo.

Taken as a whole, this student's depth of understanding is impressive, as is his or her vocabulary and carefully reasoned presentation. The essay might be improved with some examples from the text to back up some of its ideas, but its development is admirable. However, it cannot be denied that the student clearly understands how Ozick's language conveys her attitude. While diction can occasionally get away from the student, the ideas, awareness, and overall style are first rate.

Medium-Scoring Essay

Not many people think very often about the difference between an article and an essay. Cynthia Ozick, however, detachedly describes the essay as a force of the imagination using diction, structure, and imagery, but she claims the article is not as imaginative.

With adjectives precisely depicting the genuine essay, the author conjures how the essay cannot be duplicated by a article, how it defies time, shape, and form. The essay's body is "reflection and insight", not wreathed in the social heat of what's popular like an article, yet its heat is "inferior", and it defies its date of birth. In contrast, the article is its opposite, something stuck in a specific era, "Siamese-twinned to its date of birth" and in 5 years, "guaranteed not to wear well." The word "genuine" compellingly connotes the force of a true essay — it bears the stamp of strong essayists like "Montaigne . . . Hazlitt, Lamb, De Quincey, Carlyle . . . Emerson." Yet, it possesses a power outside this authorship "to coerce assent." The phrase "stroll through someone's mazy mind" also tells us how the essay functions — it allows us to see into a person's mind and be informed by this person's ideas. Also, the essay is made "out of the character & mood & temperament" of the author's imagination.

The structure of this selection also presents the essay as an imaginative force, which an article can't do. Using parallel structure, the author shows us how the essay can persuade with language its conviction. The succession of "an essay is", and "an article is" comparisons also contrast how the essay cannot be duplicated outside the imagination. The author relies upon adjectives and passive voice to convey the essay's picture.

The imagery in this selection also renders the essay a mysterious power. It paints the essay as something unreliable. It says that the essay "represents the movement of a free mind at play", and a "stroll through someone's mazy mind". The essay seems to be portrayed as a journey rather than an entity — something that is not a form that can be categorized but instead a direction that tries to persuade us in some way.

Analysis of the Medium-Scoring Essay

This essay earns a medium score because it demonstrates adequate understanding of Ozick's attitude, but it truly fails to analyze the passage. Indeed, it relies more on paraphrasing than on analyzing. The introduction begins with a fairly bland sentence that implies the writer has never before considered the thrust of Ozick's ideas about articles and essays, which is not an impressive opening. The thesis is not terribly insightful, and it remains at the obvious level.

The body paragraphs may appear to present the student's ideas, but a closer examination shows that the writer instead merely paraphrases Ozick; the analysis is either simplistic or nonexistent. The length of the body paragraphs may be deceiving, but they get stuck by simply presenting what Ozick *says*, not *how* her language establishes her attitude. The body paragraphs do distinguish that Ozick thinks essays superior to articles, but that obvious idea can only go so far. In particular, the second body paragraph is weak, promising to discuss the "structure of [the] selection" but never fulfilling that promise. It provides no examples of parallel structure to back up its assertion about that rhetorical device. This paragraph is disorganized, jumping from one idea to another, and its development is subsequently flawed. Notice, for instance, the simplistic last sentence of the paragraph; it merely states that the author uses adjectives and passive voice. Neither device has any backing, nor does the student *do* anything with this information. High-scoring essays analyze *how* these devices work; medium and lower scoring essays merely list what is in the passage.

In addition, this essay demonstrates some errors in mechanics and wording that compound its simplistic thinking. The punctuation error of placing a comma or period outside of quotation marks persists. Some phrasing is unclear, imprecise, or cumbersome; for example, reread the phrases "the author shows us how the essay can persuade with language its conviction," and "it allows us to see into a person's mind and be informed by this person's ideas." Perhaps with a stronger proofreading, the student may have clarified these sentences.

The positive elements in this essay are hidden by its weak presentation, which combines limited development, weak organization, poor word choice, and simplistic ideas.

Question 3

Scoring Guide for Question 3 (George Eliot)

8–9 Top-scoring essays persuasively defend, challenge, or qualify Eliot's assertion that our actions "determine us." These essays also examine her addendum to this idea, namely that one needs to truly understand another person's "outward and inward facts" before one can judge the other accurately. They present intelligently cohesive and carefully articulated arguments that employ appropriate evidence from the writers' experiences, observations, or collective knowledge to develop their positions. The development and organization of ideas is superior. Even though these essays may contain some minor flaws, usually a consequence of timed writing pressure, they demonstrate the ability to control language with a sophisticated flair.

6–7 These upper-level essays decently defend, challenge, or qualify Eliot's assertions, generally in a thought-provoking manner. The writers' arguments are sound and use ample evidence. While these essays are well developed, they may not be as fully realized as those that receive a top score. For the most part, the prose of these essays is strong enough to convey the writers' ideas clearly, but a few lapses in command over written conventions may be present.

5 Essays earning a score of 5 understand the task and attempt to make statements that defend, challenge or qualify Eliot's assertions. While the writers' arguments may be reasonably clear, the presentation may be more limited than that of the high-scoring essays. The writers' arguments may be superficial or the evidence offered may be only mildly relevant. The writers' logic that connects evidence to ideas may be weak or nonexistent. These essays are generally clear in their use of language, although some lapses in diction and syntax may be apparent.

3–4 These essays fail to adequately respond to the topic's task. They may oversimplify Eliot's argument or misrepresent her ideas. Evidence for the writers' ideas is frequently insufficient to convince the reader of the validity of the writers' beliefs. Quite often, development and organization are flawed, limited, and/or insubstantial. The writing style may demonstrate an immature command over written English, but meaning is generally clear.

1–2 Essays scoring at the lowest end of the scale demonstrate little or no ability to defend, challenge, or qualify Eliot's ideas. They may instead try to substitute a different task, such as writing ideas that are only tangentially relevant. They may misread Eliot's intent. Development of ideas is often slighted and simplistic, either by providing inadequate evidence or offering no examples at all to back up the writers' claims. Explanation of evidence and examples may be too limited or nonexistent. The prose of these essays may show weak control over the conventions of grammar and mechanics.

High-Scoring Essay

In her assertion, Eliot alludes to the dangerous though unavoidable human predisposition towards making presumptions about people's characters. In Joseph Conrad's <u>Heart of Darkness</u>, this universal human tendency is demonstrated through the interaction between characters Marlow and Kurtz. Conrad proves, through his character Kurtz, that Eliot is correct: a person is the result of his or her emotions, actions, and surroundings and cannot be fully understood until one can realize another's inward and outward motivations.

In the beginning of his journey, Conrad portrays Kurtz as an idealized hero. Marlow's first encounter with the notion of Kurtz occurs through the articulated opinions of others. The accountant, for instance, refers to Kurtz as a first class agent, a remarkable person. The manager, similarly, views Kurtz as the agent of greatest importance. These romanticized versions of Kurtz are based only on his outward actions, and even then only those that European society deems valuable, such as his great success in business, namely the attainment of ivory.

As Marlow begins his journey to find Kurtz, he attempts to understand Kurtz's inner nature. However, he is still dependent, as Eliot puts it, on outward facts. Marlow therefore conjures up images of Kurtz to suit his own psychological needs, and so his vision remains ideological. In comparing Kurtz to "a sleeping princess in a castle," Marlow demonstrates that he must justify Kurtz's actions so that he can convince himself that the darkness will not conquer him, too. While creating this image of Kurtz in his mind, Marlow makes presumptions about Kurtz's inner thoughts based on outward facts such as Kurtz's skill with finding ivory and the scenery of the jungle. Eliot understands the foolishness of this.

It is not, however, until the inward forces acting on Kurtz become apparent to Marlow that the truth is so clearly revealed about Kurtz. His deeds control him as much as, if not more than, he controls his actions. Kurtz is a character trapped in his solitude by a myriad of worshippers. He is ensnared by the lack of law, of societal rules, of "policemen." Kurtz's greatest admirer, the "Harlequin" admits, even, that Kurtz's life wears him out yet Kurtz does not escape from it. The reason behind this is that Kurtz's greed and pillaging lead to an even greater desire to attain ivory, to grow better at his trade. The action of attaining ivory forces him to want more. Therefore, when his ships prepare to return home, he fires on his own men. Similarly, the admiration he receives from his followers leads to a need for more veneration. Consequently, Kurtz creates a monument to himself from decapitated heads to attain the respect and wonder of his worshippers. It is not until the reader, via Marlow, is able to peer through the jungle into the darkness of Kurtz's heart, into his inward turmoil and outward surroundings, that he or she may presume to know about his character. Eliot's assertion again proves to be true, as Kurtz is indeed a *very* "peculiar combination of outward and inward facts."

Conrad, in his development of Kurtz's character shows the inadequacy of people's presumptions, bolstering the validity of Eliot's observation, by revealing Kurtz's true character only after first disclosing other people's perceptions of him. Therefore, Kurtz exemplifies a person whose actions are both controlled and guided by him and whose character is defined by factors found both inside of himself and in his outward surroundings. Eliot would smile and say, "See? I told you so."

Analysis of the High-Scoring Essay

This student clearly validates Eliot's assertion that humans prejudge others without understanding their inner motives by examining the intricate novella, *Heart of Darkness*. By acknowledging that this is a "universal human tendency" which is seen in the novella's characters, the student indeed proves "that Eliot is correct." The essay directions ask test takers to use their reading, observation, or experience to back up their position, and this student utilizes a complex piece of reading very effectively. The score does not suffer because the student did not add examples from personal observations or experiences; rather, his or her score will be rewarded for what the essay does well: staying on topic and developing ideas articulately.

The essay takes a chronological approach in its examination of *Heart of Darkness;* this approach works well in this case, as the character Marlow only discovers Kurtz's complexity as the novella unfolds. Therefore, the first body paragraph establishes what Marlow learns the other characters think of Kurtz: that he appears to be a successful businessman by European standards. This paragraph is necessary to verify that Marlow initially does what all humans are guilty of, prejudging others. In this case, Marlow judges Kurtz solely on his reputation.

The next paragraph demonstrates how Marlow is still stuck in what Eliot cautions against, namely judging others without knowing their inner ideas. The student is to be admired for remembering a quotation from the text, although AP readers never expect this. Presenting ample evidence of Marlow's molding Kurtz "to suit his own psychological needs," the student shows how Marlow follows Eliot's assertion.

The following paragraph begins to present how Marlow slowly begins to grasp the essence of Eliot's statement: that Kurtz's actions stem from inner motives that Marlow does not yet comprehend. Kurtz's confusing and contradictory character proves to be a good choice for this essay, and the student presents how Marlow's growing understanding of Kurtz fits the topic well without lapsing into simplistic plot synopsis.

The final paragraph ends the essay gracefully. While a student should be cautious whenever inventing quotations, the last apocryphal sentence works well in this essay, as it sums up Eliot's attitude toward those who judge others without understanding their inner motives. The student's writing is clear, well-developed, and shows an occasional flair, such as the parallelism in the phrasing "the lack of law, of societal laws, of 'policemen'" in the fourth paragraph. AP readers are only too happy to reward the appearance of sophistication in student writing.

Medium-Scoring Essay

In F. Scott Fitzgerald's the Great Gatsby, Jay Gatsby serves as an example of Eliot's assertion that it is unwise to make assumptions about a person's character. Jay Gatsby's character cannot fully be understood until it is possible to comprehend his outward and inward influences. It is not until these are understood that Gatsby's true situation is revealed, namely that he has become overpowered by his actions.

Gatsby is initially portrayed as a person of great wealth and renown through the perceptions of Nick Carraway, for instance, from his own home, Nick witnesses Gatsby's seeming popularity with the saturation of his house with guests, and so the reader presumes that Gatsby is a man of stature, at the top of cosmopolitan society. These presumptions are, however, based only on outward facts, with no regard to his inner character.

Gatsby, however, is revealed as a frail, insecure man once Nick is invited to Gatsby's house. Gatsby tells Nick his true motivation, namely his desire for Daisy. Consequently, Gatsby climbs socially upward to get closer to her, but becomes controlled by society's conformity. His intense longing controls his actions as he no longer guides his own life, he is a prisoner of insecurity and social hierarchy.

In fact, Gatsby's deeds ultimately conquer him as it is apparent the degree to which his inward problem takes over his outward appearance and actions. His false hopes led him to dream of an impossible life. Once he realizes, however, that no matter what action he takes his dream cannot be fulfilled, he is devastated by his fantasy. Gatsby has become the victim of his actions and ideals from which he cannot escape.

In the Great Gatsby, it is uncovered that Gatsby's apparent greatness is a falsity once Gatsby's inner thoughts are revealed, he exists, instead, as a victim of society's presumptions living timidly in the shadows of greatness.

Analysis of the Medium-Scoring Essay

This essay shows how a student can get seriously off topic, especially when using a novel for the AP Language Essay. While it shows a glimmer of proving Eliot's assertion, it turns instead into literary character analysis of Jay Gatsby. In the student's favor, he or she does point out in the introduction that Gatsby is not fully comprehended until one understands his "inward influences," but that's about all the student has to say.

The first body paragraph merely presents that Gatsby seems to be at the "top of cosmopolitan society," a presumption that is "based only on outward facts." The student needs to explore *how Gatsby relates to Eliot's assertion* much more. To simply state that he fits Eliot's idea is completely unconvincing. This undeveloped paragraph presents mere character observation, then it falls flat on its analysis of this essay topic.

The next paragraph presents simplistic plot summary and tells us why Gatsby climbs socially, but again it does not *connect* to Eliot's claim. The following paragraph has the same fault; we may understand what Gatsby is like, but the reader wonders how these brief paragraphs help validate Eliot's idea.

The conclusion does claim that Gatsby is a "victim of society's presumptions" but by now this claim provides too little, too late. Instead of proving how the novel supports Eliot's assertion, the essay seems to be trying to solicit our sympathy for poor misunderstood Gatsby. The student's writing style is as flat, as are the student's ideas. The writer also shows weak control over the conventions of written English, such as in the failure to punctuate and capitalize the novel's title properly and in the numerous run-on sentences. This essay deserves a low score because of its inability to truly examine the topic, develop ideas, and present them with any degree of sophistication.

Answer Sheet for Practice Test 5

(Remove This Sheet and Use it to Mark Your Answers)

Section I
Multiple-Choice Questions

PASSAGE 1

1 Ⓐ Ⓑ Ⓒ Ⓓ Ⓔ
2 Ⓐ Ⓑ Ⓒ Ⓓ Ⓔ
3 Ⓐ Ⓑ Ⓒ Ⓓ Ⓔ
4 Ⓐ Ⓑ Ⓒ Ⓓ Ⓔ
5 Ⓐ Ⓑ Ⓒ Ⓓ Ⓔ
6 Ⓐ Ⓑ Ⓒ Ⓓ Ⓔ
7 Ⓐ Ⓑ Ⓒ Ⓓ Ⓔ
8 Ⓐ Ⓑ Ⓒ Ⓓ Ⓔ
9 Ⓐ Ⓑ Ⓒ Ⓓ Ⓔ
10 Ⓐ Ⓑ Ⓒ Ⓓ Ⓔ
11 Ⓐ Ⓑ Ⓒ Ⓓ Ⓔ
12 Ⓐ Ⓑ Ⓒ Ⓓ Ⓔ
13 Ⓐ Ⓑ Ⓒ Ⓓ Ⓔ
14 Ⓐ Ⓑ Ⓒ Ⓓ Ⓔ

PASSAGE 2

15 Ⓐ Ⓑ Ⓒ Ⓓ Ⓔ
16 Ⓐ Ⓑ Ⓒ Ⓓ Ⓔ
17 Ⓐ Ⓑ Ⓒ Ⓓ Ⓔ
18 Ⓐ Ⓑ Ⓒ Ⓓ Ⓔ
19 Ⓐ Ⓑ Ⓒ Ⓓ Ⓔ
20 Ⓐ Ⓑ Ⓒ Ⓓ Ⓔ
21 Ⓐ Ⓑ Ⓒ Ⓓ Ⓔ
22 Ⓐ Ⓑ Ⓒ Ⓓ Ⓔ
23 Ⓐ Ⓑ Ⓒ Ⓓ Ⓔ
24 Ⓐ Ⓑ Ⓒ Ⓓ Ⓔ
25 Ⓐ Ⓑ Ⓒ Ⓓ Ⓔ
26 Ⓐ Ⓑ Ⓒ Ⓓ Ⓔ
27 Ⓐ Ⓑ Ⓒ Ⓓ Ⓔ
28 Ⓐ Ⓑ Ⓒ Ⓓ Ⓔ
29 Ⓐ Ⓑ Ⓒ Ⓓ Ⓔ

PASSAGE 3

30 Ⓐ Ⓑ Ⓒ Ⓓ Ⓔ
31 Ⓐ Ⓑ Ⓒ Ⓓ Ⓔ
32 Ⓐ Ⓑ Ⓒ Ⓓ Ⓔ
33 Ⓐ Ⓑ Ⓒ Ⓓ Ⓔ
34 Ⓐ Ⓑ Ⓒ Ⓓ Ⓔ
35 Ⓐ Ⓑ Ⓒ Ⓓ Ⓔ
36 Ⓐ Ⓑ Ⓒ Ⓓ Ⓔ
37 Ⓐ Ⓑ Ⓒ Ⓓ Ⓔ
38 Ⓐ Ⓑ Ⓒ Ⓓ Ⓔ
39 Ⓐ Ⓑ Ⓒ Ⓓ Ⓔ
40 Ⓐ Ⓑ Ⓒ Ⓓ Ⓔ
41 Ⓐ Ⓑ Ⓒ Ⓓ Ⓔ
42 Ⓐ Ⓑ Ⓒ Ⓓ Ⓔ
43 Ⓐ Ⓑ Ⓒ Ⓓ Ⓔ

PASSAGE 4

44 Ⓐ Ⓑ Ⓒ Ⓓ Ⓔ
45 Ⓐ Ⓑ Ⓒ Ⓓ Ⓔ
46 Ⓐ Ⓑ Ⓒ Ⓓ Ⓔ
47 Ⓐ Ⓑ Ⓒ Ⓓ Ⓔ
48 Ⓐ Ⓑ Ⓒ Ⓓ Ⓔ
49 Ⓐ Ⓑ Ⓒ Ⓓ Ⓔ
50 Ⓐ Ⓑ Ⓒ Ⓓ Ⓔ
51 Ⓐ Ⓑ Ⓒ Ⓓ Ⓔ
52 Ⓐ Ⓑ Ⓒ Ⓓ Ⓔ
53 Ⓐ Ⓑ Ⓒ Ⓓ Ⓔ
54 Ⓐ Ⓑ Ⓒ Ⓓ Ⓔ
55 Ⓐ Ⓑ Ⓒ Ⓓ Ⓔ

CUT HERE

Section I: Multiple-Choice Questions

Time: 60 Minutes

55 Questions

Directions: This sections consists of selections from prose works and questions on their content, style, and form, Read each selection carefully. Choose the best answer of the five choices.

Questions 1-14. Read the following passage carefully before you begin to answer the questions.

First Passage

Good and evil we know in the field of this world grow up together almost inseparably; and the knowledge of good is so involved and interwoven with the knowl-
(5) edge of evil, and in so many cunning resemblances hardly to be discerned, that those confused seeds which were imposed upon Psyche as an incessant labour to cull out, and sort asunder, were not
(10) more intermixed. It was from out the rind of one apple tasted, that the knowledge of good and evil, as two twins cleaving together, leaped forth into the world. And perhaps this is that doom which Adam
(15) fell into of knowing good and evil, that is to say, of knowing good by evil.

As therefore the state of man now is, what wisdom can there be to choose, what continence to forbear without the
(20) knowledge of evil? He that can apprehend and consider vice with all her baits and seeming pleasures, and yet abstain, and yet distinguish, and yet prefer that which is truly better, he is the true way-
(25) faring Christian. I cannot praise a fugitive and cloistered virtue, unexercised and unbreathed, that never sallies out and sees her adversary, but slinks out of the race where that immortal garland is
(30) to be run for, not without dust and heat. Assuredly we bring not innocence into the world, we bring impurity much rather: that which purifies us is trial, and trial is by what is contrary. That virtue
(35) which is but a youngling in the contemplation of evil, and knows not the utmost that vice promises to her followers, and rejects it, is but a blank virtue, not a pure; her whiteness is but an excremen-
(40) tal whiteness; which was the reason that our sage and serious poet Spenser, whom I dare be known to think a better teacher than Scotus or Aquinas, describing true temperance under the person of
(45) Guion, brings him in with his palmer[1] through the cave of Mammon[2] and the bower[3] of earthly bliss, that he might see and know, and yet abstain.

Notes: Lines 6–9 = Venus set Psyche the task of sorting out the different kinds of grain in a large mixed heap. Lines 25–26, fugitive = that which flees from life. Lines 39–40, excremental = superficial, on the surface. Line 43, Scotus, Aquinas = two great scholastic philosophers. Line 45 = Guyon is the knight of temperance in Spenser's "Faerie Queene" (1) palmer = an itinerant monk under a vow of poverty, (2) the cave of Mammon = the temptation of wealth, and (3) bower = temptation of sensual pleasure.

GO ON TO THE NEXT PAGE

1. In the first sentence of the passage, the speaker compares good and evil to

   A. children.

   B. light and darkness.

   C. plants.

   D. this world and the next.

   E. fibers.

2. In lines 15–16, "of knowing good and evil, that is to say, of knowing good by evil" is suggesting that

   A. we cannot distinguish between good and evil.

   B. we can understand good by avoiding evil.

   C. good and evil are simultaneously alike and opposites.

   D. we can know evil only by knowing good.

   E. we can know good only by knowing evil.

3. The first sentence of the second paragraph (lines 16–20) is an example of

   A. indirect question.

   B. analogy.

   C. personification.

   D. syllogism.

   E. rhetorical question.

4. In line 28, "adversary" refers to

   A. monasticism.

   B. vice.

   C. hypocrisy.

   D. virtue.

   E. trial.

5. In lines 25–30, all of the following words contribute to the same metaphor EXCEPT

   A. "cloistered," line 26.

   B. "race," line 29.

   C. "garland," line 29.

   D. "run for," line 30.

   E. "dust," line 30.

6. The "garland" of line 29 may be best understood to mean

   A. an elective office.

   B. the prize of immortality.

   C. a circlet of laurel.

   D. a collection of poems.

   E. a fantastic ornament.

7. The argument of lines 31–34 ("Assuredly we . . . is contrary.") is that

   A. no human is ever completely free of guilt.

   B. no human is wholly unfamiliar with vice and its temptations.

   C. the experience of life is like a trial in a court of law.

   D. it is experience, not innocence, that purifies humans.

   E. a child is innocent until he or she has experienced evil.

8. In line 34, the phrase "trial is by what is contrary" can best be paraphrased

    A. by refusing to fight, we may achieve victory.

    B. a true verdict can be reached only after the careful study of evidence on both sides.

    C. before we can win a victory, we must first be defeated.

    D. humans are tested by their experience of conflict.

    E. what a court determines may well be wrong.

9. The implication of the comment on Spenser in lines 41–43 is that

    A. philosophers are unqualified to teach morality.

    B. literature may teach better than philosophy.

    C. comedy may be as effective a teacher as serious writing.

    D. the first function of literature is to teach temperance.

    E. literature cannot take the place of revealed religion.

10. The passage refers to the "bower of earthly bliss" (line 47) as an example of

    A. an evil recognized and resisted.

    B. the heavenly rewards of the temperate.

    C. the sensual pleasure of literature.

    D. a state of pure innocence.

    E. the garden of Eden before Adam.

11. The central argument of this passage is that

    A. true virtue must avoid evil.

    B. good and evil are interdependent.

    C. we must understand evil to be able to resist it.

    D. if we can avoid occasions of sin, we can overcome temptations.

    E. all men and women are equally susceptible to good and evil.

12. The style of the passage is characterized by the use of all of the following EXCEPT

    A. colloquial diction.

    B. literary allusion.

    C. first person pronouns.

    D. metaphor and simile.

    E. balanced compound sentences.

13. In developing its thesis, the passage relies on all of the following EXCEPT

    A. ethical argument.

    B. personal anecdote.

    C. extended definition.

    D. abstract generalization.

    E. reference to authority.

14. Which of the following best describes the speaker of the passage?

    A. an impartial observer

    B. a cautious advisor

    C. a skeptical commentator

    D. a wry reporter

    E. a dedicated partisan

GO ON TO THE NEXT PAGE

Practice Test 5

Questions 15–29. Read the following passage carefully before you begin to answer the questions.

Second Passage

Everyone knows the popular conception of Florence Nightingale. The saintly, self-sacrificing woman, the delicate maiden of high degree who threw
(5) aside the pleasures of a life of ease to succour the afflicted, the Lady with the Lamp, gliding through the horrors of the hospital at Scutari, and consecrating with the radiance of her goodness the
(10) dying soldier's couch — the vision is familiar to all. But the truth was different. The Miss Nightingale of fact was not as facile fancy painted her. She worked in another fashion, and toward another end;
(15) she moved under the stress of an impetus which finds no place in the popular imagination. A Demon possessed her. Now demons, whatever else they may be, are full of interest. And so it happens
(20) that in the real Miss Nightingale there was more that was interesting than in the legendary one; there was also less that was agreeable.

What was the secret voice in her ear,
(25) if it was not a call? Why had she felt from her earliest years, those mysterious promptings towards . . . she hardly knew what but certainly towards something very different from anything around her?
(30) Why, as a child in the nursery, when her sister had shown a healthy pleasure in tearing her dolls to pieces, had she shown an almost morbid one in sewing them up again? Why was she driven now
(35) to minister to the poor in their cottages, to watch by sick-beds, to put her dog's wounded paw into elaborate splints as if it was a human being? Why was her head filled with the queer imaginations
(40) of the country house at Embley turned, by some enchantment, into a hospital,

with herself as matron moving among the beds? Why was even her vision of heaven itself filled with suffering pa
(45) tients to whom she was being useful? So she dreamed and wondered, and taking out her diary, she poured into it the agitations of her soul.

A weaker spirit would have been
(50) overwhelmed by the load of such distress — would have yielded or snapped. But this extraordinary young woman held firm, and fought her way to victory. With an amazing persistency, during the
(55) eight years that followed her rebuff over Salisbury Hospital, she struggled and worked and planned. While superficially she was carrying on the life of a brilliant girl in high society, while internally she
(60) was a prey to the tortures of regret and remorse, she yet possessed the energy to collect the knowledge and to undergo the experience which alone could enable her to do what she had determined she
(65) would do in the end. In secret she devoured the reports of medical commissions, the pamphlets of sanitary authorities, the histories of hospitals and homes. She spent the intervals of the
(70) London season in ragged schools and workhouses. When she went abroad with her family, she used her spare time so well that there was hardly a great hospital in Europe with which she was not
(75) acquainted, hardly a great city whose slums she had not passed through.

Three more years passed, and then at last the pressure of time told; her family seemed to realise that she was old
(80) enough and strong enough to have her way; and she became superintendent of a charitable nursing home in Harley

Street. She had gained her independence, though it was in a meagre sphere
(85) enough; and her mother was still not quite resigned: surely Florence might at least spend the summer in the country. At times, indeed, among her intimates, Mrs. Nightingale almost wept. "We

(90) are ducks," she said with tears in her eyes, "who have hatched a wild swan." But the poor lady was wrong; it was not a swan that they had hatched; it was an eagle.

15. Which of the following best describes the structure of the first paragraph?

   A. It is divided into two parts, beginning with general statements, and moving to specific commentary.

   B. It is divided into two contrasting parts, with the division coming in line 12.

   C. It alternates a short sentence followed by a long sentence through- out.

   D. It moves from the presentation of Florence Nightingale's strengths (lines 1–11) to the presentation of her weaknesses (lines 12–23)

   E. It presents Florence Nightingale first in figurative language (lines 1–11), then in literal (lines 12–23).

16. Which of the following best defines the word "succour" of line 6?

   A. oversee

   B. treat with medicines

   C. relieve

   D. rally

   E. convert

17. In the first paragraph, all of the following words and phrases are used to present the popular conception of Florence Nightingale EXCEPT

   A. saintly (line 3)

   B. self-sacrificing (line 3)

   C. the Lady with the Lamp (lines 6–7)

   D. interesting (line 22)

   E. legendary (line 22)

18. The first paragraph of the passage employs all of the following contrasts EXCEPT

   A. the vision — the truth, (lines 10–11)

   B. fact — fancy, (line 12–13)

   C. another fashion — no place in the popular imagination, (lines 14–17)

   D. the real — the legendary, (lines 20–22)

   E. more interesting — less agreeable, (lines 21–23)

19. In the first paragraph, all of the following words have specific religious meanings EXCEPT

   A. saintly, (line 3)

   B. maiden, (line 4)

   C. consecrating, (line 8)

   D. Demon, (line 17)

   E. possessed, (line 17)

GO ON TO THE NEXT PAGE

20. In which of the following sentences is the use of parallel structure most important?

   A. the first ("Everyone knows . . ." lines 1–2)

   B. the third ("But the . . ." line 11)

   C. the fourth ("The Miss . . ." lines 12–13)

   D. the seventh ("Now demons . . ." lines 18–19)

   E. the eighth ("And so . . ." lines 19–23)

21. All of the following words and phrases serve a similar purpose EXCEPT

   A. popular conception, (lines 1–2)

   B. vision, (line 10)

   C. as facile fancy painted, (line 13)

   D. demons, (line 18)

   E. the legendary one, (line 22)

22. In which sentence in the first paragraph does the author use archaic diction and cliches?

   A. the first ("Everyone knows . . ." lines 1–2)

   B. the second("The saintly . . ." lines 2–11)

   C. the third ("But the . . ." line 11)

   D. the sixth ("A Demon . . ." line 17–18)

   E. the eighth ("And so . . ." lines 19–23)

23. Which of the following phrases in the first paragraph employs BOTH hyperbole and metaphor?

   A. the Lady with the Lamp, (lines 6–7)

   B. the horrors of the hospital at Scutari, (lines 7–8)

   C. consecrating with the radiance of her goodness, (lines 8–9)

   D. as facile fancy painted her, (line 13)

   E. no place in the popular imagination, (lines 16–17)

24. The words "call" (line 25) and "mysterious" (line 26) in the second paragraph are related to the diction of the first paragraph because their meanings are associated with

   A. medicine

   B. religion

   C. social position

   D. psychology

   E. feminism

25. In the second paragraph, the sentence that is most likely to surprise the conventional expectations of a reader is the

   A. first ("What was . . ." lines 24–25)

   B. second ("Why had she . . ." lines 25–29)

   C. third ("Why, as a . . ." lines 30–34)

   D. fourth ("Why was she . . ." line 34–38)

   E. fifth ("Why was her . . ." lines 38–43)

26. The significant difference of the syntax of the second paragraph from the rest of the passage is its use of

A. both loose and periodic sentences

B. parallel structure

C. sentence fragments

D. interrogative sentences

E. connotative diction

27. The third paragraph implies a contrast between all of the following EXCEPT

A. weaker spirit . . . extraordinary young woman (lines 49–52)

B. superficially . . . internally (lines 57–59)

C. reports of the medical commissions . . . histories of hospitals (lines 66–69)

D. the London season . . . ragged school and workhouses (lines 70–71)

E. abroad with her family . . . slums (lines 71–76)

28. Which of the following best describes the structure of the passage as a whole?

A. The entire passage is developed chronologically.

B. The first paragraph gives an overview, and the second, third, and fourth develop chronologically.

C. The first paragraph uses only the point of view of the author, the second and third only that of Florence Nightingale, and the fourth only that of her mother.

D. The first and second paragraphs generalize about Florence Nightingale, while the third and fourth use specific detail.

E. The first three paragraphs use a first person narrator, while the fourth employs direct and indirect discourse.

29. Which of the following is the climactic contrast of the passage?

A. three years . . . the pressure of time (lines 77–78)

B. independence . . . meagre sphere (lines 83–84)

C. Harley Street . . . the country (lines 82–87)

D. ducks . . . wild swan (lines 90–92)

E. swan . . . eagle (lines 93–95)

GO ON TO THE NEXT PAGE

Practice Test 5

Questions 30–43. Read the following passage carefully before you begin to answer the questions.

Third Passage

It is a familiar example of irony in the degradation of words that "what a man is worth" has come to mean how much money he possesses; but there seems a
(5) deeper and more melancholy irony in the shrunken meaning that popular or polite speech assigns to "morality" and "morals." The poor part these words are made to play recalls the fate of those pa-
(10) gan divinities who, after being understood to rule the powers of the air and the destinies of men, came down to the level of insignificant demons, or were even made a farcical show for the
(15) amusement of the multitude.

I find even respectable historians of our own and of foreign countries, after showing that a king was treacherous, rapacious, and ready to sanction gross
(20) breaches in the administration of justice, end by praising him for his pure moral character; by which one must suppose them to mean that he was not lewd nor debauched, not the European twin of
(25) the typical Indian potentate whom Macaulay describes as passing his life in chewing bang and fondling dancing girls. And since we are sometimes told of such maleficent kings that they were
(30) religious, we arrive at the curious result, that the most serious wide-reaching duties of man lie quite outside both morality and religion — the one of these consisting in not keeping mistresses
(35) (and perhaps not drinking too much), and the other in certain ritual and spiritual transactions with God, which can be carried on equally well side by side with the basest conduct toward men. With

(40) such a classification as this it is no wonder, considering the strong reaction of language on thought, that many minds, dizzy with indigestion of recent science and philosophy, are far to seek for the
(45) grounds of social duty, and without entertaining any private intention of committing a perjury which would ruin an innocent man, or seeking gain by supplying bad preserved meats to our navy,
(50) feel themselves speculatively obliged to inquire why they should not do so, and are inclined to measure their intellectual subtlety by their dissatisfaction with all the answers to this "Why?" It is of little
(55) use to theorize in ethics while our habitual phraseology stamps the larger part of our social duties as something that lies aloof from the deepest needs and affections of our nature. The informal defini-
(60) tions of popular language are the only medium through which theory really affects the mass of minds, even among the nominally educated; and when a man whose business hours, the solid part of
(65) every day, are spent in an unscrupulous course of private or public action which has every calculable chance of causing wide-spread injury and misery, can be called moral because he comes home to
(70) dine with his wife and children and cherishes the happiness of his own hearth, the augury is not good for the use of high ethical and theological disputation.

1. Notes: line 27, bang = marijuana

30. In the opening sentence, the speaker calls the interpretation of the phrase "what a man is worth" a "degradation of words" because she believes that

A. "worth" should refer to material value.

B. the phrase refers only to a man, not to both men and women.

C. "worth" should refer to what a specific sum can purchase.

D. the example, ironically, is not "familiar."

E. "worth" should refer to merit.

31. In lines 8–9, the phrase "the poor part these words are made to play" is

A. part of a parallel construction.

B. a theatrical metaphor.

C. a paradox.

D. an understatement.

E. a colloquialism.

32. In lines 6–7, "popular and polite speech" refers to language that is

A. common and refined.

B. inexpressive and courteous.

C. universally admired and cultured.

D. ungrammatical and correct.

E. rude and polished.

33. The extended figure in lines 8–15 compares

A. words and actors

B. rulers and demons

C. words and gods

D. tragedy and farce

E. words and entertainers

34. In lines 26–28, the author includes the quotation from Macaulay in order to

A. refer to a well-known historian who exemplifies the fault she is exposing.

B. demonstrate the superiority of European kings.

C. strengthen her argument by referring to another writer who supports her position.

D. satirize historians by the use of overstatement.

E. attack the licentious behavior of Asian rulers.

35. In the phrase "the one of these consisting in not keeping mistresses" in lines 33–34, "the one" refers to

A. "twin," (line 24).

B. "Macaulay," (line 26).

C. "result," (line 30).

D. "morality," (lines 32–33).

E. "religion," (line 33).

GO ON TO THE NEXT PAGE

36. According to the "respectable historians" of the second paragraph, a king could be described as "moral" so long as he is not guilty of

A. injustice.

B. treachery.

C. indecency.

D. greed.

E. deceit.

37. The idea of the phrase "the strong reaction of language on thought" (lines 41–42) is repeated in

A. "without entertaining any private intention of committing a perjury," (lines 45–47).

B. "seeking gain by supplying bad preserved meats to our navy" (lines 48–49).

C. "measure their intellectual subtlety by their dissatisfaction with all the answers" (lines 52–54).

D. "our habitual phraseology stamps the larger part of our social duties as something that lies aloof from the deepest needs and affections of our nature. (lines 55–59).

E. "the informal definitions of popular language are the only medium through which theory really affects the mass of minds." (lines 59–62).

38. In its context in line 44, the idiom "are far to seek for" means

A. have difficulty finding

B. refuse to look for

C. stumble upon

D. go to any lengths in search of

E. try to avoid

39. Lines 59–73 conclude the passage with the argument that

A. the moral values of the modern world are in decline.

B. the degeneration of language will erode philosophical discussion.

C. private life and public life are at odds with one another.

D. the good husband and father is not necessarily a moral man.

E. it is easy to predict a general decline in religion and thought.

40. The concluding clause of the passage ("the augury is not good for the use of high ethical and theological disputation") is an example of

A. understatement

B. overstatement

C. parallel construction

D. ad hominem argument

E. paradox

41. All of the following words or phrases are examples of what the author calls the "degradation" of language EXCEPT

A. "what a man is worth," (lines 2–3)

B. "morality," (line 7)

C. "morals," (line 8)

D. "religious" (line 30)

E. "perjury," (line 47)

42. The primary objective of the passage is to

A. comment on a popular misconception.

B. encourage more carefully researched historical writing.

C. characterize a specific historical period.

D. deplore the abasement of language.

E. encourage a more religious view of life.

43. Which of the following current events would best support the argument of the passage?

A. A rating system evaluates films on the basis of their language and sexual content, but not on their content of violence.

B. A state senator convicted of fraud is praised for his support of family values.

C. An accused swindler is acquitted after a eight-month long trial.

D. A politician with a criminal record is elected mayor of a large city.

E. A television evangelist is accused of embezzling church funds.

Questions 44-55. Read the following passage carefully before you begin to answer the questions.

Fourth Passage

The talent of turning men into ridicule, and exposing to laughter those one con-verses with, is the qualification of little ungenerous tempers. A young man with
(5) this cast of mind cuts himself off from all manner of improvement. Everyone has his flaws and weaknesses; nay, the great-est blemishes are often found in the most shining characters; but what an absurd
(10) thing it is to pass over all the valuable parts of a man and fix our attention on his infirmities; to observe his imperfections more than his virtues; and to make use of him for the sport of others, rather than for
(15) our own improvement.

We therefore very often find that per-sons the most accomplished in ridicule, are those who are very shrewd at hitting a blot, without exerting anything mas-
(20) terly in themselves. As there are many eminent critics who never writ a good line, there are many admirable buffoons that animadvert upon every single defect in another, without ever discovering the
(25) least beauty of their own. By this means these unlucky little wits often gain repu-tation in the esteem of vulgar minds, and raise themselves above persons of much more laudable characters.

(30) If the talent of ridicule were employed to laugh men out of vice and folly, it might be of some use to the world; but instead of this, we find that it is generally made use of to laugh men out of virtue
(35) and good sense, by attacking everything that is solemn and serious, decent and praiseworthy in human life.

We may observe, that in the first ages of the world, when the great souls and
(40) masterpieces of human nature were

GO ON TO THE NEXT PAGE

produced, men shined by a noble simplicity of behaviour, and were strangers
to those little embellishments which are
so fashionable in our present conversa-
(45) tion. And it is very remarkable, that
notwithstanding we fall short at present
of the ancients in poetry, painting, oratory, history, architecture, and all the

noble arts and sciences which depend
(50) more upon genius than experience, we
exceed them as much in doggerel, humour, burlesque, and all the trivial arts
of ridicule. We meet with more raillery
among the moderns, but more good
(55) sense among the ancients.

44. Lines 9–15 ("but what an absurd . . .
our own improvement") are an example
of a(n)

A. periodic sentence.

B. parallel construction.

C. conditional sentence.

D. extended metaphor.

E. indirect question.

45. In line 24, the word "discovering" can
be best understood to mean

A. hoping to realize

B. understanding

C. concealing

D. being the first to find

E. revealing

46. The simile of the second paragraph
compares

A. defects and beauties.

B. weakness and blot.

C. critics and buffoons.

D. fault-finders and archers.

E. height and reputation.

47. The function of the second paragraph
is to

A. develop the idea of the opening
sentence of the passage.

B. suggest exceptions to the ideas of
the opening paragraph.

C. shift the focus from personal
opinion to a widely-held view.

D. provide a comic interlude in an
otherwise serious passage.

E. introduce the ideas to be developed
in the third paragraph.

48. In lines 34–35, the phrase "virtue and
good sense" is contrasted to

A. "vulgar minds," (line 27).

B. "persons of much more laudable
characters," (lines 28–29)

C. "vice and folly," (line 31).

D. "solemn and serious," (line 36).

E. "decent and praiseworthy,"
(lines 36–37).

49. In lines 36–37, the phrase "solemn and
serious, decent and praiseworthy in
human life" is used to

A. suggest the speaker's uncertainty
about condemning ridicule.

B. clarify what the speaker means by
"vice and folly" (line 31).

C. provide an example of the proper use of ridicule.

D. clarify what the speaker means by "virtue and good sense" (lines 34–35).

E. introduce the central idea of the paragraph that follows.

50. We can infer from the third paragraph that the speaker would approve of ridicule if it were directed against

A. youth

B. foolishness

C. human weakness

D. solemnity

E. raillery

51. In line 50, the contrast between "genius" and "experience" can be best understood as the contrast between

A. spiritual values and physical realities.

B. praise and ridicule.

C. natural aptitude and active participation.

D. instinctive capacity and acquired knowledge.

E. uniqueness and familiarity.

52. In the fourth paragraph, all of the following refer to kinds of comic speech or writing EXCEPT

A. embellishments (line 43)

B. doggerel (line 51)

C. humour (lines 51–52)

D. burlesque (line 52)

E. raillery (line 53)

53. According to the passage, in which of the following forms would the modern writer be most likely to surpass the ancient?

A. lyric poetry

B. tragedy

C. satire

D. epic

E. prose fiction

54. The author of this passage would be likely to agree with all of the following EXCEPT

A. No one is perfect.

B. The fine arts of the moderns are inferior to those of the ancients.

C. The best of men often have the worst of faults.

D. There are proper and improper uses of ridicule.

E. The history of the world is a record of very slow improvement.

55. Of the following literary works, which one would the author of this passage probably regard most highly?

A. ancient epics

B. drama of the Middle Ages

C. religious lyrics of the Renaissance

D. Elizabethan tragedy

E. contemporary comedy

IF YOU FINISH BEFORE TIME IS CALLED, CHECK YOUR WORK ON THIS SECTION ONLY. DO NOT WORK ON ANY OTHER SECTION IN THE TEST.

Section II: Essay Questions

Time: 2 Hours

3 Questions

Question 1

Suggested time – 40 minutes. This question counts one-third of the total essay score.

Directions: Read the following excerpt that Mary Oliver wrote, called "Building the House," in which she draws an analogy between constructing poetry and constructing a house. In a well-organized essay, analyze how the author uses metaphor and other rhetorical devices to express her attitude toward writing poetry.

I know a young man who can build almost anything — a boat, a fence, kitchen cabinets, a table, a barn, a house. And so serenely, and in so assured and right a manner, that it is a joy to watch him. All the same, what he seems to care for best — what he seems positively to desire — is the hour of interruption, of hammerless quiet, in which he will sit and write down poems or stories that have come into his mind with clambering and colorful force. Truly he is not very good at the puzzle of words — not nearly as good as he is with a mallet and the measuring tape — but this in no way lessens his pleasure. Moreover, he is in no hurry. Everything he learned, he learned at a careful pace — will not the use of words come easier at last, though he begin at the slowest amble? Also, in these intervals, he is happy. In building things, he is his familiar self, which he does not overvalue. But in the act of writing he is a grander man, a surprise to us, and even more to himself. He is beyond what he believed himself to be.

I understand his pleasure. I also know the enclosure of my skills, and am no less pert than he when some flow takes me over the edge of it. Usually, as it happens, this is toward the work in which he is so capable. There appears in my mind a form; I imagine it from boards of a certain breadth and length, and nails, and all in cheerful response to some need I have or think I have, aligned with a space I see as opportunistic. I would not pry my own tooth, or cobble my own shoes, but I deliberate unfazed the niceties of woodworking — nothing, all my life, has checked me. At my side at this moment is a small table with one leg turned in slightly. For I have never built anything perfectly, or even very well, in spite of the pleasure such labor gives me. Nor am I done yet, though time has brought obstacles and spread them before me — a stiffness of the fingers, a refusal of the eyes to follow the aim of the hammer toward the nail head, which yearly grows smaller, and smaller.

The labor of writing poems, of working with thought and emotion in the encasement (or is it the wings?) of language is strange to nature, for we are first of all creatures of motion. Only secondly — only oddly, and not naturally, at moments of contemplation, joy, grief, prayer, or terror — are we found, while awake, in the posture of deliberate or hapless inaction. But such is the posture of the poet, poor laborer. The dancer dances, the painter dips and lifts and lays on the oils; the composer reaches at least across the octaves. The poet sits. The architect draws and measures, and travels to the quarry to tramp among the gleaming stones. The poet sits, or, if it is a fluid moment, he scribbles some words upon the page. The body, under this pressure of nonexisting, begins to draw up like a muscle, and complain. An unsolvable disharmony of such work — the mind so hotly fired and the body so long quiescent — will come sooner or later to revolution, will demand action! For many years, in a place I call Blackwater Woods, I wrote while I walked. That motion, hardly more than a dreamy sauntering, worked for me; it kept my body happy while I scribbled. But sometimes it wasn't at all enough. I wanted to build, in the other way, with the teeth of the saw, and the explosions of the hammer, and the little shrieks of the screws winding down into their perfect nests.

Question 2

Suggested time – 40 minutes. This question counts one-third of the total essay score.

The following excerpt comes from Anwar F. Accawi's reflective essay titled "The Telephone," in which he looks back at his childhood in Lebanon before the first telephone had been installed and before time had much meaning.

Directions: Read the excerpt carefully. Then, in a well-organized essay, examine the rhetorical force that the author employs as he expresses his attitude toward time.

When I was growing up in Magdaluna, a small Lebanese village in the terraced, rocky mountains east of Sidon, time didn't mean much to anybody, except maybe to those who were dying, or those waiting to appear in court because they had tampered with the boundary markers on their land. In those days, there was no real need for a calendar or a watch to keep track of the hours, days, months, and years. We knew what to do, just as the Iraqi geese knew when to fly north, driven by the hot wind that blew in from the desert, and the ewes knew when to give birth to wet lambs that stood on long, shaky legs in the chilly March wind and baaed hesitantly, because they were small and cold and did not know where they were or what to do now they were here. The only timepiece we had need of then was the sun. It rose and set, and the seasons rolled by, and we sowed seed and harvested and ate and played and married our cousins and had babies who got whooping cough and chickenpox — and those children who survived grew up and married *their* cousins and had babies who got whooping cough and chickenpox. We lived and loved and toiled and died without ever needing to know what year it was, or even the time of day.

GO ON TO THE NEXT PAGE

It wasn't that we had no system for keeping track of time and of the important events in our lives. But ours was a natural — or, rather, a divine — calendar, because it was framed by acts of God. Allah himself set down the milestones with earthquakes and droughts and floods and locusts and pestilences. Simple as our calendar was, it worked just fine for us.

Take, for example, the birth date of Teta Im Khalil, the oldest woman in Magdaluna and all the surrounding villages. When I first met her, we had just returned home from Syria at the end of the Big War and were living with Grandma Mariam. Im Khahlil came by to welcome my father home and to take a long, myopic look at his foreign-born wife, my mother. Im Khahlil was so old that the skin of her cheeks looked like my father's grimy tobacco pouch, and when I kissed her (because Grandma insisted that I show her old friend affection), it was like kissing a soft suede glove that had been soaked with sweat and then left in a dark closet for a season. Im Khahlil's face got me to wondering how old one had to be to look and taste the way she did. So, soon as she had hobbled off on her cane, I asked Grandma, "How old is Teta Im Khahlil?"

Grandma had to think for a moment; then she said, "I've been told that Teta was born shortly after the big snow that caused the roof on the mayor's house to cave in."

"And when was that?" I asked.

"Oh, about the time we had the big earthquake that cracked the wall in the east room."

Well, that was enough for me. You couldn't be more accurate than that, now, could you? Satisfied with her answer, I went back to playing with a ball made from an old sock stuffed with other, much older socks.

And that's the way it was in our little village for as far back as anybody could remember: people were born so many years before or after an earthquake or a flood; they got married or died so many years before or after a long drought or a big snow or some other disaster. One of the most unusual of these dates was when Antoinette the seamstress and Saeed the barber (and tooth puller) got married. That was the year of the whirlwind during which fish and oranges fell from the sky. Incredible as it may sound, the story of the fish and the oranges was true, because men — respectable men, like Abu George the blacksmith and Abu Asaad the mule skinner, men who would not lie even to save their own souls — told and retold that story until it was incorporated into Magdaluna's calendar, just like the year of the black moon and the year of the locusts before it. My father, too, confirmed the story for me. He told me that he had been a small boy himself when it had rained fish and oranges from heaven. He'd gotten up one morning after a stormy night and walked out into the yard to find fish as long as his forearm still flopping here and there among the wet navel oranges.

Question 3

Suggested time – 40 minutes. This question counts as one-third of the total essay score.)

Fanny Burney (Mme d'Arblay) wrote in her novel, *Camilla*

> There is nothing upon the face of the earth so insipid as a medium. Give me love or hate! a friend that will go to jail for me, or an enemy that will run me through the body!

Directions: In a well thought out essay, evaluate the validity of Burney's assertion about extremes. Use evidence from your reading, observation, or experience to make your point convincing.

IF YOU FINISH BEFORE TIME IS CALLED, CHECK YOUR WORK ON THIS SECTION ONLY. DO NOT WORK ON ANY OTHER SECTION IN THE TEST.

Answer Key for Practice Test 5

Section I: Multiple-Choice Questions

First Passage

1. C
2. E
3. E
4. B
5. A
6. B
7. D
8. D
9. B
10. A
11. C
12. A
13. B
14. E

Second Passage

15. B
16. C
17. D
18. C
19. B
20. E
21. D
22. B
23. C
24. B
25. C
26. D
27. C
28. B
29. E

Third Passage

30. E

31. B

32. A

33. C

34. D

35. D

36. C

37. E

38. A

39. B

40. A

41. E

42. D

43. B

Fourth Passage

44. B

45. E

46. C

47. A

48. C

49. D

50. B

51. D

52. A

53. C

54. E

55. A

Section II: Essay Questions

Essay scoring guides, student essays, and analysis appear beginning on page 288.

Practice Test 5 Scoring Worksheet

Use the following worksheet to arrive at a probable final AP grade on Practice Test 5. Because it is sometimes difficult to be objective enough to score your own essay score you might also give your essays (along with the sample essays) to a friend or relative to score if you feel confident that the individual has the knowledge necessary to make such a judgment and that he or she will feel comfortable doing so.

Section I: Multiple-Choice Questions

$$\underset{\substack{\text{right}\\\text{answers}}}{\underline{\hspace{2cm}}} - (1/4 \text{ or } .25 \times \underset{\substack{\text{wrong}\\\text{answers}}}{\underline{\hspace{2cm}}}) = \underset{\substack{\text{multiple-choice}\\\text{raw score}}}{\underline{\hspace{2cm}}}$$

$$\underset{\substack{\text{multiple-choice}\\\text{raw score}}}{\underline{\hspace{2cm}}} \times 1.18 = \underset{\substack{\text{multiple-choice}\\\text{converted score}}}{\underline{\hspace{2cm}}} (\text{of possible } 67.5)$$

Section II: Essay Questions

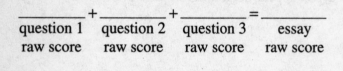

$$\underset{\substack{\text{question 1}\\\text{raw score}}}{\underline{\hspace{1.5cm}}} + \underset{\substack{\text{question 2}\\\text{raw score}}}{\underline{\hspace{1.5cm}}} + \underset{\substack{\text{question 3}\\\text{raw score}}}{\underline{\hspace{1.5cm}}} = \underset{\substack{\text{essay}\\\text{raw score}}}{\underline{\hspace{1.5cm}}}$$

$$\underset{\substack{\text{essay}\\\text{raw score}}}{\underline{\hspace{2cm}}} \times 3.055 = \underset{\substack{\text{essay}\\\text{converted score}}}{\underline{\hspace{2cm}}} (\text{of possible } 82.5)$$

Final Score

$$\underset{\substack{\text{multiple-choice}\\\text{converted score}}}{\underline{\hspace{2cm}}} + \underset{\substack{\text{essay}\\\text{converted score}}}{\underline{\hspace{2cm}}} = \underset{\substack{\text{final}\\\text{converted score}}}{\underline{\hspace{2cm}}} (\text{of possible } 150)$$

Probable Final AP Score

Final Converted Score	Probable AP Score
150–104	5
103–92	4
91–76	3
75–50	2
49–0	1

Section I: Multiple-Choice Questions

First Passage

The passage is from John Milton's *Areopagitica* (1644) in which the poet argues for printing without governmental restraints.

1. **C.** The metaphor is in the words "in the field" and "grow up." Of the five choices, only plants grow up in a field.

2. **E.** The lines are arguing that we cannot know or recognize good without knowing evil also. This idea is the central point of the passage. If we cannot recognize evil, we cannot understand good.

3. **E.** The sentence is a rhetorical question, that is, a question used for rhetorical effect, to emphasize a point with no expectation of an answer. As the passage puts the question, all we can reply is, "none."

4. **B.** The "adversary" of virtue is vice. The argument here is that virtue must not hide from its enemy, but must contend with evil directly.

5. **A.** The developed figure in the lines is a comparison of life to a footrace between good and evil, a contest to be run for the garland (prize) of immortality. The race will be hot and dusty, but true virtue will not shirk the contest.

6. **B.** The "garland" is "immortal," the reward of immortality for those who struggle in life's race and defeat evil.

7. **D.** The lines argue that we are born impure ("we bring not innocence into the world"), but we can be purified by facing evil and overcoming it. This "trial" is a contest, not a judicial proceeding.

8. **D.** Of the five choices, **D** is the best paraphrase. The phrase "by what is contrary" means by its opposite, as evil is the contrary of virtue. This passage comes from a defense of the freedom of the press, an argument against the suppression of the contrary viewpoint.

9. **B.** The passage claims that the "sage and serious poet Spenser" is a better teacher than philosophers like Scotus or Aquinas.

10. **A.** In Spenser's "Faerie Queene," the knight of temperance, Guion, visits the cave of Mammon and the bower of earthly bliss. The cave is the temptation of wealth, the bower, the temptation of sensual pleasures. To be truly temperate, Guion must be exposed to, understand, and resist these temptations.

11. **C.** The central point of the passage is that to learn to resist evil properly, we must be exposed to it. A "cloistered virtue," that is, a virtue that never faces evil directly, is inadequate.

12. **A.** The passage uses literary allusion (the references to Spenser, for example); both the singular and the plural first person ('we know' line 1; "I cannot" line 25); metaphor (lines 1–2, "field of this world") and simile (line 12, "as two twins"); and balanced sentences (lines 31–34). The language of the passage, however, is not colloquial.

13. **B.** The passage does not employ any personal anecdotes. As a whole. the piece is an ethical argument, which employs extended definition, abstract generalization, and Biblical allusions.

14. **E.** The speaker is by no means impartial, cautious, skeptical, or wry. He is a committed believer in his argument.

Second Passage

The passage is from Lytton Strachey's *Eminent Victorians* (1918).

15. **B.** The paragraph has two distinct parts. The first six lines present the "popular" idealized notion of Florence Nightingale. The division is clearly marked by the sentence "But the truth was different." The rest of the paragraph begins the presentation of what the author claims is the "real Miss Nightingale." Though the paragraph uses both long and short sentences, the alternation is not consistent. Both the third and fourth sentences are short, and the fifth is long only because it uses semi-colons in place of periods. The contrast is not between Nightingale's strength and weakness, but between a romantic conception of her and a realistic account.

16. **C.** To succour (the American spelling is succor) is to relieve, to assist at a time of distress.

17. **D.** All but "interesting" are used to present the popular idea of Florence Nightingale. The author argues the real woman was "more.. interesting" though less saintly than the woman of the legend.

18. **C.** Four of these pairs are part of the legendary versus real contrast in the paragraph. "Another fashion" and "no place in the popular imagination," however, are both part of a sentence describing the "real" woman and are not contrasts.

19. **B.** Though "maiden" might be used in a religious context, of itself it is simply the word for a virgin or an unmarried girl or woman. The four other words have specific religious denotations. As it appears here, "possessed" is used (metaphorically) to mean controlled by a spirit.

20. **E.** None of the first four options use parallel structure. The eighth sentence, however, plays "in the real" against "in the legendary" and "there was more that was interesting" against "there was less that was agreeable."

21. **D.** Four of these words or phrases refer to the popular concept of the sainted Florence Nightingale. "Demons" does not.

22. B. The second sentence employs both archaisms like "maiden of high degree" or "couch" and cliches like "saintly, self-sacrificing," "delicate maiden of high degree," "to succour the afflicted," as the author mocks the sentimental idea of Florence Nightingale. The other sentences avoid these excesses.

23. C. The "horrors of the hospital" is not hyperbolic or figurative, and "facile fancy" is not hyperbole, though it is metaphoric. The overstatement is the claim that the "radiance" (a metaphor) of Nightingale's goodness "consecrated" the dying soldiers' deathbeds. She may have made the dying more comfortable, but she did not make them sacred.

24. B. Though "call" and "mysterious" can be used without any religious reference, both have specific religious meanings. The word "call" can mean a religious vocation regarded as divinely inspired, and "mysterious" has several different religious meanings, for example, pertaining to that which only faith can explain.

25. C. Most modern readers are unlikely to expect the sister's pleasure in "tearing her dolls to pieces" to be described as "healthy," while Florence Nightingale's repairing the victims is "morbid."

26. D. Unlike the rest of the passage, the second paragraph depends almost entirely on the use of questions. Six of its seven sentences are interrogative. All of the paragraphs employ connotative diction.

27. C. The contrast of options **A** and **B** is clear. In **D** and **E,** "the London season" and "abroad with her family" suggest situations associated with the high social position of Florence's well-to-do family, but Florence's concern on these occasions is the world of poverty, of "workhouses" and "slums." The "reports" and "histories" are alike, not contrasted; they are both the subjects of Florence Nightingale's studies.

28. B. The first paragraph establishes the basic contrast of the passage, that of the conventional view of Florence Nightingale with the realistic view that this passage will present. The second, third and fourth paragraphs move chronologically from Florence Nightingale's youth, preparation, to her first success.

29. E. This final metaphor is the climax of the passage. The author has emphasized the contrast by the parallel construction of the sentence ("it was not a swan . . . it was an eagle.") The sentence is a final instance of the more genteel notion of Florence Nightingale ("a swan") and the author's vision of her strength and power ("an eagle").

Third Passage

The passage is from an essay by the nineteenth-century novelist George Eliot (Mary Ann Evans).

30. E. The author's complaint here is the replacement of what she believes ought to be a moral meaning of the word "worth" with a financial one. The noun "worth" can mean either material value or moral excellence; George Eliot regards the loss of the second meaning as an example of the "degradation of words."

31. B. The phrase is a metaphor that compares words to an actor in a play. The use of "part" (that is, the actor's role) and the verb "play" (that is, to perform) make the theatrical reference of the figure clear.

32. A. The root meaning of the word "popular" is "of the people; "common" or "in general use." The root meaning of "polite" is "polished"; "refined" is the best choice here.

33. C. Though the lines contain a metaphor in line 8 and describe the pagan gods as players in a farce in line 14, the extended figure of lines 8–15 compares the words, which have fallen to low uses, with the once-revered pagan gods, who have been trivialized. This figure of speech is a simile, since the phrase "recalls the fate" makes the comparison explicit.

34. D. The quotation from Macaulay does not tell us that he was guilty of (**A**) or even aware of (**C**) the misuse of "moral." George Eliot's use of this extravagant comment makes ridiculous the historians' calling anyone whom this description does not fit a "pure moral character."

35. D. The antecedent of "the one" is "morality" in lines 33–34, while "the other" in line 36 refers to "religion" in line 34.

36. C. The historians may call a king guilty of injustice, treachery, greed, or deceit a "moral" man, so long as he is not "lewd nor debauched."

37. E. In this phrase, the word "reaction" means "influence" or "effect." The central idea of the passage is that a debased language will lead to a debased way of thinking. Of the five choices, only **D** and **E** deal with language. Choice **D** complains of the degeneration of language ("our habitual phraseology") but does not, like **E,** deal with the effect of language ("affects") on thought ("the mass of minds").

38. A. The best choice here is "have difficulty finding." This sentence describes the difficulties of a mind already confused by contemporary science and philosophy (the passage was written at the time of the publication of the works of Darwin) undermined further by the loss of clear definitions of words like "moral" or "religious."

39. B. The point of the sentence is not that the business man is immoral, but that the decline of language indicated by his being called "moral" points to a decline to follow in ethical and religious discussion.

40. A. The best of the five choices is understatement. The use of "the augury is" and "not good," and the obvious error in the use of "moral" in lines 65–74 set against a phrase like "high ethical and theological disputation" make it clear that George Eliot is not really uncertain. None of the other four options is correct.

41. E. The word "perjury" (oath-breaking) is here not a example of a weakened use of language.

42. D. The author states her thesis in the first sentence, and makes clear her disapproval ("a more melancholy irony").

43. B. The passage attacks the "shrunken meaning" of the words "morals" and "morality" so that dishonesty in the business world can be seen as irrelevant to "morals" or "morality." The example suggests that family values are more important than honesty.

Fourth Passage

The passage is from an eighteenth-century essay written by Joseph Addison.

44. B. The lines are an example of parallel construction; it employs a series of infinitive phrases, all dependent on the phrase "what an absurd thing it is . . . to pass . . . to observe . . . to make use."

45. E. Though several of the answers are meanings that "discover" may have in other contexts, here the word means to disclose or reveal. The prefix "dis" often means "not" or "un-." This eighteenth-century usage is similar to "un-cover."

46. C. The sentence begins with a simile, introduced by "As." The figure compares "many eminent critics" and "many admirable buffoons." There is only one simile in the paragraph.

47. A. The passage begins with the criticism of the "ungenerous tempers" that are given to ridicule. The second paragraph develops this idea.

48. C. The single long sentence in this paragraph contrasts and deplores the infrequent use of ridicule to mock "vice and folly" with the more common practice of jesting at the expense of "virtue and good sense."

49. D. The phrase makes clear what the author sees as the significance of the earlier used phrase, "virtue and good sense."

50. B. The paragraph argues that ridicule would be useful if it were directed against "vice and folly," that is, immoral conduct and foolishness.

51. D. The best choice here is "instinctive capacity and acquired knowledge." The passage is contrasting the arts of the ancients that depend upon "genius" rather than "experience," the source of the inferior productions of the modern world.

52. A. In this sentence, doggerel, humour, burlesque, and raillery are forms of comic speech or writing, but "embellishments" are not necessarily comic.

53. C. Since modern writers surpass the ancient in the "arts of ridicule," they should be more accomplished in satire, the only one of these forms that depends chiefly upon ridicule.

54. E. The passage supports the first four ideas, but it suggests that men and man's productions have declined since the "first ages of the world" produced "great souls and masterpieces of human nature."

55. A. Given his praise of the "first ages," the author would probably value the ancient epics more highly than the literary works of later periods.

Section II: Essay Questions

Question 1

Scoring Guide for Question 1 (Mary Oliver)

8–9 Top scoring essays effectively analyze how Oliver uses metaphor to create her opinion about writing poetry. These high-quality essays refer to the text concretely or abstractly and show a clear understanding of how Oliver's rhetorical devices combine to create effect. Essays scored at the top are well-developed in their presentation of ideas and show outstanding organization. Although these essays may contain minor errors, the prose demonstrates an ability to control a wide range of writing elements and a flair for sophistication.

6–7 Essays that score in the upper level effectively analyze Oliver's language and how it generates effect. Typically, these essays use the text well, either directly or indirectly, to help develop ideas, and they clearly and logically connect any textual evidence to the student's thoughts. While high-scoring essays explore Oliver's rhetoric and attitude about writing poetry well, they may not be as perceptive or thorough as the top scoring essays. They are sufficiently developed and clearly organized. A few minor lapses in diction or syntax may be evident; however, the prose is well written enough to convey the writers' ideas well.

5 Essays earning a score of 5 adequately analyze the rhetoric Oliver uses, and may attempt to connect her language to her attitude, but their insights may be more pedestrian, more obvious. Quite often their development is limited by weak textual evidence, simplistic ideas, reliance on paraphrasing, or a combination of all three. The focus may be superficial. While the writing may generally convey ideas decently, lapses in written English may be present or persistent.

3–4 Lower-scoring essays inadequately respond to the topic. Their analysis of Oliver's rhetorical strategies is usually too brief. They may misunderstand or misrepresent Oliver's metaphor, or merely paraphrase her ideas. Development and/or organization may be flawed. The prose may convey the writers' ideas, but may hint at immaturity in its control of written English. Simplistic ideas coupled with a simplistic style may characterize low-scoring essays.

1–2 The lowest-scoring essays demonstrate little success in analyzing Oliver's central metaphor or any other rhetorical devices. They may ignore or pay limited attention to her techniques. They may try to discuss her attitude about writing poetry, but may not demonstrate how her language presents that attitude. Often these essays rely on paraphrasing throughout. The prose frequently reveals consistent weaknesses in writing, severely limited development and organization, and poor control over mechanics.

High-Scoring Essay

Mechanistic diction, a tautly constructed metaphor of linguistic carpentry, and the powerlessness of personification convey how the author's instinctive impulse to write poetry paralyzes her.

In a self-deprecating way, the author foils her adept, nimble-fingered handyman wunderkind's mysterious ambition and underlying impetus "in building things," which, for her, is analogous to the fabrication of a physical entity, an act that renders her ". . . a grander [human being]; a surprise to us and even more to [her]self." For holding together this desire to hammer, glue, and yoke her yearning to create houses of concrete and not just abodes of fiction are subtle rivets of mechanistic diction. Indeed, what the author does in forming fiction approximates the figure and shape of a plot, plied from "boards of a certain breadth and length and nails." The word "boards" connotes manufacturing of predestined materials, existentially directed toward a larger purpose than their unadorned, plank-wood form. As "board," "measuring tape," and "mallets" hearken visions of splinter-carrying, unhewed resources, so too is writing representative of potential constructs, pregnant with the possibility of imperfection, equally possibly a "small table with one leg turned in slightly" or a miraculous model house. Yet the promise of "contemplation, joy, grief, prayer, or terror" pushes the author to pursue woodworking with a fervor unchecked by her mediocrity. The "stiffness" of the fingers that the author depicts suggests the inflexible nature of writing poetry that possesses her; it stuns her senses into submission, makes her eye refuse to "switch easily from near to far," fatigues and ossifies her fingers. The alliterative descriptive "clamoring and colorful" force of searching for words depicts how noisy the process of writing is internally, how it acts like a fool, a hammer, in untapping the visions inside. Indeed, the imagery of the whole passage fills the senses with mechanical sounds and sensations, emphasizing the central metaphor of construction.

For Oliver, poetry writing translates into a metaphor of carpentry that is intrinsically intellectual. The implements needed for its internal foundation are understanding the perspicacity to know "the enclosure of my skills." Comparing herself to other artistic laymen, the author elucidates the unique challenge of writing poetry. Instead of fermenting external activity through introspective investigation, it begets "at moments of contemplation, joy, grief, prayer, or terror . . . the posture of deliberate or hapless inaction." Likening herself metaphorically to a carpenter, "a poor poet laborer," she mimics in the reader the sentiment of unjust powerlessness by glorifying the ecstasy of how "the dancer dances, the painter dips and lifts . . . the composer reaches . . . across the octaves." As this exultative action occurs, the poet "sits . . . scribbles some words," condemned to condense the mind's excitement to the twitching of three fingers. In this way, the author hints that writing poetry engenders this unspoken torment — the impatience of a "mind so hotly fired and . . . body so long quiescent." No matter what the poetry constructs externally, internally it ferments the disharmony of being dream-ridden, of being inactive — a state contrary to the carpenter's impulsive action.

But what can the author stymie her linguistic frustration with but with a physical reaction — building a tangible construct with nails and hammers, pounding out affirmation of her intrinsic intellectual insights, translating an image into something like a "small table." Surprisingly, what the author insinuates is that for all of its paralysis, the act of writing poetry itself wrests a personificative power over us, making for us an ephemeral flash "beyond what [we] believed [ourselves] to be." Personifying writing as a conquering agent, the writer depicts how writing invades the writer's mind like a phantom, appearing "on my mind a form," causing physical symptoms of its visitation, "stiffness . . . a refusal of my eyes to switch easily." For a small physical price, the act of writing unleashes the possibilities of bypassing a human state — instead of being consumed with action, we transcend it into mystifying lethargy. The author even endues writing "with wings" of language, making the labor of composition a figure like a bird. At the same time, writing is metaphorically painted in the screaming of the "teeth of the saw . . . explosions of the hammer . . . shrieks of screws" because the poet can be paralyzed into poetic creation by monstrous clamor of her own imagination. However, the ultimate form that writing poetry assumes is one of inner peace; it takes the form of "a flow," a stream that "appears in my mind" and ultimately one that "will demand action." Just as a carpenter will build a house of beauty, a poet will create a work of art.

Analysis of the High-Scoring Essay

The writer of this high-scoring essay clearly articulates his or her understanding of how Oliver's metaphor and other rhetorical devices combine to create her attitude about writing poetry. It begins with a thesis, one that is promising. The reader is intrigued to discover what the writer will have to say about "mechanistic diction" and "the powerlessness of personification."

The first body paragraph centers on the mechanical imagery on the passage. The student shows good insight into the sights and sounds, indeed the very feel of housing construction and how these images connect to Oliver's metaphor about constructing poetry. The writer includes apt examples from the text and explains them unambiguously. This writer also shows promise in sentence construction, pleasing the reader with such creations as, "For holding together this desire to hammer, glue, and yoke her yearning to create houses of concrete and not just abodes of fiction are subtle rivets of mechanistic diction." The alliteration is pleasing to the ear, as is the connotation of "rivets" holding diction together.

The second body paragraph explores Oliver's metaphor that connects carpentry and poetry writing. The writer's insights are sophisticated and well founded in the text. As in the previous paragraph, this writer continues to demonstrate a sense of style, for example, beginning one sentence with "Comparing herself" and another with "Likening herself." This parallelism will not go unnoticed by an experienced reader.

The final paragraph explores the thesis idea of "the powerlessness of personification," perhaps the most interesting idea in the thesis. The student understands the subtleties of Oliver's language and how the personification not only, by definition, gives life to inanimate objects, but also how it adds to the poet's feeling of mediocrity or paralysis. Not only are the ideas intriguing, but they are also convincing to the reader.

Ultimately this essay deserves a high score. It is on topic throughout, and it shows superior organization and development. Additionally, the writer's ability to present ideas with panache demonstrates the elegance that is often seen in top-scoring essays.

Medium-Scoring Essay

When somebody thinks a bit about the comparison, "building" a poem can be a lot like "building" a house. They both need to start with an idea and then "build" from there. In Mary Oliver's essay, "Building the House," she uses precise diction, varied syntax, and metaphor to liken writing poetry to constructing a house.

At first, the atmosphere of tranquility builds as Oliver uses careful-connoting sounding words to describe the effort of constructing "a boat, fence, kitchen cabinets, a table, a house." Words like "serene", "assured", "right", and "careful" show the measured, articulate labor in constructing poetry "at the slowest amble" initially. There persists an attitude of awe in these adjectives, the sense that the builder of compositions "is a surprise to himself" because he knows "the enclosure of (his) skills", and metes out his motions with his limitations marked in his mind. "Unfazed" and "aligned" also dwell upon the writer's instinct to rely on his own clear-minded, lucid independence, to envision "a form in his mind . . . to boards of a certain length" unmoved by the outside factors, "the niceties of woodworking" or the fact that he "has never built anything perfectly." The diction blueprints how Oliver explains her motivation for writing poetry as an effort that "surprises" herself, that she meticulously learns "at a careful place" and constructs painstakingly with each word.

The varied syntax deepens the imagery of Oliver's effort of writing poetry to the construction of a house. At the beginning, the sentences are interrupted by dashes; thoughts interrupted by personal insight and detail that inform us about " — what (the builder) cares for best —" and challenging questions " —

will not the use of words come easier at last . . . ?" Oliver forces the reader to break a train of thought, and the author suggests that the process of writing parallels this pause-ridden path, one that is roughened by breaths and time, one slowed down by the need to begin at a slow pace and form a firm foundation. Next, the essay evolves, into a first person commentary with a more conventional subject-verb flow, but still interlaced with intruding alien subject-verb phrases like "there appeared in my mind a form." These abrupt cadences in a sense nail together the flowing narrative walls by offering an objective sense of the author's powerlessness to the "form" imagined and "time" that brings "obstacles and spread them" before her.

The clever metaphorical construction of essay writing evolves through simple syntactic progression and the meticulous diction from the simple boards of the words to the "small table" of furniture of a completed phrase. The imagery in this selection filters through how the poet's mentally acts like an architect. The poet's internal labor sensually evokes the ruckus of constructing an edifice, "the teeth of the saw, explosions of the hammer, and the little shrieks of the screws" indivisible from woodworking. The pencil is compared to a hammer "which yearly grows smaller and smaller" as the poet "sits . . . scribbles . . . words upon a page." The essay-writing process is something that originates of "a form" like a house, miraculously of "boards of a certain breadth and length and nails," a form taut and mysteriously that possesses an essence that the poet employs the hammer and tools of language to realize.

Analysis of the Medium-Scoring Essay

This essay presents some interesting insights and it attempts to offer ideas in an analytical fashion, but it basically falls flat in both its presentation and its wording. The introductory sentences are fairly bland, and the thesis merely restates what the essay topic does, namely, it "uses . . . diction . . . syntax, and metaphor" to show how writing poetry parallels building a house. The thesis ignores the author's *attitude* about writing poetry, an important aspect of the original topic question.

The first body paragraph offers some good ideas from the writer, and it attempts to clarify that the author's attitude toward writing poetry is ambiguous or negative. However, the student's analysis is fairly superficial. The writer explains the obvious connotations of words that are listed from the essay. Also disconcerting is the fact that the thesis claims the essay will analyze "precise" diction, but this particular adjective is ignored for the most part.

The next paragraph contains some good insights about Oliver's syntax and provides some pleasing syntax in turn, for instance, in the sentence in which the writer explores Oliver's use of the dash. Similarly, the last sentence in this paragraph has a delightful play on words with the phrasing ". . . cadences . . . nail together . . . the narrative walls," but the rest of the sentence falls apart, both in its cadence and in its analysis.

The last paragraph of this essay turns into mere paraphrasing that simply does not fulfill the requirements of the topic. By this point the writer should be addressing *how* Oliver's metaphor expresses her attitude, but the writer seems to have forgotten that task.

Compounding the lapses in addressing the topic, this writer's command of English is flawed. Too many diction and mechanical errors become disconcerting. Unidiomatic expressions, such as "something that originates *of* a form" or using the wrong part of speech, such as "a form taut and *mysteriously*" both distract the reader and diminish the writer's force. The many punctuation errors in quotation usage and apostrophes also divert the reader's attention. Ultimately, the writer's insightful ideas deserve a stronger, clearer presentation.

Question 2

Scoring Guide for Question 2 (Anwar Accawi)

8–9 Astute and discerning essays earn the top score. These perceptive essays clearly understand the rhetorical devices that Accawi uses as he develops his opinion about how irrelevant time, as we understand it in the Western world, can be. These essays use the text well, both in a direct and indirect fashion, and they succinctly explain how Accawi's language establishes his attitude. Development and organization are outstanding in top-scoring essays. The writer's ability to use language effectively is demonstrated by a sophisticated style and vocabulary, although the essay may not be without minor flaws.

6–7 Upper-level essays clearly understand how Accawi's language creates meaning and attitude. These essays refer to text frequently and understand how to connect textual examples to the writer's ideas; however, those connections or insights may not be as deep or perceptive as the top-scoring essays. Upper-level essays usually show strong development and organization of ideas. While minor errors in the command of written English may be present, they do not cloud the writer's ability to make his or her meaning clear.

5 These adequate essays may attempt to complete the topic, but fall short of analysis. The student may paraphrase the action in the excerpt instead of connecting rhetorical devices to attitude. Ideas are frequently superficial and obvious in mid-scoring essays. Development and organization may be reasonable, but not as successful as in higher-scoring essays; too often the midlevel essays are simply too brief. The writing may be sufficient enough to convey meaning, but immature command of English conventions may be demonstrated.

3–4 These lower-half essays may not discuss the author's attitude or may only paraphrase the passage. These writers may miss the author's implied attitude about time or may not understand how to connect language to attitude. Inconsistent control over language may be visible, distracting the reader from the essay's ideas. Frequently, low-scoring essays wrap simple ideas in a simple package, and development and organization are equally unsophisticated.

1–2 Essays earning the lowest score fail to respond to the topic. They may misread the passage or misconstrue it to the reader. They may pay limited attention to Accawi's language or offer nothing but paraphrasing. Quite often, these lowest-scoring essays are unacceptably brief; ideas are not explored and examples are not provided. Continual weaknesses in grammar and mechanics may demonstrate a lack of control over the conventions of written English, and vocabulary usage may be overly simplistic.

High-Scoring Essay

Time, as a human invention, a theoretical concept, may not be deemed as significant a creation to some as it is to others. In the excerpt from Anwar Accawi's "The Telephone," the narrator's attitude towards time encompasses the accumulated influences of his society and cultural background, an attitude which views time as a spiritual entity and a representation of the ever-present past. This attitude is displayed through the author's implementation of contrasting imagery, forceful connotation, and the repetition of ideas.

Accawi contrasts manmade and natural imagery to express the disparity between his personal understanding of seasons and cycles and the modern idea of time. He creates a parallel between himself and the natural world by comparing his understanding of time with that of Iraqi geese and ewes.

Additionally, Accawi describes the natural "rocky mountains of Sidon" as being "terraced," obviously by man. The narrator's reaction to time is an innate, primitive perception, an almost primal behavior developed from an intuition of the cycles of life and the passing of seasons. The manmade and natural world are also juxtaposed as he pits such massive natural events (that he ironically classifies mildly as "milestones") as "earthquakes and droughts and floods and locusts and pestilences" against minute manmade objects like a suede glove or a tobacco pouch. Nature obviously takes a much larger role in the passage of time as man's puny gloves and pouches will not stand the test of time. The imagery of the "old sock stuffed with other, much older socks" further develops the relationship of the individual with time. The ball of socks represents the intertwining of time; the past is the present, and there is no differentiation between the two except that one may feel that which is in the present. Even though it is intangible, the past remains always in existence.

This basic association with the passage of time is again displayed through Accawi's employment of powerful and religious connotation, such as the narrator's use of the sun and God to determine time's passage. The narrator asserts that "the only timepiece [they] had need of then was the sun" and that theirs was a "natural — or, rather, a divine — calendar in God. The sun not only may be used to establish the passage of hours in the day but also carries with it the connotation of warmth, contentedness, and spirituality. The sun possesses a sense of power that the mechanical precision of the watch cannot. Furthermore, the religious, spiritual connotation of God overshadows the limited capability of the calendar. The passage of time is portrayed as spiritual and symbolic, not to be quantified by technological advances, after all, "Allah himself set down the milestones. . . ." In the measurement of time, the emotional qualities of past and present seem disregarded.

Accawi again represents this relationship between the past and the present in his repetition of phrases, demonstrating the repetitious pervasiveness of time. The narrator himself refers to a specific period of time as "when [his family] had just returned home from Syria at the end of the Big War," demonstrating that like those before him, he still adheres to his notion of time. The narrator then proceeds to recount a discussion with his grandmother in which she speaks of a moment in time as "shortly after the big snow" and "about the time [they] had the big earthquake." This referral to time in terms of events emphasizes the fact that occurrences influence a person's life. It demonstrates the significance that memories have in people's lives. There exists this repetition of the past in every new occurrence, every word spoken, as the past influences the future. While the concept of time attempts to label specific moments, it is impossible to differentiate the present, past, and future because they are all intertwined in each moment.

The excerpt from "The Telephone" emphasizes the impact of the past, present, and future. Accawi demonstrates that the manmade notion of time is an imposed invention, able to categorize events but unable to decipher their spiritual, emotional significance.

Analysis of the High-Scoring Essay

This excellent essay indeed demonstrates clear understanding of Accawi's multifaceted attitude toward time, comprehending that it is composed of spiritual, cultural, and individual perceptions. The introduction is specifically on topic, and, although it presents a somewhat formulaic three-part thesis statement, it is accurate and it lets the reader know what to expect: a discussion of "contrasting imagery, forceful connotation, and the repetition of ideas."

The first body paragraph examines the juxtaposition of manmade and natural imagery, amply backing up the concept with a sufficient number of relevant examples. Instead of simply walking through the essay chronologically, the student is able to pair examples from the excerpt's early paragraphs and later portions. This demonstrates that the student has an excellent grasp of detail and can gracefully articulate ideas about the particulars. The student's idea about the "old sock stuffed with other, much older socks" is an unusual one, a concept that most test takers will not observe. This kind of tangible perception separates the high-scoring essays from the medium, especially when presented with panache.

The middle body paragraph presents the force of the spiritual connotations in the passage and the direct references to God and Allah. The student shows how Accawi's divine language takes on a mystic quality, giving time an even more elevated association than mankind's time-keeping devices. This idea unmistakably parallels Accawi's attitude.

The final body paragraph scrutinizes Accawi's use of repetition. This paragraph's wording may need some refinement, however. Notice how the student claims Accawi repeats "phrases" but offers no specific examples from the passage. It appears that the student meant that Accawi repeats *concepts and ideas*, not actual phrases. Still, the student's work is executed well, and it sticks to the topic of how Accawi's attitude is developed through his language and style. An AP reader will be generous enough not to penalize the student for this wording mishap that was likely due to the pressure of time.

Even though this is a high-scoring essay, the conclusion can be viewed as a mere summary of the essay; it offers no new food for thought. However, it does finish with an important statement about time that is true to Accawi's message. Overall, this essay is a very good one; it stays on topic throughout, it is clearly organized and well developed, and uses language with a flair. It has very few flaws, something any AP reader will immediately excuse. The student's ideas are both articulate and sensitive to Accawi's subtleties. These qualities distinguish the essay and ensure its high score.

Medium-Scoring Essay

In the excerpt from The Telephone, Anwar Accawi uses imagery, anecdotes, and simile to show the author's discouragement towards measuring time with instruments such as watches and calendars and his preference towards remembering more emotional past events.

To lesson the relative importance of measured time, the narrator asserts that the sun is his timepiece and God is his calendar. This image of the sun evokes a sense of vague time, which contrasts the exactness of a ticking watch. This precision strips time of the emotion, memories, and feelings. In addition, the image of God, as a supreme omniscient being knowledgeable of both past and future, overshadows the need for the accuracy of calendars by which to remember things. The watch and calendar lack the emotions evoked by the powerful images of the sun and God.

Accawi also uses anecdotes to display the narrator's dissatisfaction with measuring time. The narrator's conversation with his grandmother expresses the idea that time should be expressed in terms of events. Events should therefore be emphasized instead of dates, hours, and minutes, which are too precise and unemotional. The narrator's story of oranges and fish covering the ground shows also that there are events that become a part of society, of memory, and which must be acknowledged as contributing to the present and future through their being mentioned in relation to the present.

Simile is similarly used to depict the importance of expressing the passage of time in terms of events. The author uses the simile of kissing the elderly woman, Im Khalil, as being "like kissing a soft suede glove that had been soaked with sweat and then left in a dark closet for a season." This usage represents the fact that time is found in the feeling of objects, the remembrance of events, not in intangible concepts. It is found in nostalgic memories and the passing of seasons, not in the ticking of clocks or in the boxes of a calendar.

Anwar Accawi, through imagery, anecdotes, and simile, expresses the beauty in life's events and the relative unimportance of the precise measurement of time. Simply because it is possible to measure the passage of time does not mean that it is personally fulfilling to do so.

Analysis for the Medium-Scoring Essay

An average essay frequently shows that although the student may be able to read a passage accurately, he or she fails to delve deeper than the obvious; this essay demonstrates just that trait. It is on topic, but it proceeds in such a simplistic fashion that the reader keeps wanting to say "yeah, but so what?" while reading the essay. The introduction is brief and one-dimensional; whereas a more sophisticated student will notice that Accawi's attitude is complex, this student merely points out that he prefers remembering emotionally tinged events instead of using watches to measure time. To prove this simple concept, the student will examine "imagery, anecdotes, and simile."

The body paragraphs all briefly explore these three devices, but they offer very few examples from the text, and they develop no more than surface-level analysis in the process. The first body paragraph simply points out that the sun is an image Accawi uses that is more imprecise than a watch, and that the image of God "overshadows the need for . . . calendars." While this paragraph has two examples, it merely paraphrases Accawi's idea without analyzing *how* his language creates attitude. The student's concept about Accawi's attitude is essentially accurate, but simultaneously simplistic and undeveloped.

The second body paragraph follows the same format as the first and reproduces the same problems. Two examples of anecdote, the conversation with the narrator's grandmother and the story of the oranges and fish, are retold, but to no great end; as with the first body paragraph, the student has nothing more significant to say than that Accawi has "dissatisfaction with measuring time."

The last body paragraph is the weakest of all; it shows that the student noticed one simile while reading and not much more. The student's reason for using this one simile is the same as in the previous paragraphs; by this time the technique produces boredom in the reader.

Ultimately, an AP reader can reward this essay for essentially being organized and remaining on topic. However, working against a higher score is the fact that it does not see the complexity of Accawi's attitude, nor does it develop paragraphs with analytical integrity. It uses no quotations from the excerpt, which makes it much harder to examine how Accawi's language works. The essay also suffers from simplicity in the student's own diction; the minimal presentation mirrors the minimal idea. If the student were to develop the ideas more deeply and then support them with stronger examples, while showing more sophistication in presentation, the essay would receive a much higher score.

Question 3

Scoring Guide for Question 3 (Fanny Burney)

8–9 Essays scoring at the high end will substantially evaluate Burney's assertion that there is "nothing so insipid as a medium." They present a well-articulated argument that offers ample evidence from the writers' reading, observations, or experiences to support the essay's ideas. The development is thorough, the organization clear and logical. The high-scoring essays present language usage and style that shows sophistication, although the writing may contain some minor errors.

6–7 Essays earning a 6 or 7 score effectively evaluate Burney's assertion in a generally interesting fashion. The writers' arguments are usually logically reliable and use sufficient support from the writers' experiences, observations, or readings. These essays are often developed quite well, but not to as great an extent as the highest-scoring essays. In general, these essays may show a few lapses in control over language usage, but demonstrate such a clear command over diction and syntax that meaning is clear to the reader.

5 The 5-scoring essay understands the task and attempts to evaluate Burney's ideas. The argument is generally clear, but frequently too narrow in scope or superficial in its concept. Development is often too limited. Evidence offered may be only tangentially relevant or may not be adequately or logically examined, leaving the reader to question the validity of examples. While some lapses in grammar and mechanics may be present, they generally do not interfere with meaning, and the reader can follow the writers' ideas.

3–4 These lower-scoring essays inadequately evaluate the topic. They may misunderstand, misrepresent, or oversimplify Burney's assertion. They may use inappropriate examples or fail to develop them in a convincing manner. Development and organization are frequently flawed. Even though the meaning is usually clear, the writing may demonstrate immature control of English conventions.

1–2 Essays scoring a 2 or 1 achieve little or no success in evaluating Burney's ideas. They may completely misread the passage or substitute a simpler task instead of developing a cohesive argument. Lack of relevant or convincing evidence typically characterizes the lowest-scoring essays, and weak, simplistic logic or nonexistent explanations of any evidence often compound the essays' problems. The prose of the lowest-scoring essays frequently reveals consistent weaknesses over diction and syntax.

High-Scoring Essay

Our fascination with extremes is a phenomenon that is unexplainable by any biological method — we have no genuine need for it, and yet Fanny Burney is accurate; this purely human condition is prevalent in nearly all of us. Burney implies a psychological explanation, simple yet multifaceted. In essence, we simply find the extreme to be more interesting. We cannot rely on any scientific techniques to measure such an abstract concept. But perhaps the most effective way to relate Burney's assertion to current public opinion is to look at the press's choices in content. When considering the stories covered by the press, while we are actually looking at events or people which an editorial staff deems newsworthy, in the interest of sales and advertising profits, we can assume that the media caters to the public's interests. Clearly, news about the best or the worst in our world sells. Clearly, the major headlines generating the most interest have all been the result of some sort of extreme. Plane crashes involving hundreds of lives lost, baseball players booming baseballs farther and more frequently, stock market jumps that affect everyone — these are the most readable, most interesting stories. Not the car crash that injured a twenty-five year old man (though it may be just as heart-wrenching); not the consistent .330 batting average of a seasoned baseball veteran (though it may be just as difficult to achieve); and certainly not the steady conglomerate (though it may be just as profitable). Certainly, our hearts and minds gravitate to stories and people that pique our interest.

Hollywood, especially, gears its entertainment to fulfilling this interest. We love to watch the over-the-top, clever and cruel arch-villains who plot to take over the universe and the overly saccharine brave young heroes who valiantly stop their plans (and win the damsel in distress while they're at it). Even ordinary Clark Kent became the strong Superman, perhaps convincing us that we too, would be able to fly, have x-ray vision, and save the world from any evil nemesis. It appears we want movies to represent extremes of good and evil, not just some "insipid" everyman. And certainly, this interest in the extreme is not a recent phenomenon. If we go back to Shakespeare's work, considered by many to be the archetypal settings and characters for so many stories to come, we see that Burney's comment holds no less truth. For instance, in *Hamlet*, we have Horatio, "a friend that will go to jail for me" and Polonius, "an enemy that will run me through the body," occupying different extremes. There can be no medium in effective drama, for our imaginations and emotions feed off characters and conflicts that are more grandiose than our daily lives. It's what the audience wants; it's what the playwright delivers.

Our insistent need for the extreme serves no harmful purpose. Indeed, it has shaped our modern conceptions of drama, comedy, and news, helping us define our psychological boundaries and sparking the imaginations of generations to come.

Analysis of the High-Scoring Essay

The student who wrote this high-scoring essay has a firm grasp of the topic and a clear view of the world. He or she appropriately uses examples from the news media, Hollywood cinema, and Shakespearean drama to prove that Fanny Burney's quotation is an accurate perception of mankind; we do relish extremes over the mediocre. The first paragraph blends the introductory material and its effective thesis into a body paragraph that explores the current state of print journalism. While the student does not use specific existing headlines or news stories as examples, he or she does not need to — for the universal point here is that the news media depicts the extreme in life, and the "generic" examples that are presented here work very well. Plane crashes, outrageous professional baseball salaries, and the excessive ups and downs of the stock market are all examples that the reader can relate to and easily connect to the student's point. The student also slips in a legitimate business rationale for these types of stories: not only does the public crave them, but the paper also profits by them. This paragraph, nicely on topic, focuses on observations of our modern life and convinces the reader that the media does present extremes in the news, which in turn reflects humanity's desire for such sensationalism.

The next paragraph explores Hollywood movies and Shakespearean drama, again effectively utilizing both to prove that mankind craves extremes in fictional characters. Everyone knows so well the "cruel arch-villain" and the "brave young hero" that Hollywood exaggerates. The student's declaration that we would all like to become a Superman and "save the world from any evil nemesis" both rings true and helps prove Burney's assertion. Middle-of-the-road personalities do not save the world; extreme ones do. The student's use of *Hamlet* gives the essay a sophisticated and cultured flair, not merely because it is a Shakespearean reference but because it also proves the student well-read and well-rounded. It helps to balance the previous contemporary examples in the essay. Perhaps the *Hamlet* discussion could be developed more, explaining how Horatio and Polonius exemplify these extremes in character, but an essay that is written under timed pressure cannot always elaborate as much as an untimed one. Remember that the AP reader will "reward the writer for what he or she does well," and this writer proves his or her point admirably.

This essay earns its high score through the development of its clear and relevant ideas, as well as its abundant examples, strong organization, and commendable control of written English. The sense of rhythm that is so pleasing to the ear through parallel construction can be observed in such areas as the repetition of the word "Clearly" to begin two sentences, the parenthetical "though it may be . . . " phrasing in the first paragraph, and in the sentence, "It's what the audience wants; it's what the playwright delivers" in the second paragraph. While parallelism is never a specific requirement, any student who effectively uses such sophisticated devices will demonstrate a sense of style that shines through to the reader.

Medium/Low-Scoring Essay

We can't help but be interested by extremes. They represent both the bad and the good of life and are interesting simply because they differ from the typical person. Like scientists who also are interested in differences from the standard, we classify and thus notice these differences. For example, the world records in running have, time and time again, deserved media coverage while the average speed of a typical healthy males may perhaps be an obscure fact. Our societies focus on the individual inevitably results in the few strongest, smartest, quickest being not only isolated but at times revered. The opposite side of the spectrum is similarly true. The publics fascination with, for example, a cereal killer, is only rivaled by its fascination with the fireman who saved twenty lives.

Everything in between (with varying degrees), is ordinary and, as Fanny Burney wrote, "insipid."

Perhaps our dedication to seeking out the extremes in life represents our own struggle to find who we are. Extremes provide a watermark to our own situation. Are we that "friend that will go to jail for me" or the "enemy that will run me through the body?" We are most likely in between. But are fascination with this scale is a symbol of our dreams. We certainly cannot achieve such heights (or such lows) but we can often live vicariously through these extreme individuals.

Analysis of the Medium-Scoring Essay

This essay attempts to agree with Burney's assertion; however, it does not make a strong point in doing so, nor does it actually convince the reader. Simply stated, the essay is not fulfilling because of its brevity. The example with which the student begins, that of track and field world records, does not work particularly well; it appears that the student has not thought it through. After all, it *does* make sense that a new world's record would "deserve media coverage" while at the same time "average speed of a typical, healthy male" would not. This "average" statistical information can be obtained, but it is not particularly newsworthy on a daily basis, so the example does not make much sense to the reader. The later example of the public's fascination with murderers and heroes is more logically sound, but it is not enough to save the entire paragraph from mediocrity.

The second paragraph appears to be a hastily drawn conclusion; it certainly offers no new examples or ideas to support the student's thesis. Although it may be philosophically interesting to ponder whether we might become a strong friend or a vile enemy, it does not persuade the reader of the validity of Burney's assertion, and therefore falls flat. This concept does not meet any of the requirements in the directions, namely using your "reading, observation, or experience" to support ideas.

The large number of diction and grammatical mistakes also hurt this essay's score. While the readers want to "reward the writer for what he or she does well," they simply cannot ignore so many errors. Notice the first two sentences. The student claims we are interested *by* extremes (an unidiomatic expression to start), then claims "they differ from the typical person," which is not possible. One cannot logically compare *extremes* to *people*. Notice also the number agreement problem in the phrase "speed of *a* typically healthy *males*." The student also has many wording and/or punctuation mistakes, such as "societies" instead of "society's," "publics" without its apostrophe, and "cereal" instead of "serial." Additionally, the homophone confusion of using "are" instead of "our" strikes the reader as yet another careless error. While an AP reader can disregard minor mistakes here and there, this essay is riddled with far too many errors to disregard without affecting the score. Therefore, this essay is an example of an extremely low "mid-range" essay. Giving it a score of 4 would be generous.

The essay earns a low score because of its combination of being barely on topic, weak development, ineffectual organization, and numerous mechanical errors.

PART VII

SUGGESTED READING LIST

Following is a list of important authors and some of their works that are similar to those used on the AP English language exam. The list is not meant to be all inclusive or required reading for every student, but reading these works extensively and analyzing the authors' use of language will give you excellent preparation for the exam.

Autobiography, Biography, Journal, and History

Maya Angelou

Gather Together in My Name
The Heart of a Woman
I Know Why the Caged Bird Sings
Singin' and Swingin' and Getting' Merry Like Christmas

Walter Jackson Bate

John Keats
Samuel Johnson

Charles A. Beard

An Economic Interpretation of the Constitution
The Rise of American Civilization (with Mary R. Beard)

James Boswell

The Life of Samuel Johnson, LL.D.

Van Wyck Brooks

An Autobiography
Days of Phoenix
From a Writer's Notebook

Thomas Carlyle

The French Revolution
Past and Present

Bruce Catton

Mr. Lincoln's Army
A Stillness at Appomattox

Sir Winston Churchill

Blood, Sweat, and Tears
Europe Unite: Speeches 1947 and 1948
A History of the English-Speaking Peoples
In the Balance: Speeches 1949 and 1950
Marlborough
My Early Life
Their Finest Hour
Triumph and Tragedy

Charles Dana

(any nonfiction)

Thomas De Quincey

Confessions of an English Opium Eater

Frederick Douglass

The Life and Times of Frederick Douglass
My Bondage and My Freedom
Narrative of the Life of Frederick Douglass

Leon Edel

Bloomsbury: A House of Lions
Henry James, A Life
The Stuff of Sleep and Dreams
Telling Lives

Richard Ellmann

Eminent Domain: Yeats among Wilde,
*   Joyce, Pound, Eliot, and Auden*
James Joyce

Antonia Fraser

King James I of England
Mary, Queen of Scots
Oliver Cromwell
The Warrior Queens
The Weaker Vessel: Women's Lot in
*   Seventeenth-Century England*

Edward Gibbon

The History of the Decline and Fall of
*   the Roman Empire*

Lillian Hellman

Scoundrel Time
An Unfinished Woman

William Dean Howells

Years of My Youth

Alfred Kazin

New York Jew
Starting Out in the Thirties
A Walker in the City

Helen Keller

The Story of My Life

Maxine Hong Kingston

China Men
The Woman Warrior

T. E. Lawrence

The Revolt in the Desert
Seven Pillars of Wisdom

Gerda Lerner

The Creation of Patriarchy
The Female Experience: An American
*   Documentary*
The Majority Finds Its Past: Placing
*   Women in History*

Thomas Macaulay

Critical and Historical Essays
History of England from the Accession
*   of James II*

Malcolm X

The Autobiography of Malcolm X

Samuel Eliot Morison

Christopher Columbus, Admiral of the
*   Ocean Sea*
The Growth of the American Republic
Harrison Gray Otis: Urbane Federalist

John Henry Newman

(any nonfiction)

Francis Parkman

The Oregon Trail
Pioneers of France in the New World

Samuel Pepys

Diary

Richard Rodriguez

Days of Obligation
Hunger of Memory

Mari Sandoz

The Battle of the Little Big Horn
Old Jules

Arthur M. Schlesinger, Jr.

The Age of Jackson
The Age of Roosevelt
The Bitter Heritage
Robert Kennedy and His Times
A Thousand Days

George Trevelyan

English Social History

Barbara Tuchman

Bible and Sword
A Distant Mirror
The Guns of August
The Proud Tower

Richard Wright

American Hunger
Black Boy

Anzia Yezierska

Bread and Givers
The Open Cage
Red Ribbon on a White Horse

Essay, Fiction, and Criticism

Joseph Addison

Selections from the *Tatler* and the
Spectator

James Agee

Collected Short Prose
A Death in a Family

Michael Arlen

An American Verdict
The Camera Age: Essays on Television
Exiles

Matthew Arnold

(any criticism)

Margaret Atwood

Cat's Eye
The Handmaid's Tale

Sir Francis Bacon

The Advancement of Learning
The New Atlantis

James Baldwin

Another Country
The Devil Finds Work
The Evidence of Things Not Seen
The First Next Time
Go Tell It on the Mountain
If Beale Street Could Talk
Notes of a Native Son

G. K. Chesterton

Heretics
St. Francis of Assisi
St. Thomas Aquinas
The Victorian Age in Literature

Kenneth Clark

Another Part of the Wood
Civilization
The Other Half

Samuel Taylor Coleridge

(any criticism)

Arlene Croce

(any criticism)

Joan Didion

A Book of Common Prayer
Salvador
Slouching Toward Bethlehem
(any essays)

Ralph Waldo Emerson

*The Journals and Miscellaneous
Notebooks*
(any essays)

Northrop Frye

Anatomy of Criticism
Fearful Symmetry
Fools of Time

Paul Fussell

Bad, or the Dumbing of America
The Great War and Modern Memory
*Thank God for the Atom Bomb and
Other Essays*

Nadine Gordimer

Face to Face
My Son's Story
Not for Publication
(any essays)

William Hazlitt

(any criticism)

Zora Neale Hurston

Dust Tracks on a Road
Jonah's Gourd Vine
Their Eyes Were Watching God

Ruth Prawer Jhabvala

Heart and Dust
In Search of Love and Beauty

Samuel Johnson

The Lives of the Poets
Selection from the *Idler* and the
Rambler

Pauline Kael

5001 Nights at the Movies
I Lost It at the Movies
State of the Art

William Hugh Kenner

A Colder Eye

Charles Lamb

Tales from Shakespeare
(any essays)

Stephen Leacock

Last Leaves
Winnowed Wisdom

Norman Mailer

Ancient Evenings
The Armies of the Night
The Naked and the Dead
Pieces and Pontifications

Mary McCarthy

Cannibals and Missionaries
Ideas and the Novel
Memories of a Catholic Girlhood
The Writing on the Wall

Scott Momaday

The Names: A Memoir
The Way to Rainy Mountain

Montaigne

(any essays)

Vladimir Nabokov

Lectures on Literature
Pnin
Speak, Memory

V. S. Naipaul

Among the Believers: An Islamic Journey
The Returns of Eva Peron

Joyce Carol Oates

Contraries: Essays
The Edge of Impossibility
First Person Singular
New Haven, New Earth
On Boxing
Woman Writer

Tillie Olsen

Mother to Daughter, Daughter to Mother
Silences
Tell Me a Riddle
Yonnonida

George Orwell

Down and Out in Paris and London
Shooting an Elephant

Cynthia Ozick

Art and Ardor
The Cannibal Galaxy

Walter Pater

(any criticism)

Adrienne Rich

Of Woman Born
On Lies, Secrets, and Silence

John Ruskin

Modern Painters
Praeterita
(any other criticism)

George Santayana

The Life of Reason, or, The Phases of Human Progress
The Sense of Beauty

George Bernard Shaw

The Intelligent Woman's Guide to Socialism and Capitalism
(any criticism)

Susan Sontag

Against Interpretation
Aids and Its Metaphors
Illness as Metaphor
Styles of Radical Will

Richard Steele

Selection from the *Spectator* and the *Tatler*

John Updike

Assorted Prose
Hugging the Shore: Essays and Criticism
Self Consciousness

Gore Vidal

Matters of Fact and Fiction
Reflections upon a Sinking Ship
View from a Window

Alice Walker

In Love and Trouble
You Can't Keep a Good Woman Down

Eudora Welty

The Eye of the Story: Selected Essays and Reviews
The Golden Apples
Losing Battles
One Writer's Beginnings

E. B. White

The Essays of E. B. White
One Man's Meat

Oscar Wilde

(any criticism)

Edmund Wilson

Axle's Castle: A Study in the Imaginative Literature of 1870 to 1930
The Devil's and Canon Barham: Ten Essays on Poets, Novelists, and Monsters
Letters on Literature and Politics
Patriotric Gore: Studies in the Literature of the American Civil War
The Shores of Light

Virginia Woolf

The Common Reader
The Death of a Moth
The Moment
Roger Fry
A Room of One's Own
Three Guineas
A Writer's Diary

Political Writing and Journalism

Roger Angell

Five Seasons: A Baseball Companion
Late Innings
Once More Around the Park

Hannah Arendy

Between Past and Future
The Human Condition
On Revolution
The Origins of Totalitarianism

Simone de Beauvoir

The Coming of Age
The Prime of Life
The Second Sex

William F. Buckley

God and Man at Yale
The Governor Listeth
On the Firing Line

Michel de Crèvecoeur

Letters from an American Farmer

Elizabeth Drew

American Journal: The Events of 1976
Washington Journal: The Events of 1973–1974

W. E. B. Du Bois

Autobiography
The Philadelphia Negro
The Souls of Black Folk
Worlds of Color

Nora Ephron

Crazy Salad: Some Things About Women
Wallflower at the Orgy

Frances Fitzgerald

America Revisited
Cities on Hill
Fire in the Lake

Janet Flanner

Janet Flanner's Uncollected Writings
Men and Monuments
Paris Was Yesterday: 1925–1939

John Kenneth Galbraith

The Affluent Society
Ambassador's Journal
The Anatomy of Power
The Nature of Mass Poverty

Charlotte Perkins Gilman

The Charlotte Perkins Gilman Reader
Herland

Ellen Goodman

At Large
Close to Home
Keeping in Touch
Making Sense

Thomas Hobbes

Leviathan
Philosophical Rudiments

Thomas Jefferson

(any writings)

George Kennan

American Diplomacy 1900–1950
Democracy and the Student Left
Sketches from a Life

Martin Luther King, Jr.

Stride Toward Freedom
A Testament of Hope
The Trumpet of Conscience

John Locke

An Essay Concerning Human Understanding
Two Treatises on Government

Andy Logan

> *The Man Who Robbed the Robber Barons*

Machiavelli

> *The Prince*

John McPhee

> *Headmaster*
> *A Sense of Who You Are*

H. L. Mencken

> *The Bathtub Hoax and Other Blasts and Bravos from the Chicago Tribune*
> *A Choice of Days*
> *H. L. Mencken's Smart Set Crticism*
> *In Defense of Women*
> *Selected Prejudices*

John Stuart Mill

> *On Liberty*
> *The Subjection of Women*
> *Utilitarianism*

Sir Thomas More

> *Utopia*

Jan Morris

> *Destinations: Essays from Rolling Stone*

Olive Schreiner

> *The Story of an African Farm*

William L. Shirer

> *Berlin Diary*
> *The Nightmare Years*
> *20th Century Journey*

Red Smith

> *The Red Smith Reader*
> *To Absent Friends*

Lincoln Steffens

> *Autobiography*
> *The Shame of the Cities*
> *The Upbuilders*

Jonathan Swift

> *Democracy in America*
> *The Old Regime and the Revolution*

Calvin Trillin

> *American Fried*
> *An Education in Georgia*
> *Third Helpings*
> *Uncivil Liberties*

T. H. White

> *Breach of Faith*
> *Fire in the Ashes*
> *In Search of History*
> *The Making of the President: 1960*

Tom Wolfe

> (any essays)

Science and Nature Writing

Isaac Asimov

The Exploding Suns
In Joy Still Felt (autobiography)
In Memory Yet Green (autobiography)
Until the Sun Dies

Jacob Bronowski

*The Origins of Knowledge and
  Imagination*
A Sense of the Future

Annie Dillard

An America Childhood
Holy the Firm
Living by Fiction
Pilgrim at Tinker Creek
*Teaching a Stone to Talk: Expeditions
  and Encounters*
The Writing Life

Gretel Ehrlich

The Solace of Open Spaces

Stephen Jay Gould

Ever Since Darwin
Hen's Teeth and Horse's Toes
The Mismeasure of Man
Time's Arrow, Time's Cycle
An Urchin in the Storm

Peter Matthiessen

At Play in the Fields of the Lord
Far Tortuga
In the Spirit of Crazy Horse
The Snow Leopard
The Tree Where Man Was Born

Margaret Mead

*And Keep Your Powder Dry: An
  Anthropologist Looks at America*
Blackberry Winter
Coming of Age in Samoa

Carl Sagan

The Dragons of Eden
A Path Where No Man Thought

Lewis Thomas

The Fragile Species
*Late Night Thoughts on Listening to
  Mahler's 9th Symphony*
*The Lives of a Cell: The Notes of a
  Biology Watcher*
The Medusa and the Snail

Final Preparation: "The Final Touches"

1. Spend your last week of preparation on general review of key concepts, test-taking strategies, and techniques.

2. Don't cram the night before the test! It's a waste of time.

3. Remember to bring the proper materials: three or four sharpened Number 2 pencils, an eraser, several ballpoint pens, and a watch.

4. Start off crisply, answering the questions you know first and then coming back to the harder ones.

5. If you can eliminate one or more of the answer choices, make an educated guess.

6. Mark in reading passages, underline key words, and jot down important information. Take advantage of being permitted to write in the test booklet.

7. Make sure that you're answering "what is being asked" and that your answer is reasonable.

8. Cross out incorrect choices immediately in the test booklet in order to avoid reconsidering a choice you've already eliminated.

9. Plan your essays carefully and monitor your timing.

Notes

Notes

Notes

Notes

Notes

Notes

Notes

Notes

Notes

Notes

Notes

CliffsNotes

LITERATURE NOTES

Absalom, Absalom!
The Aeneid
Agamemnon
Alice in Wonderland
All the King's Men
All the Pretty Horses
All Quiet on Western Front
All's Well & Merry Wives
American Poets of the 20th Century
American Tragedy
Animal Farm
Anna Karenina
Anthem
Antony and Cleopatra
Aristotle's Ethics
As I Lay Dying
The Assistant
As You Like It
Atlas Shrugged
Autobiography of Ben Franklin
Autobiography of Malcolm X
The Awakening
Babbit
Bartleby & Benito Cereno
The Bean Trees
The Bear
The Bell Jar
Beloved
Beowulf
The Bible
Billy Budd & Typee
Black Boy
Black Like Me
Bleak House
Bless Me, Ultima
The Bluest Eye & Sula
Brave New World
Brothers Karamazov
Call of Wild & White Fang
Candide
The Canterbury Tales
Catch-22
Catcher in the Rye
The Chosen
The Color Purple
Comedy of Errors...
Connecticut Yankee
The Contender
The Count of Monte Cristo
Crime and Punishment
The Crucible
Cry, the Beloved Country
Cyrano de Bergerac
Daisy Miller & Turn...Screw
David Copperfield
Death of a Salesman
The Deerslayer
Diary of Anne Frank
Divine Comedy-I. Inferno
Divine Comedy-II. Purgatorio
Divine Comedy-III. Paradiso
Doctor Faustus

Dr. Jekyll and Mr. Hyde
Don Juan
Don Quixote
Dracula
Electra & Medea
Emerson's Essays
Emily Dickinson Poems
Emma
Ethan Frome
The Faerie Queene
Fahrenheit 451
Far from Madding Crowd
A Farewell to Arms
Farewell to Manzanar
Fathers and Sons
Faulkner's Short Stories
Faust Pt. I & Pt. II
The Federalist
Flowers for Algernon
For Whom the Bell Tolls
The Fountainhead
Frankenstein
The French Lieutenant's Woman
The Giver
Glass Menagerie & Streetcar
Go Down, Moses
The Good Earth
Grapes of Wrath
Great Expectations
The Great Gatsby
Greek Classics
Gulliver's Travels
Hamlet
The Handmaid's Tale
Hard Times
Heart of Darkness & Secret Sharer
Hemingway's Short Stories
Henry IV Part 1
Henry IV Part 2
Henry V
House Made of Dawn
The House of the Seven Gables
Huckleberry Finn
I Know Why the Caged Bird Sings
Ibsen's Plays I
Ibsen's Plays II
The Idiot
Idylls of the King
The Iliad
Incidents in the Life of a Slave Girl
Inherit the Wind
Invisible Man
Ivanhoe
Jane Eyre
Joseph Andrews
The Joy Luck Club
Jude the Obscure
Julius Caesar
The Jungle
Kafka's Short Stories
Keats & Shelley
The Killer Angels
King Lear
The Kitchen God's Wife
The Last of the Mohicans

Le Morte Darthur
Leaves of Grass
Les Miserables
A Lesson Before Dying
Light in August
The Light in the Forest
Lord Jim
Lord of the Flies
Lord of the Rings
Lost Horizon
Lysistrata & Other Comedies
Macbeth
Madame Bovary
Main Street
The Mayor of Casterbridge
Measure for Measure
The Merchant of Venice
Middlemarch
A Midsummer-Night's Dream
The Mill on the Floss
Moby-Dick
Moll Flanders
Mrs. Dalloway
Much Ado About Nothing
My Ántonia
Mythology
Narr. ...Frederick Douglass
Native Son
New Testament
Night
1984
Notes from Underground
The Odyssey
Oedipus Trilogy
Of Human Bondage
Of Mice and Men
The Old Man and the Sea
Old Testament
Oliver Twist
The Once and Future King
One Day in the Life of Ivan Denisovich
One Flew Over Cuckoo's Nest
100 Years of Solitude
O'Neill's Plays
Othello
Our Town
The Outsiders
The Ox-Bow Incident
Paradise Lost
A Passage to India
The Pearl
The Pickwick Papers
The Picture of Dorian Gray
Pilgrim's Progress
The Plague
Plato's Euthyphro...
Plato's The Republic
Poe's Short Stories
A Portrait of Artist...
The Portrait of a Lady
The Power and the Glory
Pride and Prejudice
The Prince
The Prince and the Pauper
A Raisin in the Sun

The Red Badge of Courage
The Red Pony
The Return of the Native
Richard II
Richard III
The Rise of Silas Lapham
Robinson Crusoe
Roman Classics
Romeo and Juliet
The Scarlet Letter
A Separate Peace
Shakespeare's Comedies
Shakespeare's Histories Shake-
speare's Minor Plays
Shakespeare's Sonnets
Shakespeare's Tragedies
Shaw's Pygmalion & Arms...
Silas Marner
Sir Gawain...Green Knight
Sister Carrie
Slaughterhouse-Five
Snow Falling on Cedars
Song of Solomon
Sons and Lovers
The Sound and the Fury
Steppenwolf & Siddhartha
The Stranger
The Sun Also Rises
T.S. Eliot's Poems & Plays
A Tale of Two Cities
The Taming of the Shrew
Tartuffe, Misanthrope...
The Tempest
Tender Is the Night
Tess of the D'Urbervilles
Their Eyes Were Watching God
Things Fall Apart
The Three Musketeers
To Kill a Mockingbird
Tom Jones
Tom Sawyer
Treasure Island & Kidnapped
The Trial
Tristram Shandy
Troilus and Cressida
Twelfth Night
Ulysses
Uncle Tom's Cabin
The Unvanquished
Utopia
Vanity Fair
Vonnegut's Works
Waiting for Godot
Walden
Walden Two
War and Peace
Who's Afraid of Virginia...
Winesburg, Ohio
The Winter's Tale
The Woman Warrior
Worldly Philosophers
Wuthering Heights
A Yellow Raft in Blue Water